A READER IN NINETEENTH-CENTURY HISTORICAL INDO-EUROPEAN LINGUISTICS

INDIANA UNIVERSITY STUDIES
in the
HISTORY AND THEORY OF LINGUISTICS

Editorial Committee:
THOMAS A. SEBEOK, *Chairman*
CHARLES A. FERGUSON, *Stanford University*
ERIC P. HAMP, *University of Chicago*
DELL H. HYMES, *University of Pennsylvania*
Center for Applied Linguistics
ROBERT STOCKWELL, *University of California, Los Angeles*

A READER IN NINETEENTH-CENTURY HISTORICAL INDO-EUROPEAN LINGUISTICS

Edited and Translated by
WINFRED P. LEHMANN

INDIANA UNIVERSITY PRESS
BLOOMINGTON AND LONDON

Copyright © 1967 by Indiana University Press
All rights reserved
No part of this book may be reproduced or utilized in
any form or by any means, electronic or mechanical,
including photocopying and recording, or by any
information storage and retrieval system, without
permission in writing from the publisher. The
Association of American University Presses, Inc.
Resolution on Permissions constitutes the only
exception to this prohibition.
Library of Congress catalog card number: 67-63012
Manufactured in the United States of America

UNIVERSITY
LIBRARY
NOTTINGHAM

CONTENTS

v

INTRODUCTION

by W. P. Lehmann

THIS anthology has been arranged to provide easy access to some of the important works of nineteenth-century historical Indo-European linguistics. These works are not readily available to students, in part because of their language, in part because of the difficulty of obtaining the works themselves. Schlegel's book of 1808, for example, is generally placed in a special section for rare books in a library; the early issues of an important journal like the Zeitschrift für vergleichende Sprachwissenschaft may be stored in a depository; even the section in Grimm's Grammar dealing with the sound shift may be difficult for a non-specialist in German to locate. An anthology will permit students to become acquainted with some of the key works of the nineteenth century, and to learn at first hand their contributions to the development of linguistics as well as their weaknesses.

The weaknesses are readily apparent, and should not need detailed comment. Even the important contributions presented here include shortcomings we would not tolerate. Principles observed in writing, printing and editing generally seem to have been determined for the ease of the publisher rather than the reader. A very capable author like Grassmann, for example, paid little attention to editorial details. The name Panini is at one point given without a macron in his article, at another point as Pānini; similarly Samaveda and Sāmaveda. These are superficial details, but they indicate how little the editor pampered the reader. Greek forms were rarely labeled — the special type face used for Greek was considered an adequate marker — and often a reader was expected to recognize Latin and Sanskrit forms as well. Glosses for forms may be in one of a number of languages. Other such editorial practices of the nineteenth century are left to the reader to discover. Occasionally it was difficult to maintain them without seeming unfair to our great predecessors. But when Brugmann lists himself as Brugman and permits spelling his forename Carl or Karl, one has the impression that externals were of little concern in the aim to make available as quickly as possible new insights into linguistic problems.

The selections here incorporate such insights, or are credited with priority in achieving them. In making selections, I intended to present only complete essays, or complete sub-sections of a work,

1

so that the reader might himself determine the point of view of a
scholar, his contemporaries, and his publication. Excerpts may
more economically present the high points of early linguistics, but
they take from readers the pleasure of determining these; the interested student can find the history of linguistics in this way in
Hans Arens' Sprachwissenschaft. Excerpts also fail to provide the
context in which a permanent contribution was made. Jones's entire
essay is reprinted here, for example, to indicate that the celebrated
paragraph which is constantly reprinted simply makes up one small
segment of a report on Indian culture; it is instructive for students
to find out for themselves how peripheral was the concern with language at the beginning of the nineteenth century. Schlegel too discussed Indian culture in general, not simply language. Yet it did not
seem useful to demonstrate repeatedly by incorporating long passages of their writings on other matters that he and the other early
linguists assumed many intellectual responsibilities. For similar
reasons, only parts of selections 12, 13, 15, 16 and 18 are included
here.

    Each selection in the anthology is preceded by comments which
point up its contributions, and thus I do not give here a survey of the
development of nineteenth-century linguistics. I might also note that
the anthology does not reflect all advances of the nineteenth century.
Some are not represented because they were inaugurated by more
than one man, sometimes in several different works. The study of
dialect geography, for example, was encouraged by many linguists,
as the selections from von Raumer and Sievers demonstrate. Such
encouragement was not given in special essays, as the example of
Gaston Paris may indicate; his initial lecture of 1868 on the historical grammar of the French language, Mélanges linguistiques,
pp. 153-173 (Paris, 1909), reflects the views that led to the dialect
project in France, but only in a general discussion. Other advances
are not represented because they occurred to a number of linguists
almost simultaneously and were not made in any one notable work,
for example the understanding that reconstructions can be established from other segments of a linguistic system than those directly involved. The conclusion that PIE e must be assumed because of palatals in Sanskrit is the most striking example. The
gradual clarification of the vowel system of Proto-Indo-European
is also the work of many, as the excerpt from Saussure indicates.
Further, because of the length of the materials here, I have omitted
the works of the great dissenters such as Hugo Schuchardt. These
to be sure would be useful in illustrating the breadth of approaches
in linguistics, as does the Hugo Schuchardt-Brevier (Halle: Max
Niemeyer, 1922). But, as Schuchardt himself points out, his central
concern was the Romance language group, not Indo-European;

accordingly his work lies outside the area of the anthology. Moreover, like the dialect geographers, he published many of his theoretical statements in the twentieth century. For this reason too
Paul's Prinzipien is not represented; its definitive form was reached
only in 1920. For a synthesis of nineteenth-century work, I have included a chapter from Whitney.

Interpretation of the contributions of the leading nineteenth-
century linguists are happily available in a number of fine surveys.
One of the best is Language, by Otto Jespersen (London: Allen and
Unwin, 1922) pp. 19-99. The most widely read is probably Holger
Pedersen's Linguistic Science in the Nineteenth Century, translated
by John W. Spargo and republished as The Discovery of Language
(Bloomington: Indiana University Press, 1962). Pedersen's penetrating review of linguistics has a capable predecessor in Vilhelm
Thomsen: Geschichte der Sprachwissenschaft bis zum Ausgang des
19. Jahrhunderts, translated by H. Pollak (Halle: Niemeyer, 1927).
A recent short survey going beyond the nineteenth century is Perspectives in Linguistics, by John T. Waterman (Chicago: University
of Chicago Press, 1963).

Students who read German should make use of the excellent introduction to the history of linguistics through well-chosen excerpts
in Hans Arens' Sprachwissenschaft (Freiburg/München: Karl Alber,
1955). Its bibliography contains 744 items, of which items 306-321
deal with the history of linguistics.

Moreover, handbooks that provide brief surveys should not be
overlooked, such as Hermann Hirt's Indogermanische Grammatik I.
(Heidelberg: Winter, 1927) pp. 1-16, or J. Schrijnen's Einführung
in das Studium der indogermanischen Sprachwissenschaft, translated by W. Fischer (Heidelberg: Winter, 1921) pp. 20-38, or
Antoine Meillet's Introduction à l'étude comparative des langues
indo-européennes (Paris: Hachette, 1937⁸), Appendix I, pp. 453-483,
or the fine essays on individual linguists in his collected essays:
Linguistique historique et linguistique générale II. (Paris: Klinck-
sieck, 1938). All of these provide means for a better understanding
of the contributions in the selections presented here, and of the
problems their authors attempted to solve.

This Reader was undertaken in the fall of 1963. At that time
students in a course on the history of the German language were
asked to translate various essays. Of these, translations by the
following students are included, after revision: 5 by Mr. Roy A.
Boggs, 7 by Mr. Louis E. Brister, 9 by Mr. Peter Mollenhauer, 11
by Miss Carolyn Farmer, 13 by Mr. Clifford Crowe, 14 by Miss
Judy Haddon, 18 by Mr. Jerry Glenn. The other essays I have
translated. I am grateful to Catharina Breedveld for typing much
of the manuscript, and to Miss Victoria Bunye for reading all of it.

Problems of translation could be discussed at length. Among
them are shifts in the uses of terms. For Grimm <u>deutsch</u> meant
Germanic, for Schleicher West Germanic, though also German in
accordance with its current use. It is often difficult to translate
such terms accurately without providing a contemporary interpretation that reflects the increased precision in use of terminology,
and may therefore not correspond to the views of the author. More
external, but also troublesome, are items that we no longer use,
such as Bactrian rather than Avestan, or symbols like k̲ rather than
Sanskrit c̲, IE a₁ rather than e̲. The proper interpretation of these
is generally apparent. Some of the forgotten terminology one is
tempted to reintroduce, such as the youthful Saussure's symphthong
and autophthong.

In general, interpretation is left to the reader; when Grimm
uses "analogy," for example, his meaning differs from ours, but it
is instructive and not difficult to interpret his use of the term. Often
such terminology has been long maintained. It is highly important to
understand Grimm's view of the consonant shift occurring in <u>stufen</u>
"grades," in accordance with the scheme he included in his discussion; the concept of the shift as a series of steps or grades has persisted to the present, though it was probably carried to its extreme
under the neogrammarians for whom not only the various series but
also the individual items were distinct. Further, an understanding
of the methodological approach of Grimm to the consonant shift may
be instructive when viewed in relation to that maintained in our
handbooks for Indo-European ablaut.

Students who seek to follow the development of methodology in
linguistics will want to consult the originals, not merely the translations or even the selections provided here. Fuller acquaintance
with the important contributions of the past will lead to a deeper
understanding of the views we have maintained and may also provide
insights into contemporary approaches and the discussions of linguists today.

A READER IN NINETEENTH-CENTURY HISTORICAL INDO-EUROPEAN LINGUISTICS

CHAPTER ONE

SIR WILLIAM JONES

THE THIRD ANNIVERSARY DISCOURSE, ON THE HINDUS

Delivered 2 February, 1786. Works I, pp. 19-34.

Sir William Jones's celebrated discourse is given here
in full to illustrate the context from which linguistics developed in the nineteenth century. With his contemporaries,
Jones was interested in better knowledge of ancient history.
In the pursuit of this knowledge, language was only one
means. The commemorative address of his successor as
president of the Asiatick Society, Sir John Shore, states
explicitly that for Jones language was a tool, not an end in
itself. "But the judgement of Sir William Jones was too
discerning to consider language in any other light than as
the key of science, and he would have despised the reputation of a mere linguist. Knowledge and truth, were the object of all his studies, and his ambition was to be useful to
mankind; with these views, he extended his researches to
all languages, nations, and times." (Works I.p.v.) A glance
at the other annual discourses supports this statement on
Jones's wide interests and the subsidiary position of linguists, which it maintained to the middle of the nineteenth
century. Yet the "Desiderata" which Shore found among
his papers may indicate that Jones had planned to spend
additional time on linguistics: the third desideratum is "A
Grammar of the Sanscrit Language, from Panini, etc."; the
fourth, "A Dictionary of the Sanscrit Language, from thirty-
two original Vocabularies and Niructi."
These proposed undertakings, and citations from his
"Dissertation on the Orthography of Asiatick Words in Roman Letters" (Works I. pp. 175-228) may indicate that
Jones deserves a larger reputation than that for stimulating
study of the Indo-European languages and historical linguistics. The views in his third discourse on the origin of
our writing system and Devanagari are accurate; the following excerpts from the "Dissertation" indicate a knowledge of phonetics comparable with that of Grimm's successors.

7

It would be superfluous to discourse on the organs
of speech, which have been a thousand times dissected,
and as often described by musicians or anatomists; and
the several powers of which every man may perceive
either by the touch or by sight, if he will attentively observe another person pronouncing the different classes
of letters, or pronounce them himself distinctly before
a mirror: but a short analysis of articulate sounds may
be proper to introduce an examination of every separate symbol.

All things abound with errour, as the old searchers
for truth remarked with despondence; but it is really
deplorable, that our first step from total ignorance
should be into gross inaccuracy, and that we should begin our education in England with learning to read the
five vowels, two of which, as we are taught to pronounce them, are clearly diphthongs. There are, indeed, five simple vocal sounds in our language, as in
that of Rome; which occur in the words an innocent
bull, though not precisely in their natural order, for
we have retained the true arrangement of the letters,
while we capriciously disarrange them in pronunciation; so that our eyes are satisfied, and our ears dis-
appointed. The primary elements of articulation are
the soft and hard breathings, the spiritus lenis and
spiritus asper of the Latin Grammarians. If the lips
be opened ever so little, the breath suffered gently to
pass through them, and the feeblest utterance attempted,
a sound is formed of so simple a nature, that, when
lengthened, it continues nearly the same, except that,
by the least acuteness in the voice it becomes a cry,
and is probably the first sound uttered by infants; but
if, while this element is articulated, the breath be
forced with an effort through the lips, we form an aspirate more or less harsh in proportion to the force
exerted. When, in pronouncing the simple vowel, we
open our lips wider, we express a sound completely
articulated, which most nations have agreed to place
the first in their symbolical systems: by opening them
wider still with the corners of them a little drawn back,
we give birth to the second of the Roman vowels, and
by a large aperture, with a farther inflexion of the lips
and a higher elevation of the tongue, we utter the third
of them. By pursing up our lips in the least degree,
we convert the simple element into another sound of

the same nature with the first vowel, and easily con-
founded with it in a broad pronunciation: when this new
sound is lengthened, it approaches very nearly to the
fourth vowel, which we form by a bolder and stronger
rotundity of the mouth; a farther contraction of it produces the fifth vowel, which in its elongation almost
closes the lips, a small passage only being left for the
breath. These are all short vowels; and, if an Italian
were to read the words an innocent bull, he would give
the sound of each corresponding long vowel, as in the
monosyllables of his own language, sà, sì, sò, sè, sù.
Between these ten vowels are numberless gradations,
and nice inflexions, which use only can teach; and, by
the composition of them all, might be formed an hundred diphthongs, and a thousand triphthongs. . . .

   We may now consider in the same order, beginning
with the root of the tongue and ending with the perfect
close of the lips, those less musical sounds, which require the aid of a vowel, or at least of the simple
breathing, to be fully articulated; and it may here be
premised, that the harsh breathing distinctly pronounced
after each of these consonants, as they are named by
grammarians, constitutes its proper aspirate. (pp. 182-5)

   We hear much of aspirated letters; but the only
proper aspirates (those I mean, in which a strong
breathing is distinctly heard after the consonants) are
to be found in the languages of India; unless the word
cachexy, which our medical writers have borrowed
from the Greek, be thought an exception to the rule:
this aspiration may be distinguished by a comma, as
the letter before us is expressed in the word c'hanitra,
a spade. (p. 195)

   Agreeably to the preceding analysis of letters, if I
were to adopt a new mode of English orthography, I
should write Addison's description of the angel in the following manner, distinguishing the simple breathing, or
first element, which we cannot invariably omit, by a per-
pendicular line above our first or second vowel:

   Sò hwen sm énjel, bai divain cămánd,
   Widh rais¹n tempests shécs a gilti land,
   Sch az ăv lét ór pél Britanya pást,
   Cálm and s¹rín hi draivz dhi fyúryas blást,
   And, pl¹z'd dh'álmaitiz árderz tu perfórm,
   Raids in dhi hwerlwind and dairects dhi stārm.

This mode of writing poetry would be the touch-
stone of bad rhymes, which the eye as well as the ear
would instantly detect; as in the first couplet of this
description, and even in the last, according to the common pronunciation of the word perform. I close this
paper with specimens of oriental writing, not as fixed
standards of orthography, which no individual has a
right to settle, but as examples of the method, which I
recommend.... (p. 205)

Jones (1746-94) was led to his knowledge of Sanskrit
through an interest in Hindu law. At Harrow and Oxford he
studied oriental languages and literature. After achieving
a reputation as an oriental scholar, out of financial necessity he undertook the study of law. In 1783 he was appointed
judge in Calcutta, where he continued his vigorous career of
publication. His collected works were published five years
after his death, in a handsome edition, The Works of Sir
William Jones in six volumes (London: Robinson and Evans,
1799). This has been followed here, with a few orthographical changes: since ligatures and symbols like long s are
not maintained, it also seemed best to modernize spellings
like authentic for authentick, and Sanskrit for Sanscrit, except in titles. Students having the opportunity of consulting
the printing of 1799 will admire, with Sir John Shore, Jones's
"degree of knowledge" and his elegant presentation.

IN the former discourses, which I had the honor of addressing to
you, Gentlemen, on the institution and objects of our Society, I confined myself purposely to general topics; giving in the first a distant
prospect of the vast career, on which we were entering, and, in the
second, exhibiting a more diffuse, but still superficial, sketch of the
various discoveries in History, Science, and Art, which we might
justly expect from our inquiries into the literature of Asia. I now
propose to fill up that outline so comprehensively as to omit nothing
essential, yet so concisely as to avoid being tedious; and, if the state
of my health shall suffer me to continue long enough in this climate,
it is my design, with your permission, to prepare for our annual
meetings a series of short dissertations, unconnected in their titles
and subjects, but all tending to a common point of no small importance in the pursuit of interesting truths.

Of all the works, which have been published in our own age, or,
perhaps, in any other, on the History of the Ancient World, and the

first population of this habitable globe, that of Mr. Jacob Bryant,
whom I name with reverence and affection, has the best claim to the
praise of deep erudition ingeniously applied, and new theories happily illustrated by an assemblage of numberless converging rays
from a most extensive circumference: it falls, nevertheless, as
every human work must fall, short of perfection; and the least satisfactory part of it seems to be that, which relates to the derivation
of words from Asiatic languages. Etymology has, no doubt, some
use in historical researches; but it is a medium of proof so very
fallacious, that, where it elucidates one fact, it obscures a thousand,
and more frequently borders on the ridiculous, than leads to any
solid conclusion: it rarely carries with it any internal power of
conviction from a resemblance of sounds or similarity of letters;
yet often, where it is wholly unassisted by those advantages, it may
be indisputably proved by extrinsic evidence. We know à posteriori,
that both <u>fitz</u> and <u>hijo</u>, by the nature of two several dialects, are
derived from <u>filius</u>; that <u>uncle</u> comes from <u>avus</u>, and <u>stranger</u> from
<u>extra</u>; that <u>jour</u> is deducible, through the <u>Italian</u>, from <u>dies</u>; and <u>ros-</u>
<u>signol</u> from <u>luscinia</u>, or the finger in groves; that <u>sciuro</u>, <u>écureuil</u>,
and <u>squirrel</u> are compounded of two Greek words descriptive of the
animal; which etymologies, though they could not have been demonstrated à priori, might serve to confirm, if any such confirmation
were necessary, the proofs of a connection between the members of
one great Empire; but, when we derive our <u>hanger</u>, or short pendent
sword, from the Persian, because ignorant travellers thus mis-spell
the word <u>khanjar</u>, which in truth means a different weapon, or <u>san-</u>
<u>dalwood</u> from the Greek, because we suppose, that sandals were
sometimes made of it, we gain no ground in proving the affinity of
nations, and only weaken arguments, which might otherwise be
firmly supported. That <u>Cús</u> then, or, as it certainly is written in
one ancient dialect, <u>Cút</u>, and in others, probably, <u>Cás</u>, enters into
the composition of many proper names, we may very reasonably
believe; and that <u>Algeziras</u> takes its name from the Arabic word for
an island, cannot be doubted; but, when we are told from Europe,
that places and provinces in India were clearly denominated from
those words, we cannot but observe, in the first instance, that the
town, in which we now are assembled, is properly written and pronounced <u>Calicátà</u>; that both <u>Cátá</u> and <u>Cút</u> unquestionably mean places
of strength, or, in general, any inclosures; and that <u>Gujaràt</u> is at
least as remote from <u>Jezirah</u> in sound, as it is in situation.
   Another exception (and a third could hardly be discovered by
any candid criticism) to the Analysis of Ancient Mythology, is, that
the method of reasoning and arrangement of topics adopted in that
learned work are not quite agreeable to the title, but almost wholly
synthetical; and, though synthesis may be the better mode in pure

science, where the principles are undeniable, yet it seems less cal-
culated to give complete satisfaction in historical disquisitions,
where every postulatum will perhaps be refused, and every definition controverted; this may seem a slight objection, but the subject
is in itself so interesting, and the full conviction of all reasonable
men so desirable, that it may not be lost labor to discuss the same
or a similar theory in a method purely analytical, and, after beginning with facts of general notoriety or undisputed evidence, to investigate such truths, as are at first unknown or very imperfectly
discerned.

The five principal nations, who have in different ages divided
among themselves, as a kind of inheritance, the vast continent of
Asia, with the many islands depending on it, are the Indians, the
Chinese, the Tartars, the Arabs, and the Persians: who they sev-
erally were, whence, and when they came, where they now are settled, and what advantage a more perfect knowledge of them all may
bring to our European world, will be shown, I trust, in five distinct
essays; the last of which will demonstrate the connection or diversity between them, and solve the great problem, whether they had
any common origin, and whether that origin was the same, which we
generally ascribe to them.

I begin with India, not because I find reason to believe it the
true center of population or of knowledge, but, because it is the
country, which we now inhabit, and from which we may best survey
the regions around us; as, in popular language, we speak of the rising sun, and of his progress through the Zodiac, although it had long
ago been imagined, and is now demonstrated, that he is himself the
center of our planetary system. Let me here premise, that, in all
these inquiries concerning the history of India, I shall confine my
researches downwards to the Mohammedan conquests at the beginning of the eleventh century, but extend them upwards, as high as
possible, to the earliest authentic records of the human species.

India then, on its most enlarged scale, in which the ancients
appear to have understood it, comprises an area of near forty degrees on each side, including a space almost as large as all Europe;
being divided on the west from Persia by the Arachosian mountains,
limited on the east by the Chinese part of the farther peninsula, confined on the north by the wilds of Tartary, and extending to the south
as far as the isles of Java. This trapezium, therefore, comprehends
the stupendous hills of Potyid or Tibet, the beautiful valley of Cashmír, and all the domains of the old Indoscythians, the countries of
Nepál and Butánt, Cámrup or Asàm, together with Siam, Ava, Racan,
and the bordering kingdoms, as far as the Chína of the Hindus or Sín
of the Arabian Geographers; not to mention the whole western peninsula with the celebrated island of Sinhala, or Lion-like men, at its

southern extremity. By India, in short, I mean that whole extent of country, in which the primitive religion and languages of the Hindus prevail at this day with more or less of their ancient purity, and in which the Nágarí letters are still used with more or less deviation from their original form.

The Hindus themselves believe their own country, to which they give the vain epithets of Medhyama or Central, and Punyabhúmi, or the Land of Virtues, to have been the portion of Bharat, one of nine brothers, whose father had the dominion of the whole earth; and they represent the mountains of Himálaya as lying to the north, and, to the west, those of Vindhya, called also Vindian by the Greeks; beyond which the Sindhu runs in several branches to the sea, and meets it nearly opposite to the point of Dwáracà, the celebrated seat of their Shepherd God: in the south-east they place the great river Saravatya; by which they probably mean that of Ava, called also Airávati in parts of its course, and giving perhaps its ancient name to the gulf of Sabara. This domain of Bharat they consider as the middle of the Jambudwípa, which the Tibetians also call the Land of Zambu; and the appellation is extremely remarkable; for Jambu is the Sanskrit name of a delicate fruit called Jáman by the Muselmans, and by us rose-apple; but the largest and richest sort is named Amrita, or Immortal; and the Mythologists of Tibet apply the same word to a celestial tree bearing ambrosial fruit, and adjoining to four vast rocks, from which as many sacred rivers derive their several streams.

The inhabitants of this extensive tract are described by Mr. Lord with great exactness, and with a picturesque elegance peculiar to our ancient language: "A people, says he, presented themselves to mine eyes, clothed in linen garments somewhat low descending, of a gesture and garb, as I may say, maidenly and well nigh effeminate, or a countenance shy and somewhat estranged, yet smiling out a glozed and bashful familiarity." Mr. Orme, the Historian of India, who unites an exquisite taste for every fine art with an accurate knowledge of Asiatic manners, observes, in his elegant preliminary Dissertation, that this "country has been inhabited from the earliest antiquity by a people, who have no resemblance, either in their figure or manners, with any of the nations contiguous to them," and that, "although conquerors have established themselves at different times in different parts of India, yet the original inhabitants have lost very little of their original character." The ancients, in fact, give a description of them, which our early travellers confirmed, and our own personal knowledge of them nearly verifies; as you will perceive from a passage in the Geographical Poem of Dionysius, which the Analyst of Ancient Mythology has translated with great spirit:

To th' east a lovely country wide extends,
India, whose borders the wide ocean bounds;
On this the sun, new rising from the main,
Smiles pleas'd, and sheds his early orient beam.
Th' inhabitants are swart, and in their locks
Betray the tints of the dark hyacinth.
Various their functions; some the rock explore,
And from the mine extract the latent gold;
Some labor at the woof with cunning skill,
And manufacture linen; others shape
And polish iv'ry with the nicest care:
Many retire to rivers shoal, and plunge
To seek the beryl flaming in its bed,
Or glitt'ring diamond. Oft the jasper's found
Green, but diaphanous; the topaz too
Of ray serene and pleasing; last of all
The lovely amethyst, in which combine
All the mild shades of purple. The rich soil,
Wash'd by a thousand rivers, from all sides
Pours on the natives wealth without control.

Their sources of wealth are still abundant even after so many
revolutions and conquests; in their manufactures of cotton they still
surpass all the world; and their features have, most probably, remained unaltered since the time of Dionysius; nor can we reasonably
doubt, how degenerate and abased so ever the Hindus may now appear, that in some early age they were splendid in art and arms,
happy in government, wise in legislation, and eminent in various
knowledge: but, since their civil history beyond the middle of the
nineteenth century from the present time, is involved in a cloud of
fables, we seem to possess only four general media of satisfying
our curiosity concerning it; namely, first their Languages and Letters; secondly, their Philosophy and Religion; thirdly, the actual
remains of their old Sculpture and Architecture; and fourthly, the
written memorials of their Sciences and Arts.

   I. It is much to be lamented, that neither the Greeks, who attended Alexander into India, nor those who were long connected with
it under the Bactrian Princes, have left us any means of knowing
with accuracy, what vernacular languages they found on their arrival
in this Empire. The Mohammedans, we know, heard the people of
proper Hindustan, or India on a limited scale, speaking a Bháshá, or
living tongue of a very singular construction, the purest dialect of
which was current in the districts round Agrà, and chiefly on the
poetical ground of Mat'hurà; and this is commonly called the idiom
of Vraja. Five words in six, perhaps, of this language were derived

from the Sanskrit, in which books of religion and science were composed, and which appears to have been formed by an exquisite grammatical arrangement, as the name itself implies, from some un-
polished idiom; but the basis of the Hindustaní, particularly the
inflections and regimen of verbs, differed as widely from both those
tongues, as Arabic differs from Persian, or German from Greek.
Now the general effect of conquest is to leave the current language
of the conquered people unchanged, or very little altered, in its
groundwork, but to blend with it a considerable number of exotic
names both for things and for actions; as it has happened in every
country, that I can recollect, where the conquerors have not preserved their own tongue unmixed with that of the natives, like the
Turks in Greece, and the Saxons in Britain; and this analogy might
induce us to believe, that the pure Hindî, whether of Tartarian or
Chaldean origin, was primeval in Upper India, into which the
Sanskrit was introduced by conquerors from other kingdoms in some
very remote age; for we cannot doubt that the language of the Véda's
was used in the great extent of country, which has before been delineated, as long as the religion of Brahmà has prevailed in it.

The Sanskrit language, whatever be its antiquity, is of a wonderful structure; more perfect than the Greek, more copious than
the Latin, and more exquisitely refined than either, yet bearing to
both of them a stronger affinity, both in the roots of verbs and in the
forms of grammar, than could possibly have been produced by accident; so strong indeed, that no philologer could examine them all
three, without believing them to have sprung from some common
source, which, perhaps, no longer exists: there is a similar reason,
though not quite so forcible, for supposing that both the Gothic and
the Celtic, though blended with a very different idiom, had the same
origin with the Sanskrit; and the old Persian might be added to the
same family, if this were the place for discussing any question concerning the antiquities of Persia.

The characters, in which the language of India were originally
written, are called Nágarí, from Nagara, a City, with the word Déva
sometimes prefixed, because they are believed to have been taught
by the Divinity himself, who prescribed the artificial order of them
in a voice from heaven. These letters, with no greater variation in
their form by the change of straight lines to curves, or conversely,
than the Cusic alphabet has received in its way to India, are still
adopted in more than twenty kingdoms and states, from the borders
of Cashgar and Khoten, to Ráma's bridge, and from the Sindhu to the
river of Siam; nor can I help believing, although the polished and
elegant Dévanágarí may not be so ancient as the monumental characters in the caverns of Jarasandha, that the square Chaldaic letters,
in which most Hebrew books are copied, were originally the same,

or derived from the same prototype, both with the Indian and Arabian characters: that the Phenician, from which the Greek and Roman alphabets were formed by various changes and inversions, had a similar origin, there can be little doubt; and the inscriptions at Canárah, of which you now possess a most accurate copy, seem to be compounded of Nágarí and Ethiopic letters, which bear a close relation to each other, both in the mode of writing from the left hand, and in the singular manner of connecting the vowels with the consonants. These remarks may favor an opinion entertained by many, that all the symbols of sound, which at first, probably, were only rude outlines of the different organs of speech, had a common origin: the symbols of ideas, now used in China and Japan, and formerly, perhaps, in Egypt and Mexico, are quite of a distinct nature; but it is very remarkable, that the order of sounds in the Chinese grammars corresponds nearly with that observed in Tibet, and hardly differs from that, which the Hindus consider as the invention of their Gods.

II. Of the Indian Religion and Philosophy, I shall here say but little; because a full account of each would require a separate volume: it will be sufficient in this dissertation to assume, what might be proved beyond controversy, that we now live among the adorers of those very deities, who were worshipped under different names in Old Greece and Italy, and among the professors of those philosophical tenets, which the Ionic and Attic writers illustrated with all the beauties of their melodious language. On one hand we see the trident of Neptune, the eagle of Jupiter, the satyrs of Bacchus, the bow of Cupid, and the chariot of the Sun; on another we hear the cymbals of Rhea, the songs of the Muses, and the pastoral tales of Apollo Nomius. In more retired scenes, in groves, and in seminaries of learning, we may perceive the Bráhmans and the Sarmanes, mentioned by Clemens, disputing in the forms of logic, or discoursing on the vanity of human enjoyments, on the immortality of the soul, her emanation from the eternal mind, her debasement, wanderings, and final union with her source. The six philosophical schools, whose principles are explained in the Dersana Sástra, comprise all the metaphysics of the old Academy, the Stoa, the Lyceum; nor is it possible to read the Védánta, or the many fine compositions in illustration of it, without believing, that Pythagoras and Plato derived their sublime theories from the same fountain with the sages of India. The Scythian and Hyperborean doctrines and mythology may also be traced in every part of these eastern regions; nor can we doubt, that Wod or Oden, whose religion, as the northern historians admit, was introduced into Scandinavia by a foreign race, was the same with Buddh, whose rites were probably imported into India nearly at the same time, though received much later by the Chinese, who soften his name into FO'.

This may be a proper place to ascertain an important point in the Chronology of the Hindus; for the priests of Buddha left in Tibet and China the precise epoch of his appearance, real or imagined, in this Empire; and their information, which had been preserved in writing, was compared by the Christian missionaries and scholars with our own era. Couplet, De Guignes, Giorgi, and Bailly, differ a little in their accounts of this epoch, but that of Couplet seems the most correct: on taking, however, the medium of the four several dates, we may fix the time of Buddha, or the ninth great incarnation of Vishnu, in the year one thousand and fourteen before the birth of Christ, or two thousand seven hundred and ninety-nine years ago. Now the Cáshmirians, who boast of his descent in their kingdom, assert that he appeared on earth about two centuries after Crishna the Indian Apollo, who took so decided a part in the war of the Mahábhárat; and, if an Etymologist were to suppose, that the Athenians had embellished their poetical history of Pandion's expulsion and the restoration of Ægeus with the Asiatic tale of the Pándus and Yudhishtir, neither of which words they could have articulated, I should not hastily deride his conjecture: certain it is, that Pándu-mandel is called by the Greeks the country of Pandion. We have, therefore, determined another interesting epoch, by fixing the age of Crishna near the three thousandth year from the present time; and, as the three first Avatàrs, or descents of Vishnu, relate no less clearly to an Universal Deluge, in which eight persons only were saved, than the fourth and the fifth do to the punishment of impiety and the humiliation of the proud, we may for the present assume, that the second, or silver, age of the Hindus was subsequent to the dispersion from Babel; so that we have only a dark interval of about a thousand years, which were employed in the settlement of nations, the foundation of states or empires, and the cultivation of civil society. The great incarnate Gods of this intermediate age are both named Ráma but with different epithets; one of whom bears a wonderful resemblance to the Indian Bacchus, and his wars are the subject of several heroic poems. He is represented as a descendent from Súrya, or the Sun, as the husband of Sítá, and the son of a princess named Caúselyá: it is very remarkable, that the Peruvians, whose Incas boasted of the same descent, styled their greatest festival Ramasitoa; whence we may suppose, that South America was peopled by the same race, who imported into the farthest parts of Asia the rites and fabulous history of Ráma. These rites and this history are extremely curious; and, although I cannot believe with Newton, that ancient mythology was nothing but historical truth in a poetical dress, nor, with Bacon, that it consisted solely of moral and metaphysical allegories, nor with Bryant, that all the heathen divinities are only different attributes and representations of the Sun or of deceased progenitors, but conceive that the whole system of religious fables rose, like the Nile, from several distinct sources, yet I cannot but agree, that one great spring and fountain of all idolatry in the four quarters of the globe was the veneration paid by men to the vast body of fire, which "looks from his sole dominion like the God of this world"; and another, the immoderate respect shown to the memory of powerful or virtuous ancestors, especially the founders of kingdoms, legislators, and warriors, of whom the Sun or the Moon were wildly supposed to be the parents.

III. The remains of architecture and sculpture in India, which I mention here as mere monuments of antiquity, not as specimens of ancient art, seem to prove an early connection between this country and Africa: the pyramids of Egypt, the colossal statues described by Pausanias and others, the sphinx, and the Hermes Canis, which last bears a great resemblance to the Varáhávatár, or the incarnation of Vishnu in the form of a Boar, indicate the style and mythology of the same indefatigable workmen, who formed the vast excavations of Cánárah, the various temples and images of Buddha, and the idols, which are continually dug up at Gayá, or in its vicinity. The letters on many of those monuments appear, as I have before intimated, partly of Indian, and partly of Abyssinian or Ethiopic, origin; and all these indubitable facts may induce no ill-grounded opinion, that Ethiopia and Hindustàn were peopled or colonized by the same extraordinary race; in confirmation of which, it may be added, that the mountaineers of Bengal and Bahàr can hardly be distinguished in some of their features, particularly their lips and noses, from the modern Abyssinians, whom the Arabs call the children of Cúsh: and the ancient Hindus, according to Strabo, differed in nothing from the Africans, but in the straitness and smoothness of their hair, while that of the others was crisp or woolly; a difference proceeding chiefly, if not entirely, from the respective humidity or dryness of their atmospheres: hence the people who received the first light of the rising sun, according to the limited knowledge of the ancients, are said by Apuleius to be the Arü and Ethiopians, by which he clearly meant certain nations of India; where we frequently see figures of Buddha with curled hair apparently designed for a representation of it in its natural state.

IV. It is unfortunate, that the Silpi Sástra, or collection of treatises on Arts and Manufactures, which must have contained a treasure of useful information on dying, painting, and metallurgy, has been so long neglected, that few, if any, traces of it are to be found; but the labors of the Indian loom and needle have been universally celebrated; and fine linen is not improbably supposed to have been called Sindon, from the name of the river near which it

was wrought in the highest perfection: the people of Colchis were
also famed for this manufacture, and the Egyptians yet more, as we
learn from several passages in scripture, and particularly from a
beautiful chapter in Ezekial containing the most authentic delineation
of ancient commerce, of which Tyre had been the principal mart.
Silk was fabricated immemorially by the Indians, though commonly
ascribed to the people of Serica or Tancŭt, among whom probably
the word Sèr, which the Greeks applied to the silkworm, signified
gold; a sense, which it now bears in Tibet. That the Hindus were in
early ages a commercial people, we have many reasons to believe;
and in the first of their sacred law-tracts, which they suppose to
have been revealed by Menu many millions of years ago, we find a
curious passage on the legal interest of money, and the limited rate
of it in different cases, with an exception in regard to adventures at
sea; an exception, which the sense of mankind approves, and which
commerce absolutely requires, though it was not before the reign of
Charles I. that our own jurisprudence fully admitted it in respect of
maritime contracts.

We are told by the Grecian writers, that the Indians were the
wisest of nations; and in moral wisdom, they were certainly eminent:
their Nìti Sástra, or System of Ethics, is yet preserved, and the Fables of Vishnuserman, whom we ridiculously call Pilpay, are the
most beautiful, if not the most ancient, collection of apologues in the
world: they were first translated from the Sanskrit, in the sixth
century, by the order of Buzerchumihr, or Bright as the Sun, the
chief physician and afterwards Vezír of the great Anúshirevàn, and
are extant under various names in more than twenty languages; but
their original title is Hitópadésa, or Amicable Instruction; and, as
the very existence of Esop, whom the Arabs believe to have been an
Abyssinian, appears rather doubtful, I am not disinclined to suppose,
that the first moral fables, which appeared in Europe, were of Indian
or Ethiopian origin.

The Hindus are said to have boasted of three inventions, all of
which, indeed, are admirable, the method of instructing by apologues, the decimal scale adopted now by all civilized nations, and
the game of Chess, on which they have some curious treatises; but,
if their numerous works on Grammar, Logic, Rhetoric, Music, all
which are extant and accessible, were explained in some language
generally known, it would be found, that they had yet higher preten-
sions to the praise of a fertile and inventive genius. Their lighter
Poems are lively and elegant; their Epic, magnificent and sublime
in the highest degree; their Purána's comprise a series of mytho-
logical Histories in blank verse from the Creation to the supposed
incarnation of Buddha; and their Védas, as far as we can judge from
that compendium of them, which is called Upanishat, abound with

noble speculations in metaphysics, and fine discourses on the being and attributes of God. Their most ancient medical book, entitled Chereca, is believed to be the work of Siva; for each of the divinities in their Triad has at least one sacred composition ascribed to him; but, as to mere human works on History and Geography, though they are said to be extant in Cashmír, it has not been yet in my power to procure them. What their astronomical and mathematical writings contain, will not, I trust, remain long a secret: they are easily procured, and their importance cannot be doubted. The Philosopher, whose works are said to include a system of the universe founded on the principle of Attraction and the Central position of the sun, is named Yavan Achárya, because he had travelled, we are told, into Ionia: if this be true, he might have been one of those, who conversed with Pythagoras; this at least is undeniable, that a book on astronomy in Sanskrit bears the title of Yavana Jática, which may signify the Ionic Sect; nor is it improbable, that the names of the planets and Zodiacal stars, which the Arabs borrowed from the Greeks, but which we find in the oldest Indian records, were originally devised by the same ingenious and enterprizing race, from whom both Greece and India were peopled; the race, who, as Dionysius describes them,

> ... first assayed the deep,
> And wafted merchandize to coasts unknown,
> Those, who digested first the starry choir,
> Their motions mark'd, and call'd them by their names.

Of these cursory observations on the Hindus, which it would require volumes to expand and illustrate, this is the result: that they had an immemorial affinity with the old Persians, Ethiopians, and Egyptians, the Phenicians, Greeks, and Tuscans, the Scythians or Goths, and Celts, the Chinese, Japanese, and Peruvians; whence, as no reason appears for believing, that they were a colony from any one of those nations, or any of those nations from them, we may fairly conclude that they all proceeded from some central country, to investigate which will be the object of my future Discourses; and I have a sanguine hope, that your collections during the present year will bring to light many useful discoveries; although the departure for Europe of a very ingenious member, who first opened the inestimable mine of Sanskrit literature, will often deprive us of accurate and solid information concerning the languages and antiquities of India.

CHAPTER TWO

FRIEDRICH VON SCHLEGEL

ON THE LANGUAGE AND WISDOM OF THE INDIANS

From Über die Sprache und Weisheit der Indier:
Ein Beitrag zur Begründung der Alterthumskunde
(Heidelberg: Mohr und Zimmer, 1808)

Like Jones's Discourse, Friedrich von Schlegel's Über die Sprache und Weisheit der Indier prepares for the important early works in nineteenth-century linguistics. Schlegel's aim too is to encourage general study of antiquity, not only of language; the section on language makes up only approximately a fourth of his book, which goes on to deal with other "media of satisfying our curiosity concerning...the early age" of mankind. Schlegel's book was important for arousing interest in Sanskrit, especially in Germany; it also makes the first mention of aims that were to be central to linguistics, notably "comparative grammar". Because its prime importance is its encouragement to others, only excerpts are given here, though the entire book is delightful to read. I have included one paragraph of citations comparing the vocabulary of Sanskrit and German; it may illustrate the advances made over Schlegel by his successors. And his lists of grammatical criteria for establishing relationships illustrate the enthusiasm of a popularizer rather than the care of a scholar. From the selections translated, students may learn to know the contributions of Schlegel's work as well as its shortcomings.

With his successors, Schlegel is interested in finding a common source for the languages which after Jones were held to be related. In interpreting the early conception of "source" or "derived from" we must be careful to avoid our own definitions, which are based largely on the work of subsequent linguists. In his excellent introduction to the centenary edition of Rask, Ausgewählte Abhandlungen XIII-LXIII, Holger Pedersen discusses sympathetically the use of these notions at the beginning of the nineteenth century for determining the relationship of languages. Schlegel indeed speaks of a family-tree, but derives the European languages from Sanskrit on the basis of its greater antiquity, not by positing intermediate stages. Accordingly, the relationship he suggests between German and Sanskrit should not be equated with our deriving German from Proto-Indo-European.

Schlegel's emphasis on grammar in determining relationships merits great credit. His demand for precise agreement of vocabulary items may be understood when we compare the fanciful etymologies of his predecessors; insistence on rigor was essential to stop further such fabrications. Yet while he asks for complete agreement in determining cognates, Schlegel permits the use of forms which differ, though he has not yet hit upon the concept of determining "rules" for such differences; his citing of an "analogy" between Latin p and Germanic f, Latin c and Germanic h, is a step on the way to the more comprehensive sets of rules given by Rask and Grimm.

Schlegel also is applauded for introducing the term "comparative grammar" into linguistics. In basing this term on comparative anatomy and incorporating the notion of family trees for languages, he drew on biology for linguistic methodology, foreshadowing Schleicher and his reliance on Darwinism. These adoptions of methodology and the attention he drew to Sanskrit are the most important contributions of his book.

Yet in it Schlegel also suggested a further means for distinguishing language interrelationships, one that was not taken over by Bopp, Grimm and their successors, and subsequently remained peripheral to the central course of nineteenth century linguistics: the use of typology. For Schlegel there was an ancient grammar, characterized by inflection, and a more recent grammar, characterized by analytic devices. Languages of the ancient type were more kunstreich (ingenious, artistic) than are those of the newer manner. Accordingly, examination of the type of a language might contribute to determining its antiquity. Yet in dealing with Chinese, for even Schlegel this means was disappointing; the problems of typology interested some linguists of the nineteenth century, notably Humboldt and Steinthal, but its uncertainties gave it more status among non-specialists than among linguists. Even the efforts of Sapir in this century did little to encourage its application, though recent techniques may make it more useful. (See my Historical Linguistics, Chapter III.) Yet all attempts to use typology in support of genealogical classification have been completely discredited. We may wonder whether the ineffectiveness of typology as a tool for supporting genealogical classification led Schlegel's successors to disregard his interest in structure, which we find duplicated only in this century.

Apart from his book of 1808, the chief concern of Friedrich von Schlegel (1772-1829) was for literature. He began his study of Sanskrit and Indian antiquity in 1803, under Alexander Hamilton in Paris, planning a chrestomathy printed in Devanagari, but for it he lacked the necessary funds. Instead he published his book to arouse interest in Indic studies, expecting for European scholarship results comparable to those produced by the study of Greek in the fifteenth and sixteenth centuries. Yet after publication of the book, he himself abandoned his concern for Indic studies, in a shift of interest that may be reflected by his joining the Roman Catholic Church. From then to his death he directed his attention to Europe and his own literary production. His brother, August Wilhelm von Schlegel (1767-1845), who also concerned himself with the typological classification of language, came to concentrate on Indic studies, especially after he was appointed professor of literature at the University of Bonn in 1818. His work in this position is generally credited as the beginning of Indic scholarship in Germany. Apart from the contributions which increased knowledge of Indic languages made to linguistics, the importance of the brothers for linguistics is based almost entirely on Friedrich's book of 1808.

Chapter 1. On the Indic Language in General (pp. 1-3)

The Old Indic Sanskrito, that is the cultivated or perfected, also Gronthon, that is the written language or the book language, has a very close relationship with the Roman and Greek, as with the Germanic and Persian languages. The similarity consists not only in a great number of roots, which it shares with them, but it extends to the innermost structure and grammar. The agreement is accordingly not one of chance which might be explained by mixture, but rather an essential one which points to common descent. Comparison yields the further result that the Indic language is the older, the others however later and derived from it.

For Armenian, the Slavic languages and next for Celtic, the relationship with Indic is either minute, or not to be compared with the close agreement among the languages named above which we

derive from it. Yet this relationship, though minute, is not to be
completely disregarded, since it manifests itself in accordance with
the sequence in which these languages were named at least in some
grammatical forms, in such components which cannot be reckoned
among the chance features of the language but rather belong to their
inner structure.

In Hebrew and related dialects, as well as in Coptic, a goodly
number of Indic roots may possibly be found still. But this does not
prove an original relationship since it can be the result of simple
mixture. The grammar of these languages like that of Basque is
basically different from that of Indic.

The large and not yet completely determinable number of the
remaining north and south Asiatic and American languages has absolutely no essential relationship with the Indic language family. To
be sure, in the grammar of these languages, which also is quite different from that of Indic, we find a similar arrangement among several; in their roots however they are also completely different, even
among one another and so totally deviant, that there is no possibility
of being able to take them back to a common source.

The important results of this linguistic comparison for the oldest history of the origin of peoples and their earliest migrations will
be the subject of investigation in the future. In this first book we
will be content with establishing and making clear the principles
themselves, simple but very comprehensive results of conscientious
research. . . .

Chapter 2. On the Relationship of Roots (pp. 6-7)

Some examples may show most clearly that the claimed relationship does not in any sense rest on etymological elaborations,
many of which were contrived before the proper source was found,
but that it may be presented to impartial scholars as simple fact.

In making this demonstration we permit absolutely no rules of
change or replacement of letters, but rather demand complete equivalence of the word as proof of descent. To be sure, if the intermediate steps can be proved historically, then giorno may be derived
from dies; and if instead of Latin f we often find Spanish h, if Latin
p very often becomes f in the Germanic form of the same word and
Latin c not infrequently h, this certainly establishes an analogy,
also for other not quite such apparent cases. Yet as indicated, one
must be able to demonstrate the intermediate steps or the general
analogy historically; nothing can be fabricated from axioms, and the
agreement must be very precise and evident in order to permit even
the minutest variations of form.

I cite first of all some Indic words which are characteristic of Germanic. Shrityoti — er schreitet 'strides'; vindoti — er findet 'finds'; schliβyoti — er umschlieβt 'surrounds'; Onto — das Ende 'end'; Monuschyo — der Mensch 'human being'; Shvosa, Svostri — die Schwester 'sister'; Rotho — das Rad 'wheel'; Bhruvo — die Brauen der Augen 'eyebrows'; Torsho — der Durst 'thirst'; Tandovon — der Tanz 'dance'; Ondoni — die Enten 'ducks'; Noko — der Nagel 'nail'; sthiro — unbeweglich, stier 'immovable'; Oshonon — das Essen 'food', etc....

Chapter 3. Of Grammatical Structure (pp. 27-28; 32-35)

Might one however not possibly reverse this whole proof and say: the relationship is striking enough and may be established in part; but what really is the reason for assuming that Indic is the older among the related languages and their common source? May it not just as well have arisen only through mixture of the others, or at any rate have received its similarity in this way?

Not to mention that much of what has already been mentioned and also many another probability speaks against that, we will now come to something that decides the situation fully and raises it to certainty. In general the hypothesis that attempts to derive whatever Greek elements are found in India from the Seleucids in Bactria is not much happier than one which might try to explain the Egyptian pyramids from natural crystallization.

The decisive point however which will clarify everything here is the inner structure of the languages or comparative grammar, which will give us quite new information about the genealogy of languages in a similar way as comparative anatomy has illuminated the higher natural history.

Of the related languages we will first select Persian, whose grammar, which has even taken over personal suffixes from Arabic through the long and old intercourse between both peoples, agrees with that of Indic and the others far less than even that of German today, not to speak of Greek and Roman. But if one assembles all similarities, they are certainly weighty.... [to p. 32]

In Germanic grammar there are many other agreements with the Greek and Indic besides those which it shares with Persian. In Germanic as throughout in Indic, n is characteristic of the accusative, s of the genitive. The final syllable -tvon forms substantives of state in Indic, just as -thum is used in German. The subjunctive is in part marked by a change of the vowel, as in all languages which follow the old grammar. Agreeing similarly is the formation of the imperfect through change of the vowel in one type of the German

verbs. If in another type the imperfect is formed by means of an
inserted t, this to be sure is a special characteristic, just as is the
b in the Roman imperfect; the principle however is still the same,
namely that the secondary determination of the meaning for time
and other relationships does not happen through special words or
particles added outside the word, but through inner modification of
the root.

If, moreover, we add the grammar of the older dialects, of
Gothic and Anglo-Saxon for German, of Icelandic for the Scandinavian branch of our language, then we not only find a perfect with an
augment, as in Greek and Indic, a dual, more exact gender and relationship markers of the inflections, which now are somewhat worn
down and less recognizable; the third persons of the singular and
plural of verbs, for example, are complete and in perfect agreement. In a word, in the contemplation of the old monuments of the
Germanic language not the slightest doubt can remain that they formerly had a quite similar grammatical structure to that of Greek
and Roman.

Even now very many traces of these older forms of language
remain in Germanic, in German itself more than in English and the
Scandinavian dialects; but if on the whole the principle of the more
recent grammar prevails here — to form conjugation primarily
through auxiliary verbs, declension through prepositions — this
should mislead us the less, since also all the Romance languages,
which stem from the Latin, have undergone a similar change, as
have all the Hindustani dialects, as they are now spoken, which have
approximately the same relationship to Sanskrit as the Romance
dialects do to Latin. No external cause is necessary either to explain this phenomenon which shows up everywhere the same. The
ingenious structure is readily lost through wearing away by common
usage, especially in a time of barbarism, either quite gradually, or
at times also more suddenly; and the grammar with auxiliaries and
prepositions is actually the shortest and most convenient, like an
abbreviation for simple, general usage; in fact one could almost establish the general rule that a language is the easier to learn, the
more its structure has been simplified and approximated to this abbreviation. . . .

Chapter 4. Of Two Main Types of Languages according to Their Inner Structure (pp. 44-45)

The real essence of this principle of language which prevails
in Indic and in all languages derived from it is best made clear
through contrast. For not all languages follow this grammar, whose
ingenious simplicity we admire in Indic and Greek, and to whose

character we tried to call attention in the previous chapter. In many other languages and actually in the most, we find the characteristics and laws of a grammar quite different from that, indeed in complete contrast with it.

Either the secondary markings of meaning are indicated through inner change of the sound of the root, through inflection; or on the other hand always through a separate, added word, which by itself indicates plurality, past, a future obligation or other relationship concepts of manner; and these two very simple cases also designate the two main types of all languages. On closer inspection all other cases are only modifications and secondary types of these two kinds; therefore this contrast includes and completely exhausts the entire sphere of language which is immeasurable and indeterminable with regard to the variety of roots.

A notable example of a language quite without inflection, in which everything that the other languages indicate through inflection is arranged through separate words that have a meaning by themselves, is furnished by Chinese: a language which with its peculiar monosyllabicity, because of this consistency or rather perfect simplicity of structure, is very instructive for the understanding of the entire world of languages.... (to 49-50)

The series of grades of languages, which follow this grammar, is accordingly the following. In Chinese, the particles which designate the secondary marking of meaning are monosyllabic words that exist by themselves and are quite independent of the root. The language of this otherwise refined nation would accordingly stand precisely on the lowest grade; possibly, because its childhood was fixed too early through its extremely ingenious writing system. In Basque and Coptic, as in the American languages, the grammar is formed completely through suffixes and prefixes, which are almost everywhere still easy to distinguish and in part still have meaning by themselves; but the added particles are already beginning to merge and coalesce with the word itself. This is even more the case in Arabic and all related dialects, which to be sure clearly belong to this type in accordance with the greater part of their grammar, while many other things cannot be taken back to it with certainty; here and there we even find an individual agreement with grammar through inflection. Finally, in Celtic some individual traces of grammar through suffixes are found; yet in greater part the newer manner is the prevalent one, of conjugating through auxiliaries and declining through prepositions. ...

Chapter 6. Of the Variety of Related Languages and of
Some Peculiar Intermediate Languages
(conclusion, pp. 84-86)

I would really be afraid of tiring and confusing the reader if I
reported everything that had been gathered and prepared. Enough
if some order has been brought in the whole field and it has been
indicated satisfactorily, by what principles a comparative grammar
may be drawn up, and a completely historical family-tree — a true
history of the origin of language instead of the former fabricated
theories about its origin. What was said here will at least be adequate to demonstrate the importance of the study of Indic, even only
from the point of view of the language; in the following book we will
contemplate this study in relation to the history of the Oriental
spirit.

I conclude with a look back at William Jones, who first brought
light into the knowledge of language through the relationship and
derivation he demonstrated of Roman, Greek, Germanic and Persian
from Indic, and through this into the ancient history of peoples,
where previously everything had been dark and confused. When
however he wants to extend the relationship to some other cases
too, where it is much smaller — further, to reduce the indetermin-
ably great number of languages to the three main branches of the
Indic, the Arabic and the Tatar families — and finally, after he himself first determined so beautifully the total difference of Arabic
and Indic, to derive everything from one common original source
simply for the sake of unity; then we have not been able to follow
this excellent man in these matters, and in this everyone will un-
hesitatingly agree who examines the present treatise attentively.

CHAPTER THREE

RASMUS RASK

AN INVESTIGATION CONCERNING THE SOURCE
OF THE OLD NORTHERN OR ICELANDIC LANGUAGE

"Undersøgelse om det gamle Nordiske eller Islandske
Sprogs Oprindelse" (Copenhagen, 1818), in Rasmus Rask,
Ausgewählte Abhandlungen, ed. by Louis Hjelmslev, Vol. I
(Kopenhagen: Levin and Munksgaard, 1932)

Perhaps the most brilliant of the early linguists,
Rasmus Rask (1787-1832) made his primary contribution
in accordance with a topic proposed for a prize by the
Danish Academy of Sciences in 1811. The topic directed
the structure of his monograph, and according to Pedersen
led to some of its shortcomings. It requested competitors
to "examine with historical criticism and indicate with appropriate examples the source from which the old Scandinavian language is to be derived most securely; also to
indicate the character of the language and the relationship
in which it stood from the oldest periods and during the
Middle Ages on the one hand to the Nordic, on the other to
the Germanic dialects; also to determine precise principles
which must be followed in any statement of the origin and
comparison of these languages."

After discussing general principles, Rask surveyed the
evidence with regard to neighboring languages: Greenlandic
Eskimo, Celtic, Basque, Finnish, Slavic, Lettish, Thracian
and the Asiatic languages. His survey of the relationship
with Thracian (a term he adopted from Adelung to refer to
the ancestor of Greek and Latin, hence one which we might
equate with Indo-European) makes up approximately half of
his monograph and contains the well-known statement relating Icelandic obstruents to those of Greek and Latin.
Grimm himself indicated his indebtedness to this statement; after coming to know it he speedily rewrote the first
volume of his grammar of 1819 and included in the second
edition of 1822 the section presented below on the Germanic
consonant shift. Rask's statement is presented here, with
a few other excerpts to illustrate his fine grasp of linguistic principles.

As Pedersen and others have pointed out, Rask must
be credited for his use of "system" and "grammatical criteria" rather than vocabulary in carrying out the request of
the Academy. Although we applaud him for his methodological advances, we regret some of his terminology, for
example, his name Thracian for "Indo-European". Since
he did not know Sanskrit at the time he wrote his monograph, his group of Indo-European languages was still
small, though in it he accurately provided the answer to
the first request of the Academy. For the Germanic branch
he used the term Gothic, which he divided into Scandinavian
and Germanic (of which [Moeso-]Gothic was in turn a sub-
branch).

Less external is the terminology regarding "source"
and "descendant of"; a literal interpretation of these suggests that Rask was quite wrong in his genealogical classification. Yet these terms Pedersen would like to interpret
"systematically" not "historically". Students who wish to
deal with the problem fully may go to the original, admirably edited by Louis Hjelmslev, and to Pedersen's sympa-
thetic introduction. Some of Rask's other views correspond
to those of Schlegel; like him Rask thought of inflectional
languages as the most ingenious — though unlike Schlegel he
concerned himself little with typology.

The most widely discussed problem in relation to Rask
is one of priority: has he been given inadequate credit for
his accurate formulation of the Germanic consonant change,
known widely by the name of Grimm's law? The discussion
in Holger Pedersen's Linguistic Science in the Nineteenth
Century, pp. 248-254, 258-262, presents the problem with
Pedersen's well-known conciseness. In these days of cor-
porate scholarship, questions of individual credit do not
seem as important as they did in the past, when even national prestige was involved. We are much more interested
in trying to understand the views, and for them the terminology used by perceptive scholars of the past. We admire
Rask for noting the correspondences; Grimm accepted
these, supported them more fully and gave his well-known
formulation.

We also admire Rask for his efforts to learn language
in the field; the data for his conclusions are largely the result of his own collecting. After completing his monograph,
Rask undertook a journey to Russia, Persia and India, which
led to more advanced views on the Indo-European languages.
We also credit him for managing his data with a methodology

that approximates the high requirements of successors: though in the essay he still used the term "letter" for sounds as well as for writing symbols, he attempted to get at the phonetic basis of the letters. The phonetic interpretation he then compared systematically. Of further emphasis in his comparisons was grammar. This emphasis is clear from the space he devotes to grammatical comparison (pp. 190-295) of the monograph as opposed to vocabulary (295-321).

Rask's interest in learning ever more languages consumed the rest of his life after his return from his trip to the east in 1823. His failure to incorporate his new ideas in a revision of the "prize monograph" as well as its availability only in Danish led to a widespread disregard of it. The centenary edition in Danish has made up in part for previous neglect; possibly for the one hundred and fiftieth anniversary of Rask's death a complete English translation might be arranged. Rask's perceptive examination of his data and the great preponderance of methodology that accords with ours in proceeding beyond that of his predecessors would justify the translation, though most scholars might with little difficulty make their way through the Danish original.

Investigations, pp. 49-51

Grammatical agreement is a far more certain indication (than is vocabulary) of relationship or original unity; for one finds that a language which is mixed with another very rarely or never takes over changes of form or inflection from this, but on the other hand the more readily loses its own. In this way English has not taken over any Icelandic or French inflections, but on the other hand has lost many of the old inflections of Anglo-Saxon; similarly Danish has not taken over German endings, nor has Spanish taken over Gothic or Arabic endings. This kind of agreement, which is the most important and most certain, has nonetheless been almost entirely overlooked until now in tracing the source of languages, and this is the greatest error of most things written to the present on this point; it is the reason why they are so uncertain and of such small scientific value.

The language which has the most ingenious grammar is the most unmixed, the most original, oldest and nearest to the source; for the grammatical inflections and endings are constantly lost with

the formation of a new language, and it requires a very long time
and intercourse with other people to develop and rearrange itself
anew. In this way Danish is simpler than Icelandic, English simpler
than Anglo-Saxon; in the same way New Greek is related to Old
Greek, Italian to Latin, German to Moeso-Gothic, and similarly in
all situations that we know.

A language, however mixed it may be, belongs to the same class
of languages as another, when it has the most essential, concrete,
indispensable and primary words, the foundation of the language, in
common with it. On the other hand nothing can be concluded about
the original relationship of technical terms, words of politeness and
commerce or that part of the language which intercourse with others, social relations among one another, education and science have
made it necessary to add to the oldest stock of words; it depends on
many circumstances, which can only be known from history, whether
a people has borrowed these from other languages or developed
them from its own. Thus English is rightly counted to the Gothic
class of languages and in particular to the Saxon branch of the Germanic chief part of it; for all basic stems of the English stock of
words are Saxon, such as: heaven, earth, sea, land, man, head,
hair, eye, hand, foot, horse, cow, calf, ill, good, great, little, whole,
half, I, thou, he, to make, love, go, see, stand; of, out, from, together, etc. Especially substitutes (pronouns) and numerals are
lost last of all in mixing with unlike languages; in Anglo-Saxon for
example all pronouns are of Gothic and specifically Saxon origin.

When in such words one finds agreements between two languages, and that to such an extent that one can draw up rules for
the transition of letters from one to the other, then there is an
original relationship between these languages; especially when the
similarities in the inflection of languages and its formal organization correspond; e.g.

Gk	phēmē	in Latin to	fama	and		holkos	to	sulcus
Gk	mētēr	in Latin to	mater	and		bolbos	to	bulbus
Gk	phēgos	in Latin to	fagus	and		amorgē	to	amurca
Gk	pēlos	in Latin to	palus	and	Aeol.	olkhos	to	vulgus

From this one sees that Gk ē in Latin often becomes a, and o becomes u; by bringing together many words one would be able to
draw up many transition rules. And since one finds such great
agreement between Latin and Greek grammar, one can rightfully
conclude that an original relationship exists between these languages, which is also sufficiently known and does not need to be
demonstrated here again.

Thracian

(pp. 177-8) After having considered the three eastern classes
of languages: Finnish, which had little or no relation with Icelandic,
Slavic, which was closely related, and Lettish, which seemed even
nearer; we find to the south the Roman class of languages and the
New Greek. The Romance is of greatest extent; to it belong Italian,
Spanish, Portuguese and French, but all these languages are more
notable for their development, harmony and literary riches than for
age or remote origin. It is known that all of them arose after the
fall of the Roman Empire, indeed long after, when the confusion
which the wandering Gothic people caused to the old Latin began to
subside, but in such a way that the old material completely maintained the upper hand and merely was rearranged in new form. Accordingly this language could in no way contain the source for the
Gothic, which is much older; and the same can be applied to New
Greek; but the Romance languages descend, as indicated, from the
Latin, and the New Greek (hē rōmaïkē) from the old or real Greek
(hē hellenikē): we then come to the two old, rightfully famous peoples, the Greeks and Romans.

Adelung in his Mithridates has demonstrated at length and with
care that all the peoples, who were situated between the Halys River
in Asia Minor, as widely as broadly to the north and west up to Pan-
nonia, where the Germanic stock began, are to be ascribed to a single stock of peoples, whom he called the Thracian-Pelagian-Greek-
Latin, but who in my opinion might be given the shorter designation
Thracian, after the central point.

(pp. 187-8) [After stating phonetic similarities between Greek
and Icelandic, Rask discusses some differences, such as the limited
number of permitted final consonants in Greek and the loss of final
inflections in Icelandic; he continues:] But not only in endings, also
in the words themselves many changes took place; it will probably
not be out of the way to note here the most frequent of these transitions from Greek and Latin to Icelandic.

Long a becomes á or ó, as: elakhus (little) lágur (low), mater módir.

Short a to e: daman temia, scabo eg skèf, sakkos,
                                  saccus seckur.

u to o: gunē kona, purgos (tower) borg, gusto
                                  German ich koste.

Of the mute letters, they generally remain in words, becoming
usually:

p to f, e.g.:   platus (broad) flatur (flat), patēr fadir.

t to þ, e.g.:   treis (read trís) þrír, tego eg þek, tu tu þu.

k to h, e.g.:   kreas (meat) hræ (dead body), cornu horn, cutis hud.

b most often remains: blazanō (germinate) blad, bruō (spring forth) brunnr (spring), bullare at bulla.

d to t: damaō (tame) tamr (tame), dignus tíginn (elevated, noble)

g to k: gunē kona, genos kyn or kin, gena kinn, agros akr.

ph to b: phēgos Danish Bøg, fiber, Icel. bifr, phero fero eg ber.

th to d: thurā dyr; so also in Lagin, theos deus.

kh to g: khuō Danish gyder, ekhein ega, khutra grýta, kholē gall.

' to s: heks sex, hama saman, hupnos svefn, Danish Søvn.

But often they are also changed in other ways; for example, medially and after a vowel k becomes g, as in: macer (read maker) mager, ac og, taceo Icel. þegi; and t to d, as in: pater fadir, frater bródir, and the like.

(pp. 190-2) [After dealing with the phonology of the Thracian languages, Rask surveys their morphology. Only his introduction is translated here; he goes on to survey the paradigms, spending most of his time on the substantives, much less on verbs.] Both languages which we know of the Thracian class, namely Greek and Latin, are so famous and well-known that it would be superfluous here to describe them extensively; but since they have been analyzed by various language teachers, accordingly from various points of view, they have been given a more unlike appearance than they really have. Presumably none of the learned men who have worked in this area have known the related, ancient and unusual languages: Lithuanian, Slavonic, Moeso-Gothic and Icelandic; these are very closely related to the Thracian, and could contribute so very much to clarify them. Indeed these have until now been much less analyzed and known than the Thracian languages. One can accordingly not expect to find greater agreements between the proposed grammatical systems of these and the Thracian languages than between the Thracian languages themselves. From the foregoing one should also have been convinced that there is much to improve in the grammars of these

languages, in respect to system and manner of presentation. The
same is true of Thracian or the so-called ancient language, and it
is scarcely to be expected that anyone who knows only one or at
most two of these languages could find out the system which was the
correct one for all; this can only be discovered through comparison
of all of them. I have in the foregoing given briefly for each language the classification and arrangement that seems to me most
correct, especially from the basis which seems most fitting for all
of them. I will accordingly do the same here, at least to present the
reader all of them from a single point of view, which is indispens-
ably necessary, if one is to recognize and evaluate the similarities
or dissimilarities between them.

Nouns and adjectives have one and the same manner of inflection in both the Thracian languages: in Greek they distinguish three
numbers and in the singular five cases, which are best arranged as
follows: 1) nominative, 2) vocative, which is generally only an insignificant modification of the nominative, 3) accusative, 4) genitive,
and 5) dative. One might be uncertain which of the last two should
be placed first, but because of the relationship of the accusative with
the genitive in the Slavic languages, as of the natural likeness of the
endings in the Lettish and Thracian languages, the arrangement
given seems most correct. The dual has only two cases: the one
is used for the nominative, vocative and accusative; the other for
the genitive and dative. The plural has four; the nominative and
vocative are always the same here. In Latin on the other hand these
parts of speech have six cases in the singular, namely, in addition
to Greek, 6) an ablative, which however is simply a modification of
the dative. The dual is lacking entirely in Latin, but in the plural it
has the same cases as in Greek, since the vocative is included with
the nominative and the ablative with the dative. Gender and comparison are the usual three. With regard to method of inflection
these words are distinguished in both languages into two main types
or systems, as also in Gothic, Slavic and Lettish. The sub-division
in each of these, as in the languages just mentioned, is made according to gender; Neuter, which is the simplest and most original,
is to be set first, thereupon Masculine, which is directly developed
from it; and finally the Feminine, which has the most peculiarities
of its own.

In accordance with this principle of division the separate methods of inflection in these languages are as follows: [The first system contains the three genders; the second system is made up of a
neuter and a common gender.]

(p. 295) This formal organization of the Icelandic language is
much simpler than the Greek and Latin inflection, from which it has
originated in its entirety. For there is hardly a single form or

ending which is not found in them, except for those which have
arisen from combinations of parts which however are individually
found in the Thracian languages. After this one will also expect a
significant similarity also in regard to the stock of words. Since I
cannot give here an entire dictionary, however, I will limit myself
to citing a number of individual words as proof. [He cites 352.]

(pp. 321-3) This collection of words which in the Thracian and
Gothic languages, and especially in Icelandic, seem to have an original relationship to one another, could easily have been larger, but
I omitted many, though they were obvious in both classes of languages, such as all interjections: ouai, Lat. vae, Icel. vei, from
which vein and kvein as also veina and kveina, ai Icel. æ (read aj),
pheu Danish fy, and many others; and I selected these not so much
according to ease of detecting likeness, but much more according to
meaning, to demonstrate that precisely the first and most necessary
words in the language, which designate the first objects of thought,
are the same in both classes of languages. For this purpose I also
listed them according to subject matter. I do not assume that all
will agree with me on every one of these; but even if one throws out
all of those about which one might have some doubt, then nonetheless
of 352, in addition to the 48 listed above, in all 400 words, enough
will certainly remain, that combined with the grammatical comparison given above they will prove as much as the 150 words with added
grammatical notes which Sajnovics has cited as 'proof that the Hungarian and Lappish languages are one and the same'; as far as I
know, no one has subsequently denied this. After this agreement
which we have found in the stock of words and in inflection, as well
as in accordance with the agreed historical indication of our fathers'
immigration to the north from Scythia, and especially the last
main colony, which is said to have brought in the language, literature and runes, which have such a striking likeness with the oldest
Phoenician-Greek series of letters, which colony, as well-known,
came from Tanais and the Black Sea: it seems that both the North-
men and the Germanic peoples are branches of the large Thracian
stock of peoples, and that their language must also have had there
its first origin, which also agrees with what is known about the languages of the Lettish stock and its relationship to the Greek. The
Lettish stock is the nearest branch of the Thracian, next the Northern and the Germanic; the last seems to me somewhat farther away,
which is also natural as a result of our fathers' eastern and southern tribal seat. But the difference is really not great; they stand
about side by side, but in no way can the Northern be taken to stem
from the Thracian indirectly through the Germanic; this would be
contrary both to history and to the inner essence of the languages.
Similarly one can by no means say that Icelandic stems from Greek.

Greek is not the pure old Thracian. Least of all must one limit Greek to Attic, for it is just one of the latest Greek dialects, and far from the one in which relationship is shown most clearly. As great preeminence as Attic has in refinement and harmony, so great do Doric and Aeolic have in antiquity and importance for the investigator of language; for if these were lost, the identity with Latin, not to speak of Icelandic, could scarcely be proved satisfactorily. But what we can permit ourselves justified to conclude after the foregoing is that Icelandic, or Old Norse, has its source in the old Thracian, or that in its chief components it has sprung from large Thracian stock, of which Greek and Latin are the oldest and only remains, and that we can consider that its root. But for the complete etymological explanation of this we have seen that the Lettish and the Slavic classes of languages are of greatest importance, also that even Finnish was not without significant influence and use.

CHAPTER FOUR

FRANZ BOPP

ON THE CONJUGATIONAL SYSTEM
OF THE SANSKRIT LANGUAGE

In comparison with that of Greek, Latin, Persian
and the Germanic languages

From Über das Conjugationssystem der Sanskritsprache in
Vergleichung mit jenem der griechischen, lateinischen,
persischen und germanischen Sprache
(Frankfurt-am-Main: in der Andreäischen Buchhandlung, 1816)

It may be unfair to Bopp to give a selection from his
initial work. But his chief importance is in clarifying the
morphology of Indo-European, and even his final presentation has long been superseded. Accordingly the views which
he first presented are those of greatest interest to us.
Moreover, his analysis of the conjugational system of the
Sanskrit language is by no means a negligible result of four
years of independent work, carried on with little guidance
from predecessors. The extracts presented here indicate
however that Bopp's publication of 1816 was still preliminary to the important treatments in comparative linguistics.

For in 1816 Bopp is still pursuing the course of Friedrich von Schlegel. To be sure a much greater portion of
his book is devoted to the language, pp. 3-157, but as much
space is given to Indic literature, primarily to translations,
pp. 160-312. Bopp's chief aim is accordingly an understanding of Indic culture, not of the Indic language, let alone
that of the Indo-European family. His first work then resembles a comparative grammar of the Indo-European languages less than does the monograph of Rask. The publication in 1818 of Rask's work, which had been completed
earlier, may have been as beneficial to Bopp in his groping
toward a comparative grammar of the Indo-European languages as it was to Grimm.

To interpret Bopp's aims from the often tedious introduction of his teacher Windischmann, Conjugational System
i-xxxvi, may also be less than flattering to the mature
Bopp; but it gives us an insight into contemporary hopes

for comparative linguistics and accordingly some understanding of the tremendous energy with which it was pursued. According to Windischmann, ix-x, Bopp "had resolved to treat the investigation of language as a historic
and philosophic study and not to be content with understanding what was written in any given language. We may rejoice
at these efforts and intentions, which from a purely human
point of view deserve to be named before many others, for
through intimate association with the significant signs, by
which the word, this child of the spirit, expresses the deep-
est emotions and feelings, as it does the clearest and most
definite thoughts, indescribably much of the hindrances to
true self-knowledge and self-culture are dispelled." Moreover, in study of languages, such as Gothic, and their
structure, there was hope, according to Windischmann,
for additional means to illuminate the history of the Indic
and Germanic peoples and the differing cultures of each.
Such considerations led Bopp to master ever more of the
Indo-European languages — Sanskrit, Avestan, Greek, Latin,
Lithuanian and Gothic for the first volumes of his Comparative Grammar of 1833 — then Slavic, Celtic and Albanian
for remaining volumes, and the second edition of 1857-61.
The posthumous third of 1868-70 maintains some of the initial shortcomings of the early period of comparative linguistics virtually to the time of the neo-grammarians.

One shortcoming was the almost exclusive attention to
morphology. We note Grimm's similar lack of interest for
phonology. Raumer's attention to phonetics had its influence only on the successors to the great pioneers.

Another shortcoming is Bopp's attempt to discern the
origin of inflection in separate words, particularly the verb
"to be". In its crass form, this is completely superseded.
Yet many publications still emerge which seek the origin of
inflections, like the Germanic weak preterite, in simple
verbs such as do, even though highly conservative and careful linguists, e.g. H. Collitz, Das Schwache Präteritum.
Baltimore, 1912, have cited almost overwhelming evidence
against such views. The early notions on the development
of language, from non-inflected through agglutinative to inflected, have not been discarded even today, though we probably would find little receptivity for the view that certain
inflections developed because of an inherent meaning of the
symbol, such as s for the second person.

Franz Bopp is often credited with providing "the real
beginning of what we call comparative linguistics" (Pedersen,

Linguistic Science, p. 257). In keeping with this achievement his external career was distinguished. His publication resulting from four years of study in Paris, 1812-1816,
led to general recognition. After visiting London and pub-
lishing there, he became professor of Sanskrit and comparative grammar in Berlin in 1821. Teaching and publication made up the rest of his life; his publications are on
the whole admirable, except for a suggestion that the
Malayo-Polynesian languages are related to the Indo-
European. Apart from this lapse, editions, monographs
and successive editions of his grammar, with translations
into English and French, made him the dominant figure in
Indo-European comparative grammar throughout the first
half of the nineteenth century.

Chapter 1. On Verbs in General

By verb in the narrowest sense is meant that part of speech
which expresses the connection of a topic with a property, and their
relations to one another.

The verb, according to this definition, has no real meaning in
itself, but is simply the grammatical bond between subject and predicate, through whose inner change and formation their mutual relations are indicated.

Under this concept there is only a single verb, namely the so-
called verbum abstractum, sein, esse. But also with this verb, to
the extent that it is to express simply the relations between subject
and predicate, we have to remove the concept of existence, which it
comprehends in itself; in its grammatical determination this does
not need to express the existence of the subject, because this is
already expressed by the subject when we state it. Thus in the
sentence: homo est mortalis, it is not the verb, est, which expresses
the existence of the subject homo, but the existence is contained as
the first and basic characteristic in the concept expressed by the
word homo, just as the characteristic mortalis like others assumed
to be known for the concept homo is associated through the copula
est. In the sentence: der Gott ist seiend, the word sein represents
two quite different functions. In the first it determines as grammatical bond simply the relation between the subject and the predicate; in the second it expresses the property which is added to the
subject.

It seems to me therefore, that simply through lack of a completely abstract verb, a verb which embraces the concept of existence

in itself is used in most languages for the sake of a grammatical bond; and there might well be a language, which is not without a totally meaningless copula, through whose inflection or inner change the relations between subject and predicate might be expressed. In Sanskrit there are two verbs which correspond to the verb esse, namely asti and bhavati. Whether both are exchanged with one another equally frequently, and although the first is replaced by the latter in the tenses lacking to it, nonetheless for both synonyms a fine difference must exist, which may possibly have been distinguished more sharply originally. Nonetheless it seems to me from observation of the use of both, and from comparison of the substantives and adjectives derived from the roots of both, to emerge clearly that asti almost alone expressed grammatical union, that bhavati however is primarily used when existence is to be expressed. From the root bhū come the words bhāvana, svajambhū, prabhu, bhūtam, bhavān, etc., all of which point to existence. From the root as one can hardly find a noun derived other than the participle sat and its negative asat. The following verse from the Bāgavat Gīta can probably not be translated faithfully into any language:

Nāsatō vidjatae bhāvō nābhāvō vidjatae satah.

The relation of the subject with its predicate is not always expressed through a special part of speech, but is unexpressed; and the relations and secondary determinations of meaning are indicated through the inner change and inflection of the word itself that expresses the attribute. The adjectives inflected in this way make up the sphere of verbs in the usual sense.

Among all the languages known to us, the sacred language of the Indians shows itself to be one of the most capable of expressing the most varied relations and connections in a truly organic manner through inner modification and forming of the stem syllable. But disregarding this remarkable capability of modification, occasionally it is pleased to incorporate the root of the verbum abstractum, in which case the stem syllable and the incorporated verbum abstractum divide the grammatical functions of the verb.

Among the languages which are of common origin with the Old Indic we have to admire the capability of indicating the most varied determinations of relationship, most of all in the Greek. In the conjugation of the verbs it not only follows the same principle as the Sanskrit, but the inflections by which it expresses the same relations are exactly the same; and it combines in the same tenses and in the same way the verbum abstractum with the stem syllable.

The Roman language agrees with the Indic no less than does the

Greek, and one could hardly find in it a relation expressed by an inflection which is not common to it and Sanskrit. In the conjugation
of verbs however the combination of the root with an auxiliary verb
has become the prevailing principle for it. In this combination however it does not express a part of the relation, which is to be defined, through inflection of the stem syllable, as this is the case in
Indic and in Greek, but the root remains totally unchanged. —
     It is the purpose of this essay to show how in the conjugation of
the Old Indic verbs the definitions of relationship are expressed
through corresponding modifications of the root, how at times however the verbum abstractum is combined with the stem syllable to
one word, and stem syllable and auxiliary divide the grammatical
functions of the verb; to show how the same is the case in the Greek
language, how in Latin the system of combination of root with an
auxiliary has come to be dominant, and how only in this way the apparent difference of the Latin conjugation from that of Sanskrit and
Greek arose; finally to prove, that in all the languages which stem
from Sanskrit or from a mother language in common with it, no definition of relationship is indicated by an inflection which is not common to them and that original language, and that apparent exceptions
only arise from the fact that either the stem syllable is combined
with the auxiliaries into one word, or that from participles the
tempora derivativa which are customary already in Sanskrit are
derived, in the fashion as verba derivativa can be formed from substantives in Sanskrit, Greek and many other languages.
     Among the languages that stand in closest relationship with
Sanskrit I recognize especially Greek, Latin, Germanic and Persian. It is remarkable that Bengalese, which surely has undergone
the least foreign admixtures among the New Indic dialects, does not
agree in its grammar nearly so completely with Sanskrit as do the
above-mentioned languages, while on the other hand it attests a far
greater number of Old Indic words. Yet new organic modifications
have not taken the place of the Old Indic inflections, but after their
meaning and spirit have gradually vanished, their use also diminished, and tempora participialia (among which I do not understand
periphrastic forms like the Latin amatus est) replaced the tenses
which were formed in Sanskrit through inner change of the stem
syllable. Similarly in the New Germanic languages, several indications of relationship are expressed through periphrasis, which in
Gothic were designated by inflections that were already used in Sanskrit and Greek.
     In order to show in its full light the truth of these principles
which are extremely important for the history of languages, it is
necessary to become acquainted above all with the conjugational
system of the Old Indic languages, then to survey and compare the

conjugations of the Greek and the Roman, the Germanic and Persian languages, whereby we will see their identity, but will also recognize the gradual and graded destruction of the simple speech organism and observe the striving to replace it by mechanical combinations, from which an appearance of a new organism arose when their elements were no longer recognized.

Chapter 2. Conjugation of the Old Indic Language

We will go through the tenses of the Indic verbs here in the sequence in which they follow one another in the Sanskrit grammars, and in the process will give as briefly and compactly as possible the reason for every change of form and depict the manner how every modification of meaning corresponds to an individual modification of the word. From this it will become clear of itself that many tenses must be explained as compounds. Since however in my assertions I cannot support myself on the authority of others, for up to now nothing has been written about the origin of the grammatical forms, I will have to support them with cogent proofs.

Formation of the Present

In the tempus praesens the meaning of the root is limited through no added secondary indication; the subject has real use of the predicate designated by the root. Also from the root, which is the common mother of all parts of speech, the tempus praesens is formed through simple addition of the designations for person. The designation for the first person is M for the singular and plural, and for the dual V; designation of the second person is S, or H which is related to it; designation of the third person is T for all three numbers. The endings, or the accents of the personal designations serve to determine the numbers, not the formation and characterization of the tenses.

Example: ad, eat

	Sing.	Dual	Plur.
3.	atti<adti	attah<adtah	adanti
2.	atsi-adsi	atthah-adthah	attha<adtha
1.	adai	advah	admah

Note. The D of the root becomes T before T and S in accordance with the rules of euphony. (end of p. 13)

Chapter 3. Conjugation of the Greek verbs (61-2)

In Greek, as in Sanskrit, certain random letters are added to
roots, which as in Indic are maintained only in some tenses and disappear again in the others. One could, as in Sanskrit, divide the
verbs into different conjugations in accordance with these, which
then would largely correspond with the Indic in their characteristics. — The first Indic conjugation adds a to the first root; thus
patschati comes from patsch. With this one can compare those
Greek verbs which insert e, a or o between root and designation
for person. The third conjugation of Sanskrit repeats the initial
letters of the root, e.g. dadāti, tischthati, from dā and sthā. So in
Greek dídōmi, héstēmi from da and sta. The fifth Indic conjugation
adds nu to the root; e.g. sunuma "we beget" from su. To this corresponds in Greek rhēgnumen, déiknumen, dáinumen from the roots
rhēg, deik, dai. — The eighth Indic conjugation adds u, e.g. tanuma
"we extend" from the root tan. — The ninth conjugation adds the syllable nā in Sanskrit, e.g. krināmi from kri. N is often inserted in
Greek between the root and the designation for person, as in krínō,
klínō, témnō, etc., from kri, kli, tem.

Chapter 4. Conjugation of the Latin Verbs (88-89)

In order to learn to know the principle of the Latin conjugation,
it is necessary that we start out from the conjugation of the auxiliary verbs, partly because of their frequent combination with the
other verbs, partly because in their simpler change the principle
of the Latin conjugation is easier to recognize.
The Latin language has two verbs, which are used for combination between subject and the predicate expressed by an adjective or
substantive, and for the expression of their mutual relation to one
another. Their stem syllables are es and fu, corresponding to the
Indic roots of the same meaning as and bhu. As in Sanskrit bhavati
replaces those tenses that went out of use for asti, so it happened
for Latin fu. The ancients said esum; the Etruscans (=Umbrians)
for sum: esume. Esu-me is like Indic as-mi and the Greek esmi,
esmai. — The praeteritum of esum is eram, with change of the s to
the related r, accordingly eram for esam. Also in Sanskrit and in
Greek the personal designations with A are emphasized. But the
past is not expressed through this emphasis, rather through modification of the root: through replacement of the augment, through reduplication or change of the stem vowel. Eram is different from
esum; its use gives its past meaning, but this modification of the
meaning does not correspond to a particular modification of the root.

Chapter 5. Conjugation of the Persian Language
and the Old Germanic Dialects (116-17)

However much the inflections have gone out of use in other
parts of speech of the Persian language, through which in Indic and
the languages related to it important secondary specifications are
indicated, yet especially in the inflection of verbs the close bond can
be recognized which ties it to those languages whose system of conjugation we have examined. With the old Germanic dialects it affords in the principle of the change of verbs such striking agreement
that for the sake of brevity I consider myself justified to place it
with them in one class. In the Persian language and in all Germanic
dialects, the tempus praesens is derived from the root through simple affixation of the personal designations, which are known to us
from Sanskrit as from Greek and Latin. Yet these have not maintained themselves throughout, but are at times replaced through
vowels, as in Greek and Roman; eventually the designation of a definite person becomes the common ending of all others, as will be
clear from the following examples.

From the roots ber, luf, sok, mach, brenn there are made in
Persian, Anglo-Saxon, Gothic, Frankish and Icelandic the following
presents:

	Persian	Anglo-Saxon	Gothic	Frankish	Icelandic
1.	ber-em	luf-ige	sokj-a	mach-on	brenn-e
2.	-- -i	-- -ast	sokj-ais	-- -ost	-- -er
3.	-- -ed	-- -ath	sok-eith	-- -ot	-- -er

Pluralis

	Persian	Anglo-Saxon	Gothic	Frankish	Icelandic
1.	ber-im	luf-iath	sokj-am	mach-omes	brenn-um
2.	-- -id	-- -iath	sok-eith	-- -ot	-- -ed
3.	-- -end	-- -iath	sok-and	-- -ont	-- -a

CHAPTER FIVE

JACOB GRIMM

GERMANIC GRAMMAR

From Deutsche Grammatik
(Gütersloh: C. Bertelmann, 1893), I, pp. 580-592

If non-specialists know anything about historical linguistics, it is Grimm's law. The history of views on the
consonant shift is virtually a history of linguistic theory until 1875; subsequently it is equivalent to the theory of historical linguistics, from the neogrammarian position (that
each consonant should be treated individually) to that pro-
pounded today (that the entire shift be viewed as a whole).
Yet our first reaction on looking at Grimm's celebrated
statement may be surprise. He is groping through the consonants; his remarks on the liquids show great uncertainty.
The vowels are quite obscure for him. And combined with
the treatment are peripheral remarks about speech — comments on the purpose of vowels — which we would not welcome in any treatise today. Yet this formulation of the
Germanic consonant shift has indeed had "momentous consequences for the history of language." Subsequent discussion is voluminous; few Germanists, Indo-Europeanists or
even general linguists have failed to comment.

It was Grimm's conception of the shift as a unit which
made such an impact on linguistics. Although his formulation lacks the neatness we might expect, he did account
consistently for a large segment of the set of Indo-European
and Germanic consonants. His consistent account was so
overwhelming that no one doubted its validity. The items
unaccounted for were considered exceptions and were made
the object of research for the next half century.

Yet we may be even more surprised that there is no
mention of a law. Grimm has given nine rules, relating
the consonants of Germanic with those of Greek and Latin,
less commonly with Sanskrit and other Indo-European languages. Instead of rule, Regel might equally well be translated correspondence. If we did use this translation,
Grimm's formulation might be quite contemporary. He
stated the evidence fully, including exceptions, posited the

relevant correspondences, and indicated their relationships to one another. The statement is a classic example of the formulation of a problem in linguistics, and of its solution within the sphere of language.

Possibly an attempt at explanation is implicit, though even this is not certain. By viewing the shift as non-organic, Grimm apparently saw in it a deviation from the organism developed by the speakers of Indo-European languages. Just as inflection, in contrast with agglutination, seemed appropriate to the Indo-European languages, so did the system of obstruents in Greek and Latin. But we see none of the fanciful attempts at explanation which our handbooks summarize — a shift due to change of geography, or climate and so on — nor even the more sober attempts which seem appropriate to us, such as a general shift in keeping with one type of phonetic reshaping or with the modification of distinctive features. Grimm's concentration on taxonomy spared him all such ventures.

He was also fortunate in his ignorance of phonetics, which permitted him to class together consonants which were quite different in articulation, and to produce a statement which passes beyond details to the system. Examination of details, as by Raumer, Grassmann, Verner, clarified exceptions, but it also for a time undermined the unity which Grimm saw in the shift, and which a structural approach has restored.

The translation has been deliberately kept stark to illustrate Grimm's pioneering. We might well interpret "guttural" to mean velar, as it often does even among linguists who should be better informed; but that it meant "throat-sound" to Grimm is clear from his German equivalent "Kehllaut". Though we may pride ourselves on superior terminology, our estimate of the capabilities of Grimm's contemporaries is not diminished by the ease with which they were to identify examples as Greek or Latin, with no special indication.

As we update Grimm's terminology, we may wonder at terms that have not been discarded. Grimm speaks of consonant gradation. We no longer do, but our entire treatment of the Indo-European vowels is based on the assumption of gradation. Grimm viewed vowels as virtually hopeless, but brought order into the consonant system by his use of grades. Subsequent linguists brought order into the Indo-European vowel system by using grades. In maintaining their terminology, are we also maintaining an antiquated framework for the vowels?

Though we consider Jacob Grimm (1785-1863) one of
the greatest contributors to linguistics, his name is a
household word for other achievements as well. The veneration in which he is held by scholars may be indicated by
the retention of the page numbers of his original text of the
grammar, which are maintained here, as in subsequent
editions. His Germanic Grammar is still the most complete one we have. The large German dictionary, recently
completed, was inaugurated by him and his brother, Wilhelm (1786-1859). His work in other fields: medieval literature, law, mythology, folklore, is as fundamental as his
work in linguistics. After studying law at Marburg he held
small government posts, which brought him at various
times to Paris and Vienna. In 1817 he was appointed professor and librarian at Göttingen. Here he lectured in his
areas of interest until 1837, when with six other professors
he protested against the King of Hanover's abrogation of
the constitution, and was dismissed. His political action at
this time illustrates that his greatness was not confined to
academic matters. After returning to Cassel for a few
years he and his brother were invited to professorships at
Berlin in 1840, and to memberships in the Prussian Academy of Sciences. Acclaim did not hinder his work, which
involved all areas of linguistics from phonology to the
painstaking activities of a lexicographer.

A Survey of the Consonants

The above survey informs us that the vowel relationships are
uncertain and subject to various influences, but that their distribution and alternation are not arbitrary, rather, resulting from deeply
established laws that have not yet been disclosed. The law of the
ablauts will spread more light on this. One may view the vowels as
the necessary coloring or animation of all words, as the breath
without which they would not even exist. The real individuality of
the word rests on the vowel sound; it affords the finest relationships.
The form, if I may say so, on the other hand the specification is
established by the consonantism. Here the relationships appear far
more certain and lasting; dialects, whose vowels for the most part
deviate, often maintain the same consonants.
581   The four liquids are unchangeable; their fluid element preserves
them intact during the most powerful upheavals. They undergo only
occasional permutations, transpositions, losses or geminations, in

spite of which their essential significance remains the same; i.e.,
although, for example, chil che occasionally appears as chir che, r
and l remain fundamentally different in all other cases. To be
noted:

1) On the one hand l and r are closely related, on the other m
   and n. When an exchange takes place, m is the earlier and
   more delicate, n later and coarser [(cf. p. 386, 387). These
   references are to Grimm's Grammar.] Conversely, the
   harder r may be older, the softer l younger. M stands in a
   special relationship with the labials, n with the linguals (cf.
   p. 536). Thus the OHG au, ou before m and labials, ô before
   n and linguals (p. 100); l and r are associated as readily with
   labials, linguals and gutturals. — L and r disintegrate occasionally into u and i (and could therefore be called semi-
   vowels); never m and n, yet the influence of a lost n on the
   preceding vowel might be compared (gâs, for gans).
2) In the important association of r with s, of the combination
   rd with dd and sd (Goth. zd) r, rd appear as the younger
   forms which have gradually developed from s, sd (cf. p. 64,
   65, 121, 167, 210, 244, 305, 317, 343, 387, 416).

Like the liquids, the three spirants v, h, s remain essentially
unchanged throughout all the Germanic dialects. I deduce their
inner relationship in part from the ê and ô which appear in front of
them rather than ei and au (p. 91, 94), in part from the changes between h and v, w (p. 148, 403), h and s (p. 318, 416), and the association of the aspiration with the assibilation (th, ts, z); no direct exchange between v, w, and s; h and v, (the softest of all consonants,)
disappear occasionally without replacement, even initially and particularly before liquids. (v. addendum)

Relationships are completely otherwise with the remaining
consonants; a notable contrast between High German and all the
other dialects becomes obvious. In the labial, lingual and guttural
sounds, the Gothic (Saxon, Frisian, Northern) tenues correspond to
the High German aspirates; the Gothic mediae to the High German
tenues; and the Gothic aspirates to the High German mediae. The
particulars may be expressed as follows:

Goth.	P.	B.	F.	T.	D.	Þ.	K.	G.	.
OHG	F.	P.	B, (V)	Z.	T.	D.	CH.	K.	G.

582 A change has taken place by means of which each of these nine consonants in High German shifted similarly from its position.[1] There
is no doubt that the High German situation must be viewed here as

the later, the changed, and the Gothic (Saxon, Frisian, Northern) as
the earlier. This has been proved by analysis of the Old High German letters on various grounds. Observations:

1) The lingual series indicates the relationship most clearly; in
   Gothic táins, dal, þaúrnus are as necessarily distinguished
   as in Old High German Zein, Tal and Dorn.

2) The labial order also fits as soon as one acknowledges the
   second aspirate bh for the HG v in initial position and admits
   this instead of the closely related real media. For f, p, v,
   the erroneous designations ph, b, f were introduced, or occasionally others. Compare Goth. pund, baíran, filu with the
   HG funt, përan, vilo (also written phunt, bëran, filo). The
   older arrangement had visible effect in the inconsistent
   writing system; the strictest High German pronunciation,
   in which përan, pein, përag were completely current, did
   not even rise to the pure media bilo for filo, vilo. Even
   hard, upper German folk dialects do not know and cultivate
   such a b for f (certainly, however, many b for the spirant
   w). This all applies however for the initial position; in medial position the media frequently seems to me to stand in
   proper position, for example, in ëbar (aper), ëban (aequalis)
   etc. (cf. below, p. 589, fn. b.).

3) For the series of throat sounds the aspiration is lacking in
   Gothic, etc.: in High German all three gradations are found,
   but how are the High German k and g (ch assumed for Goth.
   k) to be organically divided into Gothic k? This could hardly
   be answered from the German language; the uncertainty of
   the Old High German writing system not only confuses k and
   g, but also k and ch with one another. At the same time
   however some clarification is provided by this that the OHG
   k which alternates with g never goes over to ch, and conversely, the k which alternates with ch never to g. So for
   example, gunni may not stand for chunni (genus) and chans
   never for gans (anser); for both, however, kunni and kans.
   Since in addition medial ch may not be exchanged with k (no
   sprëkan for sprëchan), then HG k for ch would be completely
   objectionable and of the two sounds, g and k, one would be
   superfluous and indeed theoretically this would be g. The
   High German language would thus not actually have any more
   throat sounds than the Gothic; ch would correspond to Goth.
   k, k however to g. Yet it appears to me that there is a third
   case where OHG g of necessity stands, i.e., where it cannot
   be replaced by k or ch; this is none other than the varying
   relationship between h and g (p. 427). Here the Goth. g

583

plays a double role; in þragjan (currere), and guma (vir) a different g appears from that in augô (oculus), and tagram (lacrimis). This can become clear only through comparison of further originally related languages.

With such comparisons, which here cannot by any means be thoroughly pursued, but rather only are intended to put our Germanic sound-relationships into proper perspective one proceeds best from the consonants. If a thoroughly grounded statement is ascertained and accepted for these, then perhaps some insights might also be gained into the history of the vowels.

First we encounter the important principle: liquids and spirants agree in all essential relationships with the manner and arrangement of the German tongue. It seems that where the branches of the Germanic languages do not deviate from one another, Latin, Greek and Indic will not deviate. Sanskrit expressly recognizes the r and l as vowels, and uses r this way often, l more rarely. The weakening of the older m into later n is common everywhere; a large group of words with m in Sanskrit and Latin receive n in Greek (see addendum); exactly as the final MHG n becomes m again in medial position (lein, leimes; arn, armes, p. 386), so ên is related to êmen (Lat. eram, eramus; compare néon with novum). Analogous modifications of the s to r are also easily found; especially Latin preferred the r, which is however always to be understood as the younger form. Alternation of the spirants v (digamma), 584 s and h is demonstrated by hespéra, vespera; heptá, for septem; hûs, sus; hérpō, serpo; hekurós, socer; hupó, sub; sas, sâ (Skt. is ea), Gk ho, hē, Goth. sa, sô; háls, sal; sasa, (Skt. lepus), haso etc.; also the initial spirant disappeared completely, e.g., Lat. anser is found for hanser (Skt. hamsa, cignus), odium for hodium (Goth. hatis), éar Lat. ver, and the Gk ídmen (Skt. vidmas, Lat. videmus, Goth. vitum) earlier had a digamma before it. V and s alternate the least, cf. sinister with winster.

Yet more astounding than the accord of the liquids and the spirants is the variation of the lip, tongue and throat sounds, not only from the Gothic, but also the Old High German arrangement. For just as Old High German has sunk one step down from the Gothic in all three grades, Gothic itself had already deviated by one step from the Latin (Greek, Sanskrit). [See supplement.] Gothic is related to Latin exactly as is Old High German to Gothic. The entire twofold sound shift, which has momentous consequences for the history of language and the rigor of etymology, can be so expressed in a table:

Gk	P.	B.	F.	T.	D.	TH.	K.	G.	CH.
Goth.	F.	P.	B.	TH.	T.	D.	-.	K.	G.
OHG	B.(V)	F.	P.	D.	Z.	T.	G.	CH.	K.

or otherwise conceived:

Gk	Goth.	OHG	Gk	Goth.	OHG	Gk	Goth.	OHG
P	F	B(V)	T	TH	D	K	-	G
B	P	F	D	T	Z	G	K	CH
F	B	P	TH	D	T	CH	G	K

From this we see now how the Goth fills the gap arising from the
departure of the throat aspirate: he uses the spiritus h initially
rather than ch, and h occasionally also medially and finally, but
frequently also the media g. In Old High German the g would appear here consistently everywhere and would be analogous to the b
and d of the other series; it may however be a remnant of the
earlier sound arrangements that the Gothic initial h has also been
carried over to Old High German because it was taken for a spirant
and not as aspirate. Only occasionally does g appear beside it.
This use of the h for ch is also remarkably found precisely in initial
position in Latin so that the gutturals, more precisely determined,
show up as follows:

Gk	Lat.	Goth.	OHG
κ	c	h,g	h,g
γ	g	k	ch
χ	h	g	k

The necessary examples for the proposed nine comparisons are:
585   I. (P. F. B,V.) 1) Initial position: pax, pacis, pacatus; Goth.
fahêds (gaudium, quies), ON feginn (contentus, laetus) --- pes,
pedis; Gk poûs, podós; Skt padas; Goth. fôtus; OHG vuoz --- piscis,
fisks, visc --- porca (sulcus), OHG vuriha --- porcus, OHG varah
--- Gk póros (iter, via), Goth. faran (ire) --- pater, Gk patér, Goth.
fadrs, OHG vatar --- patis (Skt conjux), Lith. pats, Gk posis (? Dor.
Gk pótis), Goth. brûd-faþs (sponsus) --- Gk pûr, OHG viur --- Gk
polú OHG vilo, Goth. filu --- Gk pléos, Goth. fulls, OHG vol --- Gk
prôí, OHG vruo --- pecus, Goth. faíhu, OHG vihu --- pulex, OHG
vlôh --- plecto, OHG vlihtu --- Gk pérdō, Lith. perdziu, Swed.
fjerter, OHG vërzu --- Gk palámē, Lat. palma, AS folma, OHG
volma --- Gk ptéron (for Gk petéron, like Gk petáō for Gk ptáō), ON
fiðdhur, OHG vëdar --- Gk peúkē, picea, HG vihta --- pellis, Goth.
fill, OHG vël --- pullus, Goth. fula, OHG volo --- pauci, Goth. favai,
OHG vaohê --- primus, Goth. frumists, OHG vromist. --- 2) Medial position (The Gothic medial b for f is less precise than Northern and Saxon f. bh) Gk kápros, caper, ON hafr --- Gk loipós

(reliquus), ON leifar (reliquiae), Goth. láibôs --- svapa (Skt somnus), Gk húpnos, ON svefn, OS suëbhan --- septem, AS sëofon, Goth. sibun --- aper, ON iöfur, AS ëofor, OHG ëbar --- Gk hupér, super, Goth. ufar, ON yfir, OHG ubar --- rapina, AS reáf, OHG roub.

II. (B, P, F) 1) For initial position, I know no example to support my view that the Germanic words with initial p̲, HG f̲ (p̲h̲) are lacking (above p. 55, 131, 212, 247, 397, 462). 2) Medial position: Gk kánnabis, cannabis, ON hanpr, OHG hanaf; should turba be compared with Goth. þaúrp, OHG dorof; stabulum with ON stôpull, OHG staphol; labi with hláupan, loufan?

III. (PH, B, P) The aspirate of the older languages itself still requires closer attention; Sanskrit recognizes both p̲h̲ and b̲h̲, which appear mixed in Gk p̲h̲, Lat. f̲ and b̲. 1) Initial position: The Indic root bhu, the Gk phu, the Lat. fu in the verb 'to be', compare with the AS bëon, OHG pim (sum) --- Gk phēgós, fagus, ON beyki, OHG puocha --- forare, ON bora, OHG poren --- frangere, fregi; Goth. brikan, OHG prēchan --- frui, fructus; Goth. brûkôn, OHG prûchôn --- frater, brôþar, pruoder --- flare, blasan, plasan --- fero (in
586 Skt the root bhr), Goth. baíra, OHG piru --- Gk phúllon, folium, ON blad, OHG plat --- Gk ophrús, ON brâ, OHG prawa. --- 2) Medial position: Gk eléphas, antos, Goth. ulbandus, OHG olpenta --- Gk kephalé, haubiþ, houpit --- Gk nephélē, nebula, Goth. nibls?, OHG nēpal --- Gk gráphein, Goth. graban, OHG grapan. These medials vacillate toward the first class, like: caput, AS heáfod, OHG haubit, cf. the ON nifl to which an OHG nëbal would correspond.

IV. (T. TH. D.) 1) Initial position: tauta (lett. gens, regio) Goth. þiuda, OHG diot --- tu, Goth. þu, OHG dû --- tenuis, tener, ON þunnr, OHG dunni --- Gk teínein, tendere; Goth. þanjan, OHG denen --- Gk treîs, tres; þreis; drî --- tergere, ON þërra --- Gk térsein (arefacere) Goth. þaúrsis (aridus) torridus, OHG durri --- tacere, Goth. þahan, OHG dagen --- Gk trékhein, Goth. þragjan --- Gk talân, tlân, tolerare, Goth. þulan, OHG dolen --- tectum, Goth. þak, OHG dach --- Gk taûros, ON þiór --- tad (Skt id), Gk to (for tad), Goth. þat, OHG daz --- talis, ON þvîlîkr. --- 2) Medial position: ratio, raþjô, redja --- frater, brôþar, pruoder --- Gk metá, Goth. miþ --- dantas (dens, dentis) tunþus, zand --- rota, ON hradhr (celer) OHG hrad (rota) --- iterum, Goth. viþra, OHG widar --- Gk héteros, anþar, andar --- perhaps Gk étēs, hetaîros (socius) may be compared with OS gesith, OHG sindeo --- étos (annus) with the obscure Goth. ataþni (i.e. at-aþni, OHG az-adani?).

V. (D. T. Z.) 1) Initial position: dingua, tuggo, zunga (cf. above p. 152) --- deus, divus, Lith. diéwas; Gk dís, diós (for theós is Cretan) ON tŷr; OHG ziu (cf. above p. 150, 151) --- dantas (Skt) Gk odoús odóntos; dens, dentis; Goth. tunþus, OHG zand --- Gk dia-, Lat. dis-, Saxon to-, OHG zi- --- Gk damân, domare, Goth. tamjan, OHG zemen --- Gk drûs, Goth. triu --- digitus, cf. with the Saxon têkan (signum) OHG zeichan --- Gk deiknúein, deíkein, indicare, Saxon tôgjan, HG zeigen --- Gk dólos, dolus, ON tâl, OHG zâla --- ducere, Goth. tiuhan, OHG ziohan --- Gk dúo, duo, Goth. tva, OHG zuei. --- Gk dákru, Goth. tagr, OHG zahar --- Gk deksiá, dextra, Goth. taíhsvô, OHG zēsawa. --- 2) Medial position: Gk hēdú, Goth. suti, OHG suozi --- ad, Goth. at, OHG az --- Gk hédos, sedes; sedere, Goth. sitan, OHG sizan --- Gk édein, edere; itan, ëzan --- Gk eídein, eidénai, videre, Goth. vitan, OHG wizan --- odium, Goth. hatis, OHG haz --- claudere, OHG sliozan --- laedere, HG letzen, --- radix, ON rôt --- Gk húdōr, Goth. vatô, OHG wazar --- Gk hidrós, sudor, sveiti, sueiz --- pedes, fôtjus, vuozi.

VI. (TH. D. T.) The Latins have no th (except in foreign words), 587 but often the Gk th has become the labial aspirate f of the same grade just as in Greek itself the Aeolic dialect shows ph for th (cf. Gk thumós, spiritus, animus, with fumus, Gk phúmos; thúein with fire, suffire) both remind one of the intersection of Goth. þl with fl indicated on p. 66, 67. 1) Initial position: Gk thugátēr, Goth. daúhtar, OHG tohtar --- Gk thúra, Lat. pl. fores, Goth. daúr, OHG tor --- Gk thér, Aeol. phér, Lat. fera, ON dŷr, OHG tior --- Gk tharréein (audere) Goth. ga-daúran, OHG turran, cf. the preterite ga-daúrsta, getorsta with Gk thárros, thársos, thrasús. --- Gk thénar (vola manus) OHG tënar --- Medial position: Gk méthu, AS mēdo, OHG mētu --- Gk éthos, AS sido, OHG situ.

VII. (K. H,G. H,G.) In the second grade the Goth. h is found for ch; in the third the OHG h for g. 1) Initial position: claudus, halts, halz --- Gk kánnabis, ON hanpr, OHG hanaf --- canere cf. with hano (gallus, as this with ON kalla, OHG challôn, clamare, fari) --- caput, háubiþ, houbit --- Gk kardía, cor, haírtô, hërza --- Gk kúon, canis, hunþs, hund --- Gk koîlos, hol --- celare, hilan, hëln --- Gk kálamos, calamus, halam, halm --- Gk kártos, karterós, hardus, hart --- cornu, haúrn, horn --- collum, hals --- Gk krumós, (gelu), ON hrîm --- Gk klaíein, Goth. hlahan --- Gk krázein, crocitare, Goth. hrukjan --- Gk kléptēs, Goth. hliftus. --- 2) Medial position: Gk ókos, oculus, áugo, ouga --- acies, OHG egga --- lux (lucs) liuhad, lioht, cf. Gk leukós with liuhadeins --- Gk oîkos, Goth. veihs --- lacus, AS lagu --- acus, aceris, OHG ahan, agan, --- Gk dákru, tagr, zahar --- tacere, þahan, dagen --- pecus, faíhu, viho --- Gk hekurós, socer, Goth. svaíhra, HG schwager, schwieger --- Gk mékōn (papaver), OHG mâgan, NHG mohn (? Goth. mêhan). Medially this sometimes corresponds to Skt sh: e.g. dasha, Gk déka, Lat. decem, Goth. taíhun, Lith. deszimts.

VIII. (G. K. CH.) 1) Initial position: granum, ON korn, OHG chorn --- Gk génos, genus; kuni; chunni --- Gk génus, gena, ON kinn, OHG chinni --- Gk gónu, ON knê, OHG chnio --- Gk guné, ON kona, OHG chona --- gelu (frigus) Goth. kalds, OHG chalt --- gula (guttur)

OHG chĕla --- gustare, kiusan, chiosan --- gau (Skt vacca), ON kû, OHG chua --- 2) Medial position: Gk egő, ego, Goth. ïk, OHG ih --- vigil, OHG wachar --- Gk agrós, agere, Goth. akrs, OHG achar --- Gk ágein, agere, ON aka --- Gk mégas, mégalos; mikils; michil --- rex, regis, regnum; reiks; rîchi --- jugum, juk, joch --- augere, áukan, auchôn --- Gk amélgein, mulgere, ON miólka, OHG mĕlchan.---

588   IX. (CH, H. G. K.) In Latin h is here equivalent to ch. cf. Schneider, Lateinische Grammatik, p. 202: Gk kheimőn, hiems; Gk kheír, Lat. hir; Gk khĕr, herinaceus. Frequently however, OHG g to k, which I carry out here only in theory. 1) Initial position: Gk khĕn, anser (for hanser) Goth. gans, OHG kans --- Gk khéō (fundo), Gk khutós (fusus) Goth. giutan, OHG kiozan --- Gk kholĕ, ON gall, OHG kalla --- Gk khthés, heri, hesternus, Goth. gistra, OHG kĕstar --- Gk khórtos, hortus, gards, OHG karto --- hostis (peregrinus) gasts, kast --- homo, Goth. guma, OHG komo --- Gk khthőn like khthés for khés for khőn and this for khóm, cf. khamái, humi, humus; to be compared with Goth. gauï, OHG kouwi, kou --- 2) Medial position: Gk ékhein, Goth. áigan, OHG eikan --- Gk trékhein, Doric trákhein, Goth. þragjan --- Gk lékhos, Goth. ligrs, OHG lĕkar --- Gk leíkhō, líkhō (lambo) Goth. láigo, OHG lêkôn --- Gk lukhân (insidiari), (Goth. lêgôn?), OHG lâkôn. --- (see supplement).

Notes on this comparison of consonants:

1) Even if certain of the cited samples still appear to be dubious or uncertain, the majority may be considered as clearly demonstrated because of the analogy of the gradation; the correctness of the rules in general is unmistakable. Words in which two consonants agree are doubly certain (Gk trékhein, þragjan; pódes, fôtjus); those in which one consonant agrees, another deviates, are suspicious; even more suspicious, those whose consonants showed essential equivalence in the three languages without gradation. In this case, relationship is either entirely lacking (e.g. AS pädh, padhas and Gk páthos, dolor) or the one language has borrowed from the other (e.g. scrîban is scribere itself, fruht is fructus, hence not Germanic; the same is true for OS sicor, Lat. securus).

2) In the investigations of the words, likeness or resemblance of consonants which are in general related is less important than observation of the historical course of gradation, which does not become disturbed or reversed. A High German word with p, which shows b in Gothic and f in Latin is originally related in these three languages: each possesses it unborrowed. If, however, we were to find an f in a High German word, b in Gothic and p in Latin, then the relationship

would be nonsensical, even though in the abstract exactly the
same relationships of the letters are present. The Gk t requires a Goth. þ, the Gothic t however no Gk th but rather d,
and so the identity throughout is based on the external difference.

589   3) Words, which the one or other language does not possess,
         could readily be posited for the nine consonant relationships,
         but not in the elements of vowels, liquids and spirants. All
         hypothesizing accordingly remains unprofitable; we might at
         most claim that for example Gk dáphnē would have to have
         t-b in Gothic and z-p in High German; Gk phutón b-þ in
         Gothic and p-d in High German. These nine rules are only
         touchstones for words which are available. Analogy is gen-
         erally not sufficient for new creations, for everything alive
         is incalculable and merges the laws of theory with the ex-
         ceptions found in reality.
     4) Such exceptions, i.e. instances, where the proposed com-
         parisons fail, appear:
         a) in the transition of the tenues, mediae or aspiratae, to
             tenues, mediae or aspiratae of another series. How often
             do the members of one series exchange with one another:
             p, t, k (Gk taôs, pavo; Gk pénte, Aeol. pémpe; Gk poîos,
             Ion. koîos) b, d, g (Gk obelós, Dor. odelós; Gk gê Dor. dê:
             cf. above p. 445, 446) ph, th, ch (examples above p. 587).
         b) because of the imperfection of the aspirations in most
             languages and the mixing with the related spirants and
             mediae which arises out of it. Sanskrit has aspiration
             of the mediae and tenues of each organ, so that bh, ph;
             dh, th; gh, and kh are found. Jumbled relics of these ap-
             pear in the other languages. The Greek speaker has ph,
             th, and ch; the Latin only the first (and then it is modi-
             fied; his f is close to the bh); th becomes f for him; ch
             becomes h. Also the Lithuanian and Latvian languages
             both lack f, th and ch (yes even the simple spirant h);
             Gothic etc. lack ch, which they replace with h and g. In
             other Germanic dialects, distinct traces of the bh, dh and
             gh, which can probably be found more clearly in the fu-
             ture than could happen in my presentation. The lack of
             initial Goth. p, HG ph (f), appears less striking with this
             point of view. Since in Greek and Latin the labials fluc-
             tuate, e.g. Gk kephalḗ, caput; Gk néphos, nephélē, nubes,
             nebula; thus each of the Germanic forms is justified, Goth.
             háubiþ beside gibla and the Saxon heáfod; and it must
             in general remain undecided whether OHG houbit or
             houpit, nĕpal or nĕbal deserves preference. The Latins

loved medial mediae (habeo, nobilis, mobilis, fabula, cibus, hebes, scabies, etc.; origin in v̲ is obvious in novisse, movere, etc.).

590

c) The sound shift takes place in the mass, but never neatly in individual items; words remain in the relationship of the old arrangements — the stream of innovation has passed them by. Connection with the unchangeable liquids and spirants has usually (not always) preserved them. Thus, α) some words of the Gothic etc. languages still have the stamp of the Latin and Greek order, e.g. du, dis (cited p. 152), compare with Saxon tô and OHG zuo, zi, zĕr; daddjan (dan. dîe) was erroneously cited, which is related according to the sixth comparison with Gk tháein, and has nothing to do with the AS tit. Further examples are OS sĕdel, instead of sĕtel (p. 217), the ON pt̲ instead of ft̲ (p. 314). The relationship between dies, dags, dăg-dăgr may not be interpreted otherwise. β) some of the Old High German words have the stamp of the Gothic etc., as in the words enumerated p. 154, 155, 394. γ) some Gothic and Old High German (the latter accordingly unscathed through two sound shifts) agree with the Latin and Greek e.g. the cited AS tit, Eng. teat, OHG tutto (p. 155), Gk tîtthē. Further: longus, laggs, lângr; angustus, aggvus, engi; gramen, gras etc.[2] δ) of two consonants in a word one may be shifted, the other retained, e.g. in tûnga, zunga, lingua, the g̲ remained, while d̲ (dingua) underwent gradation; the lingual does not check in prudentia, Goth. frôdei and Lith. protas; gaudere too may by closely related to Goth. gatjan (facere ut aliquis obtineat restituere, from gitan, like nasjan from nisan) and MHG ergetzen, and for the stricter form katjan (ON kâtr, laetus, beside gĕta acquirere and gĕtaz acquiescere) go to the MH erchetzen. This possibly misleading sentence should not be misused by the etymologists.

5. I have presented the Old High German sound shift (p. 127, 151, 177) as something non-organic, and admittedly it is a visible deviation from an earlier organism which is still present in vestiges. One must also consider Gothic in contrast with Greek and Latin as equally non-organic. The similarities of both changes puts them right in the proper light. They are great events in the history of our language and neither is without inner necessity.[3] It is also not to be overlooked that each gradation fills ever smaller circles. The peculiarity of the latter does not extend beyond the High

German dialect. The earlier one encompassed Gothic,
Saxon, Northern still; accordingly it had a more significant
extent. And how restricted this appears when contrasted
with the still older situation, which we must recognize for
the Latin, Greek and Indic languages, and to which in general also the Slavic and Latvian tribes adhere, perhaps with
some modifications. For example, since aspiration is lacking for the Latvians, Prussians and Lithuanians, they are
accustomed to use a media for it or sibilants (see addendum). But they possess the unmodified (Latin and Greek)
tenues and mediae, cf. the Lith. pilnas (plenus) (see addendum) pirmas (primus) pakájus (pax, pacis) piemů (poimén)
peda (vestigium) tris (tres), tu (tu) traukti (trahere) kampas
(campus) kas (quis) kélas (kéleuthos) akis (oculus) ratas
(rota) dantis (dens) antras (Goth. anþar) wertas (Goth.
vaírþs) derwâ (ON tiara, NHG zehr) trokszti (NHG dürsten)
du (duo) sedeti sedere etc. Similarly in Slavic pasti
(pascere) vepr (aper) piti (píein) pokoj (pax) mater (mater)
sjekati (secare) videti (videre) dom (domus) smrt (mors,
mortis) ptak (pterón) etc. For this reason, the Slavic and
Lettish languages are without doubt closer to the Latin and
Greek than the Gothic, and this is closer than the Old High
German.

6) The result of the sound shift brings it about that HG z (for t)
fully takes the place of the th, as HG ph for p, and ch for c.
This High German equating of the z (ts) with th is even more
remarkable, in part because in no monument known to me an
actual exchange between z and th is apparent (no trace of an
OHG thiman, thein for ziman, zein), and in part because in
the High German dialect the pure spirant h is strongly favored and never is exchanged with the spirant s. This exchange prevails precisely in the Slavic and Lettish languages, in which so many of the original gutturals appear
assibilated, cf., cor, cordis, hĕrza with the Lith. szirdis
(pronounce schirdis), Bohemian srdce; canis, hund with the
Lith. szů; centum, hundert with the Lith. ż (pronounce sh
or dsh) answers to the Gk kh, Lat. h as: żiema (kheîma,
hiems), żeme (humus, cf. humilis and khthamalós, khamalós),
żmogus, (homo, pl. żmones, homines; OPruss. smunents,
homo), żasis (khến, anser); żengti, żengimas is the Germanic
gangan, gang. One should compare, however, the AS scĕort,
Eng. short for cĕort and even the OHG scurz for churz
(above p. 175) as well as the hissing pronunciation of the
Frisian, English and Swedish initials c, k, ch.

592

The relationships of the consonants accordingly provide adequate proof of original relationship of the compared languages. Might not also, based on this, at the same time contacts between the vowels be detected? — the analogy between the High German and Gothic vowel situation not lead to the conclusion that Latin vowels too must be connected with Gothic? The connection will be even more uncertain and disrupted for this reason because in the Germanic dialects with the same consonantal gradation we meet such varying and manifold vowels. Nonetheless there are still unmistakable similarities like those given below.

Addenda

(580-581) The relationship of the semi-vowels v and j (p. 9) to the spirants v, s, h (p. 10) is still obscure. First of all, the lingual order has no semi-vowel at all. Secondly, the gutturals have a semi-vowel j which is distinct from the spirant h. Finally, the question arises whether the semi-vowel v falls together with the spirant v? I have already touched on this puzzle on p. 187. It is to be noted that semi-vowels (i.c. vowels with consonantal value) only develop from i and u, not from a, obviously not from the non-original e and o. And since further l and r can develop to u and i, they are semi-vocalic in a reverse sense, i.e. consonants with vocalic value. Is it related to the richer endownment of the throat sound series that the aspirate is occasionally withdrawn from it?

(583, 32) madidus, mador, Goth. natjan, OHG naz.

(584, 15) If one also assumed a fourth grade, then the sound would return to the first grade. Isolated items might possibly be put there, such as the ch and z in châpi, hagestolz cited in the addenda to p. 185 and 526; these however are non-organic exceptions. Never does such a thing show up in an established regular series.

(585 to 588) Some more examples are added here for the nine comparisons.

I, 1. pallidus, Lith. palwas, ON fölr, OHG valêr; Slav. post (jejunium) OHG vasta; Lith. pauksztis (avis) Goth. fugls; Slav. plst (coactile) OHG vilz; Slav. pjast (pugnus) OHG vûst; Gk péras, Goth. fêra.

I, 2. nepos, OHG nĕvo; Gk kêpos, OHG hof, hoves; copia, hûfo; hoplé, ON hôfr, OHG huof, huoves.

II, 2. Lith. obolys, Russ. jabloko, ON epli, OHG epfili; Russ. obezjana (simia) Bohemian opice, ON api, OHG affo.

IV, 1. trituro, AS þĕrsce, OHG driscu; tonitru, AS þĕrsce, OHG driscu; tonitru, AS þunor, OHG donar; Slav. trn, tern (spina) Goth. þaúrnus, OHG dorn.

V, 2. kardía, cor, cordis, haírtô, hĕrza; radix, ON rôt;
hoedus, ON geit, OHG keiz; madidus, OHG naz; kónis, kónidos, ON
nit, OHG niz (instead of hnit, hniz); nidus, Slav. gniezdo, AS nĕst,
OHG nĕst; possibly nodus, Goth. nati (consisting of knots) OHG nezi.
    VII, 1. Gk kêpos, hof; copia, hûfo; crinis, hâr; cerebrum, hirni.
    VII, 2. pulex (pulec-s) Slav. blocha, OHG vlôh.
    VIII, 1. Slav. gnjetu (premere, depsere) OHG chnĕtan).
    VIII, 2. Lith. nogas (nudus) ON naktr, OHG nacchot.
    IX, 1. hoedus (= hoidus) ON geit.
    (591, 22) In the Slavic initial position the media of the second
or third grade occasionally prevails, especially in the combinations
bl, br, gn, gr, e.g. blocha (pulex) brat (frater)(bronja) (lorica, Dobr.
p. 115) OHG prunja; gnida (kónis, kónidos Dobr. 195); graditi
(cingere, Goth. gaúrdan) etc.; to the Germanic hl, hu correspond
chl, chv, e.g. chvila (mora) hvîla; chlev, hleip and many others.
    (591, 24) pilnas, plenus, Slav. pln, poln.

Notes

    1. The modification of the initial and final sounds in Old High
German, Middle High German and Middle Low German is not taken
into consideration here.
    2. The OHG mit, miti agrees with the Gk metá, hût, hûti with
cutis, but not with Goth. miþ, ON hûdh. I doubt if other words cited
in the note p. 159 and other assumed OHG words can be judged in
the same manner. The contradiction to the comparison of the linguals is noteworthy in the words patér, métēr; pater, mater, frater;
Goth. fadrs (?), brôþar; AS fäder, môder, brôdher (cf. p. 514, 544);
OHG vatar, muotar, pruodar; the Germanic languages agree among
themselves and the Lat. frater with them; but should it be pathér and
méthēr? Hardly; all three have the same original tenues in Sanskrit.
    3. Different from individual corruptions which were not thor-
ough, e.g. from the Swedish and Danish displacement of initial lingual aspirates by tenues, while labial aspirates remain: or the
Danish media which is found medially, beside which the initial position maintains the tenuis.

CHAPTER SIX

WILHELM VON HUMBOLDT

ON THE STRUCTURAL VARIETY OF HUMAN LANGUAGE AND ITS INFLUENCE ON THE INTELLECTUAL DEVELOPMENT OF MANKIND

From Über die Verschiedenheit des menschlichen Sprachbaues und ihren Einfluss auf die geistige Entwickelung des Menschengeschlechts (Berlin: F. Dümmler, 1836), Chapter 19

An excerpt from Humboldt's highly influential monograph can do little more than indicate the far-ranging manner in which he presented his views about language. The whole is tightly organized and should be read as a unit for accurate understanding of Humboldt's position. This selection illustrates some of Humboldt's concerns, among them questions which are still occupying linguists.

One is, how should we deal with language in change. A subsequent answer was to abstract the system from speech — language from parole — and make it the essential concern of linguists. By this view linguistic analysis could arrive at items and their arrangements; linguistic forms are arranged for selection and order. After the items and their arrangements are described, the historical linguist might compare two selected stages of a language and deal with the changes between them. Humboldt's view of language as an organism in constant change does not permit such a simple answer. He would have looked with favor on the attempts to introduce linguistic methodology which does not first require reduction of language to a state — which can manage processes in a descriptive presentation.

A second concern exemplified in the excerpt is the problem that Sapir dealt with under drift. Here too Humboldt is not dogmatic. He does not hypostatize; he would probably have objected to the notion of therapeutic sound change. He simply suggests that a principle can be noted; he discusses its functioning in language and leaves it up to others to make use of this guideline in their efforts to understand language.

The excerpt also illustrates Humboldt's well-known concern with typology. Like that of the Schlegel brothers,

61

this was to be overwhelmed by the concentration on genealogical classification. The types were not exact enough to arouse enthusiasm. In discussing them, Humboldt does not propose that they are to be rated against one another, but rather against their adequacy in meeting the varied demands of the human intellect. Nor does he relate any type to historical progress or to stages of culture. The aim was simply to understand language.

Other ideas are discussed more fully in other widely cited sections of the monograph such as the eighth on form [in which Humboldt asserts that language is not a finished product (ergon) but rather an activity (energeia)] and the eleventh on the inner form of language. These have been cited especially in connection with the Sapir-Whorf hypothesis. Humboldt held that the structure of a language reflects the culture of its speaker and that the differences between languages parallel those between speakers, but he did not specify the parallels nor did he insist that it was the language which brings about the differences. These views on the close relation between language and other components of culture appeal especially to linguists such as Weisgerber and his associates, who object to a purely mechanistic approach to language.

Humboldt's primary publications dealt with language, but he was interested in the humanities in general. A close friend of Schiller and an early commentator on Goethe, Wilhelm von Humboldt (1767-1835) belonged to the leading intellectual groups of his day. Though he studied political science, he devoted himself to his interests in literature and esthetics until 1801 when he entered service with the Prussian state; repelled subsequently by its reactionary policies, he returned to his private pursuits in 1819. He was proclaimed for his knowledge of languages, among them Basque, which he made known among linguists. Although he did not travel as widely as his younger brother, Alexander (1769-1859), his control over languages extended beyond those of Europe, as illustrated in the references of the excerpt. Like the ancient Kawi language of Java, to the grammar of which the monograph is an introduction, languages were of primary interest to Humboldt for his chief concern, the relation of language and culture.

19. On the Primary Differences between Languages in Accordance with the Purity of Their Principle of Formation

Since language, as I have already mentioned frequently above, always possesses only an ideal existence in the heads and spirits of men, never a material one — even when engraved on stone or bronze — and since the force of the languages which are no longer spoken depends largely on the strength of our own capability to revivify them, to the extent in which we can still perceive them, in the same way there can never be a moment of true standstill in language, just as little as in the ceaselessly flaming thought of men. By nature it is a continuous process of development under the influence of the actual intellectual force of the speaker. Two periods which must be definitely distinguished arise of course in this process: the one in which the sound-creating force of the language is still in growth and living activity; the other in which an apparent standstill takes place after complete formation of at least the external form of language and then a visible decline of that creative, sensual force follows. But even from the period of decline new principles of life and new successful reformations of language can develop, which I will touch on in greater detail below.

In the course of development of language generally, two mutually limiting causes work together: the principle which originally determines the direction, and the influence of the material which has already been produced, whose power always stands in reverse relation to the force of the principle which is asserting itself. There can be no doubt of the presence of such a principle in each language. Just as a people, or a human capable of thought in general, adopts elements of a language, in the same way it must combine them into a unity, quite instinctively and without a clear realization of the process; for without this operation thinking by means of language in the individual and mutual understanding would be impossible. One would have to make this very assumption if one could rise to an initial creation of a language. This unity however can only be that of an exclusively prevailing principle. If this principle approximates the generally language-forming principle in man to such an extent that this permits its necessary individualization, and if it penetrates the language in full and unweakened power, then it will run through all stages of the course of its development to such an extent that in place of a diminishing power a new power will arise again and again which is suitable for the continuing course. For it is characteristic of every intellectual development that its power does not actually die but simply changes in its functions or replaces one of its organs with another. If however something which is not based on the necessity of the form of the language is already

mixed with the initial principle, or if the principle does not truly
penetrate the sound, or if something which is also wrongly formed
joins a not purely organic material and leads to greater deviation,
then a strange power becomes opposed to the natural course of development, and the language cannot gain new strength through the
pursuit of its course, as should be the case for every proper development of intellectual forces. Here too, as in the designation of the
manifold associations of thought, language needs freedom; and one
can regard it as a secure sign of the purest and most successful
linguistic structure if in it the formation of words and constructions
undergoes no other limitations than are necessary to combine regularity with freedom, that is, to assure for freedom its own existence
through limitation. For the course of development of intellectual
capability generally stands in natural harmony with the correct
course of development of language. For since the need of thinking
wakens language in man, in the same way that which flows purely
from its conception also by necessity advances the successful advance of thinking. If however a nation equipped with such a language
would sink into intellectual inertia and weakness for other reasons,
it would be able to work itself out of this state more simply through
its language. Conversely the intellectual capability must find in
itself the lever for its development, if it is equipped with a language
deviating from that correct and natural course of development. Then
the means created by this capability will have an effect on the language, not to be sure a creative one, because its creations can only
be the product of its own life-force, but constructing in it, lending
its forms meaning, and permitting a use which it had not placed in
them and to which it would not have led.

     We can then determine a difference in the countless variety of
current and lost languages which is of decisive importance for the
continuing education of mankind, namely that between languages
which have developed powerfully and consistently from a pure principle in lawful freedom and those which cannot boast of this advantage. The first are the successful fruits of the linguistic instinct
which flourishes among mankind in manifold exertions. The latter
have a deviant form in which two things combine: lack of strength
of the feeling for language, which always exists in pure form among
man originally; and a one-sided malformation which arises from the
situation that to a form of sound which does not by necessity flow
from the language others are combined, attracted by this malformation.

     The above investigations provide a guide-line to study this in
actual languages and to present it in simple form, however much
one thinks he sees a bewildering mass of detail in them initially.
For we have attempted to show what is important in the highest

principles and in this way to establish points to which linguistic
analysis can be raised. However much this path may still be clarified and smoothed, one comprehends the possibility of finding in
each language the form from which the character of its structure
flows; one can also see in the material sketched above the measure
of its advantages and its deficiencies.

If I have succeeded in depicting the inflectional method in its
total perfection, in showing how it alone provides the true, inner
firmness for the word with regard to the intellect and the ear, and
at the same time distinguishing securely the parts of the sentence
in accordance with the necessary intertwining of thoughts, then there
is no question that it exclusively preserves in itself the pure principle of linguistic structure. Since it takes each element of speech
in its twofold value, in its objective meaning and its subjective relationship to the thought and language, and designates this double
relationship in its proportional weight through forms of sound designed for the purpose, it increases the most original essence of
speech, articulation and symbolization, to its highest grades. Accordingly the question can only be, in which languages this method
is preserved most consistently, completely and freely. No real language may have reached the pinnacle. But above we saw a difference of grade between Sanskrit and the Semitic languages: in the
latter, inflection in its truest and most unmistakable form and connected with the finest symbolization, yet not carried through all
parts of the language and limited through more or less accidental
laws — the bisyllabic word form — the vowels used exclusively for
designation of inflection — the hesitation about compounding; in the
first, inflection preserved against every suspicion of agglutination
through the firmness of the word unity, carried through all parts of
the language and prevailing in it in the highest freedom.

Compared with the process of incorporation and loose attach-
ment without a true word unity, the method of inflection seems to
be a principle of genius, proceeding from the true intuition of the
language. For while such languages are anxiously concerned with
uniting the individual entity into a sentence, or with representing the
sentence immediately unified, the method of inflection indicates directly the components in accordance with a particular thought construction, and by its nature cannot separate the relationship of a
component to the thought in speech. A weakness of the language-
forming instinct at times does not permit the method of inflection
to go over to the sound, as in Chinese, and at other times not to
prevail freely and alone, as in the languages which individually follow the process of incorporation. The effect of the pure principle
can however be checked also through one-sided malformation, when
an individual form of construction, as for example the specification

of the verb by means of modifying prefixes in Malay, becomes prevalent to the neglect of all others.

However different the deviations from the purest principle may be, every language can still be characterized for the extent to which the lack of designations for relationship is visible in it, and the attempt to add them and raise them to inflections, and the expedient of characterizing as a word what speech ought to present as a sentence. From the mixture of these principles will proceed the essence of such a language, but as a rule an even more individual form will develop from the application of them. For where the full energy of the guiding force does not preserve the proper equilibrium, there a part of the language readily attains a disproportionate development with unfairness to others. From this and other circumstances individual excellences can also arise in languages in which one cannot otherwise recognize the character of being excellently suited organs of thought. No one can deny that Chinese of the old style carries an impressive dignity through the fact that only weighty concepts join one another directly, and in this way it attains a simple greatness by seeming to escape to pure thought through speech in discarding all unnecessary secondary relationships. The real Malay is not unjustly praised because of its ease and the great simplicity of its constructions. The Semitic languages preserve an admirable art of fine distinctions of meaning through many vowel gradations. Basque possesses in its word formation and in its constructions a special strength which proceeds from brevity and boldness of expression. Delaware and other American languages combine into a single word a number of concepts, for the expression of which we would need many. But all of these examples only prove that the human intellect, however unbalanced the course it may take, can always produce something great and productive of fruitfulness and enthusiasm. These individual points do not decide the preeminence of languages to one another. The true preeminence of a language is simply to develop from a principle and in a freedom which make it possible for it to maintain all the intellectual capabilities of man in vigorous activity, to serve them as a satisfactory organ, and to stimulate them constantly through the sensuous fullness and intellectual regularity which it preserves. Everything of benefit to the spirit which can develop from language exists in this formal characteristic. It is the bed in which the spirit of language can propagate its waves, in the secure confidence that the sources which they lead him to will never be exhausted. For he actually glides on it as on an indeterminable depth from which he can draw more and more, when more has already flowed to him from it. Accordingly this formal measure can be applied to languages only if one tries to bring them under a general comparison.

CHAPTER SEVEN

RUDOLF VON RAUMER

LINGUISTIC-HISTORICAL CHANGE AND THE NATURAL-HISTORICAL DEFINITION OF SOUNDS

"Die sprachgeschichtliche Umwandlung und die
naturgeschichtliche Bestimmung der Laute,"
Zeitschrift für die Österreichischen Gymnasien V (1856), 353-73

The great advance in historical linguistics after the early publications of Grimm, Bopp and others was in knowledge of phonetics. Usually we assume that this increased knowledge clarified historical problems, as in accounting for the "first set of exceptions in the consonant shift" — the retention of the voiceless stops after fricatives, for example in Gothic ist = Lat. est. But from von Raumer we learn that the influence also went in the other direction, that the problems which arose in historical linguistics led to an increasing need for competence in phonetics. In keeping with this need to move away from the "shuffling of letters," von Raumer set out to arrive at an accurate statement of articulatory phonetics.

The essay presented here recapitulates many of the conclusions presented by von Raumer in his monograph on Aspiration and the Consonant Shift, published when he was 22. In this he attempted to clarify the relationship of the Greek stops to the Germanic; he concluded that ph th kh were aspirates, like the related bh dh gh in Sanskrit. By this clarification he defined with greater precision the variety of sounds that Grimm combined in his aspiratae. He also made the suggestion for which Grassmann later was given credit — that Sanskrit never shows aspiration in two successive syllables: Aspiration and the Consonant Shift p. 74, §64: "For since Sanskrit never aspirates two successive syllables, one can assume as the original form of bud' with equal justification b'ud'. Then biudan would simply be the usual transition of b' to b." But this insight of von Raumer's was not noted by his contemporaries. Apparently review of all the relevant examples, as by Grassmann, was necessary to attract the notice of linguists.

In devoting attention to phonetics, von Raumer dealt

with the spoken dialects, citing the pronunciation of Low
German, Bavarian, Swabian variants. This attention to the
dialects was followed by specific concentration on them, as
his concern with phonetics led to the definitive treatments
of Sievers and Jespersen at the end of the century.

Rudolf von Raumer (1815-1876) had a quiet career,
completing his studies at the University of Erlangen and
holding a position there until his death. With a chair at a
university which was not a center for linguistic study he
was somewhat of a loner, who did not participate in the
struggles between the traditional grammarians and the
more rigorous linguists. Possibly his aloof position also
led to the neglect of his writings. Both in content and style,
however, they seem more modern than most linguistic
works of his time. In spite of his problems in developing
a linguistic vocabulary and his occasional faulty reasoning
(as in his interpretation of Gothic þ as an aspirate) we consider him one of the important contributors to the developing methodology of historical linguistics.

Foreword

Through the discoveries of historical linguistic investigation, the significance of phonetics has been placed in a new light.
The more the importance of phonetics becomes recognized, the
more apparent becomes the need to understand as clearly and precisely as possible its subject matter, namely the sounds themselves.
This understanding, insofar it is in the sphere of direct observation,
lies in the area of the physical sciences. Therefore it is highly desirable that important scientists should devote themselves to the
study of this subject. Among the many valuable studies, which have
been recently undertaken in this area, I intend to dwell only upon
those which Johannes Müller and Ernst Brücke have achieved for
the determination and arrangement of the sounds of language. Investigations of this type need above all a common solid foundation.
And exactly that has been furnished by Brücke's publication[1] in a
manner as clear as it is accessible. Only after agreement has been
reached on such a basis can one discuss the more complex and deep-
seated questions of scientific as well as historical investigation of
sounds. If in regard to some of these questions I maintain previously proposed findings opposed to Brücke's views, I ask that this
not be considered as personal obstinacy. I have subjected my assertions to a renewed careful examination. But the result of this
examination has only convinced me anew, that my views concerning

aspiration and the sound shift, stated in 1837, are essentially correct. The relationship, however, in which this particular sound development stands to the various types of sound change in general,
will be clarified partly by the following treatise, partly by comparison of it with my other linguistic works.

I. The Natural-historical Determination of Sounds

1. The natural-historical determination of sounds must first
devote itself solely to the sounds of the present as object of immediate observation. The chief aim of such observation is the manner
of utterance of the sounds. Differences, which the ear perceives or
believes it perceives, are not to be dismissed. But in the realm of
precise natural-historical observation they are only then to be dealt
with, when one can establish with certainty their diversity of production.[2]

2. We distinguish primarily the tones of the human voice and
the sounds of human speech. The tones are produced through the
vibration of the vocal cords in the glottis; the sounds are produced
through the deflection of the exhaled airstream against the organs
lying between the epiglottis and the lips. Of the tones produced in
the glottis, one distinguishes between loud and soft speech (vox
clandestina). Loud speech is produced when we accompany utterance of sound, as far as it is possible, with tones from the vocal
cords. Soft speech is produced when we speak without simultaneous
sounding of the vocal cords. We accompany soft speech too with a
noise, differing from the production of sounds, which we can clearly
perceive especially in whispering the vowels.[3]

3. The sounds are divided into classes on the basis of three
different criteria, namely 1) according to the position of the organs,
2) according to the type of air influx, 3) according to the organs, by
which they are produced.

4. According to the position of the speech organs, the sounds
are divided into 1) those which require for their utterance a complete closure of the organs (stops, literae explosivae), and 2) those
which are produced without a complete closure of the organs (continuants, literae continuae[4]). The latter sounds are divided again
into those, which are produced by air passing through such a narrow
passage, that the noise of air deflection becomes clearly audible
(consonantal continuants, consonantes continuae) and those for which,
because of the wideness of the opening this is not the case (vowels).

5. The second criterion of classification is the type of air influx. Usually one divides the consonants into hard and soft, so that,
for example, the German p is called hard, the b soft, and likewise

β (in gieβen) hard, and the s (in sagen, Wesen) soft. The objection
is raised against this division, however, that it is wavering and
without clearly fixed limits, for what one person calls hard, another
will consider soft. Another criterion has therefore been advanced,
which provides a definite limit, namely whether the tone of the voice
can be combined with the utterance of a sound or not. Sounds are
accordingly divided into voiced and voiceless. The difference is
most noticeable in the pronunciation of some continuants, for example, the s and the β. While one sustains the (so-called soft) s, one
can simultaneously produce a singing tone; as soon as one passes to
the (hard or sharp) β, however, the singing tone immediately ceases.
This difference, which was known already by the old Indian grammarians, is an excellent criterion, because it replaces an uncertain
and indefinable difference for the ear with a certain and verifiable
distinction in utterance. But since the tone of the voice only accom-
panies the sound and is not essential to it, one will do better by
seeking the reason why it becomes impossible for certain sounds to
combine with the tone of the voice, and then to take this cause as the
criterion for distinction. This cause, however, is none other than
this: certain sounds are produced by blowing (flare), while others
are formed through breathing (halare). But blowing and singing exclude one another; one can convince himself of this at once, if one
tries to sustain a singing tone when one passes from breathing to
blowing.[5] The difference then that one designates by voiceless and
voiced[6] I would prever to express by blown (literae flatae) and
breathed (literae halatae).[7]

     6. Concerning the division of the sounds according to the or-
gans or the places of articulation, I refer to Brücke's exhaustive
presentation; for illustration, however, I wish to give at this point
merely a survey of the common stops and spirants (consonantes
continuae spirantes) of the general New High German language. I
limit myself to these two classes, because primarily they are to be
considered in the course of this paper. I append the column for
vowels merely in order to indicate the position of the consonantal
continuants between the stops and the vowels.

     This table of the common stops and spirants of the general New
High German language conforms to the one given in my paper on
aspiration and the sound shift. Only in one single instance do I dis-
agree thereby with Brücke, in reference to the cerebral sibilant (sch
in schoen). I have repeated the experiments, which in conjunction
with the old Indian grammar, disposed me to assign this sound to the
cerebrals, and they have only convinced me again that its place of
articulation lies between that of ch (in Sichel, Brücke's X[1]) and that
of β (and s). One can convince himself of this fact, if one produces
our spirants, one after another with vox clandestina, whether the

Place of Articulation	Stops (Explosivae)		Consonantal Continuants (Conson. continuae)		Vowels (all halatae)
	blown (flatae) (= voiceless)	breathed (halatae) (= voiced)	blown (flatae)	breathed (halatae)	
I. Throat sounds (gutturales)	k	g	ch (in Sache, Brücke's X²)		are not always assignable to individual places of articulation with the same certainty as the consonants.
II. Palatal sounds (palatales)			ch (in Sichel, Brücke's X¹)	j (in jeder)	
III. Cerebral sounds (cerebrales)			sch (in schoen)		
IV. Dental sounds (dentales)	t	d	β (in gießen)	s (in sagen, Wesen)	
V. Labial sounds (labiales)	p	b	f	w² (= French V) w¹ (the u in Quelle)	

sequence be from back to front or from front to back. One may
first narrow the air passage in one such sequence by beginning with
the ch in Sache, passing then to that in Sichel, thereupon to the sch
and finally the β. Immediately upon reaching the β, one should return to the sch. It will be very easy to notice that the place of articulation of the sch lies somewhat farther back than that of the β.
This is the most usual pronunciation of the NHG sch. The determination of this sound becomes somewhat complicated, however, in
that there is a third sibilant besides β and sch, which is pronounced
somewhat farther back than the usual German sch. Sanskrit has
this sound in the palatal sibilant श, according to Bopp's designation
's). It is produced by approaching the palate with the tongue in the
same area, where we pronounce the ch in Sichel. But while we hold
the part of the tongue, which lies in front of the place of articulation,
as far as possible from the palate in pronouncing ch (in Sichel), in
pronouncing the palatal sibilant we must approach the palate with
the tongue. Through a gradual transition from the positioning of the
organs of articulation of the palatal sibilant (श, s̓) to that of the
pure cerebral sibilant (ष = s̩, sh, sch), we obtain an uninterrupted
series of traditional sibilants lying between the palatal s̓ and the
cerebral s̩. A portion of our fellow-countrymen use these sibilants
in place of the pure cerebral s̓ (= sh, sch).

II.   The Historical-Linguistic Change of Sounds

1.   In the course of time the words of language have changed
their sounds. So much is certain and, moreover, this is one of the
most important facts for the history of languages. We ascertain
that the sounds of words have changed when we compare the older
state of languages with the more recent. The process of the change
itself however has not yet been investigated enough. If we penetrate
deeper into the darkness which in many ways veils these questions,
we find a huge multitude of highly different processes at work. And
what is even more troublesome, we find that to isolate these processes becomes even more difficult, because often quite heterogeneous occurrences lead to almost the same result.

2.   When the change of languages and especially of language
sounds is spoken of, there are almost immediately references to
the "spirit of the language" and its wonders. I have no intent what-
soever of deprecating the profundity with which the more recent research distinguishes itself. But I think it is about time that we turn
our attentions to reality and its phenomena with clear and impartial
minds. When we do, we find that the "spirit of the language" in
itself and apart from people does nothing, but rather that all changes

in language actually are produced by the people. To just what extent
their production is really a product of man remains a matter of conjecture. It is enough that the changes themselves are objects of observation as soon as they become apparent.

3. If first of all we direct our observation to that which happens
before our very eyes, or better, before our ears, we will discern
the following facts:

1) Every single person changes his speech in the course of his
life. As a child, before the complete development of his speaking
ability, he speaks many words with sounds, which he later abandons.
If he attains an old age and loses his teeth, not only does the sharp-
ness of his articulation disappear, but also in more than one instance real modifications of the previously pronounced sounds become apparent.

2) From this alone it follows that not even a single family,
which consists of old people, adults and children, speaks one and
the same language.

3) But even the adults among themselves never have exactly
the same language, not even phonetically. This follows necessarily
from the principle of individuation. Every human being has his own
peculiarly formed organs of speech as well as his own particular
facial features. Now the production of sounds is conditioned by the
form of the speech organs, which confine the sound-producing air
stream. Therefore, although our ear does not perceive the resultant
difference, it is nevertheless present. But in many cases our ear is
very readily able to detect the difference.

4) A further and not infrequently occurring difference results
from the fact, that one person articulates a sound at a somewhat
different place than another, and therefore, strictly speaking, actually produces an entirely different sound.

4. If we consider the possibilities which could result from the
above discussed differences among relatively great numbers of people, we find them to be of most varied kinds. If the change of a
sound heard in an individual's speech is caused by the inability of
the vocal organs to produce the heard sound, this individual is forced
to face the particular change wherever the sound in question occurs.
Let us consider then an entire family, or an even larger social
group consisting only of individuals which suffer from the foresaid
disability. The sound pronounced earlier will necessarily disappear
in this entire group, and the other sound will take its place.

On the other hand, however, let us consider a family in which
one member, for example the father, has that peculiarity of speech,
but the mother does not. The case may then occur that the children
imitate either the father entirely or the mother. But it can also be

that, being capable of imitating both, the children imitate their
father in some words, the mother in others, and in some words
perhaps they waver between one parent and the other.

5. If the change of the heard sound is not based on the inability
of the speaker to produce the sound, but rather only on the fact, that
the changed pronunciation is easier for the speech organs than the
traditional one, then usually the results will also be different than
in the previously discussed instances. It is possible then that certain members of the group will retain the old pronunciation. But
since the change is not due to an individual peculiarity of the speaker,
but rather to the mechanism of the human speech organs in general,
among the other members of society it will also be effected, not
merely through imitation, but also through the structure of their
own speech organs. This is the case in most instances in which one
sound is altered by the environment of another.

6. A large part of the changes, which the sounds of words undergo in the course of time, can be accounted for in the ways discussed above. Especially if one remembers in addition, that the
mere inexactness of hearing and speaking causes sound changes,
which are very similar to the four discussed already. We find however another type of alterations belonging to a class of sound changes
different from those previously discussed. And these changes are
namely those in which, firstly, there is no question of mere inexactness of transmission, because they are immanent within the entire
vocabulary or at least a very large part of it. Secondly, in these
changes there exists no inability to produce the earlier sound, because the same sound, which is abandoned in one place, reappears
at another. And thirdly, in these changes it has not been possible to
prove an influence of neighboring sounds as the cause of the change.
In this category belongs the most remarkable sound change in the
Germanic languages: the sound shift of the mutes.[8]

7. The ways in which one sound changes into another can be
twofold. Either a certain sound changes swiftly into another particular sound, or it passes gradually through a continuous series of
intermediate sounds. In the case of sound changes through neighboring sounds, especially among vowels, there is often this gradual
transition. For the sound changes discussed under number 6, this
gradual transition is especially applicable.

8. It is naturally not my intention above to exhaust the diverse
types of sound change. Otherwise, sound change through analogy,
for example, would also have to be treated. But I would prefer to
reserve this and other related questions for another occasion.

III. Which Means Do We Have at Our Command
for Investigating Sound Changes?

1. We are not speaking here of the confirmation of the fact, that the sounds of words have changed. Neither is it a question of the form of words in one language or another. Rather, we are concerned about the process itself, by which the one form of words and sounds has replaced the other.

2. Neither is it a matter here of how word forms, which were already present in the spoken language, came to be taken into the written language. We are asking, rather, how one form of a word replaced another in the spoken language itself.

3. Although the question then about this process itself is different from the question concerning sounds which in one language are to be found in place of others in another language; the research on the latter question forms the basis for the investigation of the former. Indeed the excellent activity in the realm of comparative phonology and its admirable results lead us to believe that we shall also be successful in getting more clues about the above-mentioned processes. It is our very worthy linguists, whom we have to thank for the many results, and whose work has laid the foundation for all further investigations. Above all, it has been the comparative studies of the Indo-Germanic languages which have paved the way for us. I mention only the works of Rask, Bopp and Pott concerning the connection of the Asiatic and the European branches of the Indo-Germanic languages, the epochal Germanic grammar of Jakob Grimm, and the research in the Romance languages by Diez, in the Slavic languages by Miklosich and Schleicher, in the Celtic languages by Zeuβ.

4. All of these works not only furnish the material for the investigation of sound change, but they also pave the way to this objective through the contributions, which they make toward the solution to what Diez, in the second edition of his Grammar of the Romance languages, has recently accomplished in this field. In fact the works of Diez quite clearly direct our attention toward both points; research must now be primarily focussed on these. The first of these is the investigation of the living dialects in the most specific and the most general sense of the word, and secondly, the physiological investigation of not only the living languages, but also of the languages no longer spoken.

5. Besides the very worthwhile treatment of dialects of entire ethnic groups, the investigation of living dialects will have to concern itself above all with the most accurate examination and representation possible of the particular diction of individuals. These studies will give us the possibility of drawing conclusions from

the thousand-fold synchronic diversity on the diachronic succession.[9]

6. The second requisition: the investigation of sounds in non-
living languages is always attended by great difficulties. And yet
this inquiry is the indispensable pre-condition if we want to advance
from the mere demonstration of alphabetical modification to the investigation of sound change. The means at our command for con-
verting the written letters of old languages into living sounds are
quite diverse. To some extent they are provided in the structure of
the languages themselves. Physiological and euphonic sound changes
within the language concerned also offer numerous clues. Moreover,
there is the value of the sounds in meter, which gives us so much
information, especially in the classical languages and Sanskrit, and
their positions in rhyme, which is so important for many languages
of the Middle Ages. We do not want to review here all of the particular aids for determining the sounds of dead languages: the introduction of individual words in other languages, their transcription in
another alphabet, and so forth. Rather, we shall limit ourselves to
emphasizing only two means of determination relevant to the old
chief languages of the Indo-Germanic family: the statements of the
old native grammarians and the linguistic-historical change of the
sounds themselves.

7. The importance of the old grammarians for determining the
sounds is generally recognized. The general complaint, however, is
that their assertions are partially ambiguous and partially difficult
to understand. It is evident that this complaint is not entirely without foundation, in that the most discerning and candid scholars have
arrived at quite different conclusions in many of the most important
points. It should be pointed out, however, that the Indian grammarians are incomparably more accurate, more comprehensible and
more explicit in their definition of sounds than the Greeks, who are
in their own way also quite discriminating.

8. When I designate the historical-linguistic change of sounds
as one of the means for determining sounds no longer spoken, I
must first protest against a misunderstanding. In reference to Max
Müller's estimable article on the languages in the area of the oriental war, Brücke says:[10] "It must be noted that Max Müller considers the e̲ and o̲ to be diphthongs which differ from the true diphthongs, like the English J̱ and o̲u̲ in o̲u̲t only in degree. It is hardly
comprehensible how a m̄an of Max Müller's intelligence could defend
such an error, however widely accepted, after he had read the investigations of Willis. The cause of this particular error is, as it
appears to me, another error of even greater range, which he unfortunately shares with many other linguists. They believe that the
nature of a speech sound can only be determined by historical and

comparative philological research, for only this can be meant by the author when he refers to theoretical analysis. This determines how sounds replace one another at different times and among different peoples. But even if this occurred according to more immutable laws than it actually does, even then the analysis of individual sounds with regard to the conditions, under which they arise would be left to direct observation and scientific experiments." I subscribe fully to this statement of the discerning physiologist, and wish moreover that he would some day subject to a scientific examination the definition of sounds found in our otherwise quite laudable grammatical works. He would encounter there a great number of things which are almost more incredible than the above cited views of Max Müller[11] concerning the alleged diphthongal nature of the Sanskrit ē and ō. I have therefore no intention of wanting to determine the nature of sounds according to linguistic-historical processes that would be contradictory to natural-historical observation. What I assert is rather: When we are uncertain about which sound is expressed by the symbol of a non-living language, among other arguments we can consider the question: What development has the sound of this symbol undergone in the course of linguistic history? From the answer to this question we can draw conclusions on the nature of the old sound. It is quite apparent, that by this method we would never enter into conflict with scientific conditions of sound production. For our entire investigation is to serve only the purpose of finding the historically true sound belonging to the symbol among the many scientifically possible ones. I shall demonstrate this with an example. Old High German had two i's, a short and a long. Etymologically, the short i corresponds to a Gothic (short) i; the long one to a Gothic ei. For example, Old High German stilu (furor) is in Gothic stila (with a short i); on the other hand, Old High German stîgu (scando, with long i) is in Gothic steiga. Now if someone should want to conclude that the OHG î is a diphthong, because it came from Gothic ei, then he would be guilty of the error of Max Müller, which Brücke rightfully criticizes above. If he says however: "The OHG i is long, where it corresponds etymologically with a Gothic ei; but where it stands in the position of a Gothic i (always short), it is short," then he will be right, insofar as direct proofs contrary to this assumption can not be adduced from elsewhere.

IV. The Natural-Scientific Determination of the
Aspirates and the Germanic Sound-Shift

1. One of the most remarkable sound changes in the entire area

of Indo-Germanic languages is the transformation which the mutes
have undergone in the Germanic branch of this great language family. This transformation is not only among the most remarkable
because it is one of the most important for etymological research,
but rather because it runs through an entire family of sounds with
amazing regularity and, moreover, has occurred in the course of
centuries not once, but twice, according to the very same principles.
This transformation, to which Jacob Grimm gave the name "sound
shift," consists therein, as is well-known, that the Germanic languages of the Gothic stage have a tenuis in place of a Greek media,
and in place of a Greek tenuis, an aspirata, and finally in place of a
Greek aspirata, they have a media. But the same transformation,
which Gothic experienced in relation to Greek, Old High German
undergoes a second time in relation to Gothic. In spite of all re-
strictions and exceptions, which the course of this development undergoes, we have accordingly in this transformation a process which
is undeniably based on the nature of these sounds.

2. In order to comprehend the progress of this development,
however, it is absolutely necessary to determine correctly the nature of the sounds concerned in it. The tenues or blown (= voiceless) stops cause us no difficulty. The languages still living today
have them as well as the dead languages, and the essential agreement of our k̲, t̲, p̲ with the Old Greek k̲, t̲, p̲ is not disputed. The
mediae would give us somewhat more difficulty, if at the outset we
have to attempt to determine relatively exactly the meaning of this
concept, which the Old Greek grammarians identify with the expression mésa. For the moment, however, we can put aside this investigation, for the specific peculiarities of Greek pronunciation are
not our concern in dealing with the law of the sound shift, but rather
the sounds, which in the original Greek stage etymologically corresponded to the Gothic tenues, were the breathed (= voiced, = soft)
stops, accordingly in the main our g̲, d̲, b̲.

3. The difficulty lies in the determination of the sound of the
aspirates. Twenty-one years ago I made the attempt to grasp the
law of the sound shift more accurately by proceeding beyond the
mere etymological comparison of letters and trying to penetrate
into the historical-physiological process of the sound change itself.[12]
Among the results of this investigation was a more exact determination of the Greek and Sanskrit aspirates, a precise distinction of
them from mere spirants (friction noises) and the proof, that precisely the aspirates played a major role in the process of the sound
shift, a role, which the spirants, being quite different from the aspirates, were incapable of assuming. The main difference between
aspirates and spirants was found to be, that the aspirate was a stop
(explosiva) with after-sounding, while the spirant is a continual

sound (continua), produced not through the closure, but rather
through the mere constricting of the speech organs.

4. Now after many years of further research I would, of course,
modify in many respects the views which I expressed in my article
of 1837. Yet I still hold to the entire course of the investigation as
well as to its essential conclusions, believing I can refute everything
which has been said against my findings. The conclusions published
by me would receive the strongest blow if the views which a perceptive physiologist recently postulated concerning the nature of the
old aspirates had any basis. For Brücke is of the opinion in his article mentioned frequently above, that the old aspirates, the Indian
as well as the Greek, were merely fricatives (spirantes). He attempts to support his opinion with the most diverse arguments, and
I feel myself obliged, therefore, to analyze more closely his argumentation.

5. We shall first discuss the Sanskrit aspirates. Here Brücke
begins his exposition with an argument, which he draws from the
orthographical designation of the Sanskrit aspirates. "In the Dêvanâgarî," he says, "their signs have nothing in common with those
of the respective stops; only the sign for $\underline{t}^2$ ($\underline{t}$ of the cerebral group)
has an unmistakable resemblance with that of its aspirate. This
must be pointed out, because the almost complete lack of correlation of the signs is not entirely without importance for the evaluation of the nature of the sound."[13] To the same degree as the latter
is of importance precisely for the Dêvanâgarî, Brücke's argument
will obviously refute his own views, as soon as the signs for the un-
aspirated stops reveal themselves to be in evident correlation with
the signs for the corresponding aspirates. With a great number of
signs, however, this correlation is not subject to the least doubt,
and moreover is restricted by no means merely to the t of the cerebral series. One glance at the Dêvanâgarî signs will convince us of
this fact. Let us compare in the guttural series क (ka) and ख (kha),
in the palatal series ञ (dscha) and झ (dschha), and in the labial series प (pa) and फ (pha). How one wants to explain the origin of this
similarity depends naturally on the views one has in general on the
origin and development of the Dêvanâgarî.

According to the present grammatical tradition of the Indians,
"each aspirate is pronounced like its corresponding non-aspirate,
but with an accompanying, clearly perceptible h. Consequently one
may not pronounce ख ($\underline{k}$) like a German ch, फ ($\underline{p}$) not like f, or प
($\acute{t}$) like an English th; but according to Colebrooke ख ($\underline{k}$) is read
like kh in inkhorn, फ ($\underline{p}$) like ph in haphazard, and प ($\acute{t}$) like th in
nuthook. The relationship is the same with the other aspirates."[14]
Even Brücke cannot deny this. He is of the opinion, however, that
the present pronunciation of the Sanskrit aspirates is not the original,

that they were rather mere fricatives (spirants): रव (k̓) sounded
like our ch in Spruch, फ (p̓) like f and so forth.[15]

To determine whether this is in fact true, we shall have to consult the older Indian grammarians. In the annotation to Pânini's
Grammar we find a survey of the Sanskrit letters with indication of
the manner of production in regard to the several speech organs as
well as the position of these organs.[16] Here all of the aspirates k̓,
g̓, etc., as well as the corresponding non-aspirated stops are
counted among the letters, whose utterance requires sprista, that
is, the contact of the organs.[17] I would not know, how one could any
more clearly characterize the nature of the stops. But perhaps
Brücke wants to maintain that the annotations to Pânini are not old
enough for him, rather that they stood under the influence of that
later change in the pronunciation of the Indian aspirates which was
assumed by him. Let us look then for the earliest evidence of Indian grammar. In the Prâtisâkhya of the Rigvêda a representation
of the sounds of Sanskrit has been preserved, which leads us quite
far back in Indian antiquity. The very alphabet which precedes the
first patala shows us how closely the aspirates were associated with
the corresponding non-aspirates even in those very earliest times.
For the letters are represented in such a way, that every aspirate
forms a single word with the corresponding non-aspirate, which,
through the dual ending (au), indicates the copulative composition
of both letter-names. Thus ka and k̓a are joined to form the word
kak̓au, ga and g̓a to form the word gag̓au, and so on.[18] Decisive,
however, is the naming and definition of the aspirates in this old
grammatical work. For the ten Sanskrit aspirates (k̓, g̓, c̓, g̓, ṭ̓, ḍ̓,
t̓, ḍ̓, p̓, b̓) are brought together with the ten corresponding unaspi-
rated stops and the five nasal consonants under the expression
sparṣâs. This expression comes from the same word spriṣ
(tangere), to which the word spriṣta (contact) in the annotations
to Pânini belongs. All of these sounds, including the aspirates, are
accordingly designated as contact sounds by the old grammarian
and are quite expressly distinguished from the semi-vowels (j, r,
l, v) and the breathed sounds (ûṣmâ), to which h and the sibilants
are ascribed. As a clinching argument, one old annotation inter-
prets the passage to the effect, that the sparṣâs are the letters in
the utterance of which the speech organs touch one another.[19] For
all fifteen sounds, which with the aspirates form one and the same
class, there is no doubt of this contact; for also in the nasal consonants the actual speech organs are entirely closed and only the nasal
passage remains open. It is therefore quite clear what the old
grammarian means with the designation sparṣâs contact sounds.
Furthermore there can accordingly be no doubt, that also the aspirates were produced in his time through actual contact of the
speech organs, that is, as stops.

I believe herewith to have given the proof, that the Sanskrit aspirates were stops, and it only remains to put in its right place an argument especially emphasized by Brücke. Max Müller says in the above-mentioned publication:[20] "According to the Sanskrit grammarians we produce the aspirate as a modified tenuis, and not as a double consonant, in that we begin to pronounce the tenuis, but instead of breaking it off sharply, we allow it to be produced with what they call the corresponding wind (flatus, incorrectly rendered as sibilans)." From this Brücke wants to conclude:[21] "Let us first turn our attention to this passage,"[22] he says, "so far as it is concerned with the tenuis aspirates, that is, the voiceless aspirates. So far it does not give cause for the slightest doubt, since Max Müller mentions on p. 27, that the fricatives are called winds by the Sanskrit grammarians. In this passage the derivation of the voiceless fricatives from the voiceless stops is described. No one could invent a description of such simplicity and truth, if these fricative sounds did not exist in the language. The present pronunciation of the voiceless aspirates is consequently not the original." Rather according to him, the Sanskrit aspirates must have been voiceless fricatives, namely रव (k̇a), our ch in Spruch, क़ (ċa) our ch in sprich, etc.

This entire argument, however, seems to me to suffer from an inner contradiction. Even according to Brücke, the Indian grammarians have a clear and correct concept of the fricatives. They classify the sibilants, the h and a few others as belonging to these fricatives (ûśmâ, a term of the Indian grammarians, rendered wind by Max Müller). But precisely the aspirates, which are our concern here, they do not include, but rather classify them among the sparśâs, that is, sounds which require complete contact of the speech organs. What could be clearer, than that the Sanskrit aspirates were, in fact, not fricatives (spirants, ûśmânas), but rather stops?

As concerns the description of their production, which Max Müller passes on to us from the Indian grammarians, surprisingly enough it agrees completely with the statement I gave of the Old Greek aspirates twenty-one years ago. According to the description of the Indian grammarian, we have a Tenuis with a following, yet incompletely developed spirant, which, as regards the organs concerned, corresponds to the Tenuis. Twenty-one years ago I proposed to represent this undeveloped spirant with a proposed ẖ and delineated the sound in question as follows:

Non-aspirated Mutes		Spirants	
p	b	f	v
t	d	β	s
k	g	ch (spruch)	hh

From these result the hard aspirates p͡hv, t͡hs, k͡hhh. If the following spirant develops completely, then we obtain the double-consonant p͟f, tβ (new High German z̲) and k͟c͟h, which still occurs in many dialects of German-speaking Switzerland. The difference between the aspirate and the corresponding double consonant is this: with the double consonants (p͟f, tβ, k͟c͟h), after production of the Tenuis the speech organs are brought into the steady position, which is necessary for the utterance of the clearly developed spirant. They are held in this position for a time, so that the spirant produced by it is distinguished from the preceding tenuis as a separately articulated sound. Because the speech organs have this steady position, one can also hold them there as long as one likes and, for example, make the uninterrupted sound: p͟f͟f͟f͟f͟f, t$\beta\beta\beta\beta$ and so on. The situation is quite different, however, with the undeveloped after-sounding of the aspirates. This is produced only through the slow opening of the organs after the closure of the Tenuis. The organs do not remain for one moment in the same position. Therefore no clearly determined, separable sound can be produced; and just so, this sound, which is involved in a continuous change from the time of its origin until it fades away, cannot be maintained steadily. For it begins with the point of opening and ends with such an expansion of the speech organs, that the stream of flowing air no longer makes audible friction.

In order to make myself as clear as possible, I have restricted myself intentionally to the simplest circumstances.

6. I have already treated the nature of the Old Greek aspirates quite extensively in my work concerning aspiration and the sound shift.[23] From the agreement of the Old Greek grammarians with the development of the sounds within the Greek language itself as well as in the relationship of Greek to the other Indo-Germanic languages, I demonstrated the Greek aspirates to be the sounds already given in the previous paragraph: p͡hv, t͡hs, k͡hhh. I would not know very much to add to what I said then and I confess that Brücke's publication, which in other respects is highly instructive, has not shaken me the least in my convictions on this point. Brücke starts out from the fact that the Old Greek grammarians intended the same distinction with their division of the letters into phōnéenta and áphōna, as he makes in connection with the Indian grammarians between voiced and voiceless sounds. But just one condition should have prevented him from making this assumption. The Old Greek grammar does not merely have phonéenta and áphōna but also hēmíphōna. Now what shall we do with these? By Brücke's view they must have been intermediary between voiced and voiceless sounds. Admittedly there is no such thing. We maintain the assumption therefore that reproduces phonéenta as vocales, hēmíphōna

as semivocales, and áphōna as mutae. By vocales, the vowels are
understood; by semivocales those sounds, which are formed through
the narrowing of the speech organs. The division of the latter into
khilá (tenues), daséa (aspiratae), and mésa (mediae) we explain as
follows: grámma khilón designates the letter, whose sound is cut
off sharply without after-sounding; dasú designates the stop with a
strong air gust after the opening of the closure; finally méson designates a sound, which to be sure does not have the strong after-
sounding of grámma dasú, nor also the sharp cutting off of all after-
sounding like the grámma khilón. From this assumption one can
best explain the development, which not only the daséa, but also the
mésa have undergone in New Greek.

7. If we take these results as a basis, which the investigation
of the Sanskrit and Old Greek aspirates has furnished us, we find
that our present High German language actually does not have any
aspirates. The essence of the aspirates consisted therein, that it
was a stop with an undeveloped after-sounding. In this class our f,
β, and ch (in sprich as well as in Spruch) do not belong. For they
are continuant sounds (continuae), produced through narrowing, not
closure of the speech organs. Neither are our pf and our z (= tβ)
aspirates. To be sure, they begin with a stop, but do not follow this
with such an only half-developed after-sounding as we described
above (§ 5), but rather a clear, fully-developed spirant. Our pf and
z are therefore double sounds, which the Indian and Greek aspirates
were not.

8. The Germanic languages of the Gothic stage no longer have
a guttural aspirate; of the labial, they have preserved only a small
part, and these medially. On the other hand, they have the dental
aspirate initially as well as medially. The h and f, which these languages have in the positions where we might normally expect aspirates, are not aspirates but spirants. A remnant of the labial aspirates, Old Saxon possesses in its medial ƀ. All of the older
Germanic languages of the Gothic stage have the dental aspirate
th (þ). It has, however, been partly lost in the modern languages
such as Swedish, Danish, and Low German; in others its change and
eventual loss has been going on for centuries, as in English, which
still shows a slight trace of the genuine old aspirate only in those
instances, where the pronunciation of the th begins with the stop.

9. If we relate what we learn about the nature of the aspirate
from the Indian and Greek grammarians with the results of etymological research, we recognize by a clear example how a real history of sound changes only results from the combination of scientific
determination of sounds and etymological comparison of words. In
place of the Greek and Sanskrit aspirates we find etymologically the
soft (=voiced=breathed) stop in the Germanic languages of the Gothic
stage. For example:

Greek	kh	=	Gothic	g	(e.g. khéō, Gothic giuta);
Greek	th	=	Gothic	d	(e.g. thúra, Gothic daúr);
Greek	ph	=	Gothic	b	(e.g. phérō, Gothic baíra).

The same change is repeated for the second time in the relationship of High German to the Germanic languages of the Gothic
stage. But only the dental th of the Gothic stage changes to High
German d; the h does not go to g, nor the f to b. While the numerous Gothic th's consistently becomes d in High German (Gothic
thanjan, High German denen, Gothic thata, High German daʒ, etc.),
the h and f remain unchanged (Gothic haubith, High German haupt;
Gothic harjis, High German heer; Gothic fôtus, High German fuβ;
Gothic faran, High German fahren). What can be clearer than this
process? The true aspirate contains the stop in itself, which remains after the cessation of its after-sounding. The Greek-Indian
aspirates therefore become soft stops in Gothic, and similarly, centuries later Gothic th becomes High German d. On the other hand,
the spirants h and f do not contain such a stop and consequently do
not become High German g and b, but remain as they are.

10. We still have to show how precisely a media came from the
aspirate. There is, of course, no question of a general necessity.
The hard aspirate can also leave the hard stop by giving up its
after-sounding. Such has been the case of the Old Norse th in
Swedish. According to a very widespread but erroneous theory,
one is inclined perhaps to say that it is impossible for aspirates,
as we conceive of them, to begin with a soft stop. One will say:
"The hard stop requires a greater amount of air than the soft. Now
if the quantity of air pouring forth is increased further with the aspirate, how can it possibly begin with a soft stop?" But this argumentation is based on an erroneous physiological assumption. The
hardness of the stop is dependent, to be sure, upon the amount of air
emitted, but not upon this alone; it is at the same time also dependent upon the further condition, that the expelled current of air finds
a firm closure of the speech organs, which can be opened only by
strong pressure. If on the other hand the closure yields somewhat
in firmness while the mass of onrushing air pressure either remains the same or even increases, two phenomena happen, which
condition each other. First of all, a part of the breath rushes out
only after the stop is opened and so creates the circumstances necessary for producing the true aspirate. Secondly, the stop will lose
some of its hardness precisely through this premature yielding of
the closure. For only the breath, which rushes on before the opening of the closure, conditions the hardness of the sound. So we see
almost before our very eyes, the hard, non-aspirated stop (tenuis)
gradually becoming through further intensification, an aspirate with

a softer stop. For it is, in fact, the further strengthening of the breath beyond that of the tenuis, which causes the earlier opening of the closure. In this way the phonetic-historical series t - th - dh - d can result, as well as, more directly, the group t - dh - d. Old Saxon provides us with the documentary proofs for the whole process.

Notes

1. Grundzüge der Physiologie und Systematik der Sprachlaute, by Ernst Brücke. Wien, 1856.

2. I agree here with Brücke's views.

3. The noise caused by the narrowing of the glottis has been explained thus: "the vocal cords are not set into motion to produce tone, but rather the air as it passes through them causes a friction noise" (Brücke, p. 8). If my observation does not mislead me, this is not exactly the situation. For when one passes from a singing tone to the noise of whispering, one notices that the latter is not produced at the same point as the singing tone, but somewhat further up.

4. In this expression I deviate somewhat from the usual usage.

5. This opposition of blowing and breathing extends far beyond the distinction of sounds, which is actually only one manifestation of it. There are, moreover, two ways of whistling, one by breathing, the other by blowing. Whoever whistles by blowing, he will obstinately maintain that it is impossible to whistle and sing simultaneously. And he is right, insofar as he is speaking only of his own way of whistling. If, however, his assertion is extended to every way of whistling, then he will be easily refuted by the breather-whistler, who will whistle the soprano of a song to him while simultaneously singing the alto.

6. Compare Brücke, pp. 7; 31; 55ff.

7. These two classes are distinguished by the possibility of combining the singing tone with one, which the other does not permit. This is the usual difference in utterance. We will see, however, that for the hearer these two classes overlap under certain conditions, in that a soft blowing produces an effect similar to simple breathing.

8. It is naturally not my intention above to exhaust the diverse types of sound change. Otherwise, sound change through analogy, for example, would also have to be treated. But I would prefer to reserve this and other related questions for another occasion.

9. I made a suggestion toward this end in Fromanns Deutschen Mundarten, 1857, and should like to recommend once again this

suggestion as well as this most valuable journal to all those informed about language.

    10. Grundzüge etc., p. 117.

    11. It is understood that in these polemics the otherwise very
meritorious works of this excellent linguist are not being impugned.

    12. Die Aspiration und die Lautverschiebung. Eine sprachge
schichtliche Untersuchung von Rudolf von Raumer. Leipzig, 1837.

    13. Brücke, Grundzüge etc., p. 82.

    14. Bopp, Kritische Grammatik der Sanskrita-Sprache, Berlin,
1834, p. 15 ff.

    15. Brücke, p. 83.

    16. Pâninis acht Bücher grammatischer Regeln, Her. von
Böhtlingk. Bd. 1. Bonn, 1839, p. 3.

    17. I transcribe the Dêvanâgarî letters in accordance with
Bopp.

    18. See the edition of this Prâtiçâkhya by Regnier, Études sur
la Grammaire védique in Journal Asiatique. Paris, 1856. Février-
Mars, p. 169.

    19. Regnier, op. cit., p. 194.

    20. The Languages of the Seat of War in the East. London,
1855, p. XXXII.

    21. P. 83.

    22. That is, the just cited words of Max Müller.

    23. Compare also my publication: Über deutsche Rechtschreib-
ung. (Vienna, 1855), p. 65 ff.

    24. To repeat the extensive proof, which I gave in my article
on aspiration and the sound shift in support of my view would require that I merely reprint here the greater part of what I said
there. For were I to leave out a single ancient quotation or an associated argument, then the exposition given there would only lose
in effectiveness.

CHAPTER EIGHT

AUGUST SCHLEICHER

INTRODUCTION TO A COMPENDIUM OF THE
COMPARATIVE GRAMMAR OF THE INDO-EUROPEAN,
SANSKRIT, GREEK AND LATIN LANGUAGES

From Compendium der vergleichenden Grammatik der
Indogermanischen Sprachen (Weismar: Hermann Böhlau, 1871),
xlviii, 829 pp., pp. 1-9

Schleicher is generally regarded as totally superseded.
Since he flourished immediately before the neogrammarians, it is scarcely remarkable that their reputation has
eclipsed his. Probably the most commonly maintained segment of his writings is his model for displaying languages,
the family tree, though it too is held to be superseded by
other interpretations of language spread and interrelationships, such as the wave theory. In part Schleicher seems
supplanted because so many of his ideas were taken over
by his successors.

    1. Even though the Stammbaum in its simple form fal-
sifies language interrelationships, Sherman Kuhn has pointed
out it is the model by which genealogical classifications have
been achieved.

    2. The reconstructed form of a proto-language, rather
than the earliest known form of a selected language which
has developed from it, is now the accepted way of indicating
linguistic relationships. In Indo-European linguistics
Schleicher broke the practice of citing Sanskrit for this
purpose and introduced the starred form.

    3. But possibly the most important influence he has
had is that on the neogrammarians — his aim (credited to
them) to account for relationships to the extent possible and
then to admit residues. In his brief sketch of the history of
Indo-European linguistics, Compendium 15-16, he has the
following comment:

At present two tendencies confront each other in Indo-
European linguistics. The adherents of the one have
taken as their principle strict adherence to sound laws
(e.g. G. Curtius in Leipzig, Corssen in Berlin, the

author of this Compendium, and others); the other
trend (Benfey in Göttingen, Leo Meyer in Dorpat, and
others) believes that it need not be essentially hindered in the clarification and explanation of language
forms by the sound laws that have been determined up
to now. In this way it is possible for the adherents of
the latter trend to explain many things which seem
dark to the others. Particularly from this approach a
number of stem-forming suffixes of Indo-European are
taken back to a single original form. The two schools
also are importantly differentiated through this procedure. The former accepts as old and original much
that the second permits to be looked on simply as a
change of an original and primitive form. The further
historical development of our discipline will show on
what side the certain, truly scientific basis for the future flourishing of linguistics is to be sought.

When one notes that August Leskien assisted in the production of the second edition and with Johannes Schmidt brought
out the third, it is not difficult to recognize one source of
neogrammarian ideas and the continuity of development in
linguistics, even though Schleicher did not sharply formu-
late a need for complete accounting for phenomena and explanation of residues.

    The Introduction to the Compendium is given here in a
translation from the third German edition, prepared by
Herbert Bendall and published by Trübner and Company,
London, 1874. Although one of Schleicher's essays may
have been useful in representing his theoretical views,
the introduction may reflect various reasons for Schleicher's
importance.

    Schleicher looked on language as a whole. His intro-
duction states specifically that linguists should deal with the
construction of sentences — a statement found again in the
excerpt from Sievers below; but Schleicher also admits that
he cannot handle sentences adequately, and hence he confines himself to sounds and forms. This limitation was
largely maintained for the next eighty years, with the emphasis on phonology that Schleicher introduced.

    He also attempted to get away from the detail of lan-
guage to its form, using for this purpose formulae. In this
attempt he foreshadows the repeated efforts to increase
rigor in linguistics. His formulae for descriptive linguistics, referred to below in the extract from Whitney, were

not maintained though his reconstructed — or fundamental — forms have been. It should be noted that Schleicher looked on these as abstractions, not as real language material; he says specifically that he does not assert they ever existed.

Everywhere Schleicher's presentation is sober and clear. In the third edition of the Compendium he introduced external techniques which have become general, such as glossing citations in the language of the writer rather than in Latin. His conclusions have in part been superseded, as in his identification of Armenian as a dialect of Iranian. But through his lucid summary of the data that had been assembled Schleicher provided the basis for the tremendous expansion of control over historical linguistics during the last quarter of the nineteenth century.

August Schleicher (1821-68) may not have achieved a definitive work because of his short life. The first edition of his Compendium was published in 1861, on the basis of fifteen years of lecturing. Earlier he had published a morphology of Old Church Slavonic, 1852, and a grammar of Lithuanian, 1856-7, produced as a result of field work. For the second edition he modified the Compendium largely in externals. The third was published posthumously from his annotated copy. Since he examined the bases of linguistic study — the relevance of Hegel, or Darwin — and since he made use of the compendious grammars being produced for the various Indo-European dialects — for the Romance languages by Diez, 1836-44, for the Celtic by Zeuss, 1853, and for the Slavic by Miklosich, 1852ff. — he may have removed from his Compendium some of the shortcomings maintained from his predecessors if he had not died relatively early.

Introduction

I. Grammar forms one part of the science of language: this science is itself a part of the natural history of Man. Its method is in substance that of natural science generally; it consists in accurate investigation of our object and in conclusions founded upon that investigation. One of the chief problems of the science of language is the inquiry into, and description of the classes of languages or speech-stems, that is, of the languages which are derived from one and the same original tongue, and the arrangement of these classes according to a natural system. In proportion to the remainder but few speech-stems have hitherto been accurately investigated, so that the solution of this chief problem of the science must be looked for only in the future.

By grammar we mean the scientific comprehension and explanation of the sound, the form, the function of words and their parts,
and the construction of sentences. Grammar therefore treats of the
knowledge of sounds, or phonology; of forms, or morphology; of
functions, or the science of meaning and relation, and syntax. The
subject of grammar may be language in general, or one particular
language or group of languages; grammar may be universal or special: it will in most cases be concerned in explaining the language
as a product of growth, and will thus have to investigate and lay
down the development of the language according to its laws. This is
its exclusive province, and therefore its subject is the laying-down
of the 'life of language,' generally called historical grammar, or
history of language, but more correctly 'science of the life of a language' (of sound, form, function, and sentence), and this again may
be likewise as well general as more or less special.

The grammar of the Indo-European languages is therefore a
special grammar: because it treats of these languages as products
of growth, and exhibits their earlier and earliest gradations, and
would therefore be more accurately called a special historical
grammar of Indo-European language.

Note 1. By comparative grammar is meant not that grammar
which is merely descriptive, but that which throws light on speech-
forms as far as possible, because as a rule it is not confined to the
treatment of any one particular language.

Note 2. The following work embraces only two parts, viz. scientific treatment of sounds and of forms. Indo-European function
and sentence-formation we are not at present in a position to handle
in the same way as in the case of the more external and intelligible
branches — sounds and forms.

II. To assume one original universal language is impossible;
there are rather many original languages: this is a certain result
obtained by the comparative treatment of the languages of the world
which have lived till now. Since languages are continually dying out,
whilst no new ones practically arise, there must have been originally
many more languages than at present. The number of original languages was therefore certainly far larger than has been supposed
from the still-existing languages. The easiest preliminary distribution of languages which we can make is suggested by their morphological constitutions.

There are:

1. Languages which are simply composed of invariable dis-
jointed meaning-sounds, monosyllabic, e.g. Chinese, Annamese,
Siamese, Burmese. Such sounds we denote by R (radix). The Indo-
European language would be in this stage of development when the

word ai-mi (I go, $\epsilon \overset{?}{\iota} \mu \iota$) was sounded not so, but as i or i ma (formula R, or R + r).

2. Languages which can link to these invariable sounds of relation, either before, or after, or in the middle, or in more than one
place at once (denoted here as s. [suffix], p. [prefix], i. [infix]).
These are confixative languages, e.g. Finnish, Tatar, Dekhan,
Basque, the languages of the aborigines of the New World, of South
Africa (Bântu), and most languages in fact. In this step of development the word ai-mi would be i-ma or i-mi (Rs).

3. Languages which for the purpose of expressing relation can
regularly vary their roots as well as their confixes (which have
sprung from independent original roots), and can at the same time
preserve intact the means of compounding. These are inflexive languages. Such a root is regularly varied for the end of expressing
relation is here denoted by R^x (R^1, R^2, etc.), a similar suffix by s^x.

Hitherto we have become acquainted with only two speech-stems
of this class, the Semitic and the Indo-European. The latter has for
all words only one formula, viz. R^x s^x (s^x meaning one or more
than one regularly variable suffix), and consequently a regularly
variable root with a regularly variable expression of relation at the
end of the suffix, e.g. ai-mi, $\epsilon \overset{?}{\iota} \mu \iota$, $\sqrt{\iota}$.

The Indo-European is therefore a suffix-language, together with
the neighboring languages of the Finnish stem, including Tataric,
(Turkish) Mongolian, Tungusian, Samoiedish, as also with the Dra-
vidian (Dekhan) — all included in the formula Rs.

Note 1. The Semitic, which is not akin to the Indo-European,
has more word-forms, namely R^x and pR^x, forms quite strange to
Indo-European, which has only one. Besides, its vowel-system is
perfectly distinct from the Indo-European, not to mention other
marked differences. Cf. Aug. Schleicher, "Semitisch und Indoger-
manisch" in Beitr. ii. 236-244. An attempt to deduce the fundamental language of the Semitic speech-stem has been made by Justus
Olshausen in his "Lehrbuche der hebräischen Sprache", Brunswick,
1862.

Note 2. The augment in Indo-European is no relation-affix, no
prefix, but an adherent, though originally independent word, which
may moreover be omitted.

III. The life of a language (generally called its "history") falls
under two heads:

1. Development in prehistoric times. As man has developed,
so also has his language, i.e. the expression of his thoughts by
sounds: even the simplest language is the product of a gradual
growth: all higher forms of language have come out of simpler
ones, the confixative of the monosyllabic, the inflexive out of the
confixative.

2. Decline in the historic period. Language declines both in
sound and in form, and in its decay changes of meaning take place
alike in function and construction of sentences. The transition from
the first to the second period is one of slower progress. To investigate the laws by which languages change during their life is a most
important problem in the science of language, for unless we are acquainted with them we cannot possibly understand the languages in
question, especially those which are still living.

Through different developments, at different points in the province of one and the same language, the self-same tongue branches
out into the ramifications of the second period (whose beginning
however is likewise earlier than the origin of historic tradition),
and diverges into several languages (dialects); this process of differentiation may repeat itself more than once.

All these changes took place gradually and at long intervals in
the life of the language, since generally all changes in language un-
fold themselves gradually.

The languages which spring immediately from an original language we call fundamental; almost every fundamental-language has
split up into languages; all these last-named languages may further
branch into dialects; and these dialects into sub-dialects.

All the languages which are derived from one original-language
form together a class of speech or speech-stem; these again are
sub-divided into families or branches of speech.

IV. The name of Indo-European has been given to a distinct set
of languages belonging to the Asiatico-European division of the
earth, and of a constitution so consistent internally, and so different
from all other languages, that it is clearly and undoubtedly derived
from one common original language.

Within this Indo-European class of speech however certain languages geographically allied point themselves out as more closely
related to one another: thus the Indo-European speech-stem falls
into three groups or divisions.

These are:

1. The Asiatic or Aryan division, comprising the Indian, Iranian (or more correctly Eranian), families of speech, very closely
allied to one another. The oldest representative and fundamental-
language of the Indo-European family, and generally the oldest
known Indo-European language, is the Old Indian, the language of
the oldest portion of the Vêdas; later on, after it had become fixed
in a more simplified form, and subject to certain rules, as a correct written language, in opposition to the peoples' dialects, called
Sanskrit. We are not acquainted with Eranian in its original form:
the oldest known languages of this stem are the Old Baktrian or

Zend (the Eastern), and the Old Persian, the language of the Achai-
menid cuneiform inscriptions (the Western). To this family besides
is related the Armenian, which we know only from a later date, and
which must have branched off even in early times from the Eranian
fundamental-language.

2. The south-west European division, composed of the Greek,
next to which we must perhaps place the Albanian, preserved to us
only in a later form; Italian (the oldest known forms of this language
are the Latin — especially important for us is the Old-Latin, as it
was before the introduction of the correct literary language formed
under Greek influence — the Umbrian and the Oscan), Keltic, of
which family the best known, though already highly decomposed,
language is the Old Irish, Erse dating from 700 A.D. Italian and
Keltic have more in common with one another than with the Greek.

3. The North-European division, composed of the Sclavonic
family with its closely-allied Lithuanian, — the most important language for us of this group, — and the German, widely separated from
both. The oldest forms of this division are the Old-Bulgarian (Old
Church-Slavonic in MSS. dating from 1100 A.D.); the Lithuanian (and
of course the High-Lithuanian, South-Lithuanian, Prussian Lithuanian), first known to us 300 years ago, but clearly of far greater antiquity; and the Gothic from the fourth century. Beside the Gothic,
however, are the oldest representatives of German and Norse, Old
High German, and Old Norse, which we may bring forward when
they present earlier forms than Gothic.

The greatest number of archaic particulars in point of sounds
and construction of language is found in the Asiatic division, and
within it, in the Old Indian; next in point of archaicisms (i.e. preservation of similarity to the original language, by having fewer
strongly-developed and peculiar forms) comes the S.W.-division, in
which Greek is found to be most faithful; and lastly the N.-European
group, which, if regarded as a whole, may be shown to have the most
characteristic development, and to be the least faithful to the original language.

By combining these facts with the above-named relationships of
the Indo-European languages, and drawing inferences as to the process of separation of the Indo-European body of language in ancient
times, we get the following result: The Indo-European original language differentiates first, through unequal development in different
parts where it prevailed, into two fundamental-languages, viz. The
Sclavo-Teutonic, which afterwards divided itself into Teutonic and
Sclavo-Lithuanian, and the Aryo-Graeco-Italo-Keltic, the remaining
portion of the Indo-European language, which divided itself into
Graeco-Italo-Keltic and Aryan; and the Graeco-Italo-Keltic soon
split up into Greek and Italo-Keltic, while the first, the Aryan,

remained undivided for some time. Later still the Sclavo-Lithuanian, the Aryan (Indo-Eranian) and the Italo-Keltic, further divided themselves. It may be that at most or at all of the divisions there arose more languages than we now know of, since probably many Indo-European languages have died out through the lapse of time. The further eastward an Indo-European people lives, the more archaisms are found in its language; the further westward they have gone, the fewer archaicisms, and the more numerous new-formations are found in the language. From these and other indications we infer that the Sclavo-Teutonic race first began its wanderings westwards; next followed the Graeco-Italo-Keltic; and of the Aryans who remained behind, the Indians journeyed south-eastward, the Eranians south-westward. The home of the Indo-European original race must be sought in the highlands of Central Asia.

It is only of the Indians, who were the last to leave the parent stem, that it is quite certain that they expelled an aboriginal race from their later dwelling-place, a race of whose language much passed into their own; a similar process is highly probable in the case of many other Indo-European peoples.

The most ancient divisions of the Indo-European, up to the origin of the fundamental languages belonging to the families of speech formed from the speech-stem, may be seen in the following table. . . . The length of the lines shows the duration of the periods, their distances from one another, the degrees of relationship.

Note. In the present work an attempt is made to set forth the inferred Indo-European original language side by side with its really existent derived languages. Besides the advantages offered by such a plan, in setting immediately before the eyes of the student the final results of the investigation in a more concrete form, and thereby rendering easier his insight into the nature of a particular Indo-European language, there is, I think, another of no less importance gained by it, namely that it shows the baselessness of the assumption that the non-Indian Indo-European languages were derived from Old-Indian (Sanskrit), an assumption which has not yet entirely disappeared. This view has found supporters up to the present date, especially as regards Old-Baktrian (Zend). The term 'Sanskritist', not seldom applied to Indo-European philologers (meaning that we concede to Sanskrit a position which it does not deserve, by deriving other languages from Sanskrit, or explaining them by it, instead of studying them fundamentally), is likewise shown to be quite inapplicable by the plan employed in the Compendium. The disadvantage of having in certain cases Indo-European original forms inferred which are more or less doubtful, does not weigh at all against the advantages which, according to our view, are attained by the arrangement of the subject used hereafter.

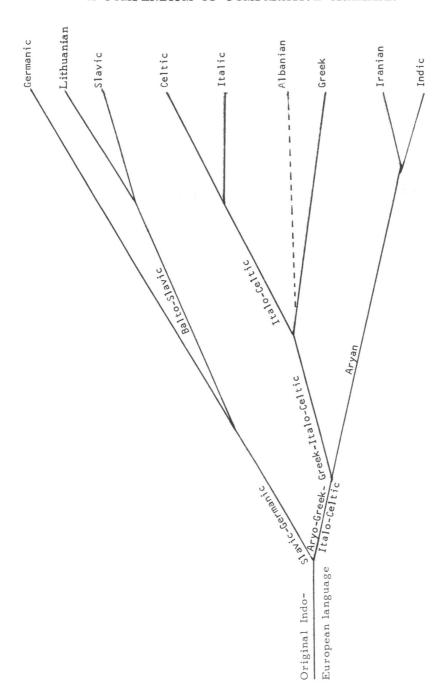

SCHLEICHER'S FAMILY TREE

A form traced back to the sound-grade of the Indo-European original language, we call a fundamental-form (f.f.) [e.g. Lat. generis, f.f ganasas; Gk γενους, f.f ganasas]. Hence it is only when forms of different sound-grades are brought to one and the same sound-grade, that we can compare them with one another. When we bring forward these fundamental-forms, we do not assert that they really were once in existence.

CHAPTER NINE

C. LOTTNER

EXCEPTIONS TO THE FIRST SOUND SHIFT

"Ausnahmen der ersten Lautverschiebung,"
Zeitschrift für vergleichende Sprachforschung auf dem Gebiete des
Deutschen, Griechischen und Lateinischen 11.3 (1862), 161-205

Lottner's cataloging article has never been given the
acclaim of Grassmann's or Verner's, which it prepared for.
Yet Lottner carefully screened the evidence and listed the
three large sets of "real" exceptions, after eliminating the
apparent ones traceable to "false comparisons", onomatopoeic words and borrowings. In his treatment of the apparent exceptions Lottner reflects the status of historical
linguistics shortly after the middle of the nineteenth century; for that reason, and because the first section of his
article is his permanent contribution to clarification of the
first sound shift, this section is presented rather fully here.
The "real exceptions", which Lottner discusses in the remaining sections of his article, may be found in the articles
of Grassmann and Verner. After Lottner's publication
there was no further confusion about the apparent exceptions. His clarification of these, and his thorough descriptive presentation of the evidence remain the essence of his
achievement.

This is not to say that Lottner's article is thoroughly
praiseworthy. The tone of it is occasionally intemperate;
at the conclusion he added a short paragraph apologizing to
Curtius for an unwise phrase in an earlier article. He also
misled Grassmann about the "third set of exceptions,"which
were clarified by Verner, by introducing the glib notion of
a Wahlverwandtschaft — elective affinity — between the resonants and the mediae. Yet with its faults, the article is an
example of the interplay of descriptive and historical linguistics: Lottner's descriptions simplified the explanations
of Grassmann and Verner. The article also illustrates that
linguistics did not advance by a series of leaps; rather,
careful scientific attention to the data led in time to its
mastery.

C. Lottner submitted the article from London. To my

knowledge he made no further contributions to historical
linguistics. From their acknowledgements we conclude
that the article was important for both Grassmann and
Verner.

Prefatory Note. In general, only those Germanic languages are considered whose consonants have really experienced only the first
sound-shift. On the other hand, High German has only then been
taken into account when it illuminates the Germanic original form
which in Old Norse, Anglo-Saxon, etc., was distorted according to
specific sound laws. Words which are only High German are not
treated for the time being.

The exceptions to the first sound-shift fall into apparent and
real exceptions.

Those words may be treated as the first class among the apparent exceptions with which the entire assumption of a violation of
Grimm's law originates simply from the fact that one has compared
things that should have remained uncompared. It is of course impossible to list all cases of such erroneous comparison since error
and caprice lack definite demarcations. I am therefore content to
observe a few examples of this kind where erroneous comparison
has enjoyed a certain popularity, whether by virtue of its apparent
plausibility or on account of its author's reputation. Of this sort
are Gothic: kara 'care' which has nothing to do with Lat. cura,
since the latter arose from coira, as is proved by OLat. coerare,
to which probably belongs Gk koíranos (cf. Landpfleger, 'prefect').
The Germanic word means primarily 'fear, anxiety, lament' (therefore OHG charôn lamentari, our NHG char-freitag), and it thus goes
with the old root GAR 'be heavy', which is present in Skt guru 'heavy'
(from garu; comparative gariyas) = Lat. gravis, Gk barús, and from
which Goth. kaurs 'difficult' is to be derived. Yet in Germanic the
meaning 'to be heavy about something', 'to take care about something', must have developed in this root at an early time. For that
is the only explanation for ON kaer-r 'dear', the original form of
which is KÁRIA and which will have to be understood as 'something
worth being cared for' with the same suffix ja which is present in
Goth. andanêmja- 'acceptable, pleasant', in Goth. unquêþja- 'impossible to utter, inexpressible', in Lat. exim-ius = eximendus and in
the many corresponding formations of Sanskrit (such as bhâr-ya
'ferendus'). This Scandinavian kaerr therefore does not in the least

have anything to do with Lat. cârus which, despite the long vowel, is
probably to be compared with OIr. caru,[1] carimm 'I love'. — The
comparison of Goth. leik with Skt dêha "body" — the transition from
d to l is as indemonstrable for Gothic as the k vs. h is objectionable
— was able to gain a dubious reputation only on account of the great
reputation of the founder of comparative grammar. The same is
true of his relation of Goth. -leiks 'like' (isolated galeiks = OE lîc,
gelîc, ON lîkr, glîkr) with Skt -dṛça, because the regularly corresponding Lith. lygus is much more plausible and because the root
dṛç, i.e. dark (Gk dérkō) 'see', from which that Sanskrit word originates, is also regularly represented in our AS torht 'light' = OHG
zor(a)ht. Goth. natjan 'moisten' would have hardly been compared with
Gk notía if one had not dismissed all too easily the connection of the
latter with Gk nótos. To compare Goth. raþs 'easy' with Gk hrádios,
as the otherwise admirable Gabelentz and Loebe do, is a monstrosity,
because the latter is contracted, as Homer's Gk hrēídios shows and
furthermore, it began with digamma in Lesbian. Our Germanic
word belongs to the root RAT, in Skt ratha 'wagon', Lat. rota, OHG
rad, Gallic riton (to be deduced from petor-ritum) and therefore
means something that 'begins'. The root itself may have been developed from AR (Skt ṛ "go" Gk or- etc.). — Goth. auhns "stove" has
often been compared with Skt agni 'fire', but since Aufrecht has related it nicely to Skt açna 'stone' the former comparison must be
considered obsolete. Bidjan 'ask for' scarcely has anything to do
with Lat. petere, because the basic meaning of the latter is 'to fly
at something,' (= Skt pat 'fly, fall'), whereas Goth. badi 'bed' seems
to indicate as the original meaning of our word: 'sternere, se pro-
sternere'. Goth. kalds 'cold', or rather its stem-verb ON kala 'be
cold' is quite regular with regard to Lat. gelu, gelidus, Skt gala
'cold, coldness, water'. For that reason OSlav. chladŭ 'cold' is
either not related at all, or it is borrowed. Lith. szaltas 'cold',
szala (3rd p. sg.) 'be cold, become cold' is however quite a different
word, which, with respect to the root, Zend çareta 'cold' and Skt
çiçira 'cold' resemble. But the two latter words point back to an
original root KAR, KAL; whether this root is to be treated as identical with GAL, I do not know. At any rate, the difference occurred
already before the language separation and we Germanic people
must be absolved from the reproach of an irregular sound-shift...
(166). With these and similar comparisons we lose ourselves completely in a territory where any words are picked up according to
their sound-similarity and, with an indubitably blessed, but highly
unscientific naïvité, are assumed to be related.

Apparent exceptions to the sound-shift can also stem from the
fact that the words under comparison are connected psychologically,
but not historically, i.e. that they are imitations of sounds, or they

fall into that category which Buschmann designates by the name
'sound of nature'. After the thorough discussion by that scholar it
may be considered certain that the consonants T, P, or in other
words the syllables ap, pa, at and ta even in non-related languages
form the basic elements in the names of the father (more infrequently in that of the mother) because of the identical physiological
make-up of the speech organs and because of identical psychological
impulses. Although the Indo-European languages possess words
from very early times to express these relationships, it must nevertheless be admitted that some of the many parental names have
been formed anew only after the time of the language separation. If
therefore Goth. atta 'father' corresponds too well to Gk átta OSlav.
otĭcĭ (OBohem. ot), then neither relationship nor borrowing is to be
assumed here, but the Gothic word has simply sprung from the ever-
flowing fountain of nature sounds. Furthermore, it can be seen from
the treatise of the aforementioned scholar that the nasals N and M
play the same role in the name of the mother (again, here too, less
frequently in the name of the father) as P and T did in the case of
the father. It must also be noted that all of these readily pronounce-
able elements, notably m(a) and p(a), serve at the same time as
children's words for 'food' and 'nourishment' and therefore frequently as expressions for the mother's breast. Such words are our
pappen, pappe, Engl. pap 'female breast', Lat. papilla, Lat. mamma,
mamilla 'mother's breast' but mamma, mammula also meaning
'mother, grandmother'. For our purposes, we must be concerned
with still another word for 'mother's breast' (beside the above-
mentioned apparently very irregular pappen) which staggers just as
unsteadily and wildly through the various consonant stages, namely
OE titte, NE teat, to which fits NHG Zitze, but also OHG tutta, MHG
and NHG tutte, Gk títthē (compare in Dieffenbach a number of related words under Goth. daddjan 'to nurse'). Yet this latter is perhaps no longer the immediate creation from a sound of nature, but
rather the reduplication of an old root dî, which corresponds to Skt
dhê 'to nurse' (from which, dhênu 'cow') and also to dhâ (in dhâ-trî
'wet nurse'), compare Gk thêsai, tithéné, thêlus, Lat. femina (?),
fellare, Umbr. felio- 'sucking', OIr. dinu 'agna', stem dîna(n)t, Lat.
filius (cf. Gk thêlē, thēlázō and Lett. dehls 'child'), OSlav. doiti 'to
nurse', dê-tę 'child.' OHG tila = Gk thélē (cf. OHG taan = Gk thêsai) is
certainly related and must be distinguished from those new formations made of sounds of nature. In all of the latter words the exact
sound correspondence stands for a genuine historical relationship.
But that the above-noted chaos of sounds in otherwise closely connected words of identical meaning can find a sufficient explanation
through the assumption of simple psychological relationship, is most
clearly demonstrated by similar sounding words from non-Indo-

Germanic languages by Dieffenbach, such as Basque thilia, dithia, titia, Hung. tsets, Eston. tis, all of which mean 'female breast'. To these may be added several onomatopoeic words in which an apparently irregular sound-shift takes place, e.g. ON klaka 'queri (de avibus)' = klökkva 'lament', NE clank, OHG klingan as against Lat. clango, Gk klaggē, klázō, to which may be joined Goth. hlahjan 'laugh', which originates from a similar formative impulse. In addition, compare NE clatter, clap, NHG klirren, klopfen, klappern. OE cancettan 'laugh' and also ceahhettan do not go with Gk kagkházō, cachinnari. Much more of this kind could be cited, if one wished to include living folk dialects. A peculiar example of this merely psychological relationship is NE lick, OE liccjan = NHG lecken. It is quite impossible to place this with Skt. lih, Gk leíkhō, Lat. lingo, OIr. ligum etc., since this root is present with regular shift in Goth. laigon. In addition, there is in Lithuanian and in Slavic a Lith. lak-ti, OSlav. lokati and beside it Lith. laiźyti (OSlav. lizati) which correspond regularly to the Greek-Sanskrit root. If one notes that similar sounds serve also in non-Indo-European languages as a designation for the act of licking (e.g. Hebr. kkl, Finn. lakkia), and that in Germanic itself there is a third form which deviates completely, but is still related in sound: ON sleikja — Gk láptō, Lat. lambo, labrum, NE lap 'lick', lip = OHG laffan, lefsa, NHG lefze, Lippe (the latter actually Low German) are admittedly more remote, but must not be ignored either — then all this leads one to conclude that only Goth. laigôn is historically connected with Skt lih, whereas the other forms with a seemingly irregular k are new root formations, or if one prefers it this way, that the old root lih is in fact present in them, but is disturbed in its regular sound shift through the influence of sound imitation and thus has been distorted to LIK, LAK (the latter with a quite preposterous a from i). This easy mode of explanation would have arisen a long time ago if the strange hypothesis had not spread in comparative linguistics that root formation cannot possibly have occurred after the Indo-European peoples had separated. I cannot grasp why such a purely exterior event like the disintegration of peoples should have suddenly cut off the capability to create language. It is paramount to denying the writer of this article the capability to create new compounds and derivatives in his mother tongue just because he emigrated to England. I should like to go on record that I have strongly protested against this mechanical, as well as lifeless and unhistoric, interpretation of the aforesaid conception which assumes the existence of a special "root-forming" era.

A similar situation is found in ON gaukr 'cuckoo', also MHG gouch, which just does not fit NHG Kuckuck, NE cuckoo, or Lat. cuculus, Gk kókkuks; all these irregularities can be explained simply by the fact that imitations of the animal's voice have been made over and over again. Only the same assumption will explain the strangely corresponding and deviating names of the crow, partially also those of the raven; compare Lat. corvus, Swed. korp; OHG hraban, ON hrafn, can just barely be related to the Latin word (although our b does not correspond to Lat. v either). Further, there is OE cráve, ON kráka, Gk koróně, Lat. cornix and further the verbs NHG krächzen, Gk krázō, Lat. crocito and finally, though applied to the 'rooster', OE crávan, our krähen. All of these are but bound together by a psychological tie.

A great number of apparent violations of the sound shift must be attributed to borrowings within or from the Germanic languages. Most of their foreign words are clearly of Greek, Latin and recently also of French origin. It is not possible to list all of them; I am content to cite those which appear in Gothic. They are from Latin: akeit 'vinegar', annó 'annual pay', arka, asilus, aurkeis (urceus), faskja, kaisar, kapillon 'shear', karkara, katils (catinus), kavstjo (cautio), kubîtus 'resting place at the table', which is related to anakumbjan 'to lie at the table', laiktjo, lukarn, maimbrana 'parchment, membrane', militon, papa, paurpaura, praitoria, pund, spaikulator, unkja and probably also vein. From Greek they are: aggilus, arkaggilus, aikklesjo, aipiskaupus, aipistaule, aivaggeli, aivlaugia (Gk eulogía), aivxaristia, probably also alev 'oil', anaþaima, apaustulus, azyme, balsan, barbarus, daimonareis, diabaulus, diakaunus, hairaisis, jota (Gk iôta), nardus, paintekuste, parakletus, paraskaive, paska, pistikeins (Gk pistikós), praizbytarei, praufetus, psalma, saban (Gk sábanon), sabbato, sakkus, satanas, sikls, sinap, skaurpjo, smyrn, spyreida (Gk spurís), synagoge; further ulbandus 'camel', with a changed meaning and strangely enough with regular sound shift from Gk eléphant. --- I pass over the borrowings of the younger dialects from the two Classical languages, as well as over the few cases where the borrowings take place into them. I also omit the many Germanic words which have gone into the Romance languages, since all of these have been exhaustively treated by Diez. Yet on the whole I must say that it is completely wrong to assume complete isolation of the Germanic peoples of heathen times. Just one word like ulbandus should speak against this, since it must have been in use for a long time in order to be Germanicized in such a form. But we also know that the Germanic heathens took over the seven day week from the Romans — where else would the pagan names of the weekdays come from? We know from Kirchhoff that the runes originate from the Roman uncials. There are Roman coins in Old Scandinavian graves from the time of Tiberius to Marcus Aurelius; and in the oldest Eddic songs we already have evidence of Roman words: tafla 'tabula', tefla 'to play a game at a board' are to be

found in the Vǫlusspâ; ketill 'kettle' appears in the Hymiskviða and
has deeply penetrated the northern heathendom, as is shown by the
names Âs-ketill, Þôr-ketill 'god's kettle, Thor's kettle'. Even the
Roman state affairs and Roman religion have influenced us early;
Kemble detected the Old English name Sāter not only in Sāteres däg
(Saturday), but also in the names of places, compare Sāteres byrig
(Saturn's castle). Saturn must therefore have enjoyed a certain
popularity, if not in fact veneration, and Caesar, as is well-known,
rose to the honor of being moved into the Old English genealogies
as the son of Vôden. Under these circumstances it will be advisable
in the future not to be too eager to disregard the possibility of borrowing even for very old Germanic words which have apparently
escaped the sound-shift.

It is of course to be expected that there was an early exchange
of words between the Germanic peoples and their neighbors to the
east and west. As regards the Celts, our connections with them
were obviously quite lively in the pagan era. This is proved by the
fact that the king of the truly Germanic Marcomannen, for instance,
had the decidedly Celtic name Maroboduus. In addition, there are
the great number of Gallic names ending in -rîx, -rîg-is and -mârus
to which the many Old Germanic names ending in -ricus, -merus
correspond very precisely. Compare, for example, Gall. Segomârus
with OGmc Sigimerus, a condition which can only be explained
through the factor of mutual influence. But since Celtic not only
resembles Germanic in lowering the old aspirates to mediae, but
also shows beginnings of a sound shift of the mediae to tenues, for
these reasons it is in most cases extremely difficult to determine
which one of the two languages has borrowed from the other, and
often whether borrowing or original relationship exists. Besides,
most words of this kind will be discussed below, because the irregularity present in them can best be explained by a comparison with
words of the other originally related languages. Therefore I mention here only Gall. bracca 'trousers', from which is borrowed ON
brôk, OE brôc, NE breech. Furthermore, the strange Goth. kelikn
Gk púrgos which is no doubt identical with celicnon, a word that recently appeared on a Gallic inscription. The fact that the word
stands alone in Gothic, as well as its strange suffix and the completely un-Germanic appearance and sound, speaks for borrowing
from Celtic.

Since earliest times Germanic has many specific agreements
with Slavic and Lettish; much of this is admittedly due to an original
kinship, but very early borrowing is not rare either. The Slavic-
Lettish languages resemble the Celtic in their consistent lowering
of the old aspirates to mediae, and they also coincide otherwise
(see below) in an anticipating manner with our sound shift. These

circumstances make it also extremely difficult to decide whether
borrowing took place and if so, from where ... (174) Although I deal
here only with those Slavic-Germanic loanwords which, not being
recognized as such, seem to constitute exceptions to the sound shift,
I cannot refrain on this occasion from drawing attention to the
strange fact that we have indeed borrowed from Slavic a great many
expressions dealing with commerce, comforts and amusements
(buying, names of coins, debt, market and translator, the beaker and
the dance), but the Slavs on the other hand have taken from us the
word for ruler (likewise the Finns their kuningas). The historic
position of the two peoples corresponds fully to this phenomenon:
throughout the Middle Ages the Germans treated the Slavs as ser-
vants; therefore our Sklave, earlier in the fifteenth century without
k, Slave, NE slave, Swed, slaf. The Scandinavians established for
the Slavs their Russian empire. It remains to be seen whether this
political position of the two peoples is going to change in the future.

Borrowings have also taken place from one Germanic language
into another, i.e. 1) from Low German into High German, 2) from
Scandinavian into English, 3) from Low German into New Scandinavian, and 4) from New High German into Low German and New
Scandinavian. Yet, in 2) and 3) the borrowing and receiving dialects
are at the same stage of the sound shift. This is admittedly not the
case with the borrowings of the first and fourth class, and some of
these indeed give the appearance of a disturbance of the sound shift
(e.g. Swed. dyster, borrowed from NHG düster, does not correspond
to OE þŷster, Lith. tamsus, Swed. an-dakt = NHG Andacht, not to
Lat. tongere). But a more detailed treatment of these mutual borrowings of the Germanic peoples must be reserved for another time.

A great number of apparent irregularities in the sound-shift
also come into being through the irregularities of the related languages. To start from the beginning, it is known that Sanskrit has
an entire class of aspirates, namely the voiceless aspirates, which
only the Iranian languages share with it. With every example one
must first determine whether — which seems mostly the case — these
voiceless aspirates come from an original tenuis or — which admittedly occurs in some cases — originated from an aspirated media.
For this Greek will generally guide us safely. Thus everything is in
good order for the Sanskrit root path, from which comes panthan
'path', equal to the Germanic root fanþ, which will have to be treated
later because of other irregularities, because Gk pátos, patéō wit-
nesses the existence of the original tenuis. But Skt nakha 'finger-
nail' is likewise quite regularly represented by OE nägel, since Gk
ónukh- shows here the age of the aspirate. There are, however,
also other cases where the Germanic only seems to be irregular
with regard to Sanskrit, for example Goth. hairto 'heart' vs. Skt

hṛd, hṛdaya. Since all European languages have here either k or its
regular substitute (Gk kardía, Lat. cord-, OIr. cride, OSlav. sridĭce,
Lith. szirdis) there really is no alternative to admitting an irregularity in Sanskrit (and Zend).

Another series of exceptions can be explained when one looks at
the history of the sound shift law. It seems to me that Curtius has
demonstrated that the sound shift began with the lowering of the aspirates to mediae, which in turn led to the raising of the genuine
mediae into tenues, and further the old tenues into aspirates. I
should like to point out in anticipation of the conclusion of this examination that there will then be another reason in support of his
view. But it would be false to believe that this lowering of the old
aspirates owed its origin to a sudden caprice of the Germanic people, for it is very deeply ingrained in our whole language development. Zend already shows b for the old bh and frequently also d for
the old dh. In OPers. bh, dh and gh always change to mediae. On
European soil this same degeneration is very old in some words;
and earlier I have pointed to the conformity of all European languages in this respect, which is attested several times as one of the
reasons which compel us to assume that there was a lasting association of the Europeans after their separation from the Asiatics.
Goth. ik, mikils, -k (suffix in mi-k, þu-k etc.), kinnus all correspond
to Gk egő, megalo-, ge, génus, to Lat. ego, mag-is, gena (the Celtic,
Slavic and Lettish languages prove nothing in this matter since all
old aspirates become mediae in them), while Sanskrit offers aham,
mahat, ha (Ved. gha) and hanu. The situation is also similar with
Skt vṛh 'to grow' 2) 'to work' — Zend verez- but Gk werg-, Goth.
vaurkjan; also with Skt vṛdh 'to grow', but Gk (b)ríza from wridja,
hrádeks, hrádamnos, with which goes Goth. vaurts, OE wyrt, and
further ON rôt, NE root, while OE rôd 'pertica', NE rood, rod, OHG
ruota agree with the Sanskrit sound level. From Gk megalo- it can
be affirmed against all doubt that the root had originally gh, for this
root is in Sanskrit manh 'crescere, augere' and has maintained Gk
kh in mēkhos, mēkhané, with which in turn Goth. magan agrees. It
may also be assumed as proved that Gk ge arose out of older Gk khe
only on European soil, in the event that Gk -khi (in hêkhi), which cannot possibly be considered a case suffix, is related to it as Skt hi is
to ha (all these little words are enclitic). With all the other examples there remains the slight possibility that originally a g stood
here and that the h of Sanskrit is a special irregularity.

Aside from these anticipations of the sound-shift, which pervade
all European languages, each language has also specific preludes to
the sound shift, as well as some peculiar irregularities of its own.
[Lottner goes on to list these pp. 177-182].

(182) Finally, apparent irregularities come into being through

dialect peculiarities of the individual Germanic languages, through which the system of their mutes is more or less altered. To this belongs above all the second sound shift of the High German which has affected some of its individual dialects more, others less, but none completely. Therefore determination of the original Germanic form meets with considerable difficulty where words have only been preserved in High German. The second sound shift, as is well-known, has penetrated the dental group most thoroughly, and of these the z (= Goth., OE, ON t). But there is an exception here too, to which insufficient attention has been paid: the groups tr, tl always remained unshifted. This not only explains our treu, OHG triuwi vs. NE true, ON trûa, Goth. trauan etc., but also cases like OHG bittar vs. OE biter, ON bitr, Goth. baitrs, where a vowel was inserted at later times. --- A great number of apparent exceptions to the first sound shift originate in Old Norse and in Old English through the almost consistent change of medial b to f (changed further in English, Low German and Danish to v, in Swedish to fv), whereas Old Saxon has preserved the intermediate grade bh. Thus, OE leof 'dear', ON liufr, OE lufjan 'love' appear to be on the same grade with Skt lubh 'cupere'. Likewise, ON stafr 'staff' OE stäf seem to fit exactly Skt stambh 'fulcire', but HG lieb, Stab, Goth. liubs, stabs show that everything is in order. In most cases of Old Norse medial d becomes þ, ð, and in Anglo-Saxon this may happen under certain conditions which, of course, gives rise to new apparent exceptions.
2) In New Norse (as well as in Low German) th is lost and is replaced by t or d. It is replaced by the former when the English form begins with a hard th, and by the latter when the English pronounce a soft th (thus Swed. du, de, den, dem, desse, än-då = Engl. thou, the, they, them, these, though). For this reason Swed. du 'you', tänka 'think' are apparently irregular when compared with Lat. tu, tongere, but in Old Norse we quite regularly have þu, þenkja. Finally, medial tenues between vowels, and final tenues after a vowel, change in Danish to mediae (rarely also in Swedish). Thus, Dan. bog 'book', vide 'know', aede 'eat' correspond, for example, to Gk phègos, wid, ed, but compare Swed. bok, veta, äta, ON bôk, vita, eta. All these special irregularities are, of course, to be revoked and the state of Primitive Germanic sounds to be restored before a comparison is possible, also when the dialect form is apparently more regular than the primitive form arrived at by a comparison of the other Germanic languages. It is, for example, uncritical to cite OE seofon 'seven' for the correct sound shift with regard to septem, because Goth. sibun as well as the High German form demonstrate clearly that here Primitive Germanic had a b.

The Gothic sound conditions of the mutes are identical with Primitive Germanic in by far the most cases, but not always, just as little as the grammar of this dialect does not always have the oldest forms. Some examples of irregular sound shift in which Gothic is corrected by other dialects will be given later. Here I cite but the two peculiar examples in which the Gothic alone has maintained an unshifted d, namely du 'to' = OSlav. do 'to', da Gk hína, OIr. do and, according to Stokes, probably also Lat. -du (in in-du = NE in-to), whereas OE tô and OHG zuo, za, zi have been shifted; and Goth. dis- = Lat. dis, but OHG zir- which presupposes an earlier regular tis.

After elimination of the apparent exceptions we can now proceed to consideration of the real exceptions.

I. Irregularities of the original tenues:

a) The tenues remain regularly (184-187).

[First Lottner cites the groups sp, st, sk, which he says are well-known; then ht and ft. Apart from these he finds little material.]

b) The old tenuis appears as media (187-197).

[Here he finds the greatest number of exceptions, especially in medial position. He cites, though not coherently, the well-known words, such as "Goth. sibun 'seven' = Skt saptan", "Goth. taihun 'ten' beside -tigus (-zig) Lat. decem". Nor can he account for subsequent changes, such as the devoicing in Goth. hlaifs beside the hlaib- of the oblique cases. Accordingly he is nowhere near a solution. In his final comment on medial mediae instead of expected aspiratae he points to the "elective affinity" between liquids and mediae and to the interchange between "aspiratae" and mediae in the same word, citing for example,

OE	veorð an	vearð	vurdon	
OHG	ziohan	zôh	zugum	zogan
NHG	leiden			gelitten

He concludes the section with the sentence: "Although to be sure examples occur, in which the older aspirates can no longer be demonstrated, it may not be too daring to presuppose in general the transition of the tenues through aspirates to mediae as a former intermediate stage." It remained to Verner to correct the phonetic statements and associate the phenomenon with the Indo-European accent.]

II. Irregularities of the original mediae (197-202):

[This section was very useful for Grassmann. Although some of Lottner's equations had to be discarded, others are:

Goth. grēdus "hunger, greed"	-	Skt. gardh "be greedy"
Goth. bindan	-	Skt. bandh
OHG bodam "floor"	-	Skt. budhna, Gk puthmḗn

The ON botn and OE botm perplexed Lottner, as did the Greek tenuis. In this section too he associated the irregularities with the liquids, but noted that there were many fewer than for tenues.]

III. Irregularities of the original aspirates (202-3):

[In this short section Lottner's examples are largely erroneous comparisons, which he himself calls uncertain.

After a brief summary Lottner concludes with a statement on the relative chronology of the sound shift.] (204) "It has been disputed where exactly the sound shift began. Grimm finds boldness in the shift of the mediae to the tenues, and accordingly seems to view this as the starting point; I heard Bopp present the entire shift as a weakening of sound, completely opposite to Grimm, and he put the change of the tenues to aspirates at the beginning. The third assumption, that the aspirates became mediae first of all, Curtius capably demonstrated as the most probable by comparing the originally related languages. Through the observation that the aspirates were shifted with greatest regularity, with somewhat less regularity the mediae and least of all the tenues, this view of Curtius gains new support."

London, 10 November, 1860.

Notes

1. The older form caru Stokes attests in Félire Oingosso Céli dé — "á ísu notcaru" — "O Jesus, I love you."

2. It is peculiar that in English the Old English medial dental mediae often appear as th; thus in together, weather, father, mother, all very common words; OE ät-gädere, vedr, fäder, môdor (the three last as exceptions to the sound shift; see below). Is this Scandinavian influence?

CHAPTER TEN

HERMANN GRASSMANN

CONCERNING THE ASPIRATES AND THEIR SIMULTANEOUS PRESENCE IN THE INITIAL AND FINAL OF ROOTS

"Ueber die Aspiraten und ihr gleichzeitiges Vorhandensein im An- und Auslaute der Wurzeln," Zeitschrift für vergleichende Sprachforschung auf dem Gebiete des Deutschen, Griechischen und Lateinischen, 12.2 (1863), 81-138

Grassmann's is one of the celebrated articles of linguistics. Rightly, because it largely led to the conviction that reconstructed languages must be set up for any language family. Before Grassmann, Sanskrit had served as the measure against which forms in the other languages were compared. On the surface it may seem that all earlier scholars viewed Sanskrit as the source of the various other Indo-European languages; but their writings indicate that they were not quite so simple. Because of the transparency of its forms Sanskrit seemed closer to the agglutinative period, through which the Indo-European languages were thought to have passed, than did any of the other languages. The unparalleled antiquity of its materials supported this view. Accordingly, sounds and forms of the other Indo-European languages might well be contrasted with those of Sanskrit. By demonstrating that Germanic actually was "older" in one phonological pattern than was Sanskrit, Grassmann undermined the position of Sanskrit as the language which was the earliest attainable in Indo-European linguistics.

By this demonstration Grassmann also undermined the notion that language developed from an analytic to a synthetic structure through an agglutinative. With it he did away with the close relationship that had been observed previously between genealogical and typological classification. After the publication of his article we find fewer and fewer references to the typological structure of a language in comparative treatments; and when typology is taken up by Finck in the definitive treatment of the nineteenth-century approach there is no reference to genealogical

classification. The appealing notion of a straightforward
development of language had been abandoned.

These contributions to general linguistic theory were
achieved by explanation of one phonological problem in
Indo-European studies. We have noted how von Raumer
had hit on the explanation earlier, but had stated it so
briefly that it remained without impact. We have also
noted Lottner's important preparatory work. Neither re-
duces Grassmann's achievement. His article is admirably
composed. First he examines previous attempts at explanation, then the data. His examination of both is complete.
When he presents his conclusions there is no question of
their validity.

His convincing explanation led linguists to deal with
entire forms, not merely with single segments. In this way
it prepared for the concern with entire utterances, demanded by Sievers. Unfortunately this concern with entire
forms and with entire utterances was often neglected subsequently in the attempt to solve the numerous minor problems within the various languages.

It is also noteworthy that Grassmann, with his back-
ground in mathematics, objects to fanciful theory — the
equilibrium theory. He insists on an "organic" approach;
speech sounds must be classified in accordance with their
organs of articulation. For an understanding of linguistic
change a knowledge of articulatory phonetics is indispensable. To be sure, he stumbles over Lottner's notion of a
Wahlverwandtschaft between mediae and liquids; but such
a notion is not completely in contrast with articulatory
phonetics, for both sets of sounds are voiced and usually
lenis in articulation. Grassmann's achievement is great,
even though he left a field for Verner to conquer. His
overall procedure is unobjectionable. All "exceptions"
have been dealt with. One could not ask for more rigorous
methods.

Hermann Grassmann (1809-1877) was a banker who
was compelled to retire because of tuberculosis. In his
leisure he occupied himself with mathematics and linguistics. He made important contributions to both fields. His
work on non-commutative algebra is an important contribution to mathematics. For linguistics, besides his clarification of the reflexes of the Indo-European aspirates, he
prepared a complete dictionary of the Rig-Veda which is
still indispensable for Indo-Europeanists and for Sanskrit-
ists. Other works which would be major for most scholars

round out his list of achievements, such as his complete
translation of the Rig-Veda. He remains one of the great
figures in linguistics.

    The question of whether there were originally roots in Indo-
European with aspirates initially and finally has in my opinion not
yet been decided. It is not surprising that, before Sanskrit and also
the comparative investigation of languages gained influence on Classical philology, many grammarians — impelled by the moving about
of aspiration, e.g. in trékhō, thréksomai — assumed roots in greatest
abundance for Greek with initial and final aspirate and in this way
defaced Greek grammar in part with roots that never existed, as
linguistic comparison showed; for Goth. þragja as well as the Celtic
root trag, PBB 1.167 beside Gk trékhō forbid setting up a form
threkh** as the original form of the root. It was natural that the
investigators starting out from comparison of languages, in their
first unhappiness about such monstrosities rejected all roots with
original initial and final aspirates; and subsequently the principle
that there were no roots of this type was held as a kind of axiom in
linguistics, though in more recent times an inclination to that older
point of view may again be recognized in various places (cf. Ahrens,
Griechische Formenlehre § 152, Schleicher Compendium § 143).
But as far as I know an actual investigation has not yet been undertaken about the matter. Encouragement of such an investigation is
to be the main purpose of the present essay. Yet it is impossible to
take up the matter without touching the disputed question whether
the hard or the soft aspirates were the original. For even if the
most essential results of the investigation are not dependent on the
answer to this disputed question, the entire point of view and the
form of the presentation in its details will be quite different, depending on the answer to this question, so that it is not possible to avoid
it here. I will therefore first treat this question and only afterwards
proceed to the actual task.

    First essay: On the presence of hard and soft aspirates before
the linguistic separation. (82-110).
    [In this essay Grassmann assumes two kinds of aspirates, the
voiceless as well as the voiced, specifying that he is dealing with
the original Indo-European language. At the end of the essay he
states that the Germanic shift began with the loss of the aspiration,
sharing this phonetic modification with Sanskrit and Greek. The
change of tenues in Germanic he views as related. And only the
change of mediae to tenues does he consider without parallel in the

other languages, though he states that it took place to restore the
balance which was lost in the first two modifications.]

Second essay: On the original presence of roots whose initial
and final contained an aspirate. (110-138).

With regard to the question about the original presence of roots
with aspirates in initial and final position it is above all necessary
to note the two following well-known euphonic laws of Greek and
Sanskrit, which I give here for the sake of clarity.

> If a root ends with an aspirate and begins with a consonant
> capable of aspiration, and if its final loses its aspiration through
> the operation of some other sound law, the aspiration moves to
> the initial. But this is true of Sanskrit only when the final of
> the root is a soft aspirate and when the initial is a non-palatal
> media; and for Greek only when the initial is τ.

For Greek only $\tau\epsilon\acute{v}\chi\omega$, $\tau v\gamma\chi\alpha\nu\omega$ with their common future $\tau\epsilon\acute{v}\xi o\mu\alpha\iota$
etc. and $\tau\rho\acute{v}\chi\omega$, future $\tau\rho\acute{v}\xi\omega$ provide exceptions. For the former,
as shown above, χ results as a later modification of the original κ,
which is also maintained in the derivations and in the aorist $\tau\epsilon\tau v\kappa\epsilon\hat{\iota}\nu$,
but this cannot be demonstrated for $\tau\rho\acute{v}$-χ-ω (from $\tau\rho\acute{v}$-ω). This law
is also valid in Greek when the final represents an originally hard
aspirate, as in $\tau\alpha\chi\acute{v}s$, Comp. $\Theta\acute{\alpha}\sigma\sigma\omega\nu$ (see the first essay), and also
when the root never contained an aspirate initially as well as finally
at the same time, as in $\tau\rho\acute{\epsilon}\chi\omega$ (= Goth. þragja), fut. $\Theta\rho\acute{\epsilon}\xi o\mu\alpha\iota$. The
second law we can express in general as follows:

> If aspirates that belong to the same root occur in two con-
> sonant groups of a word which are separated by a vowel, then
> one of them, usually the first, loses its aspiration. Only rarely
> does this happen when the aspirates belong to different roots,
> or to different suffixes, or one of them to a root and the other
> to a suffix, or when more than one vowel stands between the
> consonant groups (as in $\overset{\text{,}}{\epsilon}\kappa\epsilon$-$\chi\epsilon\iota\rho\acute{\iota}\alpha$, $\tau\eta\lambda\epsilon\Theta\acute{o}\omega\nu$).

There is no doubt that reduplication originally arose from a
repetition of the entire root syllable, as especially the formation of
intensives illustrates (e.g. dar-dhar-shi 'you hold firm' from dhar,
dhṛ, $\pi\alpha\mu\varphi\alpha\iota\nu\omega$ from the theme $\varphi\alpha\nu$); originally then the aspirate
must have been repeated as such too, and only later when the re-
peated root combined into one word and the above-stated law of
euphony entered into effect did one of the aspirates give up its aspiration. Indeed we find this aspiration often maintained still in
onomatapoeic words, but in these the above law, which would disturb
the intended imitation of the sounds of nature, is not applied (gharghara, ghurghurā, gharghurghā, ghurghura, jharjhára, jhinjhi, etc.)

The decision with regard to the form of the root itself is not so simple. It would follow from the above law that there would be no roots in Greek and Sanskrit which simultaneously showed an aspirate initially and finally in the state of the language transmitted to us. Now this is the case throughout apart from some secondary dialect forms cited by the Indic grammarians and apart from the Greek forms ἐ-Οαφ-Οην, τε-Θάφ-Θαι, τε-Θάφ-Θω, τε-Θάφ-αται (from Θάπτω), and τε-Θράφ-Θαι, ἐ-Θρέφ-Θην (from τρέφω). Nonetheless it would be unjustified to draw conclusions from this about the original presence of aspirates in initial and final position. But it is even less justified to assume without further consideration, as a kind of axiom, that that euphonic law existed from the very first beginnings of the development of language. Bopp makes this last mistake, when in his comparative grammar (§ 104) he states as grounds against assuming roots with initial and final aspirates "that in the very original arrangement of the roots (directed by the cited euphonic law) the language would have guarded against the simultaneous occurrence of aspirates in initial and final position." But it is precisely the question whether that euphonic law existed from the beginning, and in principle this is most unlikely. The sure answer to this question may only be gained on a historical basis. Now this law shows up in only two language areas: in Aryan and in Greek. In the Italic languages by contrast it does not prevail, as Latin fefelli, the Oscan forms fufans, fefacust, fefacid, feiho, hafiest prove. To be sure f and h are not genuine aspirates, but they take the place of these; and if indeed that euphonic law was valid already before the separation of the Italic branch from the entire family, it is hard to see why later on again the two spirants which take the place of aspirates should have been restored, even though the one of them had already forfeited its aspiration. Even more decisively, Gothic points to the later origin of that euphonic law and to roots with original initial and final aspirates. For if the law existed already before the separation of the Germanic branch, then on the one hand, since Gothic mediae correspond to the old aspirates, the reduplication of mediae had to be avoided, and on the other hand there should have been no roots in Gothic with initial and final mediae. Neither is true. With regard to the first we can cite Goth. gaigrot from gretan, which does not belong to Skt krand as will be shown below. With regard to the second it turns out that of all nine possible groups of roots with initial and final mutes none is represented as widely as that with initial and final mediae. To look on this as a mere play of chance seems impossible; and consequently we may assume it to be securely established that the questionable euphonic law was not yet in existence before the separation of not only the Germanic but also the Italic branch. A linguistic phenomenon that

points to the contrary has not yet been adduced by anyone, as far as
I have learned. Nonetheless the frequent recurrence of Gothic roots
with mediae initially and finally forces one to the conclusion that
there were roots with aspirates initially and finally in the common
language branch. Yet the individual roots have to be compared before this conclusion can be drawn with certainty.

If the hard aspirates of Sanskrit are excluded for the time being, especially those roots come into consideration, which begin
with a media in Sanskrit and conclude with a soft aspirate. First I
consider those beginning with b. I begin with an example among
them which can be pursued with utmost certainty through all four
language branches which are considered here, and which to a certain extent can be viewed as representative of the others; for the
phonological phenomena which appear in it are repeated almost
throughout in the others in a precisely corresponding manner,
namely:

  1. budh-nā́-s, $\pi v \Theta$-$\mu\acute{\eta}\nu$, fund-u-s, OS bod-m,

where the remaining Germanic dialects likewise all show the initial
b, while d and t vary among them in an irregular manner. The initial media of Sanskrit is replaced in Greek by the tenuis, in Latin by
the aspirate, in Germanic by the media. Of these sounds only the
Latin aspirate stands in accord with the German media; all other
five replacements are anomalous. But nonetheless the same series
of phenomena is repeated in almost all roots of the named type.
Therefore, to avoid these anomalies, on the grounds that Sanskrit
has preserved the original grades of sound, one has devised theories
through which one attempts to explain these irregularities for every
single one of the remaining language branches. To this end, first
Pott and in greater detail Benary in his Phonology have set up for
Greek the equilibrium theory, which has been adopted by most of the
more recent investigators of languages (as also by G. Curtius,
Schleicher Compendium § 143). Benary explains the phenomenon,
that for example Skt budh- is equal to Gk $\pi v \Theta$- through the fact that
since the aspirate became hard in Greek the tenuis arose medially
instead of the media in order to restore the equilibrium (p. 195).
This equilibrium he finds disrupted, if from budh, which contains
two soft sounds, *$\beta v \Theta$- had developed, which would contain one soft
and one hard sound (β); and this equilibrium is to have been restored
through the hardening of the β to π. I cannot make any other sense
of this expression (of the disrupted and then restored equilibrium),
than that the hard sounds are placed as equivalent among themselves, and similarly the soft sounds among one another; on the
other hand the hard as not equivalent to the soft — and that the Greek
language had a preference for equilibrium of the initial and final of

roots. Let us examine this preference for equilibrium in greater
detail. Four types of equilibrium are conceivable for Greek. First,
both sounds can be soft, that is, initial and final can be mediae; second, the initial can be a tenuis, the final an aspirate; or conversely,
the first can be an aspirate, the final a tenuis; or, last, both can be
tenues. With regard to the first combination of sounds there is apparent in Greek a comprehensive, but, as far as I know, not yet observed law according to which there is no root in Greek with two
mediae and a simple intermediate vowel or a vowel expanded by a
nasal. It is obvious that in the reduplicated forms, as in δίδωμι,
δαιδάλλω, δενδίλλω, or in derivations like βά-δην, βα-δ-ίζω, two
mediae can arise at both sides of the vowel, without thereby affecting the law. The single exception would be the hapax legomenon of
Theocritus δαγύs 'wax doll of magicians', if the reading for it (besides δατύs) were not doubtful, and a foreign origin not probable.
Things are not much better in the second and third equilibrium form.
Actually there seems to be hardly a Greek root which originally began with a tenuis and ended in an aspirate, or conversely — of such a
kind that in the remaining languages the regular representation
would take place. Rather, we see the first of these forms regularly
paralleling the form of Sanskrit: media, vowel, soft aspirate and
in accordance with the above presentation paralleling the forms of
the other languages related to it, as the above example illustrates.
As the only cases, which might provide a more extensive correspondence of the sort that the tenuis initially and the aspirate finally
in the root appear original, I have found: τρεχω = Goth. þrag-ja
'run', in which however the Lith. strokas 'haste' makes an originally
initial s probable; and perhaps κευΘω (theme κυΘ), compared with
OE hyd-an, hed-an, OHG huot-jan; but this second example is also
highly uncertain, since the Greek κευΘω stands in much closer relationship to the Skt gudh, guh 'conceal', which has the same meaning, and since there are only highly uncertain traces of a root *kuh
in Sanskrit, about which in addition we do not know whether the h
corresponds to a dh or to another aspirate (kuha, kúhaka, kuhana,
kuhayāmi, kuhū, kuhara, kuhūla = kukūla, kūhanā, kūhā = kujjhaṭi-kā,
which have the meanings 'juggler, deception, deceive by cheating,
new moon, cave, fog, etc.' — see the Petersburger Lexicon. In any
case the second and third equilibrium forms, which originally show
a tenuis initially and an aspirate finally, or the reverse, are accordingly only poorly represented, if at all. Only the fourth equilibrium form with tenuis initially and finally is normal in Greek, but
it is greatly outnumbered by the numerous roots in which no equilibrium of the designated type takes place; and indeed all five types
of non-equilibrium occur, and most of them in great abundance. A
preference in Greek for the equilibrium between the initial and final

of the root is accordingly out of the question. One would accordingly
have to modify the Benary law to this effect that the Greek language
attempts to maintain through all changes the relationship of weight
between initial and final, as it exists at any time, and especially
when both stand in equilibrium; but even about this we find no trace
outside the area in support of which the entire theory is to serve.
From Benary's conception that of Schleicher (op. cit.) differs only
in choice of words, for the weak sounds are designated as voiced,
the hard as voiceless; equilibrium is designated as similarity of
sound and the production of equilibrium as assimilation. In order
to explain the irregularity found in Latin (Lat. fund-u-s = Skt budh-
ná-s), Benary has made accountable the shift of the aspiration from
the final to the initial, and this assumption has also been adopted by
most of the more recent investigators of language. But such a shift
has not been demonstrated anywhere in the area of the Italic languages. Moreover, the analogy of Sanskrit is not decisive here,
since the corresponding phenomenon in Sanskrit is tied to certain
conditions which do not enter in here; and in addition, Latin treats
the medial aspirates, in contrast with Sanskrit, almost everywhere
like mediae. Finally for the anomaly of Gothic and Germanic in
general no theory has as yet been made cogent, but here the anomaly
is permitted to stand as such, as for example Curtius in No. 326,
327, 328, 329, 145, 318, 138, Schleicher in § 143. All these anomalies disappear and those highly dubious theories which have been
devised for their explanation become superfluous if one assumes in
the examples under consideration original roots with aspirates initially and finally, which were modified in all those languages in accordance with the general laws which apply in these languages. If
for example we assume in the above-cited budh-ná-s, $\pi\upsilon\Theta$-$\mu\acute{\eta}\nu$ etc.
two original aspirates (bh, dh), then in Sanskrit and Greek in the development of the above-discussed euphonic law, one, and generally
the first had to give up its aspiration; in this way, since the aspirate
was soft in Sanskrit, hard in Greek — at least from a certain time on
— there a b, here π had to arise, the latter (at least if the time when
the euphonic law came into force was after this point in time). In
Latin, on the other hand, where as shown above this law did not prevail, the aspirate was maintained as f and in Germanic it shifted
regularly to b. Instead of the three anomalies which also did not
stand in any sort of relationship to one another, one has with this
assumption organic changes everywhere, and there is no need to explain the phenomena through artificial hypotheses which lack any
other support, nor, despairing of a solution to consider the changes
as non-organic. For Greek we must examine the phenomena in still
greater detail. It turns out that when the first aspirate of the root
loses its aspiration initially before vowels, the tenuis appears

without exception; on the other hand where the second (root-final) loses it, the media arises. The latter occurs, as will be discussed further below, for example in Θυγ-άτηρ, φράσσω (theme φραγ), φεύγ-ω, Θέλγ-ω, (Θελγίν beside τελχίν), φιδ-άκ-νη beside πιΘ-άκ-νη, φέβ-ομαι, φοῖβ-os (the latter probably a reduplicated formation from <u>bhā</u> 'shine') and probably also in Θιγγάνω. It follows from this that at the time when the above-mentioned euphonic law occurred, the aspirate was already hardened initially; medially however it had still preserved its original nature (as a soft aspirate). The initial aspirates before ρ and λ also seem to have remained weak at that time still; evidence for this is given by γράφ-ω = Goth. grab-a, βρεχμό-s = OE <u>brägen</u> (see below), and also γλάφω and γλυφω (compare below also δολιχό-s). Accordingly, from the above-mentioned development we have to assume that the euphonic law — according to which the simultaneous appearance of aspirates in the initial and final of the root was avoided through the fact that one of the two aspirates was deprived of its aspiration — developed independently in the two separated branches of the Greek-Aryan language branch, and that particularly between the time of separation of Greek from Aryan and the development of this law in Greek the period must have elapsed in which the initial aspirate was hardened, except before ρ and λ. This law arose in both branches from the striving which is based on the nature of the aspirates to avoid the heaping of aspirates in the same word. The two languages did not follow the same course in this process, and particularly the Aryan languages resisted also the direct coming together of the two aspirates, while Greek did not, except for homorganic aspirates; yet the Aryan languages attempted to transfer with much greater consistency to another sound of a word the aspiration lost in one position, and by this to maintain the traces of that aspiration (e.g. Skt <u>lab-dhá-s</u> from <u>labh</u> + <u>ta-s</u>, Gk γραπ-τό-s from γραφ + το-s, Skt <u>ghoxyāmi</u> from <u>guh</u> + <u>syāmi</u>, Gk κεύσω from κυΘ + σω, both with gunation of the root vowel). Nonetheless the agreement of both branches in their treatment of the aspirates is overwhelming, and particularly in comparison with the other branches of the Indo-European language family. While these gave up the aspirates partially or completely without providing a substitute for them, the others only worked against their heaping up, but still attempted, to the extent permitted by the striving for euphony which was constantly developing toward greater perfection, to preserve the aspiration as faithfully as possible. As in general in both of these branches, also where they apparently developed independently of one another, but most prominently in Sanskrit, on the one hand a wonderfully fine feeling for euphony developed, and on the other hand the striving remained along with this to bring to view unimpaired

all phonological characteristics of the roots, especially in all of the
formations and derivations which sprang out of them, and in this
way to maintain the roots in their original and complete life. And
this agreement of both language branches is also simply another of
the many phenomena, in which the far-reaching agreement between
the Greek and the Aryan (pre-Brahmanic) spirit appears to us in
language, poetry, myth and life, and gives evidence of the tremendous intellectual development which the Greek-Aryan people underwent after the departure of the other peoples. After these digres-
sions, which seemed to me necessary for the understanding of the
whole, I return to the comparison of the individual roots and first of
all to those with an original initial bh. The citations refer to Curtius,
Grundzüge (C), where the number is cited; to Schleicher's Compendium (S), where the paragraph is; to Leo Meyer's comparative
grammar (M) and to Lottner's essay in Volume 11 of this journal
(L), where the page is cited.

> 2. budh; πυΘ; -------------- ; bud   ) C. 328, M 394
>   bódhāmi; πυνΘάνομαι; ---- ; binda) S. 143;

The Latin putare does not belong here, as was shown above.

> 3. bandh; *πενΘ, *πειΘ; *fad(?); band) C. 326
>   badhnāmi;   ; binda)
>   bandh-u-s; πενΘ-ερό-s
>   bandh-a-s; πεῖσμα ; fas-ci-s(?); HG band, bind-a.

Latin fūnis probably belongs to the secondary form with u, Skt
*bundh; and Gk πίΘο-s 'vat', πιΘάκνη = φιδάκνη, Lat. fidelia and
possibly also Lat. fīlum, if it is to be explained from *fid-lum,
seem to point to a secondary form with i. The following root also
seems to set out from the same basic meaning.

> 4. ------; πιΘ   (fĭd-es); bid, bad) C. 327
>   πείΘω; fĭd-o; bidja   )

where Gothic to be sure shows the theme bad for the preterite, but
in the present (bidja) and in the derivations (bida, bidagva) it seems
to point to a theme bid.

> 5. badh, bādh; παΘ, πενΘ; fend   ; *badv (Grimm, KZ 1.437).
>   bādhe   ; πά-σχω;   -fendo; (N böd 'battle', OE beadu).

Here Greek differs appreciably in meaning from the other languages,
for Skt badh or vadh 'strike, kill', bādh 'torture', Lat. fendo as it
appears in offendo, defendo means 'push'. With this is associated
Lith. bēdá 'need, misery' = Russ. bēdá, 'misery, woe', OSl. bēda
'compulsion'; also, to the form badh, the Slavic bodą 'stab, push'.
But the transition of meaning to Greek πάΘ-o-s, πάσχω appears

clearly in the Lithuanian and Slavic words. That Lat. pati doesn't
belong here has been shown above.

6. bāhú-s; πῆχυ-s; -----; N bōg-r [C. 176, S. 143]
7. bahú-s; παχύ-s   [S. 143].

Latin pinguis does not belong here, for neither the initial, nor the
following vowel fits. It probably belongs together with sphigî 'hip',
which belongs to Skt sphai 'swell', and more directly still with ON
spik, OE spic 'bacon'; and it presupposes an adjectival formation in
u from that extended root *sphig. The root for No. 7 is:

8. bah, baṃh 'grow', from which Goth. bag-m-s 'tree'.
9. bhuj   ; φυγ ; fug   bug)
   bhujâmi; φεύγω; fugio; biuga) C. 163

Here Gothic points to two aspirates. That in Sanskrit the second
aspirate, and not as is usual the first, has lost its aspiration, seems
to have its basis in the fact that the palatal media is not usually aspirated, except in onomatopoeic words; for this reason the law of
moving of aspiration to the initial, for example, does not take place
when this is a palatal media. This situation (that the second aspirate rather than the first loses its aspiration) occurs more frequently in Greek.

10. -----; φραγ ; -----; barg) L. 200
    ; φράσσω; -----; bairga)

To this probably

10a. -----; βρεχμό-s; -----; OE brägen (see above)
11. -----; flagellum, flīgo; bliggva (L. 200)

Gothic bliggvan (theme blaggv) 'scourge' shows a as the original
root vowel, which is maintained in Lat. flagellum, while flīgo shows
the transition to the i-series.

12. bíbhemi; φέβ-ομαι; ----- OHG bib-en, OE bif-jan 'tremble'
    (L. 201, C. 409).

The reduplication which the Sanskrit root bhi shows in the stem
syllable has here entered into the theme.

13. -----; -----; fiber; OHG biber (L. 201).

Before I proceed to the other initials, I must cite another phenomenon, which gives evidence for the previously posited roots with two
aspirates, especially those cited in numbers 1-8. Comparisons of
the words beginning with Skt. b, Gk β, Lat. b, Goth. p indicates, as
is well-known, that they do not correspond to each other in any two
of the named languages. The single exception, apart from βραχύ-s

= brevis, βοῦς = bos, is formed by the onomatopoeic words, which in the three first named language branches begin with b, and whose b accordingly also remains unshifted in Germanic, like for example, Gk βλῆ-χω, Lat. balare, OHG blā-zan, NHG blöken and Skt barbara-s, Gk βάρβαρο-s, which refer to the foreign language and imitate this at the same time; similarly the Lat. balbu-s (C. 394-397, S. 117,3). Even from this peculiar situation it is probable that initial b, except in onomatopoeic words, had not existed before the separation of the languages, and that accordingly those words with initial b (Gmc p) in those languages originally had another initial. For Latin and Greek it turns out that initial b either arose from gv (βαρύ-s, βαίνω, βοῦς, Lat. bos, βοάω, βίο-s, βιό-s, βία, βάλλω, βορά, βιβρώσκω and probably βαθύ-s, βάπτω), or from dv (bis, bellum, bonus), or from v (βούλομαι, βελτίων, βολβό-s, βλαστό-s, βρῖζα, βρέχω, βρόγχο-s) or from m before l or r (βροτό-s, βραδύ-s, βλώσκω, βλίσσω, βλάξ, βληχρό-s, βραχύ-s according to L. Meyer) or from bh (βρέμω, βάζω, βασκαίνω, βρύω, βλύω, βλέπω, bulla, balaena) or from p (βόσκω, bibo, buxu-s). And the remainder, which cannot be explained in one of these ways, or seems to be borrowed, is quite isolated and still awaits an explanation. Similarly it is also probable that the Sanskrit b too arose from other sounds initially, because otherwise it would be impossible to understand why its representatives do not show up in the related languages. Now we also see here, as in Greek, that b arises from m before r in Skt brū 'speak', for Zend mru corresponds to this, and before r, m can indeed go over to b, but not the converse. Further, as also in Latin v and b frequently interchange (bāro = vāro, batillum = vatillum), so in Sanskrit this interchange between v and b appears broadly distributed, but in such a way that in part v seems to be older, in part b. If one takes the rest of the Sanskrit words beginning with b, which either have no secondary form beside them beginning with v, or in which b seems to be older than v (which is the more common), the remainder consists almost without exception of words in which an aspirate (with or without nasal) or an l follows the first vowel. The latter are bal and bil beside the obvious dialectal secondary forms *bhal and *bhil. Since the first two are also not directly attested, one must determine their meanings from derivations. In the first place, bala-m 'strength' with its derivations does not belong here, since Latin valor etc. demonstrate v as original initial. Now we see bali-s 'nourishment, food', bāla-s 'boy, child', bālā 'girl' establish the meaning of bal which is cited by the grammarians: "sustentare nutrire" (= bhr̥), for which the example bālayati bālam pitā 'the father feeds the child' is cited. This leads at the same time to the origin from Skt bhar, bhr̥, for r changed to l, as it did so often and first generated the form *bhal, and then the bh lost its aspiration through the influence of the l at the end of the root. The exact equivalent is true of bil, from which bíla-m 'gorge, grotto' arose, and which the grammarians quite correctly explain from bhid 'split' beside the root *bhil, which is cited by them too but not attested in derivatives either. The root bhid must also be viewed as the original form for bil (see Benfey's Glossary to the Sāmaveda), for d developed to l, as happens not infrequently in the final root; accordingly *bhil arose first of all, whereupon the initial aspirate lost its aspiration through the above mentioned influence of the l. This influence of the l following the vowel on the initial (soft) aspirate is also confirmed by the fact that apart from the cited roots *bhal and *bhil the grammarians cite no root which begins with a weak aspirate and ends with l. The few words of the form: "weak aspirate, vowel, l" are either onomatopoeic, like ghulaghulārava 'a kind of dove', jhillī 'cricket' etc., or dialectal secondary forms, chiefly adduced only by the grammarians, like ghola-yāmi 'mix together', a Prakrit reformation of ghūrṇa-yāmi, or jhāla 'heat of the sun' beside jvala-s (from jval); dhūli 'dust' is the only word of this type that has a more general distribution. According to this it seems justified therefore, to assume for Sanskrit a dislike for such combinations and to hypothesize that the l following the vowel in the classical language deprived the originally (soft) aspirate of its aspiration, so that particularly bal and bil point back to the original initial bh. The remaining evidence for initial b after removal of the named forms, is limited according to the glossaries of Bopp and of Benfey (to the Samaveda) to the following words (when we exclude the words cited only by grammarians: baṇij 'merchant', where the b is weakened from p (paṇ 'sell, play dice'), the Vedic asseverative particle baṭ, which probably goes back to the original initial v (see Benfey, Glossary), bāná-s = vāná-s 'arrow' = bunda-s, bṛbád-uktha for bṛhad-uktha. I now proceed to the other initials.

14. dih;   (Θιγ); fig; dig   ) C. 145
    déhmi; (Θιγγάνω); fingo; deiga) M. 385

That Goth. deiga belongs together with Lat. fingo, with which Curtius also associated it recently, is proved by the nicely fitting meaning as well as the form. The g in Germanic shows itself to be very persistent in all dialects, and it is also maintained in Goth. deiga 'πλάσσω', digans 'ὀστρακινό-s', daig-s 'φύραμα'; only the isolated gadikis 'πλάσμα' shows a deviation. Germanic accordingly points definitely to a final aspirate, the corresponding Sanskrit form would therefore have to read digh or dih. The Sanskrit root dih has the meaning: 'coat with white material' and accordingly agrees nicely with the basic meaning of fingo. That Skt h stands for gh is proved among other things by the secondary form san-degh-a for san-deh-a.

The sounds are in complete agreement when the form with two aspirates is taken as original. The Greek Θιγγάνω also agrees in
sound, since as demonstrated above the root-final aspirate, if it
loses its aspiration, goes over to the media. But the meaning is by
no means in such exact correspondence with that which the other
languages develop, that there may not still be doubt. From the root
dih develops in Sanskrit deha-s, deha-m 'body', which however does
not yet occur in the Vedas with dehî (as feminine formation from it)
with the meaning 'mound, dike, wall'; with this agrees dehalî 'mound
before a house, step, lintel, terrace', as also dehikā 'an insect that
throws up earth'; upa-dehikā 'a kind of ant', ud-dehikā 'termite'.
And this meaning of 'heaping up' or 'formation of earth' we also
give as the basis for deha 'body'. To deha-s corresponds quite exactly Gk τοῖχο-s, and with neuter suffix τεῖχ-os, the basic meaning
of which would also be 'earthen wall'. Against the interrelationship
with Gk τεύχω (Curtius, No. 135), the vowel provides the most decisive evidence, for οι and ει are the regular gunations of i, the
first regularly with the suffix o-, the latter always with the neuter
suffix -os.

15. dáh-āmi 'burn'   --   --   OHG táht 'wick'
     áh-an 'day'   Goth. dag-s

for which I adopt the interpretation of Skt áhan from *dah-an (Bopp,
Glossary). That Gk δαίω, δαίs does not belong here, as L. Meyer
(Comparative Grammar 385) assumes, but rather stands for *δαFjω,
δαFίs, and belongs to Skt du 'burn', from which Skt dava-s,
davathu-s dāvá-s 'burning' develops, has already been indicated
by Curtius (Grundzüge, No. 258); and that Lat. fax does not belong
here, because of the contrasting final c, has been demonstrated
above.

16. duhitár; Θυγάτηρ --- dauhtar [C. 318],

in which Greek has modified the second aspirate and indeed regularly; the Goth. h is conditioned by the following t. With this belongs the root:

17. duh   --   --   dug
     dogh-mi   daug.

Skt duhitar points back to the root duh; Goth. dauhtar to the Gothic
root dug; both correspond exactly in sound. But the meaning of
Goth. dug-an (συμ-φέρειν, χρήσιμον, εἶναι), with which Grimm,
Grammar 2.23, rightly puts dauh-t-s 'guest meal, δοχή', seems to
be quite remote from the concept of the Sanskrit root duh 'milk,
give milk'; and the English dug 'teat, udder' could be suspected of
borrowing from Celtic, deogh- 'mammas sugere'. But the abstract

concept of Goth. dugan must have risen from a sensuous meaning; and the root duh of Sanskrit places this transition before our eyes. In this way the meaning 'milk' is transferred to abstract concepts: 'to exploit something, draw a use or profit from it'; and the meaning 'milk', that is 'to give milk' to the abstract concepts: 'to provide something desired (useful)'. And from this concept the meaning: 'provide a use, be useful', as Goth. dugan shows it, as well as the concept of entertainment (dauht-s as translation of δοχή could very readily develop. Lat. ducere, Goth. tiuhan clearly does not belong here.

18. druh; (Θελγ); fraud; OHG trug
druhyāmi; (Θελγω); triugu (ON draug-r).

With regard to the meaning, as well as the Gk Θέλγω (the vowel of which still raises a question), I point to Kuhn's discussion in this journal (1.180), and note only that the basic concept is: 'to injure someone, especially through trickery, treachery, witchcraft'; and that ON draugr 'ghost, shadow of the dead' agrees precisely with Skt druh 'monster, witch', Zend druj 'evil spirit'. Lat. fraus, which agrees excellently in meaning (compare Skt drógha-s, droha-s 'insult, deception') I have put here experimentally; the organically corresponding form would have to be *fraug-. Since however an exchange of the aspirates of various speech organs is not at all infrequent, and since Lat. d in fraud would represent an aspirate, this attempt did not seem too daring. In Germanic a homophonous root, but starting from another meaning, seems to have mixed with this, namely Goth. driuga (theme drug) 'do military service' compared with OE dryht, ON drött 'companions, retinue', and especially with Lith. drauga-s 'companion', draugé, and in compounds: draug- with OSl., Russ. drugŭ 'companion, friend' also in the sense 'another'. We do not find anything in Sanskrit corresponding to these meanings, which go back to the concept of companionship, if one does not want to adduce the words cited by the lexicographers: druha-s 'son', druhī 'daughter'. Lat trux would indeed correspond initially with our root in accordance with the treatment above, by which initial Lat. tr can have arisen from older dr, originally dhr; but its final, as shown above, points to another origin for it.

19. ----- τυφ-λό-s ----- Goth. daub-s, dumb-s (L. 199)
20. *drāgh; ----- traho; draga
dīrgh-á-s; δολιχ-ό-s

From the root *drāgh (drāghe) 'make long' etc. are derived dīrghá-s 'long', compar. drāgh-īyas, superl. drāgh-istha-s; drāgh-imán or drāgh-mán 'length', drāgh-áyāmi 'extend'. Of especial interest here is the secondary form with two aspirates cited by the grammarians

which offends against the euphonic law: dhrāgh-e, from which the
scholiast for Panini forms the perfect dadrāghe. It must be noted
for Gk δολιχό-s, to which OSl. dlŭgŭ, Russ. dologŭ corresponds,
that in accordance with the above the soft aspirate of Sanskrit often
changes to the media in Greek before ρ and λ, a change that is not
hindered by the (subsequently) intercalated o. The tr in Latin has
been discussed above. Compare Leo Meyer (in this journal 6.223),
who however associates HG träge, incorrectly, since this already at
the Gothic stage has tr, which as is well-known is not shifted.

    21. (jabh); κεφαλή ----- OHG gebal.

OHG gebal, gibilla means 'skull', as does the related gibil, gibili
and ON gafl 'gable', with which also NHG gipfel is connected. It is
difficult to separate from this gabala, OE gaflas pl., ON gaffal 'the
fork', and also OE geaflas pl.; this leads us to the root, Skt jabh,
jambh 'open the maw, snap at something'; in connection with its development of meaning the treatment of Kuhn, KZ 1.123ff., is to be
compared. As well the Greek, in forms like γαμφ-ηλαί, γαμφ-αί,
γόμφοs = Skt jámbha-s, γόμφιο-s = jambhya-s, as also the Germanic, in forms like OE ceafle, ceaflas pl. 'throat', ON kiaptr
'snout, throat, cheek-bone' etc., in comparison with the forms cited
above, point to a split of the root jabh attested in Sanskrit − a split
previous to the linguistic separation − into a form with original aspirate initially (Gmc gab-, Gk κεφ) and into another with the corresponding media.

    22. gadh-   ----   -----   *gad

The Sanskrit root gadh (according to the grammarians 'to be mixed')
occurs in the Vedas with ā and pari in the participial form â-gadh-
ita, pári-gadh-ita, which according to the editors of the Petersburger Dictionary probably has the meaning 'attached', 'surrounded';
gádh-ia-s 'that which one must hold fast, to exploit' also belongs to
this. Grimm (No. 5456) ascribes the meaning 'jungere' to the Germanic root *gad, which occurs in OS gigado, OE gada, gegada,
gädeling 'associate', in OHG gagat 'associated', in Goth. gadiligg
'ἀνέψιο-s', in OS, OE gador 'together' in OE gegäde 'assembly',
in NHG gatte, gatten, gattung, gatter, gitter, ON gadda 'join together', Swed. gadda sig 'conspire'. The basic meaning seems to
be that of firm, close association, possibly precisely in the special
conception of 'attaching, joining to one another'.

    23. ----- ἀγαθόs   ---   gōds (L. 197).

The Gothic word points to an original form with two aspirates and
the root vowel a, to which the Greek agrees, apart from the preposed a; for at the time when the one aspirate deprived the other of

its aspiration the medial Greek aspirate in accordance with the
statements above was soft, the initial hard; accordingly either
ἀγαθό-s or ἀκαθό-s (Hesychios) had to result, depending on whether
the α was preposed before or after that time. As root we may hypothesize No. 22, with possibly a transition of meaning through the
intermediate concept 'aptus'.

24. ----- γράφω ; (scribo); graba (L. 197)

With this the secondary forms with λ: γλάφω, γλύφω, Lat. glaber,
glūbo. With regard to the initial, for Nos. 24 and 25 the first essay
is to be consulted.

25. ---- ----- gradu-s; grid-s, ON grada (L. 198)

To the two roots given in 24 and 25 belong forms with initial s,
namely Lat. scrib-o (to γράφω) and OE scrid-e, OHG scrit-u (to
gradior), both with transfer to the i-series; further, Lat. scalp-o
(to γλάφ-ω), sculp-o (to γλύφ-ω); and as original initial either sk
is to be assumed, and then it must be posited that it changed in part
to the weak aspirate before r and l even before the linguistic separation, or more probably that gh was the original initial, before
which an s had been introduced as a type of compensation for the
abandoned aspiration.

26. grdh ----- ----- gred-u-s (L. 198)

The meaning of the Sanskrit root grdh, grdh-yāmi 'be greedy for
something' is mirrored in Goth. gredu-s 'hunger', ON grad-ug-r,
OE grædig 'greedy'.

All words cited above go back to original root forms with two
soft aspirates, which in the Germanic and Italic languages are
treated precisely as such, and of which in the Aryan and Greek languages one, generally the first, loses its aspiration. Some instances
still remain to be treated, in which the hard aspirate, whether it was
originally present or developed only later from the tenuis, exerted
in the same way an influence on an originally present, soft aspirate,
so that it lost its aspiration. For we note that like roots with two
soft aspirates, those with hard aspirate initially and soft finally, or
the converse, are avoided in Sanskrit (and Greek), apart from some
individual ones which were probably taken from the dialects, and in
addition partly secondary forms of grammarians resting on uncertain readings. Actually, Germanic makes this assumption very
probable for the following two roots:

27. chid; σχιδ; scid; skaid)
    chinadmi; σχίζω; scindo; skaido) C. 295

Here Germanic (Gothic) points to the original root final dh. But

from this does not necessarily follow a root with two aspirates;
rather it is possible, indeed probable, that the original initial was
sk and only in the common Greek-Aryan language branch did the
tenuis, as we see happen so frequently, also subsequently, after the
separation of the two branches, change under the influence of the
preceding s to the hard aspirate, which then merged with s in Sanskrit to ch. Then we would have to assume an original form *skidh,
whose final aspirate had to change to d, Gk δ, after the k was aspirated and the euphonic law became effective, by which the simultaneous occurrence of aspirates initially and finally in roots was
avoided.

      28. chad   ----   ----   skad-u-s

The meaning 'shadow' goes naturally with the meaning 'cover up,
cover over, conceal' also 'darken' of the Sanskrit root chad
(chādáyāmi). In accordance with the statements about the previous
root we would here have to assume an original form *skadh.
    If at this point we review the exceptions to the first consonant
shift, as Lottner so usefully assembled them recently, we see that
they almost vanish completely, apart from a small number of dialectal variations and from the instances to be mentioned below
which rest on a type of elective affinity between the liquids and the
following media. If we examine first the initial, then of the instances in which the media is said to remain unshifted (p. 197) the
following disappear, in connection with which I always refer to the
number in the foregoing treatment: 1. god-s (No. 23), 2. graban
(No. 24), 3. gredu-s (No. 26), 4. root drug (No. 18), 5. dauhtar
(No. 16), 6. bindan (No. 3), 7. biudan (No. 2), 8. ON botn (No. 1),
9. ON bōg-r (No. 6), 10. OE geaflas (No. 21), 11. Goth. gibla, ON
gafl (No. 21), 12. dumb-s, daub-s (No. 19), 13. dag-s (No. 15),
14. OE beado (No. 5), 15. OE drygge 'dry'; for Skt *drākh 'be dry',
which is not yet attested, actually shows the original aspirate in the
form *dhrākh (same meaning), which to be sure is similarly unattested. And this example was passed over above only because the
root simply is unattested and no derivatives from it appear; also the
vowel u of Germanic, like the irregularity of the final arouses some
suspicion. Among the remaining exceptions, Goth. gagga, OHG gā
must definitely be excluded, however much it is placed together with
Skt gā. For since Skt gam (Gk βαίνω etc.) is represented by the
Germanic root kvam (Goth. kviman etc.), and since Skt gā (Gk
βιβά-s) stands in very close relationship with it, for this reason
alone one cannot accept that equation; Skt gā, Gk βα would have to
yield Gmc ** kvā. Now for the Germanic root gā, the exactly corresponding root with the same meaning is found in Skt hā, jihāmi,
and there seems to be no reason for not equating the Germanic gā

and the reduplicated gaggan with it; this equation is established to
a certain extent through Lith. żeng-iu 'stride', for Lith. ż is virtually the regular representative of Skt h. Obviously Skt hā, jáhāmi,
jáhīvas (1. du), ptc. hīná-s, which have the meaning 'desert' and, in
the related languages and to some extent also in derivatives in Sanskrit, the meaning 'to separate, gape', are closely connected; yet in
this root an i or j often develops after the initial (* χα-, hia-re, ON
gi-a, HG gi-en. That Goth. gras does not belong to Skt gras 'devour'
has been shown in the first essay in connection with the replacement
of the initial aspirate through Latin media (No. 2); and that ON bulla
= Lat. ebullire provides no exception has been demonstrated there
(No. 11). Relationship of OE gilpan with Skt garva, garba had already been doubted by Lottner and indeed justly; rather, Skt garva
'pride' is to be associated with Skt gurú 'heavy, weighty, honorable',
compar. gárīyas, for which the form and the meaning fit excellently.
Moreover ON gala 'sing, croak', gella 'yell' are hardly to be placed
with Skt gr̥, jr̥, for these, as Lottner correctly remarks, p. 165, are
represented by ON kalla; but for these the onomatopoeic Skt
gharghara 'crackling, rustling, laughter', ghargharā and ghargharikā
'bell, lute' might possibly be adduced. In connection with placing
diup-s 'deep', daupjan 'baptize' with Gk δύπτω it must be noted that
δύπτω is an extension, though a late one, of δύω, and that Lith. dub-
u-s, dumb-u gives us no clarification about the original sounds.
Goth. dal 'valley', dail-s 'part' belongs to be sure with Skt dal
'burst', dala-m 'torn-off piece, part'; but because of the final l (see
above) it is dubious whether d or dh was the original initial; dhalila
(the name of a valley in northern India) might well speak in favor of
the latter. To be sure, Skt dal is related to dr̥, dar; but just as OE
derjan 'harm' stands beside teran 'tear', terjan 'incite', the corresponding parallelism between initial d and dh might well extend into
the time before the linguistic separation. Goth. gavi 'county', however attractive the relationship with Gk γαῖα may be, is nonetheless
not to be placed here but rather following Grimm with Gk χαμαί etc.
(see above), and the frequent change of m to v at the final of roots
must be assumed (cf. Schweizer, KZ 2.305 and 7.155). Finally,
placing ON draum-r HG traum with Skt drā 'sleep' Lat. dormire is
dubious in every respect. Gmc au, OE eá before labials generally
points back to a lost palatal [HG baum = bagm-s; haubi-þ = Skt
kakubha; ON taum-r 'bridle' = *tuhm from tuh 'pull', cf. HG zuhil,
zügel, 'bridle'; so also OE teám 'suboles, what is reared', Grimm,
Grammar 2.146, from the same root; OE hreám 'cry' beside Goth.
hruk-jan; OE seám, OHG saum = σάγμα]. A readily available root
for draum-r is the above-treated drug (No. 18), and the naming of
a dream for the deceptive or shadowy figures (cf. ON draug-r above)
with which it bewitches the mind (cf. Homer's Θέλγειν) is highly

suitable; similarly OE dreám 'music' would represent music as that
which charms and enchants the mind.

As exceptions, in which Gothic mediae are to have replaced the
old tenues, Lottner (p. 187) adduces only two examples for initial
position, which he himself however subsequently designates as dubious: gretan 'weep' to Skt krand and dragan to Lat. traho. That
the latter does not form an exception has been shown above (No. 20).
The basic meaning of krand is 'roar, bellow', partly of animal cries
(of the horse, the ox, the screaming bird), partly of the roaring of
the ocean, of the thundercloud, of crackling fire, of the creaking
wheel; then also of the cries of man, particularly of cries of battle
and sorrow. To the latter the meaning of Goth. gret-an 'weep'
might be related. Yet the sound relationships lead us to another
root of similar meaning, namely to Skt *hrād 'roar, thunder', from
which: hrādinī 'the lightning of Indra'; hrāduní 'bad weather'; and
with short vowel hradinī 'river' (named from its roaring), hradá-s
'pool', used in the Vedas of a pool into which brooks plunge with a
roar, later of the deep pool of Tartarus. Accordingly gretan can
just as well be associated with hrād, since the basic meaning coin-
cides so closely with that of krand, and hrād fits exactly with regard
to form.

According to Lottner the initial Gothic aspirates furnish no exception to the shift, though the initial tenues do, yet only to the extent they seem to correspond to old tenues in some examples (p.
185). First of all OE pād = πάτο-s along with the corresponding
forms of the old dialects provides a real exception, though only in
the special sense of 'path'; for the root fanþ (Goth. finþ-an), whose
original meaning must be 'go', and all its derivatives in use (OE
feða = OHG fendo 'pedestrian', OE feða 'stride' etc.) show the regular shift. In this way OE cal-o 'bald', which is put erroneously
among the initials by Lottner, has been demonstrated above to be a
regular correspondent of Skt khal-atí-s. If in addition Goth. tek-an
corresponds to Lat. tango, Gk τε-ταγ-ών, I believe that the irregularity exists in the old languages and is caused by a sound law demonstrated above for Greek. For Goth. tek-an would correspond to
an old *dang, *dag if regularly shifted. Now we have seen that in
Greek, roots with two mediae and between them a simple vowel or
vowel expanded by a nasal are absolutely avoided; in Latin this law
was necessarily obscured because of the representation of aspirates
through mediae. If we therefore take as original that root which
Gothic suggests, then when a disinclination against such a root form
began to develop in Greek and Latin, a change of the one sound had
to take place, by which a reason was afforded for hardening of the
initial. The remaining exceptions which Lottner cites there, all
concern Germanic k, and particularly in its position before v and r,

where however the organic forms with initial h in part occur beside
it, as in kvainon, ON hvīna, in ON kringla, hringr; and Lottner already rightly observed that here the h (which however must have
been closer in sound originally to the ch) is to be viewed as the
original sound on Germanic soil; only later (when it inclined more
towards the soft spirant), because of the difficulty to make it audible
before r, v (l, n), did it disappear in part, in part harden to k. This
can be applied to all the examples adduced there; for also the ON
kynda 'kindle' stands for *kvinda in accordance with the Old Norse
sound laws.

For medial position Lottner demonstrated (pp. 188-197), as
Grimm had already pointed out at various times, that frequently in
this position the old Germanic aspirates (which correspond to the
tenues of other languages) had sunk downward to mediae; further,
that this transition, which can be pursued historically in many individual instances, was the reason why we frequently, and in particular after liquids, find mediae corresponding to medial tenues of
other languages on the first grade of the Germanic shift, where the
more frequent aspirate would be expected. And he also showed (p.
200) that the shift of mediae is frequently not carried out, so that
here too a kind of elective affinity makes itself known between liquids and mediae (p. 196). But in all other instances the exceptions
turn out to be only apparent, if one applies the laws developed above;
or they are limited to an exceedingly small number of cases, which
in addition are nearly all dubious or limited to dialect variations.
In this way, all the exceptional instances adduced by Lottner (p. 202)
in which Gothic tenues are supposed to correspond to old aspirates
vanish first of all; for the aspirates showed up as hard originally,
and therefore, in accordance with the above, regularly correspond
to Gothic tenues. These are: 1. skip, skapan (see the first essay
towards the end, No. 8); 2. meki (No. 1); 3. OE macjan (No. 7);
4. tacan (No. 6); 5. greipan (No. 10). A similar situation applies
for the exceptions which are medially preserved mediae (p. 201),
for here the Gothic mediae correspond to original weak aspirates,
as has been demonstrated in this second essay of mine for the following instances: 1. grid-s (No. 25), for which I demonstrated at
least that also Lat. gradus can be taken back to a root with two aspirates; 2. deigan (No. 14); 3. skaidan (No. 27); 4. skadus (No. 28);
5. biben (No. 12); 6. biber (No. 13). Similarly OE glād 'be happy',
if it really belongs to Skt hlad, which however does not seem certain
to me, would point to the fact that the original final was dh, whose
aspiration had to defer later to the initial aspirate. Moreover, OHG
sweben, sweibon 'vary, waver', Goth. sveiban 'διαλείπειν', ON svīfa
'waver, hurry' seem to me to have to be separated from OHG sweif
= σοβή OS suepan, OE svīpan, svāpan 'sweep' = σοβέω, Goth. sveipan

(in midja-sveipains), which correspond exactly to the Greek forms
in meaning and form (apart from the varying vowels in Germanic).
As single exception would then remain OHG swīgan = Gk σιγάω, for
which it is not clear however whether the irregularity lies on the
side of the Germanic or Greek, or whether a relationship exists at
all.

  Most numerous are the exceptions cited by Lottner (p. 185) for
the instances in which medial tenues seem to be maintained. But
first, all those exceptions must be excluded in which the Germanic
words only correspond to words in Latin, Lithuanian, Slavic (Irish),
for in all of these languages (apart from Lat. f which represents
initial sph) the tenues are not distinguished from the original hard
aspirates; and in accordance with the statements above, Gothic tenues correspond to hard tenues. Moreover, those instances must be
excluded in which the remaining languages (as Lottner too remarks)
show mediae, which then correspond regularly to tenues on the first
grade of the shift (like hruk-jan beside κραυγ-ή, hveit-s beside Skt
çvid, ut beside ud, þata beside tad; in this connection it should be
noted that Pānini already posits these words in the forms ud and
tad). Moreover those instances should be disregarded in which the
deviation occurs only in one or the other secondary dialect form,
while all other forms and dialects show the regular correspondence
(ON spak-r 'intelligent' beside ON spā for *spah 'prophecy', OHG
spahi 'wise', spahī 'wisdom' spehon, etc.; further, OE sūcan beside
the normal sūgan etc. of Old English and the other dialects). The
situation is quite different in OE vīc, OHG wīch = Lat. vīcus, Gk
Foῖκo-s, for here only Gothic provides the regular form veih-s.
Moreover those examples are excluded in which the Gothic tenues
regularly correspond to original hard aspirates, namely in vairpan
(Essay I, No. 9), in ON flat-r (No. 5), and probably in NHG flach,
which may be recognized as a secondary form beside flat-r since
Old High German almost exclusively shows the form flaz corresponding to ON flat-r. Finally, those words are excluded whose association with those of the related languages rests on erroneous
comparison. Here I put the association of taikn-s 'sign' with
δείκνυμι, Skt diç, to which the generally distributed Germanic root
tih 'show' regularly corresponds. It seems to me that taikn-s has
lost an initial s and that it belongs to the root: Zend çtij, στιγ, Lat.
stig, Goth. stik, stak 'stick', which loses its s also in Sanskrit; this
association is demonstrated by the meaning of στίγμα 'spot, characteristic', and through Lat. signum, which Ebel in this journal 6.441
correctly explains from *stig-num and which, except for the loss of
the second element of the consonant combination, corresponds exactly with Goth. taikn-s. Further, I count as erroneous the association of ON hvat-r 'sharp' with Lat. catu-s, or with Skt katu-s; the

Latin word, to which also cōs belongs, leads to a root *ca = Skt çā
(ço) 'sharpen' (Aufrecht in this journal 7.74). Skt kaṭu-s 'sharp in
taste' does not belong with hvat-r either; for this purpose kaṭh-
ora-s 'hard, sharp' (cf. kaṭh-ina-s 'hard') is much more probable —
for the ax kuth-āra, for example, is called a kaṭhora-nemi provided
with a sharp edge, and kaṭhora (Petersburger Lexicon) is used of a
sharp bite, a sharp wind, of piercing cries (of the donkey). The associated kuṭhāra 'ax' makes an original initial of kv probable at the
same time through the exchange between a and u. The sounds then
agree very exactly, since the hard aspirate regularly corresponds
to ON t. Accordingly there remains among the exceptions cited by
Lottner only one, namely OE vīcan, ON vīka, OHG wīchan 'yield' beside Gk Fείκω, Skt vic 'separate' for which the secondary form vij
of the grammarians (or indeed a derivation from vi-yuj) cannot be
taken into consideration.

    If in this way the numerous exceptions to the first sound shift
vanish almost without a trace, as soon as one recognizes the laws
developed above, I believe I have found through this fact no neg-
ligeable confirmation of the theory I have proposed.

Stettin, 4 September 1862

CHAPTER ELEVEN

KARL VERNER

AN EXCEPTION TO THE FIRST SOUND SHIFT

"Eine Ausnahme der ersten Lautverschiebung,"
Zeitschrift für vergleichende Sprachforschung auf dem Gebiete
der Indogermanischen Sprachen, 23.2 (1875), 97-130

Verner's may be the single most influential publication
in linguistics. It is so lucid that it scarcely needs comment.
Yet since a later generation often wonders why a publication
had the impact it did, a few of the reasons may be mentioned.

First, the article is excellently written. Verner presented all the relevant material in exemplary form. Comparison with even the careful Grassmann, not to speak of
the discursive Lottner or earlier scholars, will indicate
Verner's superior marshalling of the data. The argument
too is at all times lucid and persuasive. One need only
read articles published by well-known scholars even after
Verner's time to observe the refreshing clarity of Verner.
Alone as an essay, the article is superb.

Further, through the primary purpose of the article
Verner solved the most troublesome contemporary problem
— "the last set of exceptions to Grimm's law." To be sure
an explanation had been offered and had even been acknowledged by scholars as competent as Lottner and Grassmann.
But it was fuzzy, scarcely in accordance with other observations on the functioning of language. Verner's explanation was immediately convincing. Moreover, it removed
from linguistics an awkward attempt to rely on imprecise
relationships, and it suggested that linguistic phenomena
must be accounted for with the rigor demanded in the physical sciences.

Because this explanation was at once adopted, the reasoning on which it was based and its implications for general theory had a tremendous influence. Attention was
drawn to suprasegmentals. The journals after Verner are
full of articles proposing explanations of linguistic phenomena by means of accent, such as the various attempts
to give an explanation for the development of Gmc -jj-

-ww- to -dd/ggj- -ggw- in Gothic and North Germanic.
And since such suprasegmentals came to their attention,
linguists began to devote a great deal of interest to the use
of suprasegmentals in selected patterns of language, to
metrics. This scrutiny of suprasegmentals for improved
understanding of linguistic phenomena was important, but
of greatest importance for general linguistics was the effort to account for all phonological phenomena: not only
consonants and vowels, but also stress, pitch, quantity,
juncture. Control over these was not achieved at once, but
the efforts leading to that control were largely touched off
by Verner's article.

Further, Verner saw the clinching evidence for his explanation in its accounting for morphophonemic variation.
Since there was a direct relationship between the consonant
variation, the variation in accent, and the stem changes in
the preterite and preterite participle, Verner concluded
that the variation must be regularly conditioned. This attention to morphophonemic variation led to greater examination of morphological structure in its relation to the
phonological system of language, and in this way to the
method of internal reconstruction. Verner's second article,
which stands immediately after this one, KZ 23.2.131 - 38,
dealt with Indo-European ablaut. Other linguists made the
important contributions to its understanding: Brugmann by
positing vocalic nasals; Saussure by positing laryngeals.
Both scrutinized morphological patterning in arriving at
their conclusions. Both, especially Saussure, came to be
increasingly proficient in the method of internal reconstruction.

In providing his explanation, Verner sought to account
for all the data. Grimm had recognized the general relationship between the Germanic obstruents and those in the
other Indo-European dialects, and he noted only in passing
problems like the -d- in Gothic fadar etc. Grimm's successors had clarified some particulars. In clarifying the
remainder Verner accounted for all the residues. In this
way he applied the principle of accounting for all data in a
language. His predecessors were moving toward such
methodological standards. When Lottner and Grassmann,
for example, published their articles they also discussed
the remainders which were not yet accounted for. But
since imprecise sets of exceptions remained, their articles
had not exerted the dramatic impact on general linguistics
of Verner's. After his it seemed clear that linguists could

and must provide a total accounting of the data in any given
language.

It is understandable that with its tremendous contributions to Germanic, Indo-European and general linguistics
the article led to excesses. After its publication many obscure problems were examined for possible explanation by
means of supra-segmentals, and solutions were given which
never were widely adopted. Yet of greatest general impact
was the conviction that language undergoes change regularly, even mechanically: that sound change takes place
without exception. The linguists at Leipzig, who brought
Verner down from Copenhagen, were strengthened in this
mechanical view of language by his remarkable article; his
explanation helped establish the highly influential neogrammarian school which dominated linguistics for the next two
generations.

Karl Adolf B. Verner (1846-1896) was himself very
modest. The article which brought him fame was published
at the insistence of Vilhelm Thomson. Although he was
well-known after this publication, he preferred a simple
position in a library at Halle. When there was a vacancy
in Slavic Philology at his own university, he became Reader
there in 1883 and spent the rest of his career at the University of Copenhagen. Not least of his qualities was his
capacity for self-criticism. He published very little, all of
it high in quality. The impact of his work resulted from
his capable formulation as well as the discovery itself.
For a fine account of his manner of work and his person-
ality see Otto Jespersen's essay in his volume of collected
papers, Linguistics.

In the eleventh volume of this journal (pp. 161-205), Lottner
subjected the exceptions of the first sound-shift to a careful examination. He investigated all developments of the Indo-European stops
(tenues, mediae, and aspiratae) which seem to forsake the scheme

IE	k	= Gmc	h,	IE	g	=	Gmc	k,	IE	gh	= Gmc	g
	t	=	þ,		d	=		t,		dh	=	d
	p	=	f,		b	=		p,		bh	=	b,

and the now dead researcher found essentially two categories of exceptions, exclusive of the cases where no shift occurred due to certain consonantal combinations (IE sk, st, sp = Gmc sk, st, sp; IE kt,
pt = Gmc ht, ft). On the one hand, Lottner found that g, d, b were

sometimes present in Germanic unshifted, as for example in Goth. gredu-s 'hunger' beside Skt grdh-yati 'he is eager for', Goth. dauhtar 'daughter' beside Skt duhitar 'daughter', Goth. bindan 'to bind' beside Skt bandh 'to bind', and others. On the other hand, these same Germanic voiced stops (g, d, b) appeared in many cases not as correlatives of the Indo-European aspirates, as was to be expected, but as correlatives to the Indo-European voiceless stops (k, t, p); thus, for example, the Germanic form tegu 'decade', which corresponds to IE dakan 'ten', Gmc modar = IE mâtar, OHG ebar = Lat. aper, Goth. bairand 'they carry' = Skt bharanti etc.

The first class of exceptions, however, was soon afterwards accounted for by Grassmann. In his well-known article in the twelfth volume of this journal "On the original presence of roots, whose initial and final contained an aspirate," he establishes the fact that the anomalies cited by Lottner are only apparent, since in Skt grdhyati, duhitar, bandh and the like, we do not have the original Indo-European initial sound, which was rather an aspirate, as a comparison with other Indo-European languages attests, and therefore the voiced stop in the Germanic form is fully justified.

Compared with the first very extensive class of exceptions found by Lottner, the second class may not be cleared up in such a way. Here there is really a violation of the sound laws and apparently the guilt falls exclusively on Germanic. The irregular sound change occurs only medially and then only in a voiced environment. I cite some examples of this irregular shifting with differing sound-positions medially:

Gmc g = IE k. Gmc saga f. 'saw' (ON sög, OHG saga); compare Lat. sec-o, OSl. sěką 'I hew', Lith. sýki-s 'strike, time'. Gmc sagjan 'to say' (ON segja, OS seggian, OE secgan, OHG sagian) = Lith. sak-ýti, -aú 'to say'; compare ἐν-νεπ-ε for *ἐν-σεπ-ε and OLat. in-sec-e 'quote, tell'. Goth. hals-aggan- m. 'curve of the neck', OE angan- m. 'point, arrowhead'; compare Skt anka- m. 'hook, clasp; joint, side, lap' = ὄγχο-s = Lat. uncu-s 'hook'. Gmc þegna- m. 'boy, servant, warrior' (ON þegn 'free man, warrior', OS thegan 'boy, man, warrior', OE þegn 'knight', OHG degan 'boy, servant, warrior') = τέκνο-ν 'child'. Along with this compare successively the following examples of the regular shift in similar medial sounds: Goth. haiha- 'one-eyed' = Lat. caecu-s 'blind'. Gmc hlahjan 'to laugh' (Goth. hlahjan, ON hlæja, OE hlehhan, hlyhhan, OHG hlahhan); compare Skt kark 'to laugh', κλώσσω for *κλωκ-jω 'I cluck, click (the tongue)'. Gmc fanhan 'to catch' (Goth. fâhan, ON fá, OS fâhan, OE fôn, OFris. fâ, OHG fâhan); compare Skt pâç-aya-ti 'he binds', Lat. pac-iscî, pax, pâc-is. Gmc laihna- n. 'fief' (ON lân, OE læn, OHG lêhan) derived from lêhvan 'to lend' (Goth. leihvan, ON ljá, OS far-lîhan, OHG lîhan); compare Skt ric, pres. riṇak-ti and recati 'to leave' = λείπω, έ-λιπ-ον = linquo, līqui = Lith. lĕk-u, lìk-ti.

Gmc d̲ = IE t̲. Goth. fadi- m. 'master', only in compounds, as for example brūp̲-fadi- 'bridegroom' = Skt pati- m. 'master, husband' = πόσι-s = Lith. pàt-s 'lord and master'. Gmc þeuda- f. 'people' (Goth. þiuda, OS thioda, OHG diota) = Lith. (Zemaitic) tautà, Latvian tauta, Umbrian tūtu. Gmc þridjan- 'the third' (Goth. þridjan-, ON þriði, OS thriddio, OE þridda, OHG dritjo, dritto) = Skt tṛtīya-, Lat. tertiu-s, Lith. trécza-s, OSl. tretii. Gmc fedvôr 'four' (Goth. fidvor, ON fjórir, OS fiuuar, OE feóver, OHG fior) = Skt. catvâras, τέσσαρες, quatuor, Lith. keturì, OSl. četyrije. Gmc and- 'against, ant-' (Goth. anda-, and-, ON, OE and-, OHG ant-); compare Skt anti 'against' ἀντί, ἄντα 'against'. Lat. ante. Gmc andja- m. 'end' (Goth. andja-, ON endi-r, OS endi, OE ende, OHG enti- m.n.); compare Skt. anta- m. 'end', antya- adj. 'he who is final, the last'. Gmc skordi- f. 'to shear, cut' (ON skurð-r m. i-stem, 'cutting, mowing', OHG scurt- f. 'tonsure') formed from the root skar 'to cut' by means of the suffix -di = IE -ti. Gmc skoldi- f. 'guilt' (ON skuld, skyld, OS sculd, OE scyld, OHG sculd) by means of the same suffix from the root skal 'should'. Compare with this the following cases of regular shifting: Gmc hvaþara- 'both' (Goth. hvaþar, ON hvár-r, OS hueðar, OE hväðer, OHG hwedar, wedar) = Skt katar- = πότερο-s, Ionic κότερο-s = Lith. katrà-s. Gmc hleuþa- n. 'hearing, listening, silence' (Goth. hliuþa-, ON hljóð) = OBactrian çraota- n. 'hearing'. Gmc niþja- m. 'relative, cousin' (Goth. niþja-, ON nið-r, OE niððas pl.m. 'men'); compare OSl. netii m. 'nephew', ἀ-νεψ ιό-s 'cousin, relative' from a base form *napatja-, compare Skt. napât-, naptar- 'grandson, nephew, descendant', Lat. nepôt-. Goth. saliþva- f., only in the pl. saliþvos 'shelter, lodging', formed by means of the suffix -þva = IE -tva fromthe verb stem salja- 'to put up at'. Gmc tanþu-, tanþ- m. 'tooth' (Goth. tunþu-, ON tönn f., OS tand m., OE tôð, OHG zand) = Skt. dant-, dantâ- m., ό-δoύs, ό-δόντ-os m., Lith. danti-s m. f. Gmc an-þja- n. 'forehead' (ON enni, OHG andi); cp. ἀντίο-s 'that which is opposite, opposed', Lat. antiæ 'hair on the forehead'. Gmc morþa- 'murder' (ON morð, OE morð, OS morð, OHG mord), formed from the root mar 'to die' by means of the suffix -þa = IE -ta. Goth. vulþu- m. 'grandeur' = Lat. vultu-s, from the root val 'to desire' by means of the suffix -þu = IE -tu.

Gmc. b̲ = IE p̲. Gmc seban 'seven' (Goth. sibun, ON sjau, OS, OHG sibun, siban, OE seofon) = Skt saptan, ἑπτά, septem. On the other hand with regular shifting: Gmc nefan- m. (the Germanic basic form must be posited with f̲ after OHG nevo 'nephew, sister's son, uncle, relative'; ON nefi, OE nefa); cf. Skt. napât- m. 'descendant, grandson', Lat. nepôt-.

But this differentiation of the originally voiceless stops takes

place not only, as in the above examples, in forms originating from
different roots; it also appears very frequently within word formations belonging to the same root, so that some derivations show in
Germanic voiceless fricatives in the root, the other derivations
voiced stops. Thus beside Gmc tehan 'ten' (Goth. taihun, ON tíu,
OS tỹn, OHG zehan = Skt daçan, δέκα, decem) is found a substantive
tegu- m. 'a ten' (Goth. tigu-, ON tig-r, tug-r, OHG -zig, -zog); beside Gmc hauha- 'high' (Goth. hauha-, ON há-r, OS hôh, OE heáh,
OHG hôh) a form hauga- m. 'hill' (ON haug-r, MHG houc, gen.
houges); beside teuhan 'to draw' (Goth. tiuhan, OS tiohan, OHG
ziohan = Lat. dûco) Gmc tuga- 'pull' (ON tog n., OHG zug m.), Gmc
taugi- f. 'cord' (ON taug f., OE teág) and Gmc haritugan- m.
'commander-in-chief' (ON hertogi, OS heritogo, OE heretoga,
OHG herizogo); beside Gmc fanhan 'to catch' the substantive fanga-
'catch' (ON fang n., OHG fang m.); beside Gmc slahan 'to beat'
(Goth., OS, OHG slahan, ON slá, OE sleán) Gmc slaga- 'blow' (ON
slag n., OE slagu f., OHG slaga f.); beside OHG swehur m. and OE
sveor m. 'father-in-law' (= Skt çvaçura-, ἑκυρό-s, socer, OSl.
svekrŭ, Lith. szeszura-s) OHG swigar f., OE sveger f. 'mother-
in-law' (= Skt. çvaçrû, ἑκυρά, socru-s, OSl. svekry); beside ON flá
from *flahan 'flay' ON flaga wk. f. 'layer' and flagna 'come off (the
skin from the flesh)'; beside Gmc felhan 'to hide' (Goth. filhan, ON
fela, OHG felahan) Goth. fulgina- 'hidden' and ON fjalg-r in compounds 'safe, well kept', and others. In the dental series we have for
example Goth. hinþan 'to capture, take prisoner', Swed. hinna st.verb,
Dan. dialect hinne 'to reach' beside the Germanic form connected with
it handu- 'hand' f. (Goth. handu-, ON hönd, OS hand, OE hond, OHG
hant, hand); Gmc finþan 'to find' (Goth. finþan, ON finna, OS fîðan,
OHG findan) beside ON fund-r, stem fundi- m. 'gathering'; Goth.
fraþan 'to understand, to be reasonable' beside Gmc frôda- 'intelligent, reasonable' (Goth. froda-, ON fróð-r, OS, OE frôd, OHG fruot);
Gmc lîþan 'to go' (Goth. leiþan, ON líða, OS lîða, OS lîðan, OE lîðan,
OHG lîdan) and liþu- m. 'limb' (Goth. liþu-, ON lið-r, OE lið, OHG lid)
beside Gmc laidjan 'to lead' (ON leiða, OS lêdian, OE lædan, OHG
leittan) and laida- f. 'way' (ON leið, OE lâd); Goth. soþa- m. 'satisfaction' ga-soþjan 'to sate' beside Gmc sada- 'satisfied' (Goth. sada-, ON
sað-r, OS sad, OHG satt = OSl. sytŭ cf. Lat. satur, sat, satis) and
others. In the labial series, f and b have fused through secondary
sound changes into one sound in most of the Germanic languages, thus
obliterating the differentiation originally present. From Gothic, which,
like Old High German, kept the two sounds distinct, these forms can
be cited: af-lif-nan 'remain over' beside laiba- f. 'remainder'.

If one surveys the cited examples, one may easily be tempted to
explain this entire differentiation of the originally voiceless stops
as a caprice of the language, to ascribe simply to mere chance the

appearance of the voiced stops in many cases where the voiceless
fricative would be expected. Yet just to cite still another striking
example, the three identically formed Indo-European relationship
terms bhrâtar, mâtar, patar correspond to the Germanic correlatives brôþar, môdar, fadar, though there is no apparent reason why
môdar and fadar do not follow the regularly shifted brôþar. One
cannot however persist in the hypothesis that this was a chance occurrence. Comparative linguistics cannot, to be sure, completely
deny the element of chance; but chance occurrence en masse as
here, where the instances of irregular shifting are nearly as frequent as those of regular shifting, it cannot and may not admit.
That is to say, in such a case there must be a rule for the irregularity; it only remains to discover this.

Let us first clarify the phonological event. One can readily accept the fact that the Germanic voiceless fricative resulted directly
from the Indo-European voiceless stop by a relaxing of the oral closure. On the other hand, the Germanic voiced stop cannot have resulted directly from the Indo-European voiceless stop by voicing,
for this would be a sound innovation directly counter to the main direction of the sound shift, which produced a voiceless stop from the
Indo-European voiced stop. One must therefore attempt to arrive
indirectly from the voiceless stop to the voiced stop, and then the
best proposal is Scherer's explanation in the fine section concerning
the sound-shift (Geschichte der deutschen Sprache, p. 82): "I now
assume that all irregularly shifted tenues were first shifted regularly to voiceless spirants, that these, particularly in frequently
used words (like fadar, môdar), were under the influence of the sur-
rounding voiced elements also produced with voice and then, with
the beginning of the third part of the shift, took the direction of all
the remaining voiced spirants or voiced affricates." If one wants to
assert that in the above explanation the so-called affricates (Rum-
pelt, Deutsche Grammatik I, section 27) must generally be substituted for spirants, then one may do this; it is itself of little importance and especially for our purposes will be a matter of complete
indifference, since it is enough for us to have determined that the
irregular shifts also followed at one time the sound stage of the
regular shifts; from there, however, they progressed further.[1] And
we can now phrase the question of the etymological explanation thus:
Why did the sound current of the shift in some cases stop with the
voiceless fricative and in other cases progress further through the
voiced fricative to the voiced stops?

The only person who has sought an answer to this question, as
far as I know, is Scherer in the passage just cited. He assumes that
the shift to voiced stops occurs "in frequently used words (like fadar,
môdar)"; consequently the regular shift occurs in less frequently

used words. I believe that the venerable author did not wish to attach great weight to this attempt at explanation and that he permitted himself to mention it only as a conceivable possibility. A careful scrutiny of the Germanic vocabulary is not favorable to his thesis. Is it probable that fadar and môdar were used more frequently than brôþar? In Ulfila's writings moreover môdar does not even appear, the word aiþei always being used instead; and he uses fadar only once, otherwise however atta, while his broþar has no parallel synonym at all.

Could fehu-, the Germanic epitome for material well-being, cattle, money, wealth, possessions and the like, have been a more infrequently occurring word than, for example, lagu- 'lake' (ON lög-r, OE lagu = Lat. lacu-s)? May one assume that our Germanic ancestors used the numbers 4 and 100 (fedvôr, hund) more frequently than the number 10 (tehan)? More such examples could be cited; I will, however, find occasion in what follows to demonstrate the improbability of that thesis.

An attempt to find an etymological rule for the differentiation of the Proto-Germanic voiceless fricative into voiceless fricative and voiced stop by means of a juxtaposition of the Germanic word stock with the comparable word stock of the other Indo-European languages cannot lead to any certain result; for precisely because the differentiation manifests itself so actively in word formation, one cannot be satisfied with a comparison of root-related words; rather, a juxtaposition of words which are identical wherever possible is required, and in this way the comparable materials will become too small for something reliable to be built on it. Happily, however, the investigation can be transferred to another sphere which is significantly more circumscribed and where we can find certain bases for our conjectures. Not enough importance has been placed on the fact that the differentiation of the Proto-Germanic voiceless fricative also appears in the conjugation of certain verbs.[2]

When, for example, we have for OE lî ðe 'navigo, proficiscor' a participal form lidan, then here there is apparently the same differentiation as in lið 'limb' as against lid 'vehicle'. That Germanic philology has until now so readily ignored this fact, which is very interesting in itself and demands reflection — for a modification of the root consonant for the purpose of conjugation does not belong to the realm of the commonplace — may have its basis in the fact that Gothic, from which one usually proceeds in a comparison, does not even know this differentiation in the conjugation. It can, however, be established through compilation of the relevant materials that this differentiation in the conjugation originally belonged to all the Germanic languages, and consequently that it must also at one time have been present in Gothic. The Germanic voiceless fricatives and voiced stops which arose from the Indo-European voiceless stops are so distributed in the conjugation, that all present tense verb forms (inf., pres. ind., subj., imper., and part.) as well as the singular forms of the preterite indicative show voiceless fricatives and all remaining verb forms show voiced stops. I must completely disregard the labial differentiation in the following compilation; it was alluded to above that the differentiation of the labial in word formation was almost completely effaced by later falling together of the sounds; there is no longer any trace to be found in the conjugation.

A. Verbs, whose roots in Indo-European end in k̲, in Germanic in h̲ (h̲v), g̲:

1) root slah, slag 'ferire'[3]
ON   slá, sló, slógum, sleginn.
OS   slahan, slôh (slôg), slôgun, slagan.
OE   sleán, slôh (slôg), slôgon, slägen.
OFris.   slâ, slôch, slôgon, e-slein.
OHG   slahan, sluoh (MHG sluoc), sluogum, slagan.
     OS, OE slôg, MHG sluoc through the influence of the plural forms; thus frequently in the following forms.

2) root þvah, þvag 'lavare'.
ON   þvá, þvó, þvógum, þveginn.
OS   thuahan, (thuôg), [thuôgun, thuagan].
OE   þveán, þvôh, þvôgon, þvägen.
OHG   dwahan, dwuoh (MHG dwuoc), dwuogum, dwagan.

3) root lah, lag 'vituperare'.
OS   lahan, (lôg), [lôgun, lagan].
OE   leán, lôh (lôg), lôgon, [lägen].
OHG   lahan, (luog), luogum, [lagan].

4) root flah, flag 'excoriare'.
ON   flá, fló, flógum, fleginn.

5) root klah, klag 'fricare'.
ON   klá, kló, klógum, kleginn.

6) root vah, vag 'mentionem facere'.
OHG   [ge-wahan], -wuoh, -wuogum, [-wagen].

7) root hlah, hlag 'ridere', makes its present forms by means of -ja-.
ON   hlæja, hló, hlógum, hleginn.
OS   ?   [hlôh], hlôgun, hlagan.
OE   hlehhan hlyhhan, hlôh (hlôg), hlôgon, [hlägen].
OHG   hlahhan, (hluoc)   ?   ?

8) root fah, fag 'laetari'.
OE   ge-feón, -feah, fægon, [fegen].
OHG   ge-fehan, -fah, -fâhum, -fehan has abandoned the differentiation.[4]

9) root sahv, sagv 'videre'.
OS   sehan, sah, sâgon sâuuun (sâhun), seuuan (sehan).
OE   seón, seah, sægon sâvon, seven.
OFris.   sia, (sag), sagen, sien.
OHG   sehan, sah, (sâhum), sewan (sehan).
The v, which is only manifested in the preterite forms, must also be regarded as a kind of differentiation.
ON   sjá, sá, sáum, sénn does not show the differentiation.

10) root falh, falg 'commendare, abscondere'.
ON   fela, fal, (fálum), folginn.
OE   feolan (felgan), fealh, fulgon (fêlon fælon), (folen, feolen).
ON fulgum is to be expected in the preterite plural; fálum is formed by analogy with fela fal, as if the verb belonged to the second ablaut class (stela, stal, stálum); likewise OFris. bi-fellan for *bi-felhan has gone over to the second ablaut class (bi-fel, -fælon, -felen). OS bi-felahan, -falah, -fulhun, -folhan and OHG felahan, falah, fuluhum, folohan are without differentiation.

11) root tih, tig 'demonstrare, nuntiare'.
OS   tîhan, [têh, tigun, tigan].
OE   teón tîhan, tâh, [tigon], tigen.
OHG   zîhan, zêh, zigum, zigan.
ON   tjá has become weak.

12) root þih, þig 'crescere, proficere'.
OS   thîhan, [thêh, thigun], thigan.
OE   þeon þîhan, þâh (þeah), þigon (þugon), þegen (þogen).
OHG   dîhan, dêh, digum, digan.

13) root sihv, sigv 'colare, liquare'.
OE   seón, sâh, sigon, [sigen].
OHG   sîhan, sêh, [sigum], sigan siwan (sihan).

14) root vrih, vrig 'operire'.
OE   vreón vrîhan, vrâh, vrigon, vrigen.
OHG   (int-) rîhan, [-rêh] -rigum, -rigan.

15) root lihv, ligv 'commodare'.
OS   (far)- lîhan, [-lêh], -liuuum (-lihun), -liuuan.
OE   lîhan, lâh, [ligon, ligen].
OHG   lîhan, lêh, liwum, liwan (lihan).
Compare No. 9 — ON ljá, OFris. lîa have become weak.

16) root tuh, tug 'trahere'.
    ON   -----   -----   -----   toginn.
    OS   tiohan, tôh, tugun (tuhun), togan.
    OE   teón, teáh, tugon, togen.
    OFris. tîa, tâch, tegon, tein.
    OHG   ziohan, zôh, zugum, zogan.

17) root þluh, þlug 'fugere'.
    OS   fliohan, flôh, [flugun, flogan].
    OE   fleón, fleáh, flugon, flogen.
    OFris. flîa, ----, flegen, flain.
    OHG   fliohan, flôh, flugum, flogan.

B. Verbs, whose roots in Indo-European end in t, in Germanic in þ, d.

Old Norse cannot be compared here, since þ and d medially fell together in one sound. Also in the conjugation, Old Saxon merged the two sounds in ð, while keeping them otherwise distinct. It can however be perceived from ON finna, OS fîðan, that both languages at one time recognized the difference in the conjugation, even in the dentals. In OHG, Gmc þ is shifted to d medially (in the Low Franconian Isidore to dh) and Gmc d is shifted to t (in Isidore to d).

1) root kvaþ, kvad 'dicere'.
    OE   cveðan, cväð, cvædon, cveden.
    OHG   quedan, quad, quâtum (quâdum), quetan. In Isidore
             quhedhan (quhedan), quhâdum, quhedan.

2) root fanþ, fand 'invenire'.
    ON   finna, fann, fundum (funnum), fundinn (funninn).
    OS   fîðan (findan), (fand), fundun, fundan.
    OHG   findan, fand, funtum (fundum), funtan (fundan).
    OE   findan, OFris. finda with d throughout.

3) root varþ, vard 'fieri'.
    OE   veorðan, vearð, vurdon, vorden.
    OFris. wertha, warth, worden, worden.
    OHG   werdan, ward, wurtum, wortan. In Isidore uuerdhan
             (uuerdan), (uuard), uurdum, uuordan.

4) root liþ, lid 'ire, proficisci'.
    OE   lîðan, lað, [lidon] (liðon), liden (liðen).
    OHG   lîdan, leid, litum, litan.

5) root sniþ, snid 'secare'.
    OE   snîðan, snâð, snidon, sniden.
    OFris. snîtha, snêth, sniden, snein (snithen).
    OHG   snîdan, sneid, snitum, snitan.

6) root vriþ, vrid 'ligare, torquere'.
   OE   vrîðan, vrâð, [vridon] (vriðon), [vriden] (vriðen).
   OHG   rîdan, [reid, ritum, ritan] (ridan).

7) root miþ, mid 'evitare'.
   OE   mîðan, mâð, [midon, miden] (miðen).
   OHG   mîðan, meid, mitum, mitan.

8) root skriþ, skrid 'gradi'.
   OE   scrîðan, scrâð, scridon [scriden] (scriðen).

9) root suþ, sud 'coquere'.
   OE   seóðan, seáð, sudon, soden.
   OHG   siodan, (sôt), [sutum], sotan.

10) root hruþ, hrud 'ornare'.
    OE   hreóðan, [hreáð, hrudon], hroden.

The above verbs all belong to the various ablaut classes; of the
verbs which in Germanic originally formed their preterite by means
of reduplication, only two show differentiation; they, however, do so
in such a way that the voiceless fricative is found only in the present
forms, while the preterite singular conforms to the remaining preterite forms and shows a voiced stop.

1) root fanh, fang 'capere'.
   ON   fá, fékk (for * fénk, *féng), féngum, fenginn.
   OS   fâhan, fêng, fêngun, fangan.
   OE   fôn (from *fôhan, * fonhan, *fanhan), fêng, fêngon,
           fangen.
   OFris. fâ, fêng, fêngon, fangen fenszen.
   OHG   fâhan, fiang, fiangum, fangan.

2) root hanh, hang 'pendere'.
   ON   (hanga), hékk, héngum, hanginn.
   OS   [hâhan, hêng, hêngun], hangan.
   OE   hôn, hêng, hêngon, hangen.
   OHG   hâhan, hiang, hiangum, hangan.

Certainly no one would think of interpreting all these cases as
special developments within the individual languages. It would be
quite unthinkable that the five languages here treated changed the h
in the preterite participle of slahan, for example, to g independently
of one another. The differentiation in conjugation must therefore
have existed already at a stage of development common to the five
languages; indeed even where this differentiation can be established
only for one particular language, it may be viewed as a common
possession, for a phenomenon which operates in such a special
sphere and is due to an insignificant acoustical difference would
hardly have been able to produce forms by analogy. If, however, the

differentiation in conjugation was common to the five languages, then Gothic must also once have participated in it. This language, which recognizes the differentiation in word formation, shows consistently the voiceless fricative in the conjugation of verbs, which in the other Germanic languages have the differentiation: slahan, sloh, slohum, slahans; leiþan, laiþ, liþum, liþans; vairþan, varþ, vaurþum, vaurþans; fâhan, fai-fâh, fai-fâhum, fâhans etc. The more frequently occurring present forms won out over the preterite forms and forced their root consonants on them; in this we may see a manifestation of the strong tendency toward uniformity of this language idiom, which also manifests itself elsewhere, for example, in Gothic i, u as against the e, i and o, u respectively of the other Germanic languages. The differentiation in conjugation, therefore, already belonged to the Germanic original language.

If, however, the differentiation in conjugation had its origin in the same language period in which the differentiation in word formation also originated, then it is self-evident that both are simply manifestations of one and the same sound shift; they must therefore be interpreted from one unified viewpoint, a common explanation must be sought for them. The following equation will be generally valid:

$$\frac{\text{Gmc tehan}}{\text{Gmc tegu-}} = \frac{\text{slahana- (inf. stem)}}{\text{slagana- (pret. part. stem)}} = \frac{\text{brôþar}}{\text{môdar}} = \frac{\text{kveþana- (inf.)}}{\text{kvedana- (part.)}}$$

An explanation which is suitable only for one of the differentiations or only for quite isolated cases of the differentiation[5] has thereby the appearance of improbability. Even if the above-cited explanation by Scherer could with great difficulty be adapted to the differentiation in word formation, it still could not be applied to the differentiation in conjugation because one would then have to make the foolish assertion that the plural forms of the preterite indicative, which show the voiced stop (OS slôgun), are more frequently used than the plural forms of the present indicative, which have the voiceless fricative (OS slahad), and that the preterite participle (OS slagan) is more frequent than the infinitive (OS slahan).

From the regular occurrence of differentiation in the conjugation of these verbs, the important conclusion may now be drawn that the differentiating force must be sought in a certain phonetic relationship which varyingly accompanied the conjugation. Through this conclusion the investigation is confined to rather narrow limits. The differentiation took place after the sound-shift had begun; therefore it is peculiar to Germanic. The differentiating impetus, on the other hand, must be older and may very well have already belonged to the Indo-European language. Consequently, this impetus must be sought in that language stage which has its end members in the underlying Indo-European forms on the one hand and on the other, in the forms to which one can attain through a compilation of the Germanic languages. Fortunately, the principal forms of the Germanic strong verbs are transparently clear back to Indo-European. The Indo-European conjugation is based on the following four means of formation:

1) varying ending
2) varying root vowel
3) the use or non-use of augment and reduplication
4) varying accent

These and no others.

If one now looks at a series of Germanic basic forms, for example:

kveþana-,	kvaþ,	kvâdum,	kvedana-,
slahana-,	slôh,	slôgum,	slagana-,
lîþana-,	laiþ,	lidum,	lidana,

it is readily apparent that the phonetic basis for the differentiation cannot lie in the phonological material of the endings: the endings of the infinitive stem (kveþ-ana-, slah-ana-, lîþ-ana-) is the same as that of the participle stem (kved-ana-, slag-ana-, lid-ana-) and yet differentiation is present. Secondly, the basis cannot be sought in the quantitative aspects of the roots, for the voiceless fricative appears with long as well as short root vowels (lîþana-, slôh; kveþana-, kvaþ, slahana-); the same is true of the voiced stop (slôgum; kvedana-, slagana-). And these same quantitative conditions were already present in Indo-European. Thirdly, and finally the use or non-use of reduplication — the augmented verb forms have been lost in Germanic — could not have caused the differentiation, since then we would have to have for some forms the same root consonants in the entire preterite indicative, which is not the case; for others outside the conjugation, a special explanation would have to be given for the differentiation, since reduplication is essentially a purely verbal process.

Consequently, only one explanation remains and it is no desperate hypothesis, to which I must take recourse because all other attempts at explanation have failed, but rather a decision which has of necessity thrust itself upon me by sober argumentation: The differentiation must be based on the fourth means of formation of the conjugation, on the varying Indo-European accent. This assumption is confirmed in the highest degree by a confrontation of the Germanic verb forms with the corresponding forms of the Sanskrit verbs. When the accent in Sanskrit rests on the root syllable, we have the voiceless fricative for the root final in Germanic; on the other hand,

when the accent in Sanskrit falls on the ending, the Germanic forms
show a voiced stop for the root final. In the following compilation,
I am juxtaposing to the Sanskrit forms first the etymologically corresponding Germanic paradigm and then a paradigm with the differentiation. Since we are concerned here only with the root final, I
am citing the Germanic forms with Gothic endings.

A. The accent rests in Sanskrit on the root; the root final is a
voiceless fricative in Germanic.

a. Skt pres. ind. = Gmc pres. ind.

sg.	1.	bhédâmi	=	bîta	lîþa
	2.	bhédasi	=	bîtis	lîþis
	3.	bhédati	=	bîtiþ	lîþiþ
pl.	1.	bhédâmas	=	bîtam	lîþam
	2.	bhédatha	=	bîtiþ	lîþiþ
	3.	bhédanti	=	bîtand	lîþand

b. Skt pres. potential = Gmc pres. subj.

sg.	1.	bhédeyam	=	bîtau	lîþau
	2.	bhédes	=	bîtais	lîþais
	3.	bhédet	=	bîtai	lîþai
pl.	1.	bhédema	=	bîtaima	lîþaima
	2.	bhédeta	=	bîtaiþ	lîþaiþ
	3.	bhédeyus	=	bîtaina	lîþaina

c. Skt. pres. imper. = Gmc pres. imper.

sg.	2.	bhéda	=	bît	lîþ
pl.	2.	bhédata	=	bîtiþ	lîþiþ

d. Skt pres. part. act. = Gmc pres. part. act.

bhédant-   =   bîtand-   lîþand-

e. Skt verbal substantive = Gmc infinitive

bhédana-   =   bîtan   lîþan

f. Skt perf. ind. sg. = Gmc pret. ind. sg.

1.	bibhéda	=	bait	laiþ
2.	bibhéditha	=	baist	laist[6]
3.	bibhéda	=	bait	laiþ

B. The accent in Sanskrit rests on the ending; the root final is
a voiced stop in Germanic.

a. Skt perf. ind. pl. = Gmc pret. ind. pl.

1.	bibhidimá	=	bitum	lidum
2.	bibhidá	=	bituþ	liduþ
3.	bibhidús	=	bitun	lidun

b. The Vedic Sanskrit forms vavṛjyús, tuturyáma and the like,
first recognized by Westergaard as perfect potential = Gmc preterite subjunctive.

sg.	1.	bibhidyám	=	bitjau	lidjau
	2.	bibhidyás	=	bitîs	lidîs
	3.	bibhidyát	=	biti	lidi

pl. 1. bibhidyáma = bitîma lidîma
    2. bibhidyáta = bitîþ lidîþ
    3. bibhidyús = bitîna lidîna

c. Forms in -ná- in Skt., usually called perf. part. pass. =
Gmc pret. part. pass.

      bhin-ná- for *bhid-ná- = bitana- lidana-[7]

Before I pursue further the rule which is disclosed here, I must
make a short digression concerning a relationship which has until
now remained obscure, but which finds its answer in this context. I
am referring to the relation between s and z(r) in the Germanic languages. The IE s corresponds in Gothic partly to r, partly but more
seldom and never initially, however, to z, whose phonetic value must
be established as a voiced dental fricative. The latter corresponds
in the other Germanic languages to an r, which is to be regarded as
a further development. In all respects, this differentiation of the
original s to s and z(r) in the Germanic languages is parallel to the
above-treated differentiation.

Thus we have for example Gmc auzan- n. 'ear' (ON eyra,[8] OS
ôra, OE eáre, OHG ôra = Lat. auris f. for *ausis, Lith. ausi-s f.,
OSl. ucho, stem ušes-); Gmc deuza- n. 'animal' (Goth. diuza-, ON
dýr, OS dior, OE deór, OHG tior; from the root dhus, which is in
OSl. dŭch-na-ti, dyš-ati 'to breathe', duchŭ 'anima', duša 'soul');
Gmc baza- 'bare' (ON ber, OS, OE, OHG, bar = OSl. bosŭ, Lith.
bása-s 'barefoot') etc. with voiced dental fricative; whereas Gmc
lausa- 'loose, empty' (Goth. lausa-, ON lauss, OS lôs, OE leás, OHG
lôs; from a root lus in Goth. fra-liusan 'to lose'), Gmc mûs-, mûsi-
f. 'mouse' (ON mús- f., OE mûs- f., OHG mûs- f. = Skt. mûsh-,
mûsha- m., μῦς, μυ-óς, Lat. mûs mûri-s, OSl. myšĭ- f.), Gmc nasa-
f. (ON nŏs, OE näse, OHG nasa = Skt. nâsâ f., Lat. nâsu-s, OSl.
nosŭ m., Lith. nósi-s f.) and others have preserved the voiceless
fricative.

The same differentiation is also found in the conjugation. One
example will suffice:

ON	kjósa, kaus, kurum kørum, korinn kørinn,
OS	kiosan, cos, curun, coran,
OE	ceósan, ceás, curon, coren,
OFris.	kiasa, kâs, keron, keren,
OHG	kiosan, kôs, kurum, koran.

Therefore, s and z(r) are distributed in the conjugation in full accord with the distribution of h g, and of þ d.

Here too Gothic avoids the differentiation, i.e. the voiceless
fricative of the present forms has spread to all the forms of kiusan,
friusan, fraliusan, driusan, visan etc.

All this demonstrates sufficiently that the differentiation of the

$\underline{s}$ to $\underline{s}$ and $\underline{z}(\underline{r})$ must in every way be viewed like the differentiation of the Proto-Germanic voiceless fricatives to Germanic voiceless fricatives and voiced stops. If at a certain time and under certain circumstances the three voiceless fricatives of the language: $\underline{h}$ (Brücke's χ^2), β (B.'s $\underline{s}^4$) and $\underline{f}$ (B.'s f^1) were voiced, i.e., to the sounds which Brücke designates by $\underline{y}^z$, z^4, w^1, it follows almost out of necessity that the fourth and last voiceless fricative of the language: $\underline{s}$ (B.'s $\underline{s}^3$) must also have been voiced (B.'s $\underline{z}^3$) at the same time and under the same conditions.[9] Therefore the basis for the differentiation of $\underline{s}$ to $\underline{s}$ and $\underline{z}(\underline{r})$ must likewise be sought in earlier accentual relationships, and we can augment the equation set up on p. 144 by the two members:

$$= \frac{\text{Gmc mûsi-}}{\text{Gmc deuza}} = \frac{\text{keusana-}}{\text{kuzana-}}$$

For the differentiation in its entirety, as will be clear from what follows, where the instances of differentiation also occurring outside root syllable are taken into consideration, the discovered rule must be formulated as follows:

IE $\underline{k}$, $\underline{t}$, $\underline{p}$ first shifted to $\underline{h}$, β, $\underline{f}$ in all environments; the voiceless fricatives thus originating, together with the voiceless fricative $\underline{s}$ inherited from Indo-European, then became voiced medially in voiced environments, but remained voiceless when they were the final sounds of accented syllables.

A simulated Indo-European word *akasatam developed in the Germanic region first to * $ax^2as^3as^4am$ (with Brücke's notation), then, however, further to *$\acute{a}x^2az^3az^4a$(m), *$ay^2\acute{a}s^3az^4a$(m), *$ay^2az^3\acute{a}s^4a$(m), *$ay^2az^3az^4\acute{a}$(m), according to whether the accent rested on the first, second, third, or fourth syllable. Later, the new Germanic accent principle came into being; z^3 remained a fricative; the other voiced fricatives, however, shifted to voiced stops; and IE *akasatam would then have appeared in Gothic in one of the following forms: *ahazad(am), *agasad(am), *agazaþ(am), *agazad(am).

The fact that the voiceless fricatives did not follow the general tendency and become voiced in accented syllables, is easy to explain physiologically. For the older period of Germanic we have to start with an accent which was not purely chromatic like the accent in Sanskrit and the Classical languages, but which, like modern accentuation, had something expiratory[10] about it, that is, was based on greater activity of the muscles of expiration and to the subsequently stronger exhalation of air. The essential distinction between the voiceless and voiced consonants is dependent on the position of the vocal cords (Brücke, Grundzüge der Physiologie, p. 8.56). For voiceless consonants, the vocal cords are wide open; the air stream

from the chest cavity has free passage: it is therefore more force-
ful than for voiced consonants, and this stronger expiration of air
manifests itself in the stops by a more rigid muscular occlusion and
a more powerful explosion. For voiced consonants on the other
hand, the vocal cords are brought together almost until they touch;
the narrow glottis hinders the free expiration of air; the air-stream
is therefore weaker, the occlusion in the oral cavity accompanying
the voiced stops and the explosion itself are not as energetic as
those of the voiceless stops. Therefore, the stronger expiration of
air is an element which the expiratory accent has in common with
the voiceless consonants. Accordingly the intensified air-stream
in the accented syllable could keep the voiceless fricative voiceless;
that is, it could hinder the vocal cords from becoming narrowed for
voicing, as happened with the normal expiration of air in the unaccented syllable.

I probably need not remark that here we must not employ the
modern hyphenation fa-dar, fin-þan; all the consonants following the
vowels belonged to the preceding syllable (fad-ar, finþ-an), as indeed
Germanic versification also attests (the Old Norse hendingar, asso-
nance rimes).

I have deduced my rule from the presence of differentiation in
the conjugation and it has been shown above that it suffices completely for the explanation of the root final in the conjugation. This
is, however, not enough. If the rule is to have general validity, then
it must also be able to explain the differentiation in all other cases;
it must also be applicable to those root consonants outside the conjugation and finally even for the endings, both inflectional and deri-
vational. I shall now turn my attention to this final test. I shall
conscientiously bring up even those isolated cases where the law is
not valid. I must again use Sanskrit as comparative member; only
rarely do I bring in Slavic and Lithuanian.

The enigma brôþar, môdar, fadar is resolved first of all. The
Sanskrit accentuation is bhrátar-, but mātár-, pitár-, and according
to the rule, in Germanic we must have brôþar in contrast with
môdar, fadar. Among other kinship names can be cited: Gmc snuza
f. 'daughter-in-law' (OHG snura, OE snóru f., ON snør f.), which
entirely corresponds with the Sanskrit word of the same meaning
snushā (= νυό-s, Lat. nuru-s, OSl. snŭcha, Russ. snochá). Gmc
nefan- m. 'descendant, nephew' = Skt nápât. Gmc svehra- m.
'father-in-law' (OE sveor, OHG swehur, MHG sweher; Goth.
svaihran-) = Skt. çváçura-, 'father-in-law' (ἑκυρό-s, Lat. socer,
Lith. szészura-s, OSl. svekrŭ, Russ. svjókor), whereas Gmc svegrâ
f 'mother-in-law' (OE sveger f., OHG swigar f.) goes back to Skt
çvaçrû f. 'mother-in-law' (ἑκυρά, Lat. socru-s, OSl. svekry, Russ.
svekróv' f.).

Of the numerals, Skt. daçan 'ten' and pañcan 'five' are paroxytone; to these correspond in Germanic tehan and fimf (Goth. fimf,
ON fimm, OS fîf, OE fîf, OHG fimf, finf = πέντε, πέμπε, Lat. quinque,
Lith. penkì, pènkios, OSl. pęti). On the other hand are Gmc fedvôr
'four' and hunda- n. 'hundred' (Goth. hunda- n., ON hund, OS hund,
OHG hunt) = Skt. catváras m., catvári n., catúr- and çatá- n., for
*çantá- (ἑ-κατό-ν, Lat. centu-m, Lith. szìmta-s, OSl. sŭto, Russ.
sto n.). Gmc seban 'seven' corresponds to Skt. saptán (Vedic Sanskrit, in the classical language accented sáptan = ἑπτά, Lat. septem).
Lith. túkstanti-s, OSl. tysąšta, tysęšta f. (for *tysantjâ), Russ.
týsjača f. 'thousand' is Gmc þúsundja- f.n. (Goth. þúsundi f., þúsundja
n.pl., ON þúsund f., OS thûsint n.pl., OE þûsend n., OHG dûsunt n pl.).
Gmc þridjan- 'third' corresponds to Skt. trtîya-. Gmc fedvôrþan-
'fourth' (ON fjórði, OS fiorðo, OE feóverða, feórða, OHG viordo)
does not correspond to Skt. caturthá-; perhaps the accentuation in
Gmc fedvôrþan- was however in agreement with the accentuation of
the Sanskrit cardinal number; cf. Lith. ketvîrta-s, Russ. četvjórtyj,
Bulg. četvrŭti.

Other comparable words are:

Gmc fehu-n. 'cattle' (Goth. faihu n., ON fé, OS fehu, OE feó, OHG
   fihu) is completely identical with Skt. páçu n. 'cattle' (so accented in the Vedas; the masculine form paçú-s is oxytone;
   Lat. pecu n.).

Gmc ehva- m. 'horse' (ON jó-r, OE eoh, OS ehu-skalk 'groom') =
   Skt. áçva- m. 'horse' (ἵππο-s Lat. equu-s).

Gmc volfa- m 'wolf' (Goth. vulfa- m., ON ulf-r, OS uulf, OE vulf,
   OHG wolf: the f of the Germanic base form assured by Gothic
   and OHG f) corresponds to Skt. vŕka- m 'wolf' (λύκο-s, Lat.
   lupu-s, Lith. vìlka-s, OSl. vlŭkŭ, Russ. voĺk, gen. vóĺka).

Gmc angan- m. 'curve, arrowhead' corresponds to Skt. aṅká- m.

Gmc haidu- m. 'appearance, way, manner' (Goth. haidu- m., ON
   heið-r, OE hâd, OHG heit m., cf. Einheit, Gleichheit etc.). Skt.
   ketú- m. 'appearance of light, brightness, clarity; appearance,
   form, figure'.

Gmc raþa- n. 'wheel' (OHG rad n.) = Skt. rátha- m. 'vehicle' for
   *rata- (Lat. rota, Lith. ráta-s).

Gmc hardu- 'hard, stringent' (Goth. hardu-s, ON harð-r, OS hard,
   OE heard, OHG hart) = κρατύ-s.

Gmc anþara- 'the other' (Goth. anþar, ON annar-r, OS ôðar, OE
   ôðer, OHG andar) = Skt. ántara- 'the other' (Lith. àntra-s).

Gmc undar- adv. and prep. 'under' (Goth. undar, ON undir, OS
   undar, OE under, OHG untar) = Skt antár adv. 'within', prep.
   'under' (Lat. inter, Oscan Umbrian anter).

Gmc tanþu-, tanþ- m. 'tooth' = Skt. dánta- m. 'tooth'.

Gmc sanþa- 'true' (ON sann-r, OS sôð, OE sôð) = Skt. sánt-,

present participle of the root as 'to be' (ἐόντ-, Lat. prae-
sent-)

Gmc anadi-f. 'duck' (ON ŏnd, OE ened, OHG anut) = Skt. âtí- f. 'a
certain waterfowl' νῆσσα, Lat. anati-, Lith. ánti-s f.).

Gmc maþla- n. 'speech' (Goth. maþla- n., 'place of assembly', but
maþljan, 'to speak'; ON mál, OE mäðel) = Skt. mántra- m.
'saying, poem, agreement, advice' (cf. OSl. moli-ti 'to ask,
pray', Bohem. modliti, Pol. modlić for *motliti = Lith. maldý-ti
'to ask', Goth. maþljan 'to speak'; Pol. modly f.pl. 'prayers',
Lith. maldà f. 'prayer').

Gmc hleuþra- n 'hearing' (OE hleóðor) = Skt. çrótra- n, 'hearing,
ear' (Avestan çraothra- n. 'hearing, causing to hear, singing').

Gmc þaþrô 'there' (Goth. þaþro, þaðra) = Skt. tátra 'there'.

Gmc feþra f. 'feather' (ON fjŏðr, OS feðara weak f., OE feðer st.f.,
OHG fedara) = Skt. pátra-, páttra- m. and n. 'wing, feather'
(πτέρο-ν, OSl. pero n.).

Gmc rôþra- m.n. 'oar, rudder' (ON rôðr m., OHG ruodar n.) = Skt
arítra- m. 'rudder', áritra- and arítra- n. 'steering rudder'.

Gmc nôsa f. 'nose' (OE nôsu; cf. ON nŏs f., OE näse f., OHG nasa f.)
= Skt. nâsâ f. 'nose' (Lat. nâsu-s, Lith. nósi-s f., OSl. nosŭ m.).

Gmc hazan- m. 'hare' (ON héri, OE hare, OHG haso, in which z has
reverted to s) = Skt çaçá- m. for *çasá- 'hare'.

Gmc fersna f. 'heel' (Goth. fairzna, OE fiersn, OHG fersna) = Skt.
pârshṇi f. 'heel' (= πτέρνα).

Goth. amsa- m. 'shoulder' = Skt. ámsa- m.n. 'shoulder' (ὦμο-s,
Lat. umeru-s).

Of the words for which the rule is not valid, I have noted the
following:

Gmc hvaþara- 'both' (Goth. hvaþar, ON hvár-r, OS hueðar, OHG
hwedar), but Skt. katará- (πότερο-s, Ionic κότερο-s, Lith.
katrà-s).

Gmc hersan- m. 'head' (ON hjarsi, hjassi), but Skt. çîrshán- n.
'head'.

Gmc hvehvla- n. 'wheel' (ON hjól, OE hveól, hveohl), but Skt. cakrá-
m.n. 'cart-wheel, circle' (= κύκλο-s).

Gmc maisa- m.f. 'sack, basket' (ON meis-s, OHG meisa), but Skt.
meshá- m. 'ram, the fleece of the sheep and what is made from
it' (Lith. maísza-s 'large sack', OSl. mĕchŭ m. 'hide, skin':
Bugge, Zeitschr. XX, p. 1).

Gmc fadi- m. 'master, husband', only as the last member of a compound (Goth. fadi- m.), but Skt. páti- m. 'master, husband'
(πόσι-s, Lith, pàti-s, pat-s).

In the Sanskrit causatives, the accent falls on the ending:
bhâráya- sâdáya-, vedáya-, etc. The Germanic causatives agree
with this accentuation, as may be seen from the following examples:

Gmc hlôgjan 'to make laugh' (ON hlœgja; Goth. uf-hlohjan with h by
   analogy with the basic verb), causative of hlahjan 'to laugh'.
Gmc hangjan 'to cause to hang' tr. (ON hengja, OHG hengan, henkan),
   causative of hanhan 'to hang' intr.
Gmc laidjan 'to lead' (ON leiða, OS lêdian, OE lædan, OHG leittan),
   causative of lîþan 'to go'.
Gmc fra-vardjan 'to spoil', causative of Goth. fra-vairþan 'to be
   ruined'.
Gmc sandjan 'to send' (Goth. sandjan, ON senda, OS sendian, OHG
   sentan; cf. Lith. siunczù 'I send'), causative of a lost verb
   sinþan 'to go', cf. sinþa- m. 'course, time' (Goth. sinþa-, ON
   sinn n., OS sîð, OHG sind).
Gmc nazjan 'to save' (OS nerian, OE nerjan, OFris. nera, OHG
   nerian: Gothic again by analogy nasjan), causative of nesan 'to
   recover'.
Gmc laizjan 'to teach' (ON læra, OS lêrian, OE læren, OHG lêran:
   Gothic by analogy laisjan), causative of a verb lîsan 'to know'
   inferable from Goth. lais 'I know'.
On the other hand, no Germanic causatives occur with h̲, þ, s̲, as
root final, since lausjan 'to loosen' (Goth. lausjan, ON leysa, OS,
OHG lôsian, OE lŷsan) is not the causative of leusan 'to lose', but
rather the denominative of lausa- 'loose'. We can therefore (as a
pre-Germanic form of the Skt. sâdáya- 'to set') assume a form
*satája-, more correctly perhaps *satíja. With the appearance of
the new principle of accentuation, we would have sátija-, and only
then the earlier stressed vowel of the ending was lost and satja-
resulted. In hlôgjan as against hlahjan, the evident contrast between
the causative-forming and the present tense-forming -ja should be
observed by the way; the latter required root stress (the fourth
class in Sanskrit).
   In Sanskrit, from the substantives which signify a masculine
being, the corresponding feminine forms are frequently constructed
by means of the suffix -î: devá- m., 'god', devî̃- f. 'goddess';
putrá- m. 'son', putrî̃- f. 'daughter'; meshá- m. 'ram', meshî̃- f.
'ewe'; sûkará- m. 'boar', sûkarî̃ f. 'sow'; mátsya- m. 'fish̃, f.
matsî̃; çván- 'dog' f. çunî̃; tákshan- m. 'carpenter', takshnî̃ f. 'wife
of the carpenter'; dhártar- 'carrier, supporter', f. -trî̃; bhártar-
'supporter, maintainer', f. -trî̃ etc. The feminine form is oxytone
even when the masculine form is accented otherwise. The Indo-
European form of this suffix must be posited as -yâ, as may be seen
from the corresponding Greek forms: σώτειρα for *σώτερ-ja,
τέκταινα for *τέκταν-ja = Skt. takshnî̃ for *takshan-yâ. This
feminine-forming suffix is also evident in Germanic, although more
seldom; thus we have from þeva- m. 'boy, servant' (Goth. þiu-s,
stem þiva-, þEWAR in the oldest Runic language, OE þeóv) a form

þivja- f. 'woman slave, maid-servant' (Goth. þivi, stem þiuja-, ON
þý, gen. þýjar, OS thiui, OHG diuwa) against galtu- m. 'castrated
swine' (ON gölt-r) a form goltja- f. 'sow' (ON gylt-r f.). Also explained thus is ON ylg-r f. 'she-wolf', stem ylgja-; the Germanic
form is *volgja, the feminine of volfa- m., which stands for *volhva-,
just as fimf for *finhv.[11] Gmc *volgja, therefore, also agrees in its
accentuation with vṛkī́ of the same meaning, just as volhva- agrees
with Skt. vṛ́ka-.

As can be seen, those cases of the differentiation of root consonants occurring outside the conjugation fit very nicely into the proposed rule. All that now remains is to establish the validity of the
rule even for those cases of differentiation occurring in the endings. In the above, we have already encountered an example in Gmc
þûsundja-; if the Pre-Germanic accent was situated on the first
syllable of this word, then the t of the ending had to appear in Germanic as d. Since the strong verbs in Germanic can, with only a
few isolated exceptions, be traced back to verbs of the first and
fourth Sanskrit classes, which accentuate the root syllable, we have
to expect Gmc d for the frequent t in the Indo-European conjugational endings. This is, in fact, the case. So we have Gmc d for IE
t in the following endings:

Gmc 3rd sg. pres. ind. berid (OS -d, OHG -t, Goth. -þ, according to
    the Gothic law of finals for -d, which also occurs) = Skt. bhárati,
    φέρει, fert.

Gmc 2nd pl. pres. ind. berid (Goth. -þ, for -d, which also occurs;
    OHG -t) = Skt. bháratha, φέρετε, fertis.

Gmc 2nd pl. pres. subj. beraid (Goth. -þ for -d, which also occurs;
    OHG -t) = Skt. bháreta, φέροιτε, ferâtis.

Gmc 2nd pl. pres. imper. berid (Goth. -þ, -d, OS -d, OHG -t) = Skt.
    bhárata, φέρετε, ferte.

Gmc 3rd pl. pres. ind. berand (Goth. -nd, OHG -nt) = Skt. bháranti,
    φέρουσι, ferunt.

Goth. 3rd sg. pres. ind. pass. bairada = Skt. bhárate, φέρεται.

Goth. 3rd sg. pres. subj. pass. bairaidau = Skt. bháreta, φέροιτο.

Goth. 3rd pl. pres. ind. pass. bairanda = Skt. bhárante, φέρονται.

Goth. 3rd pl. pres. subj. pass. bairaindau = φέροιντο (Skt. bháreran).

Goth. 3rd sg. imper. (mid.) bhairadau (atsteigadau ƒ Matthew 27, 42)
    = Skt. bháratâm.

Goth. 3rd pl. imper. (mid.) bhairandau (liugandau I Cor. 7,9) = Skt.
    bhárantâm.

Gmc pres. part. act. berand = Skt. bhárant-, φέροντ-, ferent-.

The s in the Indo-European conjugational endings becomes z in
the Goth. 2nd sg. pres. ind. pass. bairaza = Skt. bhárase, φέρῃ; in
subjunctive bairaiza = φέροιο (Skt. bhárethâs).

The second singular present form causes difficulties. The 2nd

sg. pres. ind. bhárasi in Sanskrit would according to our rule lead
to a Germanic basic form beriz. ON berr presupposes this basic
form; Goth. bairis can be traced back to beriz or beris; OS, OHG
biris only to beris; OE byrest and OFris. berst have been extended
by an epenthetic t. The 2nd sg. pres. subj. bháres, φέροις, ferâs
would lead to the Germanic basic form beraiz, which may also be
assumed from ON berir, OE and OFris. bere; Goth. bairais on the
other hand can be traced back to beraiz or to berais, OS beras and
OHG berês only to berais. I shall attempt an explanation of these
irregularities. For all the Germanic languages the basic form
beriz was at one time valid in the second singular present indicative.
The -z must have become -s in the special life of Gothic. In Old
Norse the -z remained and became -r in the further course of the
sound development. In the West Germanic languages, the -z should
have disappeared in accordance with the laws of finals applicable to
these languages; see Scherer, Zur Geschichte der deutschen Sprache,
p. 97ff. One would therefore expect in the West Germanic area a
form *beri or *ber for beriz; this apocopated form was, however,
too short for the language and could easily have been confused with
other forms; hence, the language sought, for the purpose of clarity,
to preserve the fuller form, a fact which so affected Old Saxon and
Old High German that they made the -z, which was impossible in
final position, voiceless; whereas Old English and Old Frisian
changed the -t originating in the 2nd person of the preterite-present
(OE þearf-t, vil-t, OFris. skal-t, wil-t) to s. The situation of the
subjunctive form is similar; the posited basic form beraiz regularly
becomes ON berir, Goth. bairais, OE, OFris. bere, whereas Old
Saxon and Old High German on the other hand have again established
-s.

The ending -tá- in the perfect participle passive in Sanskrit
corresponds in the Germanic weak verbs to the ending of the preterite participle passive -da-: Goth. tami-da = Skt. dami-tá, Lat.
domi-tu-s; Goth. sati-da = Skt. sâdi-tá-; frijô-da-, habai-da- etc.
With this same suffix are formed: Goth. munda- 'believed', participle of munan = Skt. matá- for *mantá-. Gmc kunda- (Goth. goda-
kunda- 'of good birth', OE feorran-cund 'originating from afar' =
Skt. jâtá- 'born' for *jantá-. Gmc hlûda- 'loud' (OE hlûd, OHG hlût)
Skt. çrutá- 'heard', κλυτό-s, Lat. (in)clutu-s. Gmc kalda- 'cold'
(Goth. kalda-, ON kald-r, OS kald, OE ceald, OHG calt) from the
root kal, ON kala strong verb 'to freeze': cf. Lat. gelu, gelidus,
gelare. Gmc alda- 'old' (OS ald, OE eald, OHG alt) = Lat. altus, cf.
ad-ultu-s, from the root al in ON ala = Lat. alere. Gmc dauða-
'dead' (ON dau ð-r, OS dôd, OE deád, OHG tôt, but Goth. dauþa- with
þ by analogy with the juxtaposed substantive Gmc dauþu- m., Goth.
dauþu, ON dau ðr, OS dô ð, OE deá ð, OHG tôd), from a root dau, ON

deyja, OS dôian, 'to die'. Probably here belongs also the fem. Gmc
þeuda 'people' from the Indo-European root tu, 'to grow' = Lith.
dialect tautâ, Latvian tauta, Umbrian tūtu).[12]

In Sanskrit, the primary suffix -ti- forms the feminine nomina
actionis, which are sometimes paroxytone, sometimes oxytone:
gáti- 'way, going' from the root gam 'to go', sthíti- 'standing' from
the root sthâ 'to stand', yúti- 'joining' from the root yu 'to yoke',
pītí- 'drink' from the root pā 'to drink', pūrtí- 'filling, granting'
from the root pṛ 'to fill', etc. That oxytonation was more widespread earlier is seen from the fact that a great many of these
forms are oxytone in the language of the Vedas which appear as
paroxytone in the later classical language; so for example kīrtí-
'thinking, mentioning', ishtí- 'impulse, wish', paktí- 'cooking, di-
gestion', bhūtí- 'powerful existence, vitality', matí- 'devotion, opinion, insight', râti-, 'bestowal, gift', vittí- 'finding, discovery', vītí-
'enjoyment', vṛshṭí- 'raining' and others; in the Classical language
kīrti-, íshti-, pákti- etc. In Germanic this suffix is -þi- or -di-.
Only rarely does it occur in the form -þi-: Goth. ga-qum-þi f.
'meeting', cf. the above-cited Skt. gáti- for *gámti-; Goth. gabaurþi-
f. 'birth' (root bar 'to bear'); more frequently, however, the suffix
occurs in the form -di-: Goth. ga-mun-di- f. 'memory' = Skt. matí-
for *mantí- 'understanding, opinion', Gmc spôdi- f. 'success' (OS
spôd, OE spêd, OHG spuot) = Skt. sphâtí-[13] 'growth, thriving', root
sphâ, sphâ-yati 'he puts on weight, becomes stouter' = OSl. spě-jetĭ
'he has success' = Lith. spė́-ja 'he has time, opportunity' = OE spê-
v-eđ 'he succeeds'; Gmc sâdi- f. 'seed' (Goth. m. mana-sedi-
'crowd of men', ON sáđ, OHG sât) from the root sâ 'to sow'; Gmc
skordi- f. 'shearing' (OHG scurt 'tonsure'), root skar 'to shear,
cut', cf. κάρσι-s 'shearing' and others.

By means of the secondary suffix -tâ f., Sanskrit quite frequently forms abstracts from adjective stems; which accent the
syllable preceding the suffix, as for example çuklátâ 'white substance' from çúkla- 'white' âryátâ 'an honorable bearing' from
ârya- 'Aryan, venerable', nyūnátâ 'defective condition' from nyûna-
'defective', krūrátâ 'cruelty' from krūrá- 'cruel', pangútâ 'lame-
ness' from pangú 'lame', pṛthútâ 'breadth' from pṛthú 'broad' etc.
The formations in -þa f. in Germanic which correspond in every
way are very numerous: so for example Gmc follíþa f. 'fullness'
(OHG fullida) = Skt. pûrnátâ 'fullness', from Gmc folla- 'full' (Goth.
fulla-, ON full-r, OS full, OE ful, OHG fol) = Skt. pûrná-, 'fullness';
Goth. gauriþa f. 'grief' from Goth. gaura- 'grieved', which is perhaps to be compared with Skt. ghorátâ 'horribleness' from ghorá-
'horrible'; Gmc hailiþa f. 'health' (OHG heilida) from haila- 'healthy,
well' (Goth. haila-, ON heil-l, OS hêl, OE hâl, OHG heil), to which
Skt. *kalyátâ from kalya- 'well' would correspond; Gmc sâliþa f.

'happiness' (OS sâlð̆a, OE sælð̆, OHG sâlida) from sâla-, sâlja 'happy' (Goth. sela-, ON sæl-l, OE sêl); Gmc deupiþa f. 'depth' (Goth. diupiþa, ON dýpt) from deupa- 'deep' (Goth. diupa-, ON djúp-r, OS diop, OE deóp, OHG tiuf) etc.

Goth. þivadva- n. 'servitude' from þiva- m. 'servant' corresponds to the frequent Sanskrit secondary forms in -tva-, as for example pitr̥tvá- n. 'fatherhood' from pitár- 'father'; patitvá- n. 'wedlock' from páti- m. 'husband, master'; jñātitvá- n. 'kinship' from jñāti- m. 'kinsman'; brâhmaṇatvá- n. 'Brahmin priesthood' from brâhmaṇá- m. 'Brahmin'. I do not know the feminine form of this suffix for Sanskrit; it appears however in Gothic in fijaþva f. 'enmity' from fijan 'to hate', frijaþva f. 'love' from frijon 'to love', saliþva, only pl. f. saliþvos 'lodgings, quarters' from saljan 'to stop at', and seems to be used for forming abstracts from verbal stems and in this is like the corresponding OSl. suffix tva- f., for example in žrŭ-tva- f. 'sacrifice' from the root žrŭ, inf. žrĕ-ti 'to sacrifice'; bitva f. 'battle' from bi-ti 'to beat'; klętva 'oath' from klę-ti 'to swear'; žętva 'harvest' from žę-ti 'to reap'; molitva 'prayer' from moli-ti 'to pray'; lovitva 'hunt, chase' from lovi-ti 'to chase'; selitva 'settling, dwelling' from seli-ti sę 'to settle, establish oneself'; cf. O někotorychŭ zakonachŭ Russkago udarenija Ja. Grota, St. Petersburg 1858, p. 41 (off-print from the Reports of the Second Department of the Academy, vol. VII). The newer Slavic languages which have maintained the free accent show an accentuation of the syllable preceding the suffix: Russ. žértva; Russ. bítva; Russ. kljátva = Bulg. klétvŭ = Serb. klêtva, which according to certain laws[14] stands for klétva; Russ. žátva = Bulg. žétvŭ = Serb. žètva for žetva; Russ. molítva = Bulg. molítvŭ = Serb. mòlitva for molítva; Russ. ƒovíta. The þ in the Germanic form of the suffix agrees with this accentuation; perhaps Goth. saliþva from saljan is the same word as OSl. selitva from seliti, although the latter goes back to *sedlitva from *sedliti (Bohem. sedliti, Pol. siedlić).

The primary suffix -as in Sanskrit forms neuter substantives which in meaning are usually nomina actionis and have the accent on the root syllable. Forms of this sort are found in all Indo-European languages; thus in Greek the neuter substantives in -ες-, nom. -ος, also with the accent always on the first syllable, in Latin in -or-, -er-, nom. -us: Skt. jánas = γένος = Lat. genus, Skt. árças 'wound' = ἕλκος = ulcus 'ulcer', Skt. sádas 'seat' = ἕδος, Skt. ándhas 'herb, plant' = ἄνθος 'flower', Skt. vácas 'word' = ἔπος, Skt. çrávas 'fame' = κλέος, Skt. sáras 'water' = ἕλος 'swamp', Skt. mánas 'spirit' = μένος 'courage, power', Skt. nábhas 'cloud' = νέφος, Skt. rájas 'dust, darkness' = ἔρεβος 'darkness of the underworld', Skt. yáças 'fame' = Lat. decus, Skt. ápas 'work' = opus, Skt. rádhas 'strength, wealth' = Lat. rôbur, Skt. áyas 'metal, bronze' = Lat. aes. In

agreement with the accentuation in Sanskrit the suffix in Germanic
has the form -ez(a); so Gmc aiza- n. for *ajez- 'ore' (Goth. aiza-,
ON eir, OE ær, OHG êr) = Skt. áyas, Lat. aes; Gmc seteza- n. 'seat'
(ON setr n. 'domicile', sólarsetr n. 'sunset') = Skt. sádas, ἔδος;
Gmc rekveza- n. 'darkness' (Goth. riqiza-, ON rökkr n.) = Skt.
rájas, ἔρεβος; Gmc bareza- n. 'barley' (ON barr n., Gothic in
bariz-eina- adj. 'barley') = Lat. far, gen. farr-is 'spelt'; Gmc
hateza- 'hate' (Goth. hatiza-, ON hatr); Gmc faheza- n. 'sheep' (ON
fær, OSwed., ODan. fár; see Steffensen in Tidskrift for filologi, New
Series, II, p. 70) = Lat. pecus, oris 'cattle'. Here Fick's correlation of Gmc aruza- n. 'scar' (ON ǫrr n.) with Skt. árus n. 'wound'
can also find its place.

 The Sanskrit gradation suffixes, comparative îyaṁs- and su-
perlative ishṭha- require accentuation of the stem syllable, even
when the accent falls on the endings in the positive degree: vára-
'excellent', váríyaṁs-, várishṭha-: dîrghá- 'long', drâghîyaṁs-,
drâghishṭha-; gurú-, βαρύς, gáríyaṁs-, gárishṭha-. This retracting
of the accent also occurs in Greek, as is well-known: ἡδύ- 'sweet'
= Skt. svâdú-, comp. ἥδιον = Skt. svâdíyaṁs-, sup. ἥδιστο- = Skt.
svâdishṭha; ἐλαχύ 'easy' = Skt. laghú-, comp. ἔλασσον- = Skt.
lághíyaṁs-, sup. ἐλάχιστο- = Skt. lághishṭha-; κακό- 'bad' κάκιον-,
κάκιστο-, etc. The accentuation of the newer Slvaic languages also
indicates this accent change, which may therefore be established as
Indo-European. In agreement with the root accentuation attested by
Sanskrit, Greek, and Slavic in gradation, the comparative suffix in
Germanic appears in the form -izan-, -ôzan-, in the adverbially
used neuter forms as -iz, -ôz: Gmc batizan-, 'the better' (Goth.
batizan-, ON betri, OS betiro, OE betra, OHG beʒiro); Gmc blindô-
zan- 'the blinder one' (Goth. blindozan-, ON blindari, OS blindoro,
OE blindra, OHG blindoro); Gmc batiz adv. 'better' (ON betr, OS
bat, bet, OE bet, OHG baʒ); Gmc nâhviz, nâhvôz adv. 'nearer' (Goth.
nehvis for nehviz, ON nærr, OS OHG nâhor); Gmc sîþôz adv. 'later'
(ON sîðar, OS sîðor, OHG sîdor). In Gmc junga- 'young' (Goth.
jugga-, ON ung-r, OS OHG jung, OE geong = Skt. yuvaçá- 'youthful',
Lat. juvencu-s, basic form *yuvanka-), comp. Gmc junhizan - (Goth.
jûhizan- for *junhizan-, ON œri, according to Thórodd with nasal œ
for *jôhizan-, *junhizan-) and superl. ON œst-r for *junhista-, may
reflect the change of accent in svâdú-, svâdiyaṁs-, svâdishṭha-,
ἡδύ-, ἥδιον-, ἥδιστο-; ON yngri, yngstr, OS jungaro, OE geongra,
gyngra, geongost, gyngest, OHG jungiro and the like may then be
viewed as later analogy formations.

 Finally, what may be said about the s, which occurs frequently
in Indo-European declensional endings? In the nominative singular
masculine the ending -s was to be expected according to our rule
for all originally oxytone and one-syllable stems: jungás, daudás,

hardús, haidús, kûs = Skt. gaus 'cow', hvas = Skt. kas 'who' etc.; for
all other stems, the ending -z: vólfaz, ámsaz, máisaz, sanþaz,
ánþaraz, dáuþuz, éhuz etc. In the genitive singular of the feminine
a-stems, -s and -z would similarly be expected according to the
accentuation: snuzós, þeudós, but nôsôz, férsnôz, follíþôz, salíþvôz
etc. So too in other declensional endings which include IE s. Germanic, however, generally shows only -z[15]: n. sg. m. volfaz (Goth.
vulfs, according to the Gothic law for finals for *vulfz, ON ulfr,
oldest Runic language -AR; in the West Germanic languages with
regular loss of the -z: OS uulf, OE vulf, OHG wolf); gen. sg. fem.
gebôz (Goth. gibos for *giboz, ON gjafar, OS gebo, geba, OE gife,
OHG gebo); n. pl. m. volfôz (Goth. vulfos for *vulfoz, ON ulfar, OHG
wolfa) etc. The language observed unity of inflectional endings.
Where the phonetic development would have impaired unity, the language suspended the sound law and monopolized the most frequently
occurring ending, and in the above case, that was the inflectional
ending of the non-oxytone stems. The third pl. ind. sind (Goth., OS,
OE sind, OHG sint) is just like this; Skt. sánti led to Gmc *sinþ; the
ending of the third plural indicative was -nd elsewhere however, and
sinþ had to submit to this.

We can now survey in broad outline the history of Germanic accentuation from the oldest Indo-European time up to the present.
The Indo-European accent was by nature purely chromatic, in position absolutely free. We must assume that in the Sanskrit accentuation — when we disregard the clearly non-original Svarita — we possess a relatively true picture of that ancient accentuation. In the
common European language period, the accent still had its original
character: that it was still purely chromatic is assured by the accent of the Classical languages; that, moreover, it still had its full
freedom is assured by the free accentuation of Lithuanian and several New Slavic languages. Only after Germanic had separated from
its closest neighbor, Slavo-Lithuanian, and had begun its special life,
do we encounter the accent somewhat changed in nature; it had become expiratory or perhaps, since it probably still retained along
with the expiratory accent its chromatic character, chromatic-
expiratory. But the Proto-Germanic accentuation had maintained,
with surprising integrity, the second characteristic feature of the
Indo-European accent, freedom. The transition to fixed accentuation (root accentuation) which followed is an analogical formation
which was thoroughly carried out. Those instances in which the accent rested on the root syllable were already in the majority under
the old accent principle, and this method of accentuation then spread
in Proto-Germanic, when those word forms which had the accent on
the ending gradually retracted it to the root syllable. From the
strict carrying out of root accentuation in all living Germanic

languages, it might be surmised that the transition to the new accent principle was already accomplished before the Germanic basic languages split into dialects. Contrary to this, however, are the pronominal forms unsih, inan, imo, iru, ira, which often count as oxytone in Old High German versification; their accentuation is difficult to explain otherwise than as an inheritance from the time of free accentuation, for the last four forms correspond successively to the Sanskrit oxytone forms imám, asmaí, asyaí, asyás (cf. Scherer, Z.G., p. 152). It must therefore be accepted, that, in the division of the Germanic basic language, the accentuation of the root syllable was indeed dominant, that, however, at the same time, forms with the old accentuation still survived which only gradually conformed in the individual languages to the main trend.

The conclusions, to which my investigation has led me, will perhaps be considered highly remarkable. It may of course seem strange that an accentual principle which perished in grey antiquity may be subsequently traced today still in the Germanic verbal forms ziehen gezogen, sieden gesotten, schneiden geschnitten. It is astounding that Germanic consonantism gives us the key to the proethnic accentuation, whereas this had formerly been sought vainly in the Germanic vocalism. If my conclusions, however, are found to be remarkable, then I hope that they will not to the same degree be found improbable. Remember the course of the investigation. Proceeding from a seemingly irregular point in the conjugation by apagogic reasoning — a means of proof which is not despised even by exact mathematics — I have arrived at an explanation which was not only completely satisfactory for that point; but at the same time a series of language phenomena also viewed previously as irregularities were proved in this way to be completely organic products of the development of the language. Precisely in the harmonic interrelationship of various language phenomena with one another and with the total development of language as discovered through this explanation, I find the best confirmation for the correctness of my demonstration.

If my conclusions are accepted by the critics, we have in them a starting point for a further investigation into Proto-Germanic accentuation. In that way we will get nearer to the great question of the origin of ablaut. That the basic principle in Holtzmann's ablaut theory, the assumption of a far-reaching influence of accentuation on the vocalism, is certain, is for me a settled matter; but the form which Holtzmann has given his theory can not be brought into accord with the one arrived at here and must be completely modified.

The most important new results of the above investigation are briefly the following:

1) Germanic still had the free Indo-European accent after the beginning of the sound-shift.

2) The accent however, was no longer purely chromatic as in Indo-European, but was at the same time expiratory.

3) If IE k̲ t̲ p̲ are sometimes found in Germanic as h þ f, sometimes as g̲ d̲ b̲, this was conditioned by that older accentuation.

4) Likewise, the bifurcation of IE s̲ into Gmc s̲ and z̲ medially depends on the earlier accentuation.

5) The first sound-shift — making allowance for the unconditional non-shift in certain consonant complexes — allows no large groups of exceptions.

Copenhagen, July 1875

Notes

1. It is therefore incorrect, for example, to speak of a differentiation of IE t̲ into Gmc þ and d̲; it was Gmc þ that divided into þ and d̲.

2. Compare Braune's essay "Ueber den grammatischen Wechsel in der deutschen Verbalflexion" in the Beiträge zur Geschichte der deutschen Sprache und Literatur by H. Paul and W. Braune, I, 513ff. Footnote by editor (presumably A. Kuhn).

3. The forms in ( ) are analogical formations; the forms in [ ] do not occur, or more correctly, I cannot verify them.

4. The Old Norse adj. feginn 'happy' may in form be the preterite participle passive to the root fah fag (compare Old English); it is however better attributed to OS fagan, OE fagen, which have the same meaning; umlaut was then caused by the palatal (k, g with following e, i) as frequently happens in ON: lengi adv. = OS, OHG lango, OE lange; degi dative sg. of dag-r; the participles ekinn, tekinn, dreginn, sleginn, fenginn, etc.

5. This is true, for example, of Pauli's attempt (Zeitschrift XIV, p. 102) to explain the d in fadar, môdar as against the þ in brôþar by a folk etymological association with Germanic fôjan 'pascere' or môdi- f 'anger, courage'. Apart from the fact that it requires very vivid, popular linguistic fantasy to associate the concept present in 'mother' with that in 'anger, courage', the explanatory words themselves require an explanation, since fôdjan and môdi likewise have a d from IE t̲. Do we then have to assume a folk etymological association for these words also?

6. The second person preterite indicative in the West Germanic languages (OS biti, lidi; OE bite, lide; OHG bizi, liti) is the subjunctive form which has penetrated into the indicative = Goth. biteis, liþeis.

7. Leo Meyer relates the Germanic preterite passive with the Sanskrit forms in -ǎnǎ- with reduplication, thus bitana = bibhidǎnǎ-; also in this case the voiced stop in lidana- agrees with the Sanskrit accentuation.

8. The z arising from r brings about in Old Norse (very seldom in Old Swedish and Old Danish) umlaut of the directly preceding root vowel: ker, 'vessel', gær 'yesterday', dýr 'animal' dreyri 'blood', ber 'loose, empty', reyr 'reed', frörinn 'frozen', kýr 'cow' sýr 'sow'. Cf. Bugge, Tidskrift for Philologi VII, p. 320; Wimmer, Fornnordisk Formlära, Lund 1874, Section 12, note 2; Steffensen, Tidskrift, new series, II, p. 71.

9. The following additional conclusion would be tempting: If at one time all voiceless fricatives of Germanic came to be voiced under certain conditions, then the voiceless stops k, t, p under like circumstances must also have become voiced (g, d, b). This however, as is known, did not occur. Therefore — as can be inferred — the differentiation took place at a time when the language did not yet know these sounds in a voiced environment, i.e., before the last part of the sound-shift, the transition of the IE g, d, b, to k, t, p, had taken place. Such a conclusion is, however, inadmissible. Latin shows a similar transition of Proto-Latin h, þ, f (Ascoli, Zeitschr. XVII, p. 241), arising from IE gh, dh, bh, which also became voiced in a voiced environment. The s here too follows the other voiceless fricatives and develops further to r. Medial c, t, p were, however, not at all affected by this sound shift.

10. The accent is of twofold nature in the Indo-European languages. Either the accentuation of a syllable occurs by the vocal cords becoming more strongly tensed; in that way a higher pitch is produced in opposition to the lower pitch of the unaccented syllables. The Sanskrit and Classical accent was of such a kind, and this is also the original meaning of the name accentus, προσῳδία. I call this accent chromatic. On the other hand the accentuation of the syllable consists in this that the muscles of expiration are set in greater activity, the stronger expiration of air intensifies the voice, and thus a relative forte is produced in opposition to the piano of the unaccented syllables. This may be called expiratory accent; Brücke describes it in his work: Die physiologischen Grundlagen der neuhochdeutschen Verskunst, Vienna 1871, p. 2. There is also a combination of both accents when the voice in the accented syllable can not only be raised, but also intensified, and in the cited work, p. 3, Brücke shows how the expiratory accent tends to take on a stronger or weaker chromatic coloring. This accent must be called a chromatic-expiratory accent. Skt mánas, Gk μένος have the pure chromatic accent on the first syllable; this can be given the musical expression ♩⌐. The Serbian accusative vodu 'aquam' has the pure

expiratory accent on the first syllable, musically expressed 𝄐 ; Vuk Stefanović denotes this accent by \\ . In the nominative of this same word, voda, on the other hand, a chromatic-expiratory accent is found on the first syllable, which might be indicated by ⌐ ; this accent Vuk Stefanović denotes by \. When Brücke (in the above-cited work) asserts "it is incorrect to attempt to distinguish a word accent consisting in tone elevation from a word accent consisting in tone intensification," then on this point I cannot agree with this expert in physiology. Anyone who has heard the Swedes pronounce the peculiar articulation of their kalla, gata, ögon, syster, saker and such words, will have to admit, firstly that the syllable with the expiratory accent does not necessarily lie higher on the tone scale than the unaccented syllables; secondly, that there can be a raising of the voice (chromatic accent) in addition to and independent of the expiratory accent; for in these Swedish words the expiratory accent rests on the root syllable, but the voice is raised on the final syllable at the same time that it decreases in expiratory power ("hvaruti, om ån utan ljudvigt, rösten liksom svänger sig uppför," Rydqvist, Svenska språkets lagar IV, p. 211). This pronunciation could be musically designated thus: ♩ . Therefore, the mentioned words have two accents, so to speak, a purely expiratory one on the root syllable and a purely chromatic one on the final syllable. An ancient Greek ear would perceive only the last syllable as accented (kalla = καλλά); the Swedish ear hears only the accent on the first syllable, which is why the native grammarians speak of a "low tone" ("låg ton") for this syllable, though this, of course, is not quite correct, since the syllable is not beneath but on the level of the normal speech tone, while the final syllable is raised above that level. Norwegian also has this method of accentuation. In an article in Christiania Videnskabs-Selskabs Forhandlinger 1874, p. 296, Joh. Storm explains: En général les syllabes atones ont ici un ton plus haut. Ceci est contraire à l'usage de la plupart des langues européennes et montre que l'élévation de la voix (angl. pitch) et le renforcement ou l'appui (angl. force) sont deux choses différentes, comme l'a très bien fait ressortir M. Ellis dans son travail sur l'accent (Transactions of the Philological Society, 1873-4, Part I p. 113 ff).

11. The sound change xv-(xf-) f is also known elsewhere. It is found, for example, in the South Slavic languages: Bulg. falŭ, Serb. fala, OSl. chvala 'praise'; Bulg., Serb. fat 'a linear measure' for chvat; Bulg. fraste 'branches' for chvraste and others. Furthermore, in Lapp loan-words: fadno = ON hvönn, feres = ON hverr, fales = ON hvalr; see Thomsen "Ueber den Einfluss der germanischen Sprachen auf die finnischlappischen", p. 68.

12. Gmc kunþa- 'known', (Goth. kunþa-, ON kunn-r, OS kûð, OE cûð, OHG kund; pret. part. pass. of kunnan) may not be cited as

contrary to the rule. The phonetic phenomena accompanying the nn
of certain roots are still not clear. One should remember, that an
s was often inserted (as one likes to term it) in word formation along
with these: OHG cun-s-t, Goth. an-s-ti-, Goth. ala-brun-s-ti-, German gun-s-t and that the nn can change a following d = IE dh to þ:
Gmc unþa (ON unna, OE ûðe, OHG onda) pret. ind. of unnan for
*unnda; Gmc kunþa (Goth. kunþa, ON kunna, OE cûðe, OHG conda),
pret. ind. of kunnan for *kunn-da. If, however, the pret. ind. kunþa
represents the expected *kunnda, then the pret. part. pass. kunþa
can also represent *kunnda-.

13. As accented by Benfey, Vollständige Grammatik, p. 162
above; the Petersburg dictionary does not give the accentuation for
this word.

14. See C.W. Smith, De verbis imperfectivis et perfectivis in
lingvis Slavonicis (Universitätsprogramm, Copenhagen 1875), p. 31f.

15. In the genitive singular of the masculine and neuter a-
stems, the ending is Gmc -s, volfas (Goth. vulfis, ON ulfs, oldest
Runic language -AS, OS uulfes, OE vulfes, OHG wolfes). The s was
retained here, because it was actually ss and, as such, had to retain
its voiceless character (IE várkasya = Gmc *volf-asj, *volf-ass,
volfas), see Ebel in Zeitschr. IV p. 149 bottom.

CHAPTER TWELVE

HEINRICH HÜBSCHMANN

ON THE POSITION OF ARMENIAN IN THE SPHERE OF THE INDO-EUROPEAN LANGUAGES

"Ueber die Stellung des Armenischen im Kreise der indogermanischen Sprachen," Zeitschrift für vergleichende Sprachforschung auf dem Gebiete der Indogermanischen Sprachen, 23.1 (1875), 5-49

Hübschmann's is another of the articles published in 1875 which indicate the maturing of linguistics. Making use of the increased control over the data in the Indo-European languages, and over linguistic methodology, Hübschmann by this article established Armenian as an independent branch of the Indo-European group.

Hübschmann's minute attention to data enabled him to sort out the evidence for distinguishing between native Armenian forms and those borrowed from Iranian. In this way his is one of the last important articles to deal with a problem which vexed early Indo-European linguistics: identification of the various strata in a language so that its original relationships could be determined. By sorting out the non-native forms, and establishing the phonological correspondence between Germanic and the other Indo-European languages, Grimm, Rask and the early historical linguists laid down the methodological principles for their field. Using these principles in a more difficult area, Hübschmann at once demonstrated their validity and gave a definitive solution to the problem he was investigating.

It is clear why Hübschmann's solution was so satisfactory: after dealing with morphological characteristics he concentrated on phonological correlations rather than on the vocabulary. His procedure might still be emulated by linguists seeking to establish genetic interrelationships in other language groups.

Even with his accomplishment, Hübschmann's understanding of Indo-European phonology was not completely accurate. Although he was aware of secondary palatalization in Indo-Iranian, he still assumed a single short vowel a for Proto-Indo-European, with a split into the vowels of

the European languages. The correct view became generally apparent shortly after his article was published.
Other misconceptions in his article are obvious to the
reader. But since Hübschmann's aim was to determine
the relation of Armenian to the other dialects, his conception of Proto-Indo-European was not crucial in achieving
this aim.

Nor were some of his methodological views, such as
those on residues. A few of these he dismisses as chance
phenomena. The sections of his long article with such
comments are not reproduced here. But it is to Hübschmann's credit that he recognized before his article was
printed that he had slighted some of the material in Armenian. Subsequently he rectified any omission by his
comprehensive Armenische Etymologie (Leipzig, 1897), the
first part of his planned grammar of Armenian. Moreover,
residues are still being explained in Armenian today, thanks
to his solid work on its phonology.

Hübschmann's concern with thorough descriptive analysis enabled him to clarify other interrelationships, such
as that of Ossetic as well as that of Afghan (which in his
first excursus, pp. 43-46 [not included here], he demonstrated to be an Iranian and not an Indic language). The
pioneering work that was necessary in Iranian as well as
Armenian may be recognized from the preliminary note to
his article, in which he deals with the transcription for Armenian. Though he modified it, he was unfortunately prevented by the editors of the Zeitschrift from revising the
transcription for Iranian, which in the form he used suggests pronunciation like that of Sanskrit.

Besides his insistence on careful descriptive techniques, Hübschmann's conception of the interrelationships
between the languages in one family was admirable. The
family tree model as proposed by earlier linguists seemed
far too rigid. His identification of shared characteristics
in Armenian and the European languages as well as in Armenian and Indo-Iranian gave excellent support to the wave
theory which had been proposed three years earlier by
Schmidt. The resulting conception of the position of the
early Indo-European dialects prepared for the more real-
istic view of interrelationship between languages which
followed further studies in dialect geography.

The interest in broadening the study of the Indo-
European languages at this time is strikingly illustrated
by the editorial comment at the beginning of the twenty-third

volume of the Zeitschrift, on its increased scope beyond
Germanic, Greek and Latin. Hübschmann's own boldness
concerning the Indo-European family may be demonstrated
by the concluding comment in the second excursus to his
article, pp. 46-49 (not included here). After suggesting
that Phrygian may have been closely related to Armenian,
he ends with the statement: "Possibly these languages
formed a separate branch with other languages of Asia
Minor, which in accordance with our contributions on Armenian above, might be placed between Iranian and Balto-
Slavic." The separate branch has indeed been uncovered,
but with a position in the Indo-European family somewhat
different from that which Hübschmann had forecast. His
concentration on interpreting the Iranian and Armenian
data permitted little further speculation of this sort. But
the interpretations he provided of these data remain permanent contributions on the position of these languages.

    Johann Heinrich Hübschmann (1848-1908), after a
post-doctorate period of four years at Leipzig, spent his
entire career at Strasburg. Scornful of academic jockey-
ing, he rejected offers to move closer to the contemporary
centers of linguistic research. Though he dealt with many
of the Indo-European languages, his concern with Armenian
extended beyond linguistics to Oriental studies. His primary achievement was in the elucidation of Armenian.
Though it has never been one of the languages of central
interest to Indo-Europeanists, Hübschmann holds a position
of great respect not only as founder of scientific Armenian
studies but also for his capable application of linguistic
method.

    My attempt to assign to the Armenian language its position
among its relatives is not the first. The Armenians themselves
have proposed views about it which flatter their national vanity but
lack every scientific foundation. And European scholars of previous
centuries have made everything of this language since they could do
nothing with it. But immediately after the establishment of linguistics by Bopp, Petermann in his Grammatica linguae Armeniacae
(Berlin, 1837), on the basis of etymologies given at the beginning of
it was able to furnish the proof that Armenian is an Indo-European
language. Nine years later, in 1846, and independently of the work
of Petermann, Windischmann published in the Abhandlungen of the
Bavarian Academy (IV,2) an excellent treatise about Armenian, in

which he comes to the conclusion that Armenian goes back to an
older dialect which must have had great similarity with Avestan and
Old Persian but to which foreign elements had been added early.
But while Pott doubted that Armenian is an Aryan language and only
wanted to admit a strong influence of Aryan on Armenian, Diefen-
bach on the other hand observed that this assumption did not suffice
to explain the close relationship of Armenian to Indic and Persian,
a view which Gosche also adopted in his dissertation: De Ariana
linguae gentisque Armeniacae indole (Berlin, 1847). Three years
later in the Zeitschrift der Deutschen Morgenländischen Gesellschaft IV, p. 347 ff., under the title "Vergleichung der armenischen
consonanten mit denen des Sanskrit" de Lagarde gave a list of 283
Armenian words with their etymologies (which he also had found independently of Windischmann), without however dealing in greater
detail about the character of the language. In the preface to the
second edition of his Comparative Grammar, 1857, Bopp designated
Armenian as Iranian and attempted, though without success, to explain its inflectional elements. Fr. Müller, who since 1861 had
busied himself successfully with the etymological and grammatical
explanation of Armenian in a series of treatises (Sitzungsberichte
der Wiener Akademie), penetrated much more deeply in the essence
of this language, which he explained as certainly Iranian. In general
Patkanoff follows him in his summarizing treatise "Über die bildung
der armenischen sprache," which was translated from Russian into
French, Journal asiatique, XVI, Série 6, 1870, p. 126 ff. Even though
de Lagarde in his Gesammelten Abhandlungen (1866), p. 291, asserted that three components are to be distinguished in Armenian:
the original basis; an Old Iranian alluvium resting on it; and a similar New Iranian, added after the founding of the Parthian kingdom,
nonetheless he did not give the distinguishing characteristics of
these three layers, and for this reason his opinion has not been
taken into further consideration. In any case Müller's view, that
Armenian is Iranian, has not been disproved, and must be designated as the best established and the prevailing one at present.
     The aim of the following is to investigate whether it is tenable.
     It is a primary defect of Müller's investigations that he has not
undertaken to demonstrate that the Armenian words which correspond phonologically with the corresponding Persian are not borrowed from Persian. If however the oldest Armenian that we know
contains loanwords from Aramaic and Greek, we may expect that
since the Armenians lived for centuries under the influence of the
mightier and more cultured Persians, they also would have taken
from their language no small number of words.[1] If this is admitted,
then one can also suspect a great number of words to be borrowed;
and if one has given way to this suspicion, then faith in the Iranian

character of the language also disappears rapidly. And this suspicion can be very easily supported. In numerous Armenian compounds, for example, we find the word dast 'hand', while the usual
word for 'hand' is dzer'n; now dast corresponds to Persian dasta,
which in contrast with Av. zasta, Skt hasta is demonstrated to be
specifically Persian through the sound change from z to d, and accordingly must be a loanword in Armenian. Accordingly also dastak,
dastakert are foreign words, OP *dastaka, *dastakarta. It is further
clear that Armenian regularly prefixes a or e to words with originally initial r: for this reason r'azm 'battle array, battle', r'ah
'way', r'ocik 'content'[2], which we also find in Persian, are loanwords from Persian, just as all words beginning with r' in Armenian
are foreign words, cf. r'abbi 'master'. Further, since final h in
Persian corresponds to original ç or dental, final h in Armenian to
original s or tr (and original ç corresponds to Armenian s, original
dental between vowels to Armenian dental or y), final h in Persian
is accordingly etymologically different from that in Armenian;[3] accordingly Arm. akah 'well-informed' = NP âgâh < âkâça, gah 'throne,
seat' = NP gâh, Av. gâtu, zrah 'armor' = Av. zrâdha, NP zirih are
loanwords from Persian. Further, if below we find the sound law
that Skt j = Av. z = Arm. ts and accordingly Skt jan 'be born' = Av.
zan = Arm. tsn (< tsin, tsen), then azat 'free' = Pers. âzâd, Av.
âzâta, from the root zan, must be regarded as a foreign word. Similarly if it is demonstrated below that Skt han = Av. jan in accordance with the sound laws would have to be represented in Armenian
by gan and is so represented, then Arm. zen- 'slaughter, offer' is
suspected of being borrowed because it corresponds to Av. jan, NP
zan-. If in the same way Skt aj in accordance with the sound laws is
Av. az, Arm. ats, then gavazan 'stick' = Av. gavâz cannot be an
original word — it would have to be kovatsan — and also not xarazan
'whip', instead of which išatsan would be expected. Finally, Skt. yaj
= Av. yaz 'worship' in accordance with the sound laws would have to
be lats or dzats in Armenian (Skt. j = Av. z = Arm. ts, see below;
originally initial y becomes Arm. l or dz, z; where y is initial in
Armenian, it is a newly added prefix, as can be easily demonstrated);
the form however is yaz and accordingly it is borrowed. The same
is true of yašt 'offering' = Av. yêsh'ti. Also to be considered as
loanwords: dev = Av. daêva, instead of which tiv would be expected
in accordance with the laws of the sound shift which are to be set up
below; likewise, I am convinced, bag- 'god' = Av. bagha, and den[4]
'religion' = Av. daêna, words which came to Armenia with the Zoro-
astrian religion. Likewise, without being able to furnish proof, I
would also like to look on words like thošak = Pers. tôshah 'viati-
cum', ambox = Pers. anboh 'quantity', zĕndan = Pers. zindân 'jail'
as having come from Persia to Armenia; but of words like dipak

'brocade' = Pers. dîbâh, Arab. dîbâj, crag 'candle' = Pers. cirâgh, Arba. sirâj, thuthak 'parrot' = Pers. tûtak, tûtî, kerpas 'silk' = NPers. kirpâs, Arba. kirbâs, Skt karpâsa, Gk. kárpasos etc. there can be no doubt that they are foreign material. If it has been so easy for me to separate as loanwords no small number of the words[5] treated by Fr. Müller, how greatly would this number be increased if an expert like de Lagarde would undertake to separate the foreign elements from the entire Armenian lexicon? Possibly also two groups of these could be distinguished, an older and a younger, and in this way the two layers would be found which according to de Lagarde were deposited on the Armenian basis.

If now we have become suspicious of the lexicon, we may turn with greater confidence to the grammar; for in all living languages this is surely the palladium that a foreign influence cannot touch. How wild is the lexicon of Afghan and New Persian, or English, and how clearly does the grammar teach us that in the former we have Iranian at hand, in the latter Germanic! And we may expect to find clarification from the grammar much more readily in Armenian, because it displays a relatively rich inflection. For Armenian still has four cases of nouns distinguished by endings and five of pronouns; and in verbs, without considering the infinitive and participles, it distinguishes by means of inflection active and passive, indicative, subjunctive and imperative, present, imperfect, simple and compound aorist, and corresponding to these double futures. Since I must treat of the grammar here briefly, it may be permitted to adduce a paradigm for the inflection of the noun and the verb:

a) Noun:
Stem: mardo "human" (Gk. broto-), anwan "name" (= anman).

	Sg.	Pl.
Nom.	mard, anun	mardkh
Acc.	z mard, z anun	z mards
Gen.-Dat.	mardoy, anwan	mardoჳ
Abl.	i mardoy, y anwanê	i mardoჳ
Dat. (pron. decl.)	mardum[6] -----	---
Instr.	mardov, anwamb	mardovkh

b) Verb: ger-el 'take captive'

	Active	Passive
1. p. sg. pres. ind.	gerem	gerim
-- subj.	geriჳem	geriჳim
imperf.	gerêi	gerêi
comp. aor.	gereჳi	gereჳay

simple aor. of		
gt-an-el "find"	gti	gtay
future	gereʒiʒ	gereʒaiʒ
	gtiʒ	gtaiʒ

m, s, y, mkh, ykh, n serve as primary verbal endings, and i, ir, r, akh, ikh, in as secondary.

If however one views the total structure of Armenian, it gives the impression of a language which has undergone great changes,[7] having lost much of the old material of stem and word formational elements; but it replaced what was lost by new inflectional elements. In this way the subjunctive turns out to be a new formation from the present stem and the subjunctive of the substantive verb: em (pronounce yem) = Lat. sum, iʒem = Lat. sim; accordingly gerem -- geriʒem, aḷam--aḷaiʒem; similarly, the future is formed from the aorist stem and the aorist subjunctive, with little change of the coalescing components: gereʒ + iʒem = gereʒiʒ instead of gereʒiʒem, 2. p. gereʒ + iʒes = geresʒes instead of gereʒiʒes; and the imperfect similarly might be a new formation from the present stem and the imperfect of the substantive verb: em 'sum', êi "eram" — gerem — gerêi, but Fr. Müller claims to find a formation with the suffix ya in the imperfect: berêi = berey-i,[8] with reference to the a-class, which forms ayi not êi: aḷam — aḷayi. Moreover, the main factor in new linguistic formations, analogy, has of course been powerfully effective, just as it also essentially brought about the remodeling of the Old Armenian inflection to the New Armenian. For example, the passive marker is i; if it is added to present stems in -u, wi results (zenu-l, pass. zenwi-l, l-nu-l, pass. lnwi-l); and this wi, which of course was originally only the present marker of the passive of a very limited number of verbs, has become the general passive marker in modern Armenian; cf. NArm. kordzwil 'be done' = OArm. gortsil, act. gortsel. In this situation it is readily understandable why the elements of the Armenian inflection are still so obscure to us. I do not know how one is to explain the ʒ[9] which forms the compound aorist and the ʒ in iʒem, etc. If one identified with them the s of the Indo-European aorist and the sy of syâm, the opt. of as, then Armenian could not be Iranian, for in Iranian s would have to be represented by h and sy by hy. Equally obscure are the secondary verbal endings; on the other hand the primary are clearer, among them m = mi, n = nti, y = ti, mkh = masi; accordingly ykh (= tkh) could go back to tasi, the original Indo-European form assumed by Schleicher, in contrast with which Sanskrit and Avestan show tha. But ykh is probably an analogical formation to mkh of the first person, and kh is to be regarded as added on later, so that y likewise goes back to tha or a similar form. The suffix of the 2. p. sg. s

refutes the Iranian character of Armenian, since Iranian shows h
rather than s; yet also Ossetic, certainly an Iranian language, has s
in the same form, for which explanations must still be provided.

Among the case forming suffixes of the plural, ʒ too is unclear,
kh probably goes back to as (or in accordance with Fr. Müller to
âsas, Iran. âhah) s to ans; in the instrumental we have the instrumental marker of the singular, to which the plural marker kh was
added. Among the suffixes of the singular, m of the dative-locative
goes back to the pronominal -hmâi, hmi; the ê of the ablative prepares difficulties. Fr. Müller would like to derive it from âdha, a
shape of the ablative suffix found occasionally in the Avesta; I would
rather think of the adverbial suffix tas = Av. tô, if ê can really not
be = at. The instrumental suffix b remains to be considered. While
this suffix was formerly identified with the one suffix of the Indo-
European instrumental bhí, recently Fr. Müller and I have attempted
to see in it a new formation, to be sure for no other reason than that
this suffix contradicted the Iranian character of Armenian which had
been asserted by us. For like Aryan in general, Iranian too does not
know the instrumental suffix bhi. Our conclusion was accordingly:
because Armenian is Iranian, it may not have the instrumental suffix
bhi. But suppose one should rather conclude: because Armenian
has this suffix, it is not Iranian. Now in accordance with Armenian
sound laws, b surely points to bhi; and an original anmanbhi,
martabhi had to become Armenian anmanb, martob, subsequently
anwamb, mardov, as the instrumental of anun, mard actually is attested. And since in its function as well the case with b is a pure
instrumental, there can be no objection to the equation: Arm. b =
IE bhi. Some scholars have claimed to find this suffix bhi in Greek,
Germanic and Balto-Slavic. But φι could also be a reflex of the
other suffixes compounded with bhi (bhiam, bhiams, bhiâms, bhis).
In Germanic the instrumental in mi = bhi is actually not found.[10]
Accordingly it remains only in Balto-Slavic, where bhi is found as
OCS mi, Lith. mi. Accordingly bhi as instrumental suffix of the
singular can be assigned with certainty only to Armenian and Balto-
Slavic.

Result: In the inflection of Armenian we cannot demonstrate
any specific Iranian characteristics; on the contrary it differs in an
important point with Aryan and agrees with Balto-Slavic.

Since the inflection does not give us enough information about
the character of Armenian, we will turn to the phonology.

Part I.

In order to decide whether or not Armenian is Iranian with

reference to its sounds, the question must first be answered: what are the characteristic features of the sound system of Iranian in contrast with the other Indo-European languages?

They are as follows:

A.1 The dental s, when not protected by a directly preceding or following consonant, consistently becomes h, and

2 correspondingly sv becomes hv,

3 but when i, u or ai, au precedes, it becomes sh. In the latter point Iranian agrees with Sanskrit (except for final position, where Sanskrit preserves the s); but Slavic between vowels always develops instead of that sh the fricative ch (sluchŭ = sraosha). In the change of s to h on the other hand, Greek agrees with Iranian; but unlike Iranian, in Greek this change is not carried through consistently. Further, also in Celtic sv becomes hv, chw; cf. Cornish huir, Breton choar 'sister' = NPers. khvâhar; Welsh chwech (= sves) 'six'.

4 Iranian shows a disinclination for aspirates but an inclination for the formation of spirants, of which it is particularly fond of kh, gh, f and w. Yet the oldest Iranian dialects, those of the Gathas and of the Old Persian cuneiform inscriptions, do not yet know the voiced spirants (gh, dh, w, which are present in the usual Avestan);[11] and Ossetic has shifted the voiceless stops (k and t) to aspirates. Baloci too knows aspirates (see at the end of this discussion), but they probably arose through the influence of Indic.

5 In consonant clusters spirants arise from stops through the influence of following t, sh, r, v; accordingly original kt, pt, tt become kht, ft, st; khsh, kra, pra, tra become khra, fra, thra.

6 Notable is the lack of l in Old Iranian,[12] the shift of çv to sp, and in contrast with Indic the form of the preposition pati (= Skt prati), of the adverb us, uz (= Skt ut, ud, but similarly in Old Persian), words like gaosha with the meaning 'ear', etc.

B. The aspirated voiced stops are lacking in Iranian; through loss of aspiration they fell together with the voiced stops and like them often became spirants subsequently. Balto-Slavic also merged voiced stops and voiced aspirated stops.

C. The change of the original palato-velars k, g, gh to the palatals c, j and s, z must be considered a primary characteristic of Iranian. But Sanskrit shares in the formation of palatals from palato-velars, and Balto-Slavic in the change of the palato-velars to slit fricatives.

Accordingly every single one of these characteristics is found in other Indo-European languages, and only the occurrence of all of them makes up the character of an Iranian language. We ask now whether all these characteristics occur in Armenian.

A.1 Original s generally appears in Armenian as h; cf. hin 'old'

= Av. hana, Lat. senex; mahik, diminutive of mah "moon", = Skt
mâsa, Av. mâoṅha; this h is lost for example in the root arb 'drink'
= original sarbh (Lat. sorbeo, Lith. srebiù), evthn 'seven', Ossetic
awd = original saptan. In inflection this h shows up as kh (now pronounced as an aspirate), just as also in Persian h is closed to the
spirant kh. s has been maintained as s in amis 'month', mis 'meat',
us 'shoulder', in which the maintenance of s is explained by an originally preceding n: amis developed from mens, mis from memsa
and us from amsa. The s in the accusative plural may probably be
explained similarly: mards (now pronounced mártŭs) developed
from mardins = martans. Accordingly the maintenance of s in these
cases would not contradict the Iranian sound law set up above, even
though Avestan would also change s to h after n; cf. maṅh = mans,
aorist stem of the root man, = man + s. In one case to be sure (before original v) s seems to be maintained even contrary to the sound
law: skesur 'mother-in-law', cf. Avestan qaçura 'father-in-law',
NPers. khusur; here v may first have changed to g[13] and this to k
after the s on the pattern of skund 'puppy' = çvan-. Windischmann,
Grundlage des Armenischen, p. 20, already wanted to regard the
colloquial by-form kesur as the original form, and derive k from kh
= sv; s would then have been added inorganically. But this explanation does not seem probable to me.
    2 sv becomes kh or v in Armenian, both probably having
arisen from hv: khoir, now pronounced khuir, = NPers. khvâhar,
pronounced khâhar, originally svasar, and veʒ = sechs = Gk sweks,
Welsh chwech.
    3 Aryan sh = s after i, u and their various grades is found in
dž = Av. duzh from dush, cf. dž-goh 'discontented' and in zguiš
'careful' = *uzgaosha, actually 'with pricked up ears' — two genuine
Iranian formations, of which the latter itself would prove the Iranian
character of Armenian. And zguiš is so well established in Armenian that one cannot readily assume it to be borrowed. This sh
shows up also in uš 'memory, reason' = Av. ushi 'reason'. Elsewhere this š may indeed have developed further to s, e.g. ls-el
'hear' = Av. srush in sraosha (Lith. klausà, OCS sluchŭ), nist 'sit-
ting' = nsit = niseda = nishadah, as in Ossetic where in ghos 'ear',
ars 'bear', aχsawa 'night', ast 'eight' s is found instead of sh. Accordingly de Lagarde is probably right in deriving gusan 'singer,
musician' from the root Skt ghush 'make noise, resound'. Yet this
material is not sufficient in order to discuss this point adequately.
    4 Armenian is fond of the (voiceless) aspirates, of which it
possesses a complete set: kh, th, ph; but of the voiceless spirants
it knows only χ. Yet of the voiceless spirants Afghan possesses
only χ (kh), but not f, which is frequent in Ossetic and Persian.
    5 χt = original kt is found in uχt 'vow, treaty', Av. ukhti, aχt

suffering, sickness' = Av. akhti; and dustr 'daughter' (beside duχt = Pers. dukht) may also be derived from duχtr, when we find bast beside baχt, drast beside draχt ('garden, paradise' Pers. dirakht 'tree'). ft for original pt cannot be found in Armenian, since f is missing; yet Avestan too still has pt instead of ft: gerepta, haptan, but NPers. giriftah, haft. For the change of tt to st I do not find an example, but it seems certain because of Arm. azd 'information' = OPers. azdâ, Skt addhâ 'certainly'. Aryan ksh = Iran. khsh appears metathesized in Armenian as šχ: išχel 'govern' = Av. khshi; bašχel 'distribute' = Av. bakhsh; ašχarh 'land' = Av. khshathra. Iranian khra appears as Arm. χra in χrat 'theme' χratu 'admonition, counsel', Av. khratu, NPers. khirad; Iran. fr as Arm. hr: hra = pra, Av. fra; Iran. thr as Arm. rh: ašχarh 'land' = Av. khshathra.

6 l is not absent in Armenian; but it also occurs in all contemporary Iranian languages, so that the presence of l in Armenian would prove nothing of itself. But we will see later that Armenian is distinct from Iranian by the manner of occurrence of l. . . .

B. As far as the aspirated voiced stops are concerned, we might assume that the original Iranian language had already given up aspiration and merged the aspirated voiced stops with the voiced stops. Before this happened, Armenian must have separated from Iranian (if we set up a family tree); for in Armenian voiced stops and aspirated voiced stops do not fall together but rather have always been kept distinct. For while the aspirated voiced stops were shifted to voiced stops, the voiced stops developed to voiceless stops; the voiceless stops however remained unchanged or became aspirates or spirants. Accordingly the original series

gh	g	k
dh	d	t
bh		p

undergo in Armenian a conversion to:

g	k	k, kh
d	t	t, th, y
b		p, ph, h

Examples are as follows:

a. Dental series:

Arm. d = original dh: Arm. d-ne-l = original dhâ "set, do" . . . (Other examples follow.)

Arm. t = original d: atamn (a-ta-mn) "tooth" = dant. (Other examples follow.)

Original t was maintained when protected by neighboring consonants: astḷ 'star', dustr 'daughter'; or it developed to d: du (from túam) = NHG du; leard 'liver' = yakart; mard 'human being' = Gk.

brotós; ôd 'wind' = vâta; or it developed to an aspirate: tharm
'fresh, young' = Skt taruṇa; tharšam 'wilted' (in an-tharšam 'not
wilting', tharšameʒuʒanel 'wilt' trans.), root tars, Lat. torreo,
tarsós; evthn 'seven' = saptan; uth 'eight' = ashtan; thandzr 'thick'
root tañc; artsath 'silver' = Skt rajata; or between vowels it developed to y: hair (written hayr) 'father'; mair 'mother'; berê 'he
bears' = bereti, etc.

b. Labial series:

Arm. b = original bh: band, bant 'prison', root bhandh... (Other
examples follow.)

p is maintained as voiceless stop in kapel = capere; partkh
(stem partu-) 'debt', Av. par (in pesha, peretha) 'involve in debt,
forfeit through debt'; pšnul "observe" = Skt paç; patmel 'narrate' =
pati + mâ; it was shifted to an aspirate[14] in phoši 'dust' = Av. pāsnu;
phetur = NHG Feder; phut 'foul' = Skt pûti 'foul, stinking', Phl.
pûtak; and initially it went over to h in: hair 'father' = patar; hing
'five' = pankan; harʒanel 'question' = NPers. purs-îdan; heru 'last
year' = Osset. fâre 'in the previous year', falwâre (= farfâre) 'in the
second last year', Pers. pâr 'the past year'.

c. Palato-velar series: (H's term: Gutturalreihe)

Arm. g = original gh: gari 'barley' = hordeum, originally
ghardha, Phl. jurdâk 'grain, barley', Baloci zurth-ânî 'a kind of
grain'; mêg 'mist' = mêgha; vagr 'tiger' = Skt vyâghra.

Arm. k = original g: kov 'cow' = gâu; klanel 'devour', keri 'I
ate', root gar; keal 'life', root giv; kin 'woman' = ganâ; kr'unk
'crane' = géranos; eki 'I came', root ga, of which the present however is ga-m. gravel too does not agree with Skt grabh, Av. garb;
yet the same irregular shift occurs in Goth. greipan. For further
details, see below. (not included here) The voiceless stop was
maintained as k in akn 'eye'; kam-il 'desire' Skt. kâma; kerp = Lat.
corpus; kapel = Lat. capere; in final position it became g: erg 'song'
= Skt arka; infrequently it became an aspirate: kharšel 'pull' = Av.
karesh; khên 'hatred, revenge' = Av. kaêna, NPers. kîn; khandel
'destroy' (khand-el denominative ?) from Av. kan, Skt khan.

On the shift of another series (g^1 -- gh^1) see below.

This is the first sound shift of Armenian. The New Armenian
of the west has undergone a second: the relationship of voiced and
voiceless stops, as established after the first sound shift, is reversed, so that the original voiced aspirates are now voiceless
stops, the original voiced stops as well as a part of the original
voiceless stops are now voiced stops, but the aspirates and h-sounds
remained unshifted. In Armenian accordingly, voiced stops and aspirated voiced stops did not fall together as in Iranian.

C. The last point remains to be discussed, the development of
spirants from original palato-velars. In this point Iranian and

Balto-Slavic have much in common, so that Johannes Schmidt protested with this support against a separation of Iranian and Slavic
and of Aryan and European in the early period; and he overthrew the
family tree of the Indo-European languages which has been proposed
up to now. For not only in the split of original k to k and k^1 = ç, s
do Balto-Slavic and Aryan agree closely,[15] but also in accordance
with Ascoli's demonstration in that of g to g and g^1 = Iranian, Balto-
Slavic ż, z and that of gh to gh and gh^1 = Iranian, Balto-Slavic ż, z.
This knowledge however is not adequate for our following purpose,
and in order to be able to compare the split of the palato-velars in
Armenian with that in Aryan and Balto-Slavic we have to set up
these series of splits completely, as I now do.

    I. Split of g to g and g^1.

    a. g appears in Sanskrit as g, in Avestan as g, Armenian k,
Balto-Slavic g.

    Note 1: Skt. gâ, gam 'go', Av. gâ in gâma, gâya, ga in gata, apa-
gaiti, gam in ja-ghm-aṭ, aibî-gemen, Arm. eki 'I came', ek 'the
stranger' (baínō, venio)... (Other examples follow.)

    The g above we see developing to j in some examples; thus be-
side Skt. gam, Av. gâ even the root and present stem appear as jam,
jim, jas, though the original g was maintained where it was protected
by a consonant: jaghmaṭ... Beside Skt. yuga : yuj we find Av. yuj.
So we may also posit original g = Skt. j = Av. j = Arm. k, Balto-
Slavic g; note Skt. rajas 'sphere of air, fog, darkness', = Arm. erek
'evening', Gk. Érebos, Goth. riqis.... The complete g-series accordingly shows up as follows:

Skt g,	Av. g,	Arm. k,	Balto-Slavic g
j	j, zh	k, ž	

    b. g^1 appears in Sanskrit as j, Avestan z, Arm. ts, Slav. z,
Lith. z.

    cf. Skt. aja, ajâ 'buck, goat', Av. azi, Arm. aits, Lith ožýs
'buck', aíks... (Other examples follow.)

    II. Split of the gh to gh and gh^1.

    a. gh appears in Sanskrit as gh, Av. g, gh, Arm. g, Balto-
Slavic g.

    cf. Skt. megha = Av. maêgha 'cloud', Osset. miegha 'fog, cloud',
Arm. mêg 'fog', Lith. miglâ, OCS mĭgla 'fog, clouds'... (Other examples follow.)

    Just as g occasionally became j in Sanskrit and j, zh in Avestan,
so gh occasionally becomes h in Sanskrit, j, zh in Avestan, ž in
Armenian.

    Skt. druh 'vex', drogha 'insult', Av. druj, druzh 'lie, deceive'

beside draogha 'deceitful', Arm. džr-el, drž-el 'deceive, miss, of-
fend'... (Other examples follow.)

Accordingly the gh-series shows up as:

$$\text{Skt. gh} = \text{Av. g, gh,} \quad \text{Arm. g,} \qquad \text{Balto-Slavic g}$$

$$\qquad \quad | \qquad \qquad \; | \qquad \qquad \; |$$

$$\qquad \quad \text{h} \qquad \quad \text{j, zh} \qquad \text{g, ž}$$

b. gh^1 = Skt h, Av. z, Arm. z, dz, Slavic z, Lith ż.

Skt. aham 'I', Av. azem, Arm. es (from ez), OCS azŭ, Lith aż
(asz)... (Other examples follow.)

Some apparent anomalies must be noted here, from which the
relation of g to g^1, gh to gh^1 becomes clear. We saw above that Skt.
yuj = Av. yuj must go back to a root yug, the g of which must have
been present in Armenian as palato-velar, as it is actually found
that zuig = *yôga. Now we also find however lts-el 'hitch up in a
yoke', which goes back to original yug^1 (which is not present in Sanskrit and Avestan); and accordingly we must posit for Armenian two
roots, yug and yug^1, which of course were identical originally. Then
the two g's are not originally different, but the one g has split in
two, in part remaining g, in part becoming g^1. The same is true of
Aryan g in the root gabh (and of forms with gh and k that H. cites).
... This can only mean: originally there was only one k, one g, one
gh, which later split to k, k^1, g, g^1, gh, gh^1....

If one now compares the k series with the g and gh series, in
accordance with the previous investigations:

	k	= Skt k,	Av. k,	Arm. k,	Balto-Slavic k	
k						
		c	c	?		
	k^1 =	ç	s	s (š,ʒ́)	Slav. s, Lith. sz	
	g	=	g	g	k,	g
g			j	j, zh	k, ž	
	g^1 =	j	z	ts	Slav. z, Lith ż	
	gh	=	gh	g (gh)	g	g
gh			h	j, zh	g, ž	
	gh^1 =	h	z	z, dz	Slav. z, Lith. ż	

there is complete agreement between these series, from which it
must be concluded that in the original period the Aryans, Armenians
and Balto-Slavic speakers were in especially close contact with one

another. For this common development of the palato-velars k, g, gh in two directions: to k, g, gh and k^1, g^1, gh^1 cannot be purely accidental — or if it is, all characteristics of languages, by which we determine their conditions of relationship, must be purely accidental.

If we consider especially the relationship of Armenian to Aryan and Balto-Slavic, it turns out first of all that by its strict distinction of g (= k and ts) and gh (= g and z, dz) it is at an older stage than Balto-Slavic and Iranian, which as may be seen from the above table have merged both of these. This phenomenon agrees totally with the other phonological relationships of these languages. For if Sanskrit and Armenian in general maintain the distinction between voiced aspirated stops and simple voiced stops (gh-g, dh-d), which Iranian and Balto-Slavic have abandoned, then we must also expect that the two first-named languages retained the distinction between original gh^1 and g^1, and the last named language groups gave it up, i.e. they merged gh^1 and g^1 to g^1 and developed this to a spirant (Av. z = Slav. z = Lith. ż). On their part Sanskrit and Armenian are differentiated because Sanskrit, in contrast with Avestan and Balto-Slavic, merges part of the original g, gh with g^1, gh^1 (so that Sanskrit j = g and g^1, Sanskrit h = gh and gh^1); Armenian on the other hand not only continues the distinction of voiced stops and voiced aspirates, but also g, gh and g^1, gh^1, and accordingly in this respect it maintains the original phonological relationship more faithfully than Aryan and Balto-Slavic.

But we must also examine the relationship of Armenian to Aryan and Balto-Slavic in another and more important area. For the chief difference between the language families named above consists in this that Balto-Slavic at first maintains its palato-velars (g, k) unchanged, Aryan on the other hand changes them to palatals. For the Old Aryan sounds k, g, gh in part remained velars, in part also developed to the palatals: Skt c, j, h (h from jh) and Av. c, zh, j, primarily in three cases: 1. if i or y followed them originally, e.g. jîv 'live'; 2. in the reduplicating syllable; 3. in root final position, when they were not protected by a following consonant, or when they were maintained unchanged before vowels in nominal derivations, as happened in part, e.g. pac 'cook', vac 'speak', but pâka and ukta. But palatalization has also taken place beyond these limits, if not widely, and in this situation k has been affected more frequently, g and gh less; cf. Aryan ca 'and', catvar 'four', car 'go, drive', pañcan 'five', Skt jaṭhara 'belly', Skt han = Av. jan 'strike'. The agreement with which Indic and Iranian have carried out this process of palatalization provides certain proof that it took place already in the common Aryan period. And since it did not occur in this way in any other Indo-European group, this formation of palatals is particularly characteristic for Aryan. For that reason it must also serve as a test to determine whether Armenian is Iranian or not.

Now we have already noted (in a portion not given here) that:
Arm. uiž, baž, buž = Aryan aujas, bhaj, bhuj, possibly also žtel =
Av. jad, žir = Skt jîra, and držel, džrel = Skt druh, Av. druzh, iž =
Av. azhi, aržani = Skt arh, Av. arej (NPers. arzân), and may because of these examples designate Armenian as Aryan. But only
one thing is unclear: why do we find in uiž, baž, buž the sound ž
corresponding to Aryan j, since in accordance with the sound shift
we would expect c? No example at all has been found for Arm. j =
Aryan jh and Arm. c = Aryan j; for this reason one must assume
first of all that j and c arose only late in the separate existence of
Armenian[16] (accordingly ž would have arisen for j and c in Aryan
times?). Arm. c = Pers. c is found frequently by the way; cf. cank,
cang 'hook' = NPers. cang; caš 'eat' with its derivatives: cašel,
cašak, cašakel 'taste' = NPers. cashîdan; capuk- = NPers. câbuk
'nimble'; carp 'fat' = Phl. carp; crag = NPers. cirâgh 'lamp'; vcar-
'solvere' = NPers. guzâr (from vicar); r'ocik 'support' = NPers.
rûzeh; rûzî, Av. raocaṅh 'day', etc. But these examples prove too
much; the agreement with Persian is here too great, for otherwise
we find no trace of such agreement. And since words like crag and
r'ocik are certainly borrowed (they are also found in Georgian), the
above words other than these are probably also loanwords. The
same is probably true of patmucan = Phl. patmucan 'dress', while
the c of mucak = NPers. mûzah could only have arisen from the k of
the underlying word muik 'shoe' = Phl. môk (Afghan moc-ařah f.
'shoe') in Armenian.

But in accordance with the sound shift, the Aryan palatal c is
found in Armenian as ch in: chorkh[17] 'four' = catvar; gochel
'scream', kochel 'name' = Lat. vocare; and it has become a dental
in mrʒ-il 'battle, fight' = Av. mereñc, nasalized from marc (for
the meaning, cf. márnatai 'he fights' = Skt mṛnáti 'he crushes'),
haʒ 'bread' = pac, thandzr (from thanʒr 'thick', Av. tañcish ta, and
finally in luis 'light' = Av. raocanh, NPers. rôz[18]. Is Armenian then
Aryan?

Compare now the Armenian words eki 'I came', keal 'life', kov
'cow', kin 'woman', erek 'evening', bek 'broken', gan 'strike' with
their Aryan related words as well as hing (from penkan) 'five' with
Aryan pañcan and lkh-anel 'leave' with Aryan ric (erg "song" = Skt
arka, root arc and khan = Lat. quam, khanak = quantum, Av. cvañṭ,
NPers. cand do not come into consideration); it then turns out that
precisely in those forms to which especially value is to be ascribed
after Ascoli's splendid studies concerning the Aryan palatals, Armenian is decisively separated from Aryan and agrees with Balto-
Slavic.

After the above remarks we can now complete the k-series set
up above as follows:

IE k = Skt k, Av. k, Arm. k,   Balto-Slavic k
         c   c   k, kh; ch, ʒ, s

and the parallelism with the g and gh series is now completely established.

From the whole preceding investigation we obtain as total result:

In accordance with its development of original palato-velars to spirants Armenian belongs to the sphere of the Aryan and Balto-Slavic languages. It agrees in part with the Aryan languages in the palatalization of the palato-velars, but in another area it also preserves palato-velars unchanged, like Balto-Slavic; for this reason it can neither be subordinated to Aryan (in the usual sense) nor be taken away from it. For this reason too it cannot be designated as Iranian, even though it like Iranian changes s to h and treats many consonants and groups of consonants (like Arm. šχ = Iran. χš = Aryan kš) in a similar or in the same way. For this reason it must be set up as an independent branch between Iranian and Balto-Slavic.

Part II.

If however Armenian stands between Iranian and Slavic, that is between Aryan and European, we must still examine its position to the special peculiarities of the European languages, through which these are sharply separated from the Aryan languages; that is, we must examine whether Armenian knows the European split of a to a and e, that of r to r and l, and whether or not it presents important points of contact in vocabulary with European. We will proceed at once to answer these questions.

1. Split of a to a and e.

Nothing is more correct than Fick's view that the most important difference between European and Aryan in vocalism consists in the split and non-split of a to a and e. It is certain that no Indic and no Iranian language knows this split. To be sure we write numerous e, i.e. short ä, in New Persian words, but short a simply becomes ä throughout (pronounced as pure a in India),[19] and of a split there is no question here. Ossetic, in the Caucasus, has o and e for and beside a, but e is rare and obviously late; it appears beside ä and both beside a, which a stricter, and older, manner of speaking preserves; and also o = a seems to be only a later darkening of the a in the neighborhood of n and r,[20] but does not enter into consideration here at all. Accordingly Aryan does not know this split.

Armenian on the other hand splits the a completely to a, e, o in the European manner, and is thereby distinguished sharply from the

Aryan related languages, even if it may not coincide in individual examples with the European. But in order to be able to undertake a comparison of the individual examples, we must first survey the vocalism of Armenian in general. The scheme for it is:

basic vowel	lengthening[21]
a	
a e, i, zero	â
o, u, zero	
i, zero	ê, î
u, zero	ui, û

and the accentual law which controls the vocalism is as follows: the accent moved to the penultimate syllable of the word and caused the loss of the last, or the loss of its vowel, so that now the last syllable always has the accent. Short i and u as well as their lengthened forms ê and ui can be maintained only by the accent, that is, if they stand in the last syllable now; if however they lose the accent through the addition of a new syllable, then ê becomes î, ui becomes û, i and u on the other hand are lost.   e.g. i: root vid 'find' = Arm. git, but in the infinitive gt-anél; original vinâça = NPers. gunâh = Arm. vnás; lengthening: mêg 'fog', root migh; mêz 'urine', root migh[1], Skt mih, but in the genitive: mîgi, mîzi[22]. u: root yuj, Arm. luts, infinitive ltsel 'yoke'; lengthening: luis 'light' from raucah, root ruc, but in the genitive lûsóy. From this it is clear at once that gitém 'I know', lizem 'I lick' go back to gêt-em, lêz-em, that is, that in these verbs the lengthened present stem occurs (gêt-em = vêda + later added em = âmi, lêzem = leigh[1]-âmi), except when we deal with denominative verbs, as may be true of mizel 'urinate' beside mêz 'urine'. On the other hand a, â cannot be changed: bazúm 'much' = Skt bahu; bazúk 'arm' = Skt bâhu; asél 'say', Skt. ah. The same is true of o,[23] cf. gochél 'cry', root vac; gortsél 'do' beside gorts 'work' = wérgon. e too generally remains, cf. mets 'great', Gk mégas, genitive: metsi; but it has dropped out occasionally, e.g. vtak 'rivulet' beside get 'river'; astl̦ 'star' = aster; tagr 'brother-in-law' = dawer, genitive = astél, tagér. But if this e comes to stand before nasals and double consonants, it regularly goes over to i,[24] hing = quinque; hin 'alt' = senex; sirt = Herz; and like original i, this i is elided when it loses the accent: hin 'old', hn-anal 'become old'; sirt 'heart', gen. srti. Accordingly e must be assumed everywhere in Armenian where instead of the a-vowel to be expected in accordance with the etymology, e, i or total loss of the vowel has occurred. Accordingly, if Armenian is to take part in the chief characteristic of European, we have to expect to find a) Arm. a (o) = European a (o) and b) Arm. e, i, zero = European e.

a. Arm. a (o) = European a (o). For this correspondence it is adequate to cite few examples: akn 'eye', Lith. akîs, oculus; atsem = ágō; tal 'give' = dare; ail = állos; aits = aíks; hair = patér. gochel = vocare; chorkh 'four' = quatuor; gorts = wérgon; kov 'cow' = bow-ós; ordz 'testicle' = órkhis; orb 'orphan' = orphanós. In addition one should note for inflection that the a-stems — apart from proper names — went completely over to o-stems; for this reason original marta-, Gk broto- appears in Armenian as mardo-, cf. gen. dat. mardoy, instr. mardov, gen. pl. mardoჳ, instr. mardovkh. In this respect Armenian agrees with Latin and Greek.

b. Arm. e = European e. In his book, Die ehemalige sprachein-heit der Indo-germanen Europas, p. 425, Fick listed the original European words to which e must be ascribed. Of these I find the following in Armenian: Arm. sirt = Eur. k^1erd 'heart'; tsnôt (= tsen-ôt) = genu 'chin'; inn (= inun = invan from envan = nevan) = nevan 'nine'; hing = penkan 'five'; mets = mega 'large'; mêj (from medyo) = medhia 'middle'; melr 'honey', melu 'bee' (mélissa) = melita 'honey'; nist (= nsit = ni-sedas) = Eur. sedas 'seat'; hin = sena 'old'; evthn = septan 'seven'; astḷ 'star' = ster; skesur 'mother-in-law' = $svek^1$ura, $sved^1$rû 'in-law'; veჳ = sveks 'six'.... For inflection e is important in nominal suffixes like ter = original tar, therefore dústr 'daughter', gen. dstér; in verbs as the stem-forming verb of the most widely distributed class: berem, beres, berê, etc.; as augment, to the extent it appears: eki 'I came', edi 'I set',[25] etu 'I gave', etes 'he saw', egit 'he found'....

2. Split of the r to r and l.

l is found in Armenian beside two r sounds (rʽ and r) and an ḷ, which is now pronounced by the western Armenians as γ, but in former days transcribes Gk. l. In European l also corresponds to the first l, while r is found in European corresponding to the rʽ, r and ḷ.

a. l = European l: lal 'bewail, weep' root lâ... (Other examples follow.)

b. Arm. r, rʽ, ḷ = European r:
sirt 'heart' = cor... (Other examples follow.)

3. There are various words which go back to a different phonological structure in the European languages than in the Aryan.... (Of the twelve found in Armenian) the Aryan forms compare with the European in the proportion of 3 : 9 = 1 : 3.

4. The last point to be discussed here, the question about the relationship of the Armenian vocabulary to that of the European languages, I have to leave untouched for the time being, because the greater part of the Armenian words are still not yet etymologically clarified.... But in future studies numerous "European" words will be demonstrated to exist in Armenian.

Through the last part of our investigation, such a tight bond has without question been constructed between Armenian and European that it would be easier to tear Armenian from Aryan than from European. Among the European languages it stands closest to Balto-Slavic because of the spirants, with which it was also especially connected by the instrumental suffix bhi, which is common to only these two. In this situation, friends of the family tree, like Fick, will certainly be inclined to separate Armenian completely from Aryan and make it a purely European language. Against this view I might first refer to the fact that Armenian does not take part completely in the split of a and r. . . .

The result of my entire investigation is accordingly as follows:

Armenian stands in the sphere of the Aryan-Balto-Slavic languages between Iranian and Balto-Slavic.

If further research makes this preliminary conclusion definitive, then the impossibility of setting up a family tree of the Indo-European languages would be strikingly demonstrated. For Armenian would be the connecting ring of both parts in the chain of the Aryan-Balto-Slavic languages, not a branch between two branches. And then too the family tree, which Johannes Schmidt's vigorous might has overturned, would remain lying forever.

But if Armenian is to be the connecting member between Iranian and Balto-Slavic, between Aryan and European, then in my opinion it must have played the role of an intermediary at a time when they were still very similar to one another, when the historical period had not yet drawn the present sharp boundary between them, but when they were still related to one another as dialects. Just as Upper Italian folk dialects with their nasal vowels, with ü instead of u and with other characteristics approach French, so that one might expect that Italian at the boundary of France is almost an intermediate between French and Italian, in the same way Armenian might once have been intermediate between the Aryan and the European dialects and therefore have taken part in the characteristics of both. For if we see that the archaic languages of the Avesta and the Veda still stand quite close to one another and that a reconstructed Iranian and an Indic Proto-language would be related to each other in the very same way as dialects, why shouldn't the European languages once have stood in this relationship to one another and Armenian as intermediate dialect between the two types? In this way the peculiar hybrid structure of Armenian can easily be explained. After the wave of the splitting of a and r had arisen in the Western dialects and that of the splitting of the palato-velars in the Eastern, the former penetrated beyond Balto-Slavic and spread further over Armenian, while the latter penetrated outside of Armenian and spread further over Balto-Slavic. The former changed, whether

directly or through a subsequent effect, the a of the Indo-European
numeral dakan to e in Balto-Slavic, and the latter changed the k of
the same word to k^1, so that instead of the IE dakan the Balto-Slavic
basic form dek^1an resulted. When later in Aryan the wave of the
subsequent split of the palato-velars (to velars and palatals) arose,
it was still able, whether it was of itself too weak or whether the
dialects had already begun to separate more and more, to spread
completely over Iranian, but only over Armenian in some offshoots,
so that we find to be sure chorkh = catvar, but also hing = pañcan.

However that may be, if we must view the development of Skt c,
j, h and Av. c, j from k, g, gh in the same forms as proof for the
connection of the Aryan languages, then also the development in the
table below must be viewed as proof for the connection of Aryan with
Armenian and Balto-Slavic:

IE	k,	g,	gh to
Aryan-Arm.-Balto-Slavic	k^1	g^1	gh^1
i.e.Skt.	ç	j	h
Av.	s	z	z
Arm.	s (š, ʒ)	ts	dz,z
Slavic	s	z	z
Lith.	sz	ż	ż

It is obvious that the minute difference between sounds in the individual languages proves nothing against this conclusion, for only the
later phonological propensities[26] of the individual languages are responsible for their existence. For Gothic even confronts the European e with i; and the l of the individual languages which has arisen
from European l is certainly not the same everywhere, as the Gk l
in Armenian transcription is always given by ļ (etymologically = r,
now = γ), never by l. If nonetheless we prove the original connection of the European languages with this e and l, we must also prove
through those spirants the former connection of Aryan, Armenian
and Balto-Slavic. What's sauce for the goose is sauce for the
gander. And finally, as compelled as we are to derive the Aryan
palatals from the pre-Aryan palato-velars, we are equally justified
in deriving the series of the Aryan-Armenian-Balto-Slavic sounds
k^1, g^1, gh^1, to which we take back those spirants, from the series of
the Indo-European palato-velars. For a split of the palato-velars
took place twice in a similar manner but in different extent.

But if one might claim both series for the Indo-European original language, as Fick did with k and k^1, then our argumentation
would be untenable and no closer relationship would be proved between Aryan, Armenian and Balto-Slavic; yet even so the common
formation of the palatals in Aryan, in which Armenian participates,

if only in part, would prove nothing for the closer connection of
Indic-Iranian-Armenian:

k	=	Skt. c,	Av. c	Arm. ch, ʒ, s
g	=	j	j, zh	(k) ž
gh	=	h	j, zh	(g) ž

But then, to be just and consistent, one ought also declare meaningless the few reasons for which Balto-Slavic and Germanic as well
as Greek and Italic or Italo-Greek and Celtic have been generally
assumed to be connected; for they are by no means of greater significance than those by which one can connect Aryan with Balto-
Slavic or Armenian with both of these. Then we would arrive at a
skeptical point of view, and would hold that European e and l too
prove nothing: just as in the one group spirants would arise from
palato-velars in certain cases without motivation, so in the other a
would become e and r would become l in certain cases without motivation. Or if one assumes two basically different k for Indo-
European, why not also two originally different a and r, which had
fallen together in Aryan just as randomly as often happened in
European with Fick's k and k[1]? No one can claim that this point
of view is nonsensical; only Fick will not be inclined to adopt it.

From this point of view there would be nothing further to say
about Armenian than that it is an individual branch of Indo-European.
And as such we will also have to view it from the other point of view,
however its relationship to European and Iranian is to be conceived.
Unfortunately — and to this I'd like to point in conclusion — the etymological investigation of Armenian is still in its beginning, and we
are working with such a minute portion of the Armenian vocabulary
that we cannot foresee what further investigations will uncover; and
it was probably unjustified to erect at this time such bold constructions on such an uncertain basis as was done above. It is by far
most important to separate the Iranian loanwords from Armenian
and to arrive at pure Armenian material. Only when this has been
done can one determine the more precise phonological characteristics of Armenian and thereupon loosen or tighten the bond that con-
nects it with Iranian. But whether this bond is firm or slack, the
close connection of Armenian to European remains undeniable, such
as the formation of the instrumental singular with original bhi, the
(partial) preservation of the palato-velars in contrast with the Aryan
palatals, and the split of a to a and e, that of r to r and l demonstrate. For the time being there are not yet many deviations and
agreements in the vocabulary to be given, since up to now neither
Armenian nor Iranian has been investigated enough etymologically.
Therefore the question of the lexical relationship of Armenian to

Iranian and Slavic must still be viewed as quite open, just as we
have intended to broach the question of the position of Armenian in
the sphere of the Indo-European languages, not to have settled it
decisively.

Notes

1. Fr. Müller also admits this in general, since in a friendly
letter (28 July 1874), in which he wants to have Armenian energetically reclaimed for Iranian and not viewed as a transitional language, he writes: "That there are many foreign words in Armenian
which have penetrated from Proto-Pehlevi is an evident fact; I fear
however that many a word that is good Armenian is regarded as a
foreign word only to be able to deny the Iranian character of Armenian." But it is not adequate to admit this in general; if one wishes
to judge about the character of a language, one must be certain in
every individual instance that the material with which one works is
not foreign stuff. Moreoever, in the interest of the theory which is
presented below I would like very much to have Fr. Müller prove to
me that I have gone too far in the assumption of loanwords.
2. Pers. rôzî, to which lûsik and not r'ocik would have to correspond in Armenian, since Pers. rôz "day" = Arm. luis.
3. Alike only if both go back to s: Arm. mah-ik = NPers. mâh
'moon', from mâsa.
4. Also designated as Persian in the Armenian-Italian dictionary of Caχcaχ.
5. To these must still be added the foreign personal names,
which are sharply distinguished from the real Armenian ones: the
latter have a very characteristic sound and are etymologically obscure; the former are old acquaintances from Persian, like Artavan
= Av. ashavan, and accordingly OPers. *artavan; Artavazd = Av.
ashavaz-daṅh, and accordingly OPers. *artavazdah (the former =
Gk Artábanos Artabanus, the latter = Gk Artabázēs or Artaouásdēs,
Artavasdes) etc. Therefore it is unfortunate to claim to prove
merely from proper names the Iranian character of a people who
are neighbors to the Persians.
6. In the modern dialect of Tiflis, um, which can only be pronominal in origin, consistently forms the locative, while the genitive
and dative have fallen together. This New Armenian therefore has
one case more in nominal inflection — to be sure one newly formed
— than Classical Armenian.
7. One example may demonstrate this: the pronoun of the second person plural is dukh 'you', formed from the singular du =
'thou' with the plural sign of nouns kh = as originally. Probably no
other Indo-European language has gone so far.

8. Also êi, êir, êr etc. would remain unexplained, while in this way we could assume that this imperfect of ah has gone over to the analogical influence of the other verbs; this is also true in part for the present, where ê 'is' is not explained from asti, but probably through analogy from berê 'he bears' = bereti.

9. ⅄ is emphatic ts, just as ch is emphatic tš (c).

10. On the Old High German instrumental in u, see Braune, "Ueber die quantität der ahd. endsilbcn," p. 40.

11. For further information see Spiegel, Grammar p. 345.

12. That Old Iranian had no l is clear from the fact that the modern Iranian languages do not agree in the use of l; compare for example the following examples: Ossetic stal 'star', khalm 'crawling animal (snake)', nal 'man', malin 'die' with NPers. sitârah, kirim, nar, murdan; and conversely: NPers. gulû (gula 'throat') with Ossetic qur = ghur, Afghan ghârah, fem. 'throat'; NPers. talkh 'bitter' with Afghan trîχ, fem. tarχah, NPers. kulâgh = Baloci gurâgh 'crow' (Afghan kârghĕh 'crow' ?). For this reason, in spite of Oppert's objections, Revue de linguistique IV, p. 209), l will have to be denied for Old Iranian.

13. This change is frequent: gail 'wolf' = European valka; get 'river' beside vtak, root vad; gin 'price' venum, original vasna; gini 'wine', vinum; gitel 'know', root vid; gtanel 'find', root vid, vind; gortsel 'work', Av. verez, werg-; tagr 'brother-in-law', dawer-; gochel 'cry' = vac, garun 'spring' = Av. vaṅhra, gišer 'night' = vesper, gar'n 'lamb' = warên, warnós. Old Persian too causes v to change to g, cf. gurg 'wolf' = Arm. gail; but otherwise in different forms than in Armenian: gul 'rose' = Arm. vard, gunâh 'pass' = vnas, etc. Both languages have carried out this change quite independently of each other.

14. Found also in loanwords: phartham 'rich', Phl. fratum; phuršiš 'process' = Pers. pursish; phiḷ 'elephant' = Pers. pîl. In loanwords however which had initial f rather than p, Armenian substituted the similar h, since it had no f: hrasaχ = Arab. farsaχ, Pers. farsang 'parasang'; hraman 'order' = Pers. farmân; hreštak 'envoy, angel' = Pers. firishtah. The Kurds too have changed their f to h, but maintained it in loanwords, e.g. in firman (Justi, Die kurdischen Spiranten, p. 15). The Ossetes on the other hand change initial p consistently to f: farsun 'ask', fondz 'five', fathan 'broad', so that p is initial still only in loanwords, while Afghan substitutes v for f and uses f only in Arabic and Persian loanwords.

15. The series are: original k = Skt k, Iran. k, Arm. k (kh), Balto-Slavic k; and k^1 = Skt ç, Iran s, Arm. s, Slav. s, Lith sz. Armenian agrees with Iranian and Slavic, cf. tasn 'ten'. Occasionally however š is found instead of s, as in šun 'dog' = Skt çvan, pš-nul 'observe', Skt paç, as in NPers. shâkh 'twig' instead of sâkh = çâkhâ,

shustan 'purify' = çudh, an indication that the sharp s of Iranian stands very close to the sh = Skt ç. And when for that reason sz is found in Lithuanian as opposed to Slav. s = k^1, and Indic ç, now pronounced sh, as opposed to Iranian s = k^1, we will consider this difference irrelevant, with Johannes Schmidt against Fick. From the sole Aryan-Balto-Slavic çvan, çuni arose only late the various Skt çvan, gen. çunas, and çuni, Av. sûnô, sûni, Arm. šun, gen. šan, Old Prussian sunis, Lith. szů, gen. szůns. But whatever is valid for Slavic s = Lith. sz must also be valid for Slavic z = Lith. z, original g^1 and gh^1.

16. Through secondary palatalization in the separate existence of Armenian there arose: jerm 'warm' = Skt gharma, NPers. garm and šeram 'silkworm' = Skt kṛmi, Phl. kirm.

17. The secondary form kharʻ is related to chor- as is Av. tûirya to Av. cathware, tûirya = tvar-ya, and kharʻ = tvar; kh = tv as in khsan 'twenty' = dvi-çanti.

18. Add to this: Arm. ch = Skt ch = original sk in the present stem forming sk = Gk sk: Arm. can-ach-em = gignṓskō, Aor. tsaneay, and in chu 'walking' = original sku, Ascoli, Vorles. p. 189.

19. Accordingly in this essay I have written instead of ä, as it is now pronounced in Persia itself, the older a, from which it developed.

20. See barzond 'high', zarond "old" = geront, zond, zund 'knowledge', zônun 'know', fondz 'five', dzorun 'speak', χor 'sun' (= svar), χorun 'eat' (= svar-). How little o means here is shown by kharôn = Av. karana, which forms in the plural: Tagauric kharatthä, Digoric kharanthä.

21. I should like to note that the quantity of vowels is not marked in the Armenian writing system; therefore elsewhere as well I have not indicated a long mark. But this is only a shortcoming of the writing system, with reference to which it must be noted that a, i, u, where they are lengthened forms of the basic vowels a, i, u, must have formerly counted as long or still do. Only e and o are always short.

22. I write here î, as in the following û; for from mĭgí, mĭzí: mgí, mzí would have had to develop, and similarly from lŭsóy: lsóy.

23. Petermann, Grammar p. 37: "omnium vocalium constantissima, quae fere nunquam abjicitur seu mutatur." (The most constant of all vowels, which almost never is lost or changed.)

24. This change of e to i has been carried through completely in the modern dialect of Tiflis, in which o has also become u throughout. In older Armenian u from o = a is found more infrequently: a sure example is probably the suffix forming the decades: -sun, gen. -sni, e.g. innsun, gen. innŭsni '90' = enenḗkonta.

25. The present is dnel = d-ne-l, which according to the sound

laws must go back to de-ne-l. If one compares this with the present tal 'give', then the equation results: Arm. de 'set' : ta 'give' = Gk the : do.

26. Consider how s in Sanskrit, where it was to be voiced, develops to everything, only not z, and how jh, instead of which h shows up, is almost prohibited. It is therefore not remarkable that we do not find in Sanskrit z, to which it was completely opposed, instead of the original g[1]. Notable is the preference of Iranian, Armenian and Slavic (in their oldest form) for the dental spirants over against the palatals of Sanskrit and the linguals of Lithuanian; but nothing is proved by this about the closer relationship of these languages to one another.

CHAPTER THIRTEEN

KARL BRUGMAN

NASALIS SONANS IN THE ORIGINAL INDO-EUROPEAN LANGUAGE

"Nasalis sonans in der indogermanischen Grundsprache,"
<u>Curtius Studien</u> 9 (1876), 287-338

Brugmann's article is included here for two reasons: it illustrates the growing control over articulatory phonetics; it reflects an awareness that the phonological and morphological levels of language are distinct, and that the one can be examined for insights into the other. Only a small portion of the article is given. The remainder is important for comparative Indo-European grammar — the excerpt presented here, for general theory, especially for the assertion that there were vocalic nasals in Proto-Indo-European.

The recognition that PIE m and n were also vocalic led to considerable clarification of the ablaut in the Indo-European languages. Eventually the six resonants — y w r l m n — were classed together, for the clarification of many interrelationships in Indo-European grammar, such as an understanding of the Germanic strong verb bases. Brugmann's formulations are awkward in part — another reason for merely providing excerpts. But publication of the article eventually led to the general assumption of vocalic resonants.

Verner's explanation of the phonological variation in sets like

OHG   ziohan   zōh   zugum   zogen

illustrated that phonological change did not occur by morphological sets but rather in similar phonological environments. Accordingly, aberrancies in morphological sets might point to earlier phonological change. Brugmann led off the investigation of vocalic nasals by scrutinizing patterns in a morphological set, the n̠-stems. His procedure leads to that now known as internal reconstruction; in using it Brugmann is not as precise as is Saussure, but through its use he added conviction to conclusions which were supported by reference to general phonetic observations.

190

The article illustrates a tremendous number published
in the last quarter of the nineteenth century which gradually
clarified the important problems in the Indo-European family. Most dealt with minor problems and received little
lasting acclaim. But their results led to the great compila-
tions, such as Brugmann's Grundriss and to the grammars
of the individual languages, such as Streitberg's, Pedersen's, Meillet's, Hirt's which are still widely used.

Karl Brugmann (1849-1919) is one of the great Indo-
Europeanists. His capacity for work was enormous. He
produced the Grundriss der vergleichenden Grammatik der
indogermanischen Sprachen, second edition 1897-1916,
which will never be superseded, for it is reliable, thorough
and representative of Indo-European studies when many of
the important problems had been clarified. Even though
his writing was prolific, Brugmann was, however, not as
clear and compact as Verner. His article on vocalic nasals lacks the immediate impact of Verner's, though it was
as important for clarification of the Indo-European vowel
system as was Verner's for the Indo-European accent.

Osthoff's essay "On the Question of the Origin of the Germanic
n-Declension," just published in Paul and Braune's Beiträgen III
1 ff., which I became acquainted with several months ago through
a special printing, I will not hesitate to characterize as a work that
will exert for a long time a most profound influence on research in
the field of nominal stem formation and inflection. Its principles,
to be sure, are not new, but its application to the given facts is new
in many instances, and opens a great many quite new and far-
reaching perspectives. I will treat the most essential results of
the essay at another opportunity, in order to use them as a basis
to clear up various phenomena of stem gradation which remain obscure. Here I will deal with a matter which Osthoff handled only in
passing, and which led him to a result whose validity I must question.

I.

As is well known, the accusative plural in Old Indic is for the
most part a weak case in those consonantal declensions, in which
stem gradation occurs. For example, the accusative forms ap-ás
'waters', path-ás 'paths', ukshn-ás 'oxen', tudat-ás 'pushing' stand
in contrast to the nominative plurals áp-as, pánthān-as, ukshán-as

and tudánt-as, and to the accusative singulars áp-am, pánthān-am,
ukshán-am and tudánt-am. A different situation exists in the European languages, which along with the Aryan took part in stem gradation, and have this appear often, though never as clearly and
openly as does the Old Indic. In the European languages the accusative plural is throughout a strong case, so that Osthoff sets up as
basic form for his model the Indo-European stem uks-án-, uksᵃn-as
in the Aryan languages and uksán-as in the European languages.
Naturally now, only one of these two forms can be considered the
original Indo-European form. Either the Aryan or the European
has altered the original relationship.

   Osthoff decides on pages 35ff. in favor of the Aryan languages,
and consequently asserts that the accusative plural in the original
language was a weak case with a weak stem form and a stressed
case ending. If I understand correctly, three considerations lead
him to this assumption:

   1. If uksán-as is taken in the original form, then a shift of the
accent from the stem suffix to the ending has to be assumed for Old
Indic. Shifts of the accent did indeed often occur in Old Indic toward
the beginning of the word, but never in the other direction.

   2. One encounters attempts in many places during the historical period of the Indo-European languages to assimilate the nominative and accusative towards each other in form. Now if uksán-as is
assumed to be the original form, so that in the original language the
nominative and accusative plural were formed alike on the one hand,
and the accusative singular and the accusative plural were on the
other hand accented alike, then Aryan would have taken exactly the
opposite course and would have disturbed the original agreement of
cases.

   3. It is a quite unprovable hypothesis that the original form of
the suffix of our case was -ams or -ans: the whole group of languages points only to -as. This proposition plays a role to the extent that it implies that the accusative plural was not formed by
simply attaching the plural -s to the singular form in -am. Accordingly, there would not necessarily need to be agreement between the
singular and plural as far as the stem gradation is concerned.

   In contrast to these statements let us weigh the following:

   1. Among themes which undergo stem gradation the accusative
plural often appears in Vedic as a strong case with regard to the
form as well as to the accent; for example, áp-as beside ap-ás,
ukshán-as beside ukshn-ás, vŕshan-as beside vŕshn-as. Among
monosyllables without stem gradation, the accusative plural in
Vedic is at times accented as a strong case, at other times as a
weak case, thus rāj-as and rāj-ás, vāk-as and vāk-ás.[1] In themes
of this sort, in later Sanskrit some words appear with the stress on

the stem syllable, such as nắv-as and vāḱ-as, others with the stress
on the case ending, such as mās-ás (Benfey, Vollständige Grammatik p. 318, IV). In Old Bactrian furthermore the accusative plural is probably about as prevalent in the strong form, and thus like
the nominative plural in sound as in the weak form; in the strong,
for example, in çpānō from çpā 'dog', dātārō from dātar 'giver'.
urvānō or urvānō from urvan- 'soul' (See Spiegel Grammar p. 119).[2]
The Vedic ukshánas corresponds very closely to Goth. auhsans; similarly, vāḱas and nắvas to the Gk ópas and nēas. If therefore all the
Indo-European languages are familiar with the accusative plural as
a strong case and only the Aryan, beside the general Indo-European
relationship, exhibits a different one, characteristically peculiar
only to itself, it follows as a matter of course that this exclusively
Aryan form, which even in the Aryan languages is not regular, is
not the original form.

2. The fact that Greek from earliest times on does not use the
same form for the accusative and nominative plural, but shows the
ending -as (ópas) for the former and -es (ópes) for the latter, remains quite enigmatical in Osthoff's conception. For the view that
in the common Indo-European language state, the ending of the nominative plural -as had already undergone weakening to -es, while at
the same time the original form of the accusative plural uks^{a}n-ás
persisted, and that precisely the old stress of the case ending
caused Greek to preserve the pure -a-sound is to my mind highly
artificial; and one must object to it above all, that the assumption
that the high pitch on the end syllable -as prevented any departure
from a pure a-sound is absolutely without basis. For where else in
Greek is such an influence of the accent to be found? I look in vain
for analogies and believe that instances like the genitive op-ós = Old
Indic vāḱ-ás simply demolish Osthoff's hypothesis.

3. Everything indicates that our Indo-European ending -as actually originated from -ams. The m of pad-am (pedem) is without
doubt essentially the same element as the m of akva-m (equum). If
now, as no one doubts, the plural of akva-m was originally akva-ms,
and from that form akva-ns, perhaps already in the original language; this form, however, differs from the singular only by the addition of the plural characteristic s,[3] it is extremely probable that
the plural of pad-am was pad-ams. None of the various languages
prevents our establishing this as the original Indo-European form;
Greek as a matter of fact, points to it most decisively. I will prove
the correctness of this assertion below at relatively great extent.

If we are to consider -ams accordingly as the original form of
the case suffix, then it necessarily follows that the accusative plural
in the original Indo-European period belonged to the strong cases....

(293) We now arrive at the central point of our argument, at the

demonstration that no phonetic obstacle exists to setting up -ams as
the original form, and that Greek -as must necessarily be derived
from -ans.

The vowel of the case suffix -am in Old Indic pád-am, Gk pód-a
Lat. ped-em, etc. has been called a connecting vowel. For the sake
of brevity let us maintain this name provisionally, without wishing
to make any statement about the origin of the vowel. It is surely the
same vowel which we encounter in the inflection of the verb before
endings beginning with -nt, as in the third person plural before -nti,
-nt, and -ntai, -nta, when these endings appear on themes which end
with consonants, such as the Old Indic third person plural dvish-ánti
(cf. first person plural dvish-más). We then call this too a connecting vowel. But now in both Aryan and European a significant difference is shown in the treatment of a when it is a connecting vowel and
when it is thematic (part of the stem suffix); this holds true in nouns
as well as in verbs, so that we are forced to conclude that the thematic a, for example from ákva-m Gk híppo-n and bhára-nti Gk
phéro-nti, was already pronounced differently from the connecting
vowel in the original Indo-European, for example pád-am Gk pód-a
and as-ánti Gk é-anti. As these Greek forms set beside the original
forms show, the difference in this language is still clearly distinct.

In Old Indic, the difference between the two a-sounds can be arrived at from a hard and fast rule, whose operation we will now examine more closely.

It is a constant rule that after a thematic a which is followed by
a consonant,[4] a nasal never disappears without a trace, and conversely that a nasal after a connecting vowel a disappears completely, if its syllable has low tone.

Let us begin with the verb. First, compare the indicative
bhára-nti (Class I) and bíbhr-ati (Class III); the imperative bhára-
ntu and bíbhr-atu; the participial accusative singular bhára-ntam
and bíbhr-atam. Contrast further bíbhr-ati (Class III) and dvish-
ánti (Class II), bíbhr-atu and dvish-ántu, bíbhr-atam and dvish-
ántam. The law to be noted here is not invalidated by the fact that
the third person plural middle of Classes II, V, VII, VIII and IX
lacks the nasal, in spite of the accent on the connecting vowel, as in
dvish-áté, kinv-áté, juñg-áté, tanv-áté and jun-áté. The fact that
this stress is more recent and that the accent originally stood on
the end syllable is proved by such Vedic forms as indh-até, tanv-até,
etc. (Delbrück, Das altindische Verbum p. 74). There is the same
type of relationship between the later tanváté and the Vedic tanvaté
as there is between the later máti- fem. (mens) and the Vedic form
matí-, which also has lost the nasal because of influence of the conditions of the accent; more on this below.

If we now compare the formation of the accusative plural of the a-stems and the consonant stems, we find that áçvān i.e. (*áçva-ns) is like bhára-nti; conversely vā́K-as, i.e. (*vā́K-ans) like bíbhr-ati. We therefore find that ending -as, with which this investigation began, has appeared in complete accordance with the sound laws for Indo-European -ans....

(303) This is the place to go into the articulatory phonetics of our question.... E. Sievers, in his splendid Grundzügen der Lautphysiologie, sets forth the principle, p. 24ff., that the liquids r and l and the nasals ṅ, n, and m can be vowels just as well as consonants. He teaches that, for example, in the usual pronunciation of ritten and handel, rittn and handl, n and l form the whole second syllable, and actually made up a syllable, and are to be designated as actual vowels. Accordingly, a strong distinction should be made between the nasalis sonans as in rittn, ātm and the nasalis consonans as in berittne, ātme; in the first words the nasal carries the accent of the final syllable, while in the second the accent is placed on the e. The sonore nasalis can carry the main stress of the word, as for example in the bisyllabic ń-nein and ń-ja as I know them for the expression of unwilling negation and heated asseveration in the Wiesbaden dialect. Now if we designate vocalic nasal m and n in contrast with the consonantal m and n, I am convinced that we have to establish for the original language beside ákva-m, ákva-ms the forms pád-m, pád-ms, and beside bhára-nti, bhára-ntai the forms as-ńti, ās-ńtai. By means of svarabhakti, i.e. the appearance of a short vowel from resonant consonants before m and n (cf. Sievers, Lautphysiologie p. 142) all the above-cited forms -m, -ms, -nti, etc., developed. First of all, therefore, svarabhakti developed in such forms as patár-m, and then spread also to those instances where a voiceless sound preceded the nasal.

My friend Osthoff urged me on to this conception. During a conversation in which I told him the main results of my study, he said: "One will probably have to posit the nasal in the original language precisely as a vowel" (in the sense of Sievers).[5]

With this assumption, we gain a double advantage. First, we can unite as one the double suffix forms -am, -anti, etc., (in consonant stems) with -m, -nti, etc., (in vowel stems). Second, all the qualitative vowel differences in the various languages which were cited above are simply solved, and I hope, some other difficulties too....

Notes

1. Vā́k-ás as accusative plural Rigveda 1.113.17 according to Grassmann under the word sjūman and Ludwig 1.p.12.

2. In Old Persian the accusative plural of stems ending in consonants is not attested.

3. Compare the instrumental singular -bhim, plural -bhim-s etc.; see Leskien, Die Declination im Slavisch-Litauischen und Germanischen, p. 99ff. 1876.

4. An apparent exception is formed by the participle bhára-nt- in the weak cases, e.g. gen. bháratas; concerning this see the excursus at the end of the article (not included here).

5. Earlier I had explained the difference to myself by ascribing to the vowel designated as connecting vowel the value of an irrational vowel in the original language.

CHAPTER FOURTEEN

HERMANN OSTHOFF AND KARL BRUGMANN
PREFACE TO MORPHOLOGICAL INVESTIGATIONS IN THE SPHERE OF THE INDO-EUROPEAN LANGUAGES I

From Morphologische Untersuchungen auf dem Gebiete der indogermanischen Sprachen I (Leipzig: S. Hirzel, 1878) pp. iii-xx

By 1878 the young linguists at Leipzig were confident enough of their methodology to undertake investigations of virtually all Indo-European problems. To publish their views Osthoff and Brugmann founded a journal of their own, which continued until 1890.

The preface to this journal, written by Brugmann but also signed by Osthoff, states the principles which they and their colleagues followed. The central axiom, that sound laws have no exceptions, was first published by the oldest of the group, August Leskien in Die Declination im Slavisch-litauischen und Germanischen (1876). With Leskien, Wilhelm Scherer, as the preface indicates, gave the initial impulse to the group. One of Scherer's contributions was his rejection of the old notion that the languages of today represent a decline from those of the past; in this way he freed linguistics from some of the burden maintained from the first part of the century.

The principles elaborated by Brugmann were also applied by the other notable neogrammarians: Braune, Delbrück, Paul, and Sievers in addition to those mentioned above. Their shortcomings have been widely discussed. Students who have heard primarily about these may be surprised at the restraint of the preface: the insistence on oral, not paper, language; the study of speech as one of the cultural activities of men; the concern with contemporary language, even with dialects; the suspicion of theory — even today the last sentence of footnote 3 is not without validity; the temperate statement of the neogrammarian axiom and concomitant recognition of analogical modification. After reading the preface one may wonder how it could have led to the shortcomings for which the neogrammarians are blamed. It is clear how on these principles many of the phonological and morphological problems of the Indo-European languages were clarified.

*   *   *

Since the appearance of Scherer's book <u>Zur Geschichte der</u> <u>deutschen Sprache</u> (Berlin, 1868), and principally through the impulses that went out from this book, the physiognomy of comparative linguistics has changed considerably. A method of research has been instituted since then and is winning more and more supporters; it differs in essential respects from the method by which comparative linguistics proceeded in the first half-century of its existence.

The older linguistics, as no one can deny, approached its object of investigation, the Indo-European languages, without first having formed a clear idea of how human speech really lives and develops, which factors are active in speaking, and how these factors working together cause the progression and modification of the substance of speech. Languages were indeed investigated most eagerly, but the man who speaks, much too little.

The human speech mechanism has a twofold aspect, a mental and a physical. To come to a clear understanding of its activity must be a main goal of the comparative linguist. For only on the basis of a more exact knowledge of the arrangement and mode of operation of this psychophysical mechanism can he get an idea of what is possible in language in general — by that one should not think of the language on paper, for on paper almost everything is possible. Moreover, only through this knowledge can the comparative linguist obtain the correct view of the way in which linguistic innovations, proceeding from individuals, gain currency in the speech community, and only thus can he acquire the methodological principles which have to guide him in all his investigations in historical linguistics. Articulatory phonetics concerns itself with the purely physical aspect of the speech mechanism. This science is several decades old, and the older linguistics, since about the 1850's, has also profited by its results; for this we must give it great credit. But the matter is far from ending with articulatory phonetics alone, if one wants to acquire a clear understanding of man's speech activity and of the formal innovations that man undertakes in speaking. Even the commonest sound changes, as, for example, the change of <u>nb</u> to <u>mb</u>, or <u>bn</u> to <u>mn</u>, or the metathesis of <u>ar</u> to <u>ra</u>, are incomprehensible if one proceeds solely from the standpoint of the physical production of sounds. In addition, there must necessarily be a science which undertakes extensive observations of the operation of the psychological factors which are at work in countless sound changes and innovations as well as in all so-called analogical formations. The first outlines of this science were drawn by Steinthal in the essay "Assimilation und Attraction, psychologisch beleuchtet" (Zeitschrift für Völkerpsychologie, I, 93-179), which up to now has received little notice from linguistic science and articulatory phonetics. In the work named below (KZ 24,50f), one of the two authors will soon try to demonstrate fully, starting from this essay of Steinthal, how important it is to form a clear idea of the extent to which sound innovations are on the one hand of a purely psychomechanical nature and on the other hand the physical reflections of psychological processes. Further, the author will there examine thoroughly the effect of association of ideas in speech activity, and the creation of speech forms through the association of forms; and he will attempt to develop the methodological principles relative to it. The older comparative linguistics, while it readily accepted and utilized the teachings of articulatory phonetics, hardly concerned itself at all with the psychological aspect of the speech process, and as a consequence it fell into numerous errors. Only in very recent times is one becoming more aware of that neglect. Fortunately the movement starting with Scherer's efforts, the "neo-grammarian" movement, has already done away with some of the fundamental errors which dominated the entire older linguistics. These errors originated in that very failure to recognize the fact that even the changes and modifications taking place solely in the external speech form and affecting only the phonetic expression of thought are due to a psychological process which takes place prior to the materialization of the sound by the vocal organs. In this regard future research will of course have to investigate many things more carefully and in more detail, and many other viewpoints important to the method of historical linguistics will presumably be disclosed through this association, when historical linguistics and psychology will have entered into a closer relationship with each other than they have maintained up to now.

The insufficient investigation of the speech mechanism, especially the almost total disregard of its psychological side, was in itself a drawback which, in the older comparative linguistics, impeded and retarded the acquisition of correct guiding principles for the investigation of form change and formal innovations in our Indo-European languages. But in addition there was something which had a far worse effect and which gave rise to an error that made the discovery of these methodological principles flatly impossible as long as it persisted.

Formerly the reconstruction of the Indo-European parent language was always the chief goal and focal point of the whole of comparative linguistics. The consequence was that all investigations were constantly directed toward this original language. Within the individual languages known to us through written documents, within the development of the Indian, Iranian, Greek languages, etc., almost exclusive interest was held by the oldest periods, those lying closest to the original language, such as Old Indic, here again especially Vedic, Old Iranian, Old Greek, here chiefly the Homeric dialect, etc.

The more recent language developments were thought of as stages
of decay, of decline, of aging, and with a certain amount of disdain
they were disregarded as much as possible. From the forms of the
earliest historically accessible periods the original Indo-European
forms were constructed. And the latter were made the generally
held criterion for evaluating the structures of attested language formations; so much so that comparative linguistics acquired its general ideas of how languages live, are maintained and change primarily on the basis of the original Indo-European forms. That this,
however, was not the right way to arrive at correct guiding principles for the investigation of form change and form innovation in our
Indo-European languages is so very obvious that one must be surprised at how many have not yet become clear about it. Is not, after
all, the authenticity, the scientific probability, of the original Indo-
European forms, which are of course all purely hypothetical creations, totally dependent on whether they agree in general with the
proper conception of the development of linguistic forms and on
whether they are constructed according to correct methodological
principles? Thus the investigators went around in the most obvious
circles, and even today many still do so, without knowing it or wanting to admit it.

    We have a picture of the manner in which linguistic forms in
general are maintained, not by means of the hypothetical reconstructions in the original language, nor by means of the oldest forms
known to us of Indic, Iranian, Greek, etc., whose prehistory can be
inferred only by way of hypothesis and reconstruction, but — according to the principle that one has to start with the known and from
there advance to the unknown — by means of those linguistic developments whose previous history can be pursued at some length on
the basis of texts and whose starting-point is directly known to us.
The more linguistic material is made available for our observation
in an unbroken written tradition extending through the centuries, the
better off we are; and the farther, with reference to the present, a
stage of a language is removed from the point where its historical
tradition begins, the more informative it necessarily becomes.
Therefore, the comparative linguist must turn his attention from
the original language to the present if he wants to arrive at a correct idea of the manner in which language is maintained, and he
must once and for all rid himself completely of the thought that as
a comparative Indo-Europeanist one need concern himself with the
later stages of the Indo-European languages only when they offer
linguistic material that is of importance for the reconstruction of
the original Indo-European language.

    Language fields like Germanic, Romance and Slavic are without
doubt the ones where comparative linguistics can most securely

acquire its methodological principles. In the first place, the main
condition is met here: we can pursue the development, the process
of change of linguistic forms through many centuries on the basis of
texts. Further we are here to a much greater extent involved with
genuine popular speech, with the common language of communication
and colloquial speech than in such languages as Old Indic, Old Greek,
and Latin. What we know about the old Indo-European languages
through the texts handed down to us is in such a way and to such an
extent literarily influenced speech — the word "literary" taken in its
broadest sense — that we scarcely get to know the genuine, natural,
spontaneous, everyday language of the old Indians, Greeks, and Romans. But it is precisely this latter way of communication of
thoughts which one must have clearly in mind in order to acquire
the correct standpoint for evaluating the linguistic change taking
place in the vernacular and especially for the evaluation of all prehistoric language development. Furthermore, the younger languages
referred to are also by far superior to the ancient languages with
reference to the purpose under discussion, because their development in everyday use, which can be pursued for centuries on the
basis of texts, terminates in a living language abounding in dialects;
but this language does not yet differ so sharply from the older state
of the language of centuries ago, accessible solely in a written reproduction, that it could not furnish an excellent corrective against
the errors that must necessarily creep in repeatedly with exclusive
dependence on this written reproduction of the speech forms of
earlier centuries. Everyone knows, for example, how we can establish the history of High German sounds in the individual dialects
from the Old High German period up to the present day far more
reliably than we can establish the history of Greek sounds in the Old
Greek period, because the living sounds of the present permit the
possibility of correctly understanding the characters through which
the Germans tried to represent their sounds in past centuries. Letters are indeed crude and awkward, and very often actually misleading representations of the spoken sound. It is not possible at all to
get an exact idea of the course of the process of changes, for example, of an Old Greek or Latin dialect.

Precisely the most recent stages of the newer Indo-European
languages, the living dialects, are of great significance for the
methodology of comparative linguistics in many other respects too.
Here I may especially emphasize only one other thing to which linguistic research has paid much too little attention until now, simply
because of the belief that whenever possible it must turn its back on
the language life of the more recent and of most recent times. In
all living dialects the shapes of sounds peculiar to the dialect always
appear much more consistently carried out throughout the entire

linguistic material and maintained by the members of the linguistic
community than one would expect from the study of the older languages accessible merely through the medium of writing; this consistency often extends into the finest shades of a sound. Whoever
is not in the position of making this observation in his native dialect
or elsewhere may refer to the excellent work by J. Winteler Die
Kerenzer Mundart des Kantons Glarus (Leipzig and Heidelberg,
1876) where he can convince himself of the accuracy of what has
been said.[1] And should not they now take this fact to heart, who so
willingly and so often admit of unmotivated exceptions of the mechanical sound laws? When the linguist can hear with his own ears
how things happen in the life of a language, why does he prefer to
form his ideas about the consistency and inconsistency in phonological systems solely on the basis of the inexact and unreliable written
transmission of older languages? If someone wants to study the
anatomical structure of an organic body, and if the most excellent
preparations stand at his disposal, will he then take recourse to
notoriously inexact diagrams and leave the preparations unexam-
ined?

Therefore: only that comparative linguist who for once emerges
from the hypotheses-beclouded atmosphere of the workshop in which
the original Indo-European forms are forced, and steps into the
clear air of tangible reality and of the present in order to get information about those things which gray theory can never reveal to
him, and only he who renounces forever that formerly widespread
but still used method of investigation according to which people observe language only on paper and resolve everything into terminology, systems of rules, and grammatical formalism and believe
they have then fathomed the essence of the phenomena when they
have devised a name for the thing — only he can arrive at a correct
idea of the way in which linguistic forms live and change, and only
he can acquire those methodological principles without which no
credible results can be obtained at all in investigations in historical
linguistics and without which any penetration into the periods of the
past which lie behind the historical tradition of a language is like a
sea voyage without a compass.

The picture of the life of language that someone gets, on the one
hand, through the study of more recent language developments and
of the living dialects and, on the other hand, through a consideration
of those things which an observation of the psychological and physical speech mechanisms place at his immediate disposal — this picture differs in essential features from that other picture which
comparative linguistics formerly saw arising out of the original
Indo-European fog when it was still looking only for the primitive
language; this picture is still the guiding form for many investigators

today. And precisely because this discrepancy exists, there remains, we believe, no other choice than: to reform the previous
methodological principles of our science and to abandon forever
that hazy picture which can in no way disavow its foggy home.

That is by no means to say that the whole structure of comparative linguistics, as far as it has been erected till now, should
be torn down and built up again from the beginning. In spite of the
above-mentioned shortcomings of the method of investigation, such
an abundance of important, and so it seems, permanently reliable
results have been achieved through the discernment and industry of
the investigators who have been active in our field, that one can look
back with pride upon the history of our science so far. But it is not
to be denied that many faulty and untenable things are mixed in with
the many good ones, even though many investigators at present still
regard the untenable components as certain conclusions. Before
one builds further, the whole structure, as far as it now stands, has
need of a thoroughgoing revision. Even the foundations contain numerous unsolid places. That part of the masonry which is already
set on top of these must necessarily be brought down again. The
other part of the masonry, which already towers fairly high in the
air, can remain standing or need only be touched up because it rests
on a good foundation.

As was already indicated above, it is Scherer's achievement to
have effectively broached the question of how changes and innovations take place in a language. To the horror of not a few fellow
investigators, but luckily for the discipline itself, Scherer in the
book named above, made ample use of the principle of leveling in
his explanations. Many forms of even the oldest historically accessible stages were suddenly according to him nothing other than formations by "false analogy";[2] until then investigators had always regarded these as purely phonetic developments from the original
Indo-European forms. That was against all tradition and hence
aroused distrust and opposition at the outset. Now, in many points
Scherer was without doubt wrong; in not a few, however, also without doubt correct. And no one can contest his right to that one
achievement which overshadows all errors and which can hardly
be valued highly enough: because of him investigators were for the
first time faced with the question of whether the way in which they
had previously been accustomed to judging form changes in old
stages of a language, as in Old Indic, Old Greek, etc., could be the
right one, and of whether these languages did not have to be treated
from the same point of view as the newer languages in which they
had readily admitted "formations by false analogy" in rather great
measure.

Some linguists, particularly a few most directly concerned

passed over the question and, abruptly rejecting it, remained satisfied with the old way. No wonder. When serious attempts at upset
are directed against a procedure that one is used to and with which
one feels comfortable, one is always more readily stimulated to
ward off the disturbance than to undertake a thorough revision and
possible alteration of the accustomed procedure.

But with others, especially younger scholars, the seed scattered
by Scherer fell on fruitful ground. Leskien above all seized upon
the thought, and since he reflected on the concept of "sound law" and
"exception to the law" more profoundly than had been done before,
he arrived at a set of methodological principles which he at first
made fruitful in his university lectures in Leipzig. Then other
younger investigators, personally stimulated by him (among them
also the authors of these Untersuchungen), tried and still do try to
bring them to wider acceptance and recognition. These principles
are based on a two-fold concept, whose truth is immediately obvious: first, that language is not a thing which leads a life of its own
outside of and above human beings, but that it has its true existence
only in the individual, and hence that all changes in the life of a language can only proceed from the individual speaker;[3] and second,
that the mental and physical activity of man must have been at all
times essentially the same when he acquired a language inherited
from his ancestors and reproduced and modified the speech forms
which had been absorbed into his consciousness.

The two most important principles of the "neogrammarian"
movement are the following:[4]

First, every sound change, inasmuch as it occurs mechanically, takes place according to laws that admit no exception. That
is, the direction of the sound shift is always the same for all the
members of a linguistic community except where a split into dialects occurs; and all words in which the sound subjected to the
change appears in the same relationship are affected by the change
without exception.

Second, since it is clear that form association, that is, the creation of new linguistic forms by analogy, plays a very important role
in the life of the more recent languages, this type of linguistic innovation is to be recognized without hesitation for older periods too,
and even for the oldest. This principle is not only to be recognized,
but is also to be utilized in the same way as it is employed for the
explanation of linguistic phenomena of later periods. And it ought
not strike us as the least bit peculiar if analogical formations confront us in the older and in the oldest periods of a language in the
same measure or even in still greater measure than in the more or
most recent periods.

This is not the place for going into further particulars. Yet let us here briefly call attention to two other main points so that we may justify our method in the face of some objections made to it recently.

One of them is this. Only he who adheres strictly to the principle of sound laws, this mainstay of our whole science, has firm ground under his feet in his investigations. There are, on the one hand, those who needlessly, only to be able to satisfy certain desires, admit of exceptions to the sound laws governing a dialect,[5] who except either individual words or classes of words from a sound change which has demonstrably affected all other forms of the same type, or who postulate a sporadic sound change which has taken place only in isolated forms and which has not affected all other forms of the same kind; and finally, there are those who will say that the same sound, in the very same environment, has changed in some words one way, in other words another. He who does this and who in addition sees in all these unmotivated exceptions which are favored by him, something very normal which he thinks follows from the very nature of mechanical sound change, and he who then even — as very frequently happens — makes these exceptions the basis of further conclusions, which are to abolish the consistency of the sound law that is otherwise observed,[6] he necessarily falls victim to subjectivism and arbitrariness. In such instances he can indeed put out quite ingenious conjectures, but none that merit belief, and he must not then complain when he is faced with cold rejection. That the "neogrammarian" movement is not yet in a position to explain all "exceptions" to the sound laws is, of course, no basis for an objection against its principle.

And secondly, a few more brief words about the use of the principle of analogy in the investigation of the older periods of a language.

Many believe that analogical formations arise principally in those stages of a language in which the "feeling for the language" has "degenerated" or, as one also says, in which "the awareness of language has grown dim"; and thus they believe that one cannot expect analogical formations in the older periods of a language to the same extent as in the later.[7] A strange way of looking at things! This point of view arose among those who think that a language and the forms of a language lead a life to themselves, apart from the individual speakers and who permit themselves to be governed to such an extent by terminology that they continually regard metaphorical expressions as reality itself and even incorporate into the language concepts which are only the ways in which the grammarian looks at things. If someone could once and for all manage to get rid of these generally harmful expressions "youth" and "old age" of languages! These and many other in themselves quite innocent grammatical

terms have so far been almost exclusively a curse, hardly a bless-
ing. For the child who was born in Greece in the Homeric age, who
became aware of the speech forms of his linguistic community by
hearing them, and who then reproduced them in order to make himself understood by his fellow men — for that child were these speech
forms ancient? Did he feel and handle them differently from the
way in which a Greek of the Alexandrian age or someone of still
later times felt and handled them?[8] If today a Greek dialect of the
20th century B.C. or a Germanic dialect of the 8th century B.C. suddenly became known to a grammarian, would not he then immediately alter his conception of antiquity, which he associates with the
Homeric and Gothic dialects, and henceforth call old things young?
And would he not in all probability henceforth drop the notion that
the Greeks of Homeric times and the Goths of the 4th century A.D.
were people with a "degenerate feeling for language," with a "dim
awareness of language"? And do such predications have anything at
all to do with the thing itself? Or might the older Indo-European
peoples, suspecting what was coming, not have analogized the forms
of their time a great deal in order to satisfy the grammatical desires of their offspring and not make the business of reconstructing
the Indo-European parent language too difficult? We believe: as
sure as we are that our Indo-European forefathers had need, just as
we do, of their lips, tongue, teeth, etc. for the articulation of the
sounds of their language, just as sure can we be of the fact that the
entire psychological aspect of their speech activity (the emergence
of sound images preserved in the memory from a subconscious
state, and the development of concepts of sounds to words and sentences) was influenced by the association of ideas in the same way
and in the same measure as today and as long as people are people.
One must also understand that the difference in overall make-up
which exists between the individual old Indo-European languages,
the descendants of the same original Indo-European language, would
not be nearly so considerable if in prehistoric periods regular phonetic change of the original forms had only taken place and if reformations and new formations by analogy had not supplemented it to a
very great extent. Therefore there is nothing to that difference between old and young.

At first glance another objection which has been raised against
us recently in order to discredit our efforts makes more sense. It
is said: whoever operates with the concept of analogy can here and
there perhaps hit upon the right thing with a stroke of luck, but in
the main he can only appeal to faith. Now, that latter statement is
quite right, and everybody who deals with the principle of analogy is
also clearly aware of it. But consider the following. First: if, for
example, the suffixal ending of the nominative plural Gk hippoi, Lat.

equi can not be reconciled with that of Osc. Núvulanús, Goth. vulfôs, Old Ind. açvâs on the basis of the sound laws, and if we have come to the conclusion that one of the two formations must be an analogical creation, is it such a bold stroke if we assume that híppoi and equi were formed according to the pronominal declension (such as originally tai, from ta-, Old Ind. te, Gk toí, etc.)? Of the same or similar simplicity are, however, countless other instances where we have recourse to our principle, whereas others arbitrarily stretch and bend the sound laws in order not to let the speaking peoples be bad grammarians who did not remember their forms and paradigms properly. Second: A principle which we strictly maintain, to the best of our ability, is: only then to take recourse to analogy when the sound laws compel to us. Form-association is for us too an "ultimum refugium." The difference is only that we see ourselves confronted with this much sooner and much more often than are the others, precisely because we are so punctilious about the sound laws and because we are convinced that the boldest assumption of the operation of analogy always has more claim to be "believed" than arbitrary evasions of the mechanical sound laws. Third: It was not long ago that the beginning was made to establish rights for the principle of analogy. Hence it is, on the one hand, very probable, indeed sure, that blunders have been made here and there in the assumption of form associations. But, on the other hand, it is also very probable that more general principles will gradually be found to cover the diverse tendencies of association, especially when the modern languages have been investigated more thoroughly with regard to their analogical formations. In this way a probability scale can also gradually be established for the assumption of association. The essential thing in the meantime is for people to have the good intention of permitting themselves to be instructed by the facts of modern language developments and then for them to conscientiously apply what they have learned to the older periods of a language.

Thus we believe that the objection that our work with the principle of analogy is reprovable because it terminates in mere conjecture has been proven to be unjustified, and we want to add one more thing in conclusion of this discussion. If the "neogrammarian" movement with its methodological principles gives up many of the original Indo-European forms which have circulated for a long time in our science and which are probably very dear to many, and if the movement is not now in a position to go along on the "idealistic flight" into the periods of primitive and pre-primitive language — as this flight is now so often attempted — and if the neogrammarian movement with its skeptical attitude seems to lag behind those who are always looking toward the primitive language and if it appears inferior in its efficiency to the older movement, it can surely console itself with the thought that for a young science, as comparative linguistics is in spite of its sixty years, it must be of more concern to fly as safely rather than as far as possible. On the other hand, it can cherish the hope that what it gives away in primitive and primitive-primitive linguistic niceties will be amply made up for through the attainment of a deeper understanding of the mental activity of human beings in general and of the individual Indo-European peoples.

We believed that we should preface the present Untersuchungen with our creed because they are to contribute primarily to bringing the "neogrammarian" movement into more and more general acceptance. We may also, however, here ask our several critics to keep in mind constantly the principles by which we have decided in favor of this or that assumption. In the last years people have unfortunately passed numerous unfavorable judgements on our movement or on some of the opinions advanced by this movement; they only prove that the judges in question have not considered at all what motives led us to follow just this method and no other. An understanding and agreement between the different movements in our science which are at present battling with each other can not be brought about by such occasional skirmishings which skirt the basic questions and not by directing one's blame solely against details, but only by taking aim at the leading motives and principles. That is not to say, of course, that we, for our part, would not be heartily grateful for a detailed demonstration of mistakes and errors.

Heidelberg and Leipzig, June, 1878

Notes

1. One should give special consideration to the remarks this phonetician (p. 233) makes in general about the unreliability of the usual representation of the spoken word and about the dangers which result from it for linguists.
2. Thus Scherer maintained, for example, (which one of the authors, O., still disputed unjustly in his Forschungen, II, 137) that Old Indic bhárâmi "I carry" was not the phonetic descendant of an original Indo-European form bharâmi, but that in Indo-European one said bharâ and that Old Indic bhárâmi was a new creation by analogy with athematic verbs like dádâmi.
3. This had previously been accepted in theory. But the fact that people were accustomed to seeing language only on paper as

well as the fact that people always said "language" when, strictly
speaking, they ought to have said "the men who speak" — it was not,
for example, the Greek language which was averse to spirants,
dropped final t, changed thíthēmi to títhēmi, etc., but those among
the Greeks with whom the sound change in question started — had as
a consequence that people frequently forgot the true state of affairs
and attached a completely false idea to the term "language." Terminology and nomenclature are often a very dangerous enemy of
science.

4. The following have expressed themselves (in general) about
these principles: more briefly: Leskien, Die Declination im
Slavisch-litauischen und Germanischen (Leipzig, 1876), Merzdorf,
Curtius' Stud., IX, 231 f.; 341, Osthoff, Das Verbum in der Nominal-
composition (Jena, 1878); more extensively, Brugman, Stud., IX, 317
ff. and Kuhn's Zeitschr., XXIV, 3 ff.; 51 ff. and especially Paul,
Beitr. zur Gesch. der deutschen Sprache u. Liter., IV, 320 ff. In
addition, most recently Brückner, "Zur Lehre von den sprachlichen
Neubildungen im Litauischen," Archiv für slav. Phil., III, 233 ff. and
Osthoff's review of Ascoli's Studi critici in Jena Lit.-zeit., 1878,
no. 33.

5. We are of course speaking here only of mechanical sound
change, not of certain phenomena of dissimilation and metathesis.
The reason for the latter lies in the peculiarity of the words in which
they appear; they are always the physical reflections of purely psychological stimuli and in no way nullify the concept of sound law.

6. Reference is made to such an example below p. 156, fn. 1.
(not included here).

7. Often one encounters the statement in linguistic works that
a given form stems from too ancient a period to be considered a
formation by false analogy.

8. Naturally we are here speaking only of common colloquial
speech and of the people who approached language with no literary
or grammatical training.

CHAPTER FIFTEEN

EDUARD SIEVERS

ON THE ACCENT AND PHONOLOGY OF THE
GERMANIC LANGUAGES. III. ON THE LAW OF
VOCALIC FINALS

"Zur Accent- und Lautlehre der germanischen Sprachen. III.
Zum vocalischen auslautsgesetz," Beiträge zur Geschichte
der Deutschen Sprache und Literatur, 5 (1878), 63-163

In a long discussion on "accent and phonology in the
Germanic languages" Eduard Sievers proposed a solution
for the difference between the endings of Gothic harjis and
hairdeis which illustrates his capabilities in analysis and
the initial steps towards recognizing allophonic variation
in language. The solution came to be known as Sievers's
law, now occasionally Sievers-Edgerton's law, after two
important articles by the late Franklin Edgerton: "Sievers's
law and IE weak-grade vocalism," Language 10. 235-65
(1934) and "The Indo-European Semivowels," Language 19.
83-124 (1943). In its current form it proposes that [i],[y],
and [iy] were allophones of PIE /y/, determined by its phonological environment; also that the other Proto-Indo-
European resonants underwent the same allophonic variation.
    Sievers recognized the "law", but did not describe the
conditioning features thoroughly; nor did he apply it to the
Indo-European resonants other than /y w/. His recognition
was achieved before it was generally accepted that Proto-
Indo-European has "several a vowels"; see the excerpt below from Saussure. The segment of Sievers's discussion
included here illustrates the concern with accent, with more
precise definition of other phonological entities, and with
the relations between morphological and phonological structures that was general after Verner's article. It also reflects the increasing preoccupation with metrics.
    Eduard Sievers (1850-1932) was probably the most
brilliant of the neogrammarians. He had a remarkably fine
capability for analyzing language. Among his legendary ac-
complishments was the identification of the Old English
Genesis as a translation from Old Saxon before there was

evidence for an Old Saxon poem on Genesis; it was later
discovered in the Vatican. Another is his early recognition
of the relationship between the accent and the phenomenon
clarified by Verner. Like Verner he made his initial suggestion in a letter; this letter, written to Braune 24 March
1874, Sievers himself never published, nor did he proceed
to a thorough formulation of the discovery as did Verner.
Streitberg published a part of the letter in <u>Germanisch</u>, pp.
287-8:

> But the verbs in -<u>ja</u>? Should one think of the influence
> of the accent, for those in -áyati, -ā́yati originally have
> the accent after the stem syllable just as the preterite
> plurals do? According to the root vowel and the Slavic
> accentuation -énŭ the preterite participle also must
> have had an accent like *numánas. But how are accent
> and weakening related? The -<u>da</u> of the preterite par-
> ticiple of the weak verbs, such as *<u>nas-i-dá-s</u> is
> surely also pertinent; cf. Skt <u>uktá</u> etc., Gk <u>plek-tós</u>,
> etc.; also Gk -<u>ikós</u> = Goth. *<u>ei-ga-s</u> etc. A pity that
> we still do not have the beginnings of a sensible theory
> of accent; and who can understand German sound
> changes without an understanding of shifts of accent?

Fortunately Sievers made ample contributions to linguistics
without pursuing this idea. A professor at 21, his long career at Leipzig made it one of the leading centers in linguistics.

The multiple recognition of the role of accent in language change is a further indication of the maturing of linguistics. It also illustrates that discoveries were not simply made by men of genius, but by capable workers in a
developing field; and credit goes to those who formulated
the discovery. The most notable multiple recognition at
the time was that of the "law of palatals." During the 1870's
it became clear to a number of linguists — Ascoli, Thomsen,
Verner, Tegnér, Saussure, Collitz, Schmidt — that Sanskrit
palatals were found in environments where the European
languages had <u>e</u>. This observation led to the conclusion
that more than one vowel must be assumed for late Proto-
Indo-European and to the assumption of <u>e a o</u> where
Schleicher posited <u>a</u>; it also contributed further to reducing the reliance on Sanskrit for comparative purposes, and
instead to the reconstruction of Proto-Indo-European. Like
the excerpt presented here, formulation of the "law of palatals" was only one of a great number of fine observations

which were being published in the last quarter of the nineteenth century, often to be refined later, as Edgerton did
for Sievers's law.

[125-31] A further reason against the assumption of general
Germanic syncope of a I take from the inflection of the ja-stems.
In order to clarify everything here, however, I must expand some-
what.

It is a question of the explanation of the groups of sounds: -ji
and -ei in harjis, hairdeis and the corresponding verbal forms
nasjis, sôkeis; on these compare Scherer, Zur Geschichte der
Deutschen Sprache 113f.; Zimmer, Zeitschrift für deutsches Altertum 19.419; Amelung, ibid. 21. 230f.; Osthoff, Zeitschrift für
vergleichende Sprachforschung 22.89f.

Scherer, whose view Zimmer and Amelung accept, as is known
derives harjis and hairdeis from *harijas and *hairdijas through
syncope of the a; in complete accordance with the views of Scherer,
Zimmer and Amelung interpreted the latter forms as hárijàs,
hairdìjas. This in turn presupposes the validity of the law of the
Middle High German low accent, which I believe I have disproved
for the original Germanic language; according to the principles proposed in Beiträge 4. 522ff., I can make no other assumption than
that those forms, presupposing three syllables, were each pronounced hárijàs, hairdijàs. Why shouldn't both have developed similarly to harjis, *hairdjis, as the group of sounds ji is maintained
undisturbed in the genitive singular neuter in reikjis, kunþjis etc. or
in fairnjin etc.; or why isn't it *hareis, like hairdeis, after the analogy of naveis and gasteis from *navijiz and *gastijiz? [The ending
-iz is supported by OE fêt, ON fœtr = *fôtiz; see above 111.] There
is also a strong physiological question concerning the assumed loss
of the vowel a between the consonants j and s; but I would not like to
press this too strongly here, for the discussion necessary for its
support might find little support.

I can come to terms still less with the view of Osthoff than with
this conception, which one might call the general point of view and
which one has to agree is consistent and logical in its point of view.
A development of *hairdjas, *harjas through *hairdjs and *harjs to
*hairdjis and harjis by means of the development of an auxiliary
vowel from the j may indeed be represented graphically but not be
made credible for the written language. If this a was actually lost
after the j, then according to the laws developed in Lautphysiologie
§ 22 this j should have become the vowel i, and we would get only
*hairdis, *haris. If one wanted to take refuge in the fact that j may

not have been a semivowel, but rather a spirant or obstruent, then
the development of an auxiliary i could not be conceived, nor its
contraction with a completely non-homogeneous vowel. Finally, the
objection that Scherer's hypothesis necessarily requires the dative
form *hairdija does not hold up any better, for the development of a
medial ija to ja is without question in sôkja and similar forms.

But if the assumption of harjis and hairdeis as general Germanic forms raises so many problems, one might simply ask
whether they indeed have any claim to this status. North Germanic
does not play a decisive role here; its forms niðr, hirðir = Goth.
niþjis, hairdeis have the same phonological relationship as do ON
biðr, sœkir = Goth. bidjis, sôkeis; hirðir, sœkir however are justified by means of analogies like ástir, nœmir = Goth. ansteis, nêmeis,
whose i is certain in the Germanic period. Accordingly in the
northern languages there is no sound law which hinders our equating
hirðir directly with Goth. hairdeis.

It's quite different in West Germanic. The older Anglo-Saxon,
Old Saxon and Old High German attest in weak verbs with short syllables instead of Goth. ji only i, e without lengthening of the preceding consonant. Compare, for example, from the Old Kentish psalter
(Ed. Stevenson, London and Edinburgh, 1844) reces 2, 9, seleð 7, 8
etc., seles 15, 10 etc., cweceð 7, 13, ðeneð 7, 13, sites 7, 4 etc.,
swereð 14, 4, gestes 17, 44 etc., segeð 18, 2 (cf. J. Grimm, Grammatik I⁴, 822f.); Old Saxon fremis, frumid, habis, habid, hugis,
hugid, letid, sagis, sagið, telid; Old High German examples, Grimm
Grammatik I⁴, 788. [In Old High German, this law was broken
through early by the sound shift, like many other things. The form
of the infinitive, of the plural and subjunctive present is carried
through everywhere where there was too great difference of the
sound; accordingly, sezzis, deckis, like sazta, not *se33iz, *dechis
etc., = OE setes, þeces]. The j was merged here throughout to a
simple vowel with i of the verbal ending, which was proved to be
general Germanic through its causing umlaut in the strong verb at
a very early time, before the beginning of the consonant lengthening.
Differently among the nouns. Here we have nominatives and accu-
satives like OE hrycg, mecg, slecg, wecg, þrymm, neuter cynn,
webb, bedd, nett, flett, OS hruggi, nt. bed, flet(ti), net(ti), siukki,
kunni, webbi, OHG hrukki, nt. kunni, tenni, stukki, giuuiggi, âuuiggi,
stuppi, uueppi, betti, antlutti, nezzi, uuizzi, etc.; further, adjectives
like OE nytt, gesibb, OS middi, thriddi, luggi, OHG luggi, fluggi,
âuuiggi, sibbi, nuzzi, accordingly throughout lengthening of the consonant before the ending. I believe that this proves that a j was
still present in West Germanic before the final vowel; and since
analogy with the verb has just showed us that ji was not possible in
West Germanic the final vowel must have been other than i. Where

else might this questionable vowel arise other than from the thematic a? As the last general Germanic original form of the short syllable stems we must therefore not assume harjis, kuni, but only *harjəz, *kunjə; in these ə may designate the vowel sound that cannot be determined, which developed gradually under the influence of the j from the thematic vowel a². But also for the long syllable stems non-shortened forms with ia or iə must be assumed. For if the Germanic original form of the neuters had been, for example, rîki or even *rîkî, then the i would have been compelled to drop in Old English and Old Norse as in the imperatives OE sêc, ON sœk = Goth. sôkei, or in the feminines OE bend, hôeð, ON heið-r (with non-original r) = Goth. bandi, haiþi. Details are given about this below. [A further proof for the non-originality of the i in the nominative of the neuters is given by ON hey = Goth. havi. If havi were original Germanic, then the i would have been compelled to drop in North Germanic after short syllable without producing umlaut. Proto-Germanic *naviz regularly yielded ON há-r, as *favaz yielded fár; or in order to give an analogy for the medial position as well, as beside the verbs *haujan, *þraujan = ON heyja (OE hêgan), þreyja the preterites *haviða, *þraviða, i.e. ON háða, þráða regularly occur. ON hey can accordingly stand only for Gmc *hauja, *haujə (cf. Lappish avje, Thomson 131). On the other hand one may not adduce the analogy of mœr, þý = Proto-Norse *mavi-r, *þivi, for these forms actually have the ending Gmc -î, as will become clear later. But the inflection mœr, meyjar can warn us not to view the nominative-accusative hey prematurely as possible analogical formations to the other cases.] None of the forms discussed can be explained through analogical formation, for apart from them there is nowhere a pattern by which they could have been formed. There are clearly three groups: ja-stems that have remained short, with e in the nominative-accusative, e.g. here and the borrowing ele; those that have become long (through consonant gemination) without vocalic ending, hrycg, cynn; old long syllables with e, hyrde, rîce.

Examination of the genitive singular of the ja stems leads to similar results with regard to the non-originality of the Gothic forms. For in order to maintain hairdeis as common form, one must first of all seize upon the highly questionable assumption of a Proto-Germanic contraction of ie to î in the penultimate (while the e of the genitive elsewhere did not become i, does not cause umlaut); then however one must explain all West Germanic forms as new formations (OE hyrdes, rîces, OS hirdies, rîkies, OHG hirtes, rîches). Only the North Germanic hirðis, rîkis can with some difficulty be compared with the Gothic. Shouldn't one then rather admit that the Gothic hairdeis owes its development only to

the specifically Gothic aversion to the sound e, with which was apparently also associated an effect from the nominative? Only in
this way do the neuters, with their prevailing genitives in -jis, receive their due: kunþjis, reikjis, faírgunjis, andbahtjis, valdufnjis,
gavaírþjis beside andbahteis, valdufneis, gavaírþeis, trausteis,
fauramaþleis (see the list in Heyne, Ulfilas § 23). The lack of a
nominative similar in sound helped to preserve the older forms
here.

Accordingly: the i in Goth. harjis is a remainder of the thematic a; it did not develop from the derivative suffix i or j but was
only conditioned in its color by these. The same remainder is found
also in haírdeis, which we have to resolve first of all in a previous
three-syllabic *herðiiz or *herðijiz, whose treatment corresponds
completely with that of naveis, ansteis (cf. p. 125). Goth. naveis is
particularly welcome as evidence that the contraction has nothing to
do with quantity or with an accentual law dependent on quantity, as
we objected above. For the language it's quite immaterial which of
two similar contracted vowels had the accent; I need only recall the
well-known elementary rules of Greek grammar.

The difference between the short and long syllable ja-stems accordingly consists only in the fact (as Scherer already recognized,
though in my view without adequate justification) that the former had
consonantal j, the latter vocalic, i.e. syllabic, i in their suffixes.

But where does this difference arise, if it does not depend on
the low accent law? One would scarcely assume with no further
evidence an earlier, general Germanic existence of this law in the
Lachmann version, and a later complete reversal especially in West
Germanic! On what should we base our suggestions? We will
therefore have to go farther back and hold to the original Indo-
European language.

If one may take confidence in the investigations of Benfey
(Abhandlungen der Göttingen Gesellschaft der Wissenschaften 16.
91ff., 1871), the suffix ia was used interchangeably in the Veda as
monosyllabic or bisyllabic. If one however examines the situation
more precisely, a quite definite law stands out: unaccented (without
svarita) i or u before a vowel is consonantal after a short syllable,
vocalic after a long syllable, without regard for the other accentual
situation of the word. Compare examples like the following:

ajuryá:	asûriá	ávya:	mártia
aryá	kâviá	-búdhya	ayásia
anishavyá	taugriá	-avadhya	árdhia
kavyá	pûrviá	íbhya	açmásia
gavyá	bhâviá	gávya	áçvia
divyá	açâsiá	mádhya	aria etc.

[For the references, see Grassmann. Here I must withhold giving
the proof for the above principle at length or discussing the regular
exceptions which occur and the violations against it, which in part
are not insignificant criteria for determining the age of Vedic
hymns. I will only note here that that principle is only a segment
of an extensive rhythmical law in oldest Sanskrit and Indo-European,
particularly concerning the relationship of the vowels i, u and the
semivowels y, v; for years I have been collecting material in support of it. Precise observation of these principles will be useful not
only for metrics but also for grammar itself. It turns out, for example, that the lengthenings before r + consonant were still foreign
to the living Vedic language; that ūr, īr always developed through r,
and the like.] Exceptions are the suffixes beginning with a consonant like -bhyās, -bhyām, -tva, to the extent that these (like word-
initial consonants + y, v in general) were used interchangeably after
long syllables (after short syllables only with consonantal y, v, i.e.
monosyllabic); further certain short syllabic adjectives, especially
verbal adjectives with bisyllabic suffix (Grassmann's Part. IV):
gádhia, gúhia, gopayátia, carkṛ́tia, tújia, dábhia, dṛ́çia (mádia,
yújia?), çásia, çrútia, hávia (while for example the suffix of the
so-called ya-class or the passive follows the rule).

I may report that Hübschmann has recently established the
same laws for Old Bactrian, starting from another point of view,
so that three languages may already be called upon as mutual wit-
nesses for the great age of the phenomenon. In the remaining languages the old difference seems to have been eliminated early; at
any rate none of them shows such an obvious observance of the law
as do the three named. But scholars will doubtless succeed in finding remnants of the rule still in details. I'd like to direct attention
to one such still: the Greek adjectives hágios and stúgios, which
correspond to hádzomai i.e. *hagjomai and similar forms in the
same way as do the Sanskrit verbal adjectives to the corresponding
verbs.

Probably the most general formulation of the law discovered
here may be given as follows: the vowel of a syllable of derivation
is and remains heavier after a preceding long than after a preceding
short (therefore ia, ua remain bisyllabic in the first case; in the
second they become monosyllabic).

CHAPTER SIXTEEN

FERDINAND DE SAUSSURE

MÉMOIRE ON THE PRIMITIVE SYSTEM
OF VOWELS IN THE INDO-EUROPEAN LANGUAGES

Mémoire sur le système primitif des voyelles
dans les langues indo-européennes (Paris: Vieweg, 1887),
authorized reprint of the 1879 edition

Saussure's achievement in his Mémoire is phenomenal.
Published during his student days, actually in 1878 rather
than the indicated 1879, it was far in advance of his time.
Applying the method of internal reconstruction to Proto-
Indo-European, he proposed the hypothesis that the long
vowels had developed from short vowel plus sonant coefficients. His hypothesis was confirmed after Hittite was discovered. J. Kurylowicz in 1927 pointed out that the Hittite
consonants transcribed with ḫ corresponded in some cognates to those which Saussurē had suggested purely on the
basis of phonological analysis of morphological patterns.
The Mémoire is accordingly a fine example of the method
of internal reconstruction, possibly the most dramatic application that has been made.
　　The consonants proposed by Saussure were related to
Semitic by Hermann Möller in the following year, and have
subsequently been known as laryngeals; their position in
the phonological system of Proto-Indo-European and pre-
Indo-European has subsequently been one of the intriguing
questions of Indo-European linguistics. As is clear from
the excerpts presented here, Saussure's chief interest was
clarification of the Indo-European ablaut relationships generally, not merely of the roots with long vowels. These
excerpts also illustrate the various uncertainties about the
phonological system of Indo-European during the seventies.
Only at the end of the decade was the "law of palatals" understood and with it the vowel system of late Proto-Indo-
European as we know it was proposed.
　　Although the contributions of Ferdinand de Saussure
(1857-1913) to historical linguistics were great, those to
descriptive linguistics overshadow them. He is known as
the founder of modern linguistics. His influence was

largely exerted through a posthumous publication based on
lecture notes: the celebrated Cours de linguistique générale, edited by C. Bally and A. Sechehaye. A student at
Leipzig, he is largely responsible for establishing the eminent linguistic group in Paris, through his position at the
École des Hautes Études, 1881-1891, which after him was
led so long by his student, Antoine Meillet (1866-1936). He
himself found life more congenial in Geneva, where he gave
the lectures on which the Cours was based. His contributions have been capably discussed, as by Rulon Wells, "De
Saussure's System of Linguistics," Word 3. 1-31 (1947) and
Meillet, Linguistique historique et linguistique générale II.
174-183. We may note that his view of language as a system is apparent in the very title of the Mémoire which he
wrote when he was barely twenty-one, and that from this
view he made his notable analysis.

(1-6) The immediate object of this small work is to study the
various forms under which is manifested what is referred to as IE
a; the remaining vowels are not taken into consideration except to
the extent that the phenomena related to a require. But if after we
have come to the end of such a limited field the table of the Indo-
European vocalism is little by little modified under our eyes so that
we see it grouped entirely around a, and we take a new view of it,
clearly it is the system of vowels in its entirety on which our observations will center and which should be indicated at the start.

Nothing is more disputed: the opinions are almost infinitely
divided and various authors have rarely made a completely rigorous
application of their ideas. In addition, the problem of the a is related to a series of phonological and morphological difficulties,
some of which have yet to be solved, but many have not yet been
stated. Thus in the course of our peregrination we will often tra-
verse the most unexplored regions of Indo-European linguistics. If
nonetheless we set out, though convinced in advance that our inexpe-
rience will often lead us into a maze, it is not recklessness, as is
often said, that compels anyone who occupies himself with these
studies to attack such questions: rather it is a necessity, it is the
first school one must pass. For the question is not one of speculations of a transcendant order but of research into elementary facts
without which everything drifts, everything is arbitrary and uncertainty.

I must withdraw some opinions which I have published in an
article in the Mémoire de la Société de Linguistique de Paris,

entitled: An Essay on a Distinction between different IE a's. Particularly the resemblance of Ar with the phonemes arising from r
led me to reject, very reluctantly, the theory of vocalic liquids and
nasals, to which I now return after mature reflection.

Bopp and those who immediately followed the illustrious author
of the Comparative Grammar limited themselves to stating that in
regard to the three vowels a e o of the European languages, the
Aryan uniformly showed a. The e and o were then considered weak-
enings characteristic of the idioms of the West and relatively recent
developments from a single IE a.

The work of Curtius in the Sitzungsberichte der Kgl. Sächs.
Gesellschaft der Wissenschaften (1864) enriched our understanding
greatly: Curtius showed that e appeared in the same place in all the
languages of Europe, so that it cannot have developed independently
in each of them. And departing from the accepted idea that the
mother language only possessed the three vowels a i u, he concluded
that all the European peoples must have passed through a common
period, during which they still spoke the same language. Also, that
during this period a part of the a's were weakened to e, under an
unknown influence, while the rest persisted as a. Later the various
languages, separately from one another, had carried out a second
split of the a, which yielded o. Yet in southern Europe this vowel
must have arisen before the end of the Greco-Italic period, in view
of the agreement of the o of the two classical languages, notably in
the declension of the masculine stems in -a (Gk híppos = equos).

We believe we are representing exactly the system of Curtius
by the following table:

Indo-European	a	ā
European	a; e	ā
Later	a o; e	ā

[It is necessary, however, to add the following remark of the
Grundzüge, p. 54: "the original dualism (Zweiklang) gan (Skt
ǵan-â-mi) and gân (Skt perf. ǵa-ǵân-a), bhar (Skt bhar-â-mi) and
bhâr (Skt bhâra-s 'bundle') arose by an imperceptible substitution
at the start: gen gan, bher bhar, then gon (Gk genésthai, gégona),
bher, bhor (Gk phérō, phóros). But nothing can make us believe that
there had ever been a time when Gk gen and gon, pher and phor
would have been interchanged arbitrarily, of a kind so that one
might have said Gk gonésthai, phórō or inversely gégena, phéros."
Here accordingly the learned professor admits an original distinction of e and o, and derives the o of Gk gégona from IE ā.]

Fick's statement, Spracheinheit der Indogermanen Europas, p.

176ff., reproduces in general the preceding system. The ancient a
is divided into a and e in the European period. When a word shows
e in all the languages, it is necessary to assume that the change of
its a to e goes back to this period. On the contrary it seems for a
or o, that although this appears in a single language, it is necessary
to admit that a still remained at the time of the community. The
ablaut of Gk dérkomai dédorka, but above all of Gmc ita, at, is an
admirable utilization of the splitting of a. On this last point see
Curtius in the quotation above.

The system of Schleicher is different. Admitting in each vocalic series two degrees of reinforcement produced by the addition
of one or two a's, he places for the series of a the three expressions: a aa āa.

He finds these three degrees in Greek: a is represented ordi-
narily by ε (e.g. Gk édō), but also by o (Gk podós) and by α (Gk ákōn).
The first reinforcement, a + a, is represented by o when it is produced from ε, i.e. "Gk gé-gon-a, the first form: ga-gān-a; Skt ǵa-
ǵān-a beside Gk e-gen-ómēn." This same degree is transmitted
under the form of ā, ē, when it has a for base: Gk élakon, lélāka.
The second reinforcement is ō: érrōga. Gothic possesses the three
degrees too; the other languages have confused the two reinforce-
ments.

Since the genealogical tree of languages as Schleicher constructed it was not that which most of the other scholars had adopted
and did not include a European period, it is clear that the e of the
languages of Europe does not go back for him to a common origin.
In particular, Goth. i has a different place from that of Gk e in his
Compendium; the latter is considered the regular representative of
IE a, Goth. i as an abnormal weakening. In formulating the following scheme according to Schleicher's system we therefore avoid the
idea of a historically common development of the European vocalism:

| Indo-European | a | | aa | | āa |
| European | a e o | | a o ā | | ā |

It is also necessary to note that Gk a and Lat. a are not mentioned
as reinforced degrees.

In a small work entitled: "Die Bildung der Tempusstämme
durch Vocalsteigerung," Berlin, 1871, the Germanist Amelung, prematurely lost to our science, has attempted to apply the system of
Schleicher in a very consistent manner and to combine it with the
fact of common European e. In his eyes, this e is the normal representative of the non-reinforced a. The European a — with which
he also includes o as Curtius had done — goes back to the first reinforcement which he designates by ā; and the second reinforcement

(â) is long ā in the European languages. Presents, such as Goth.
fara, Gk ágō, ózō accordingly show a reinforced vowel, and it is
necessary to admit that they are denominatives. — In a word, the
dualism: e a is original, and the relation existing between them is
that of simple to reinforced vowel. Note the table:

Indo-European	a	ā	â
(Aryan	a	a ā	ā)
European	e	a	ā
Gothic	i	a	ō
Greek	e	a o	ā ō

The debate which Amelung had on this question with Leo Meyer
in KZ 21 and 22 did not bring any essential modification to this system, which has been presented in detail a second time in the Zeitschrift für deutsches Altertum 16. 161ff.

Brugman, Studien 9. 367ff. KZ 24.2 traces the existence of e, as
a distinct vowel from every other, to the Indo-European period,
without pretending by this that its pronunciation had been that of an
e from its origin; and he designates its proto-type by a_1. Concur-
rently with this vowel the same scholar finds in Greek, Latin, Slavic
o = Lithuanian, Gothic a = Sanskrit ā (at least in open syllables) a
stronger phoneme which he calls a_2 and the origin of which was determined by the accent.

In accordance with this theory one generally arranges the following table, which nonetheless is certainly not that approved by
Brugman himself, for he alludes (Studien 9.381) to the possibility of
a great number of original a's:

	(a)		
Indo-European	a_1	a_2	ā
European	e	a	ā

In sum, one sees that for the languages of the West, the different authors, whatever their point of view, operate with three entities:
the e, a, ā of the European languages. It will be our task to clarify
the fact that there are really four different units, not three; that the
languages of the North confused two fundamentally distinct phonemes
still distinguished in southern Europe: a, a simple vowel, opposed
to e; and o, a reinforced vowel, which is merely e in its higher form
of expression. The dispute between those who favor the split (original a weakened partially to e) and those who favor a twofold original
a (a_1, a_2 becoming e and a) — this dispute, it is necessary to state,
gets us nowhere, because by the a of the languages of Europe is understood an aggregate which has no organic unity.

These four kinds of a̲ which we are going to try to find at the basis of the European vocalism we will pursue further still and arrive at the conclusion that they even belonged to the mother language from which the languages of the East and West arose.

Chapter I. The sonant liquids and nasals.

Before beginning the study of a̲ it is necessary to determine carefully the limits of its domain, and at this point the question of the sonant liquids and nasals is presented. For anyone who admits these phonemes for the mother language will consider a number of vowels of the historical periods of the language recent and distinct from the question of the a̲.

The hypothesis of sonant nasals was first proposed and developed by Brugman, Studien 9. 287ff. In the same work (325) the author also touched on the subject of the sonant liquids, of which apparently the first notion is due to Osthoff.

1. Sonant liquids.

In the Indo-European mother language, the liquid, or liquids, if one accepts two of them, existed not only in the state of consonants but also in the state of sonants, that is to say, that they were able to carry a syllabic accent, capable of forming a syllable. This took place, as is known, in historical times, in Sanskrit. Everything leads one to believe that the sonant liquids never arose except through weakening, because of which the a̲ which preceded the liquid was expelled; but this does not hinder our placing them, as we shall see, on the very same plane with i̲ and u̲. . . .

(8) 1. Root syllable.

The order adopted here to distinguish the different instances in which r̲ appears is based on a new classification of roots, which can only be justified later but should not confuse the reader in the meantime.

We will deal only with the roots containing e̲. — Every root which contains e in the languages of Europe has the ability of expelling this e and in this way taking on a weaker form, on the sole condition that the phonetic combinations so produced can be readily pronounced.

To be arranged under the roots containing e̲ are those in which are found the diphthongs ei̲ and eu̲ and which one is accustomed to cite under their weakened form, deprived of e̲: thus, kei, sreu, deik, bheugh (ki, sru, dik, bhugh).

The i̲ and u̲ of these roots, as well as the liquid and nasal of roots such as derk bhendh can be called sonant coefficients (coefficient sonantique).

They are parallel in vocalism of the root. Depending on whether the e remains or disappears, their function varies: r l m n develop from consonants to sonants; i and u pass from a symphthongic state to an autophthongic.

A. Roots ending with a sonant coefficient.

Examples kei (weak form ki) sreu (w.f. sru) bher (w.f. bhr) men (w.f. mn).

B. Roots including a sonant coefficient followed by a consonant.

Examples deik (w.f. dik) bheugh (w.f. bhugh) derk (w.f. dṛk) bhendh (w.f. bhṇdh).

C. Roots without a sonant coefficient, ended by a consonant.

Examples pet (w.f. pt) sek (w.f. sk) sed (w.f. zd)....

(51) How then could the a and o of the languages of the South have arisen from one and the same original a? By what miracle could this old a be colored to o, and never to a, in all the times that it is found to vary with e? — Conclusion: the twofold a and o of the classical languages is original, and it must be that in the single a of the North two phonemes were confused.

Confirmation: when a root contains a in Greek or in Latin and this root is found in the languages of the North, one observes in the first place that it there still shows the vowel a, but what is the important fact, that this a never alternates with e, as is the case when Greek corresponds with an o. Thus Goth. vagja = Gk okhéō, hlaf = Gk (ké)klopha are accompanied by viga and hlifa. But agis (a-) = Gk ákhos, or ala = Lat. alo do not have a parent form with e. On the other hand, the roots of the latter type have a characteristic, unknown among the first type: the ability to lengthen their a (agis: ōg, ala: ōl) of which we will have to take account below.

Brugman has designated with a_1 the prototype of European e; his a_2 is the phoneme which we have called o up to now. As to this third phoneme which is Greco-Italic a and which constitutes a portion of the a's of the languages of the North, we will designate it by the letter A, after noting well that it is not the parent of e (a_1) nor of o (a_2). — Excluding for the time being the other possible kinds of a one obtains the following table:

Languages of the North	Primordial state	Greco-Italic
e	a_1	e
	a_2	o
a {		
	A	a

(134-135) § 11. Grammatical role of the phonemes A and Q. Complete system of the primordial vowels.

When one considers the following cases of the permutation a_1a_2:

Goth. <u>hilfa</u> <u>hlaf</u>, Gk <u>klépto</u> <u>kéklopha</u>, Gk. <u>híppos</u> <u>híppe</u>, and when one compares with them the following cases of the permutation A $\overline{A}$: Goth. <u>saka</u> <u>sōk</u>, Gk <u>láskō</u> <u>lélāka</u>, Gk <u>númphā</u> <u>númphă</u>, the temptation is strong, assuredly, to set up the proportion $\overline{A} : A = a_2 : a_1$. But this would be to get involved in a course without result and to misunderstand the true character of the phenomena. For greater clarity we are going to construct at once the system of vowels such as we understand it. For the time being we are concerned only with root syllables.

The phoneme a_1 is the root vowel of all roots. It can be alone in forming the vocalism of the root or it can be followed by a second sonant which we have called sonant coefficient (p. 8).

Under certain conditions which are not known, a_1 is replaced by a_2; under others, better known, it is expelled.

When a_1 is expelled, the root remains without vowel when it does not contain a sonant coefficient. When it does, the sonant coefficient comes to be alone, or in an autophthongic state (p. 8), and provides a vowel to the root.

The phonemes A and Q are sonant coefficients. They cannot appear alone except in the reduced state of the root. In the normal state of the root, it is necessary that they be preceded by a_1, and the combinations $a_1 + A$, $a_1 + Q$ give rise to the longs $\overline{A}$, $\overline{Q}$. The permutation $a_1 : a_2$ takes place before A and Q as elsewhere.

Vocalism of the roots in Indo-European								
Full root	a_1	a_1i	a_1u	a_1n	a_1m	a_1r	a_1A	a_1Q
	a_2	a_2i	a_2u	a_2n	a_2m	a_2r	a_2A	a_2Q
Reduced root	-	-i	-u	-n̥	-m̥	-r̥	-A	-Q

Useful designations

For a_1A and a_1Q after contraction: $\overline{A_1}$ and $\overline{Q_1}$.

For a_2A and a_2Q after contraction: $\overline{A_2}$ and $\overline{Q_2}$.

The theory summed up in this table has been applied to all the types of roots above except those which contain A and Q....

CHAPTER SEVENTEEN

WILLIAM DWIGHT WHITNEY
LANGUAGE AND THE STUDY OF LANGUAGE, LECTURE X

New York: Charles Scribner's Sons, 1892[5], pp. 356-394

By the latter part of the nineteenth century, sufficient
work had been done in linguistics to suggest the need for
general handbooks. The most representative of these is
Whitney's. In 1864 he was asked to present six lectures
"on the principles of linguistic science" at the Smithsonian
Institution in Washington, D.C. These were expanded to twelve
when presented in Boston, and published essentially in that
form. In his preface Whitney acknowledges obligations to
Heinrich Steinthal and August Schleicher, and refers to his
frequent antagonist, the great popularizer Max Müller.
Since Whitney was at home in the linguistic centers of Europe, his statements on the "science of language" may be
taken as representative of views of the time. His book was
first published in 1867. Bloomfield, Language 16, says of
it and its successor The Life and Growth of Language (New
York, 1874). Today they seem incomplete, but scarcely antiquated, and still serve as an excellent introduction to language study." Readers may make their own judgements of
Whitney's views through the segment presented here.
Lecture X surveys the problem which pervades much
of nineteenth-century linguistics — linguistic classification
both genealogical and typological. It also deals with the
relationship between language and other elements of culture, as well as race. Although some of Whitney's views
may not have been immediately adopted, they are in large
part the ones that we now hold, such as the view that there
is little evidence for proposing a relationship between Indo-
European and Afro-Asiatic; or that there is little likelihood
of establishing interrelationships beyond a certain time, on
the basis of the materials we now know. As Bloomfield
indicated, the matter of Lecture X is therefore scarcely
antiquated. Whitney's interest in Schleicher's attempts
at linguistic formalization is also in keeping with current
activities.

225

William Dwight Whitney (1827-1894) was called by Jespersen, Language 88, "the leading exponent of general linguistics after the death of Schleicher." We hold him in
high regard for his temperate views; as Jespersen remarked, "he was opposed to all kinds of mysticism, and
words were to him conventional signs." All who have used
his Sanskrit Grammar (Leipzig and Boston, 1896[3]) can
scarcely have failed to be amused by the first sentences
of its preface: "It was in June, 1875, as I chanced to be
for a day or two in Leipzig, that I was unexpectedly invited
to prepare the Sanskrit grammar for the Indo-European
series projected by Messrs. Breitkopf and Härtel. After
some consideration, and consultation with friends, I accepted the task, and have since devoted to it what time
could be spared from regular duties, after the satisfaction
of engagements earlier formed. If the delay was a long
one, ..." In four years he completed, presumably in his
spare time, the grammar which has remained standard
ever since. A professor at Yale University, Whitney is
responsible for its early eminence in linguistics. Any
member of the Linguistic Society of America knows the
veneration still accorded him.

Classification of languages. Morphological classifications; their
defects. Schleicher's morphological notation. Classification by
general rank. Superior value of genetic division. Bearing of linguistic science on ethnology. Comparative advantages and disad-
vantages of linguistic and physical evidence of race. Indo-European
languages and race mainly coincident. Difficulty of the ethnological
problem. Inability of language to prove either unity or variety of
human species. Accidental correspondences; futility of root comparisons.

Our inquiries into the history and relations of human languages
have last brought us to a review and brief examination of their
groupings into families, so far as yet accomplished by the labors
of linguistic students. The families may be briefly recapitulated as
follows. First in rank and importance is the Indo-European, filling
nearly the whole of central and southern Europe, together with no
inconsiderable portion of south-west Asia, and with colonies in
every quarter of the globe; it includes the languages of nearly all
the modern, and of some of the most important of the ancient, civilized and civilizing races. Next is the Semitic, of prominence in

the world's history second only to the Indo-European, having its station in Arabia and the neighboring regions of Asia and Africa. Then follows the loosely aggregated family of the Scythian dialects, as we chose to term them, ranging from Norway almost to Behring's Straits, and occupying a good part of central Asia also, with outliers in southern Europe (Hungary and Turkey), and possibly in southern-most Asia (the Dekhan, or peninsula of India). Further, the south-eastern Asiatic or monosyllabic family, in China and Farther India, and countries adjacent to these; the Malay-Polynesian and Melane-sian, scattered over the numberless islands of the Pacific and Indian Oceans; the Hamitic, composed of the Egyptian and its congeners, chiefly in northern Africa; the South-African, filling Africa about and below the equator; and the American, covering with its greatly varied forms our western continent, from the Arctic Ocean to the Antarctic. Besides these great families, we took note of several isolated languages or lesser groups, of doubtful or wholly unknown relationship: as those in extreme north-eastern Asia, in the Cauca-sian mountains, in central Africa; as the Basque in the Pyrenees, the Albanian in north-western Greece, the Yenisean in Siberia, and the extinct Etruscan in northern Italy.

The scheme of classification, as thus drawn out, was a genetical one, founded on actual historical relationship. Each family or group was intended to be made up of those tongues which there is found sufficient reason to regard as kindred dialects, as common descen-dants of the same original. We were obliged, however, to confess that our classification had not everywhere the same value, as the evidences of relationship were not of an equally unequivocal charac-ter in all the families, or else had been thus far incompletely gath-ered in and examined. Where, as in the case of Indo-European and Semitic speech, we find structural accordance combined with iden-tity of material, as traced out and determined by long-continued and penetrating study on the part of many investigators, there the unity of the families is placed beyond the reach of reasonable doubt. But it is unfortunately true that these two are the only groups of wide extent and first-rate importance respecting which the linguistic stu-dent can speak with such fullness of confidence; everywhere else, there is either some present deficiency of information, which time may or may not remove, or the conditions are such that our belief in the genetic relationship must rest upon the more questionable ground of correspondence in structural development. We may by no means deny that morphological accordance is capable of rising to such a value as should make it a sufficient and convincing evi-dence of genetic unity; but it is evidently of a less direct and unmis-takable character than material identity, and requires for its estima-tion a wider range of knowledge, a more acute insight, and a more

cautious judgement. If two languages agree in the very material of
which their words and apparatus of grammatical inflection are composed, to a degree beyond what can possibly be regarded as the effect of accident or of borrowing, the conclusion that they are akin is
inevitable; nothing but community of linguistic tradition can explain
such phenomena: but agreement in the style only in which words
are composed and thought expressed admits of being attributed to
cause other than historical — to equality of mental endowment, of intellectual force and training. We may look hopefully forward to the
time when linguistic science shall have reached such a pitch of perfection, shall have so thoroughly mastered the infinitely varied phenomena of universal human language and traced out their causes,
that she shall be able to separate with certainty the effects of ethnic
capacity from those of transmitted habit: but that time has certainly
not yet come; and, as the value of morphological accordances as
evidence of genetic connection has hitherto been repeatedly overrated, so it will long, and always in unskilful or incautious hands, be
peculiarly liable to a like mistreatment.

We have already had occasions to refer to and describe some of
the principal structural peculiarities which are illustrated in the
variety of human tongues; but it will be worth while here to bestow
a few words farther upon them, and upon the systems of morphological classification to which they have served as foundation.

The languages of mankind have been divided into two grand
classes, the monosyllabic (otherwise called isolating, or radical)
and the polysyllabic (or inflectional). To the former belong the
tongues of China and Farther India, with their relatives in the same
quarter of Asia, and perhaps one or two idioms in other parts of the
world. In them there is a formal identity of root and word; none of
their vocables are made up of radical and formative elements, the
one giving the principal idea, the other indicating its limitation, application, or relation; they possess no formally distinguished parts
of speech. Usage may assign to some of their roots the offices
which in inflectional tongues are filled by inflective endings, suffixes
or prefixes; it may also stamp some as adjectives, others as nouns,
as pronouns, as verbs, and so on: yet means of this sort can only
partially supply their lack of the resources possessed by more happily developed languages; categories undistinguished in expression
are but imperfectly, if at all, distinguished in apprehension; thought
is but brokenly represented and feebly aided by its instrument. To
the latter, or inflectional class, belong all the other languages of the
world, which, whatever and however great their differences, have at
least this in common, that their signs of category and relation are
not always separate words, but parts of other words, that their vocables are, to some extent, made up of at least two elements, the

one radical, the other formative. There can be, it is evident, no
more fundamental difference in linguistics structure than this. And
yet, it is not an absolute and determinate one. It lies in the nature
of the case that, as the inflectional languages have grown out of a
monosyllabic and noninflecting stage, there should be certain
tongues, as there are in other tongues certain forms, which stand
so closely upon the line of division between the two stages, that it
is hard to tell whether they are the one thing or the other. In our
own tongue, there is no definite division-line to be drawn anywhere
in the series of steps that conducts from a mere collocation to a
pure form-word — from house floor to house-top, from tear-filled
to tearful, from godlike to godly; and, in like manner, it is often a
matter of doubt, in languages of low development, where isolation
ends and where a loose agglutination begins. Thus, even the Chinese, the purest type of all the isolating structure, is by some regarded as, in its colloquial forms, and yet more in some of its dialects, a language of compounded words; and the possession of one or
two real formative elements has been claimed for the Burmese;
while the Himalaya is likely to furnish dialects whose character, as
isolated or agglutinative, will be much disputed.

But the main objection to the classification we are considering
is not so much its want of absolute distinctness (a defect incident to
all classification, in every department of science) as its one-
sidedness: it is too much like the proverbial lover's division of
the world into two parts, that where the beloved object is and that
where she is not: it leaves almost all human tongues in one huge
class together. Accordingly a much more popular and current system distinguishes three primary orders, separating the mass of inflectional languages into such as are agglutinative, or attach their
formative elements somewhat loosely to a root which is not liable
to variation; and such as are inflective, or unite more thoroughly
their radical and formative elements, and make internal changes of
the root itself bear their part, either primarily or secondarily, in
the expression of grammatical relations. The distinction between
these three orders is well expressed by Professor Max Müller in
the following terms:

1. Roots may be used as words, each root preserving its
full independence.
2. Two roots may be joined together to form words, and in
these compounds one root may lose its independence.
3. Two roots may be joined together to form words, and in
these compounds both roots lose their independence.[1]

No better scheme of division, of a simple and comprehensive
character, has yet been devised than this, and it is likely to maintain

itself long in use. It faithfully represents, in the main, three successive stages in the history of language, three ascending grades of
linguistic development. But its value must not be overrated, nor its
defects passed without notice. In the first place, it does not include
all the possible and actually realized varieties in the mode of formation of words. It leaves altogether out of account that internal
change of vowels which, as was shown in the eighth lecture, is the
characteristic and principal means of grammatical inflection in the
Semitic tongues. The distinctions of qatala 'he killed', qutila 'he
was killed', qattala 'he massacred', qātala 'he tried to kill', aqtala
'he caused to kill' and the like, are not explainable by any composition of roots and loss of their independence, even though the somewhat analogous differences of man and men, lead and led, sing and
sang, sit and set, do admit of such explanation. In the second place,
it is liable to something of the same reproach of one-sidedness
which lies against the former, the double method of classification.
It puts into a separate class, as inflective languages, only two families, the Indo-European and the Semitic: these are, to be sure, of
wide extent and unapproached importance; yet the mass of spoken
tongues is still left in one immense and heterogeneous body. And
finally, a yet more fundamental objection to the scheme is this het-
erogeneity, which characterizes not its middle class alone, but its
highest also. It classes Indo-European and Semitic speech together,
as morphologically alike, while yet their structural discordance is
vastly greater than that which separates Indo-European from many
of the agglutinative tongues — in some respects, even greater than
that which separates Indo-European from the generality of agglutinative and from the isolating tongues. Not only are the higher
Scythian dialects, as the Finnish and Hungarian, almost inflective,
and inflective upon a plan which is sufficiently analogous with the
Indo-European, but, from a theoretical point of view (however the
case may be historically), Chinese, Scythian, and Indo-European are
so many steps in one line and direction of progress, differing in degree but not in kind: Semitic speech, on the other hand, if it started
originally from the same or a like center, has reached an equally
distant point in a wholly different direction. The two inflective families may lie upon the same circumference, but they are separated
by the whole length of the diameter, being twice as far from one another as is either from the indifferent middle. A less fundamental
discordance, perhaps, but an equal variety of structure, belongs to
those tongues which are classed together as agglutinative. The
order includes such extremes in degree of agglutination as the barren and almost isolating Manchu or Egyptian, on the one hand, and,
on the other, the exuberantly aggregative Turkish and the often ex-
cessively agglomerative American or Basque; it includes such

differences in the mode of agglutination as are presented by the
Scythian, which makes its combinations solely by suffixes, and the
Malay or South-African, which form theirs mainly by prefixes.
Here, again, it may be made a question whether the morphological
relationship of Scythian and Indo-European be not closer than that
of Scythian and Malay. The principle which divides the former is,
it is true, reasonably to be regarded as of a higher order than that
which divides the two latter; yet it is more teleological than morphological; it concerns rather the end attained than the means of attainment. The reach and value, too, of the distinctively inflective
principle, as developed in Indo-European language, is, as I cannot
but think, not infrequently overrated. In no small part of the materials of our own tongue, for example, the root or theme maintains
its own form and distinction from the affixes, and these their distinction from one another, not less completely than is the case in
Scythian. All the derivatives of love, as love-d, lov-ing, lov-er,
love-ly; the derivatives of true, as tru-ly, tru-th, tru-th-ful, tru-
th-ful-ly, un-tru-th-ful-ly — these, and the host of formations like
them, are strictly agglutinative in type: but we do not recognize in
them any inferiority as means of expression to those derivatives in
which the radical part has undergone a more marked fusion, or dis-
guising change. Loved from love is as good a preterit as led from
lead, or sang from sing; truth from true is as good an abstract as
length from long, or filth from foul; nor is the Latin lædo-r, 'I am
hurt', from lædo, 'I hurt', inferior to the nearly equivalent Arabic
qutila, from qatala. The claim might plausibly enough be set up that
the unity which the Scythian gives to its derivative words by making
the vowels of their suffixes sympathize with that of the principal or
radical element, is at least as valuable, in itself considered, as the
capacity of an Indo-European root to be phonetically affected by the
ending that is attached to it — a subjection of the superior to the inferior element. Not that the actual working-out of the latter principle in the tongues of our family has not produced results of higher
value than the former has led to; but this may be owing in great
measure to the way in which the two have been handled respectively.

The immensely comprehensive order of agglutinative languages
is sometimes reduced a little by setting apart from it a polysynthetic or incorporative class, composed of the Basque and the
American family. This, however, is rather a subdivision of one of
the members of the triple system than the establishment of a new,
a quadruple, scheme of classification.

Professor Müller[2] seeks to find a support and explanation of the
threefold division of human language which we are now considering
by paralleling it with the threefold condition of human society, as
patriarchal, nomadic, and political. Monosyllabic or "family

languages" are in place, according to him, among the members of a
family, whose intimacy, and full knowledge of one another's disposi-
tions and thoughts, make it possible for each to understand the other
upon the briefest and most imperfect hints. Agglutinative or "nomadic languages" are required by the circumstances of a wandering
and unsettled life; the constantly separating and reassembling tribes
could not keep up a mutual intelligence if they did not maintain the
integrity of the radical elements of their speech. Inflective or
"state languages" are rendered possible by a regulated and stable
condition of society, where uninterrupted intercourse and constant
tradition facilitate mutual comprehension, notwithstanding the fusion
and integration of root and affix. The comparison is ingenious and
entertaining, but it is too little favored by either linguistic philosophy or linguistic history to be entitled to any other praise. It would
fain introduce into the processes of linguistic life an element of re-
flective anticipation, of prevision and deliberate provision, which is
altogether foreign to them. That wandering tribes should, in view of
their scanty intercourse, their frequent partings to be followed by
possible meetings, conclude that they ought to keep their roots unmodified, is quite inconceivable; nor is it easy to see what purpose
the resolution should serve, if the endings are at the same time to
be suffered to vary so rapidly that mutual unintelligibility is soon
brought about. In every uncultivated community, the language is left
to take care of itself; it becomes what the exigencies of practical
use make it, not what a forecasting view of future possibilities leads
its speakers to think that it might with advantage be made to be: let
two tribes be parted from one another, and neither has any regard
to the welfare of its fellow in shaping its own daily speech. In point
of fact, moreover, Indo-European languages were inflective, were
"state languages", long before the tribes had formed states — while
many of them were as nomadic in their habits as the wildest of the
so-called Turanian tribes. And to denominate the immense and
highly-organized Chinese empire a mere exaggerated family, and
account for the peculiarities of its speech by reference to the conditions of a family, is fanciful in the extreme. No nomenclature
founded on such unsubstantial considerations has a good claim to the
acceptance of linguistic scholars; and the one in question has, it is
believed, won no general currency.

A very noteworthy attempt has been made within a short time
by Professor Schleicher, of Jena,[3] to give greater fulness and precision to the morphological classification and description of language, by a more thorough analysis, and a kind of algebraic notation,
of morphological characteristics. A pure root, used as a word without variation of form or addition of formative elements, he denotes
by a capital letter, as A: a connected sentence expressed by a

series of such elements, as is sometimes the case in Chinese, he would represent by A B C, and so on. Such a sentence we may rudely illustrate by an English phrase like fish like water in which each word is a simple root or theme, without formal designation of relations.[4] A root which, while retaining its substantial independence, is so modified in signification and restricted in application as to form an auxiliary or adjunct to another root (which was shown in the last lecture to be a frequent phenomenon in the isolating languages), is marked by an accented letter, as A': thus, in the English shall like would be represented by A' + A; shall have put, by A' + B' + A: the interposed sign of addition indicating the closeness of relation between the elements. The position of the accented letters in the formula would point out whether the auxiliaries are placed after the main word, as in Burmese, or before it, as in Siamese, or on either or both sides, as sometimes in Chinese.

If, now, the formative element is combined with the radical into a single word, it is indicated by a small letter, which is put before or after the capital which stands for the root, according to the actual position of the elements in combination. Thus, if we represent true by A, untrue would be aA; truly or truth would be Aa; untruly, aAb; untruthfully, aAbcd; and so on. Expressions of this kind belong to the agglutinative type of structure; and they are, it is plain, capable of very considerable variation, so as to be made to denote the various kinds and degrees of agglutination. It is possible, for example, to distinguish the endings of inflection from those of derivation, or elements of pronominal from those of predicative origin, by the use of a different series of letters (as the Greek) to indicate one of the classes: thus, truths might be $Aa\alpha$, but truthful, Aab; babalarumdan, in Turkish (see above, p. 318), might be $Aa\beta\gamma$, but sevishdirilememek, Aabcdef. An adroit use of such means of distinction might enable one even to set forth with sufficient clearness the peculiarities and intricacies of polysynthetic tongues.

Again, an inflective change of the root itself for the expression of grammatical relations is denotable by exponents attached to the root-symbol. Thus, man being A, men would be A^a; men's, $A^a a$, sang, sung, song, from sing, would be denoted by A^a, A^b, A^c; spoken from speak, would be $A^{\overline{a}} a$; its German counterpart, gesprochen, $aA^a b$. And in the Semitic tongues, where the root never appears without a vocalization which is formal and significant, the constant radical emblem would be A^a.[5]

Compounds, finally, would be expressed in this method by putting side by side the symbols expressive of their separate members, the capital letters with their modifications and adjuncts. House-top, would be AB; songwriter, A^aBa; and so on.

It is unnecessary to explain with any more of detail Professor

Schleicher's system of morphological notation, or to spend many
words in pointing out its convenience and value. It may evidently be
made a means of apprehending distinctly, and setting forth clearly,
the main structural features of any language. It will not, indeed,
enable us to put in a brief and compact form of statement the whole
morphological character of every spoken tongue. Most tongues admit no small variety of formations; each must be judged by its prevailing modes of formation, by the average of highest and lowest
modes, by their respective frequency of application, and the purposes they are made to serve. It does not help us to a simple and
facile scale and classification of all the dialects of mankind; but this
is to be imputed to it as a merit, not as a fault: it thus fairly represents the exceeding variety of languages, the complexity of the
characteristics which distinguish them, and their incapacity of separation into a few sharply defined classes.

No single trait or class of traits, however fundamental may be
its importance, can be admitted as a definite criterion by which the
character of a language shall be judged, and its rank determined.
We saw reason above to challenge the absolute superiority of the
inflective principle, strongly as it may indicate a valuable tendency
in language-making. Certainly it is wholly conceivable that some
language of the agglutinative class may decidedly surpass in strength
and suppleness, in adaptedness to its use as the instrument and aid
of thought, some other language or languages of the inflective class.
Not morphological character alone is to be taken account of; for not
every race of equal mental endowment has originated and shaped a
language, any more than an art, of equivalent formal merit. Some
one needed item of capacity was wanting, and the product remains
unartistic; or the work of the earliest period, which has determined
the grand features of the whole after-development, was unadroitly
performed; the first generations left to their successors a body of
constraining usages and misguiding analogies, the influence of which
is not to be shaken off; and the mental power of the race is shown by
the skill and force, with which it wields an imperfect instrument.
Many a tongue thus stands higher, or lower, in virtue of the sum of
its qualities, than its morphological character would naturally indicate. The Chinese is one of the most striking instances of such a
discordance; though so nearly formless, in a morphological sense,
it is nevertheless placed by Wilhelm von Humboldt and Steinthal[6] in
their higher class of "form languages", along with the Indo-European
and Semitic, as being a not unsuitable incorporation of clear logical
thought; as, though not distinctly indicating relations and categories,
yet not cumbering their conception, their mental apprehension, by
material adjuncts which weaken and confuse the thought.

But further, apart from this whole matter of morphological

form, of grammatical structure, of the indication, expressed or implied, of relations, another department contributes essentially to our
estimate of the value of a language: namely, its material content,
or what is signified by its words. The universe, with all its objects
and their qualities, is put before the language-makers to be com-
prehended and expressed, and the different races, and tribes, and
communities, have solved the problem after a very different fashion.
Names-giving implies not merely the distinction of individual things,
but no less, classification and analysis, in every kind, and of every
degree of subtlety. There are conceptions, and classes of conceptions, of so obvious and practical character, that their designations
are to be found in every language that exists or ever has existed:
there are hosts of others which one community, or many, or the
most, have never reached. Does a given tongue show that the race
which speaks it has devoted its exclusive attention to the more triv-
ial matters in the world without and within us, or has it apprehended
higher things? Has it, for example, so studied and noted the aspects
of nature that it can describe them in terms of picturesque power?
Has it distinguished with intellectual acuteness and spiritual insight
the powers and operations of our internal nature, our mind and soul,
so that it can discuss psychological questions with significance and
precision? Any dialect, isolating or inflective, monosyllabic or
polysynthetic, may be raised or lowered in the scale of languages
by the characteristics which such inquiries bring to light. In these,
too, there is the widest diversity, depending on original capacity, on
acquired information and civilization, and on variety of external cir-
cumstance and condition — a diversity among different branches of
the same race, different periods of the same history, and, where
culture and education introduce their separating influences, between
different classes of the same community. Our earliest inquiries (in
the first three lectures) into the processes of linguistic growth
showed us that the changes which bring about this diversity, the ac-
cretions to the vocabulary of a tongue, the deepening of the meaning
of its words, are the easiest of all to make, the most pervading and
irrepressible in their action, throughout every period of its existence. Here, then, more than in any other department, it is practicable for later generations to amend and complete the work of
earlier; and yet, such is the power of linguistic habit that, even
here, original infelicities sometimes adhere to a language during
its whole development.

  To make out a satisfactory scheme of arrangement for all human tongues upon the ground of their comparative value, accordingly, will be a task of extreme difficulty, and one of the last results
reached by linguistic science. It will require a degree of penetration into the inmost secrets of structure and usage, an acuteness of

perception and freedom from prejudice in estimating merits of diverse character, and a breadth and reach of learning, which will be found attainable only by a few master-minds. Great play is here afforded for subjective views, for inherited prepossessions, for sway of mental habits. Who of us can be trusted fairly to compare the advantages of his own and of any other language?

There can be no question that, of all the modes of classification with which linguistic scholars have had to do, the one of first and most fundamental importance is the genetical, or that which groups together, and holds apart from others, languages giving evidence of derivation from the same original. It underlies and furnishes the foundation of all the remaining modes. There can be no tie between any two dialects so strong as that of a common descent. Every great family has a structural character of its own, whereby, whatever may be the varying development of its members, it is made a unit, and more or less strikingly distinguished from the rest. Whatever other criterion we may apply is analogous in its character and bearings with the distinction of apetalous, monopetalous, and polypetalous, or of monogynous, digynous, etc., or of exogenous and endogenous, or of phenogamous and cryptogamous, in the science of botany — all of them possessing real importance in different degrees, variously crossing one another, and marking out certain general divisions; while the arrangement of linguistic families corresponds with the division of plants into natural orders, founded upon a consideration of the whole complicate structure of the things classified, contemplating the sum of their characteristic qualities; fixing, therefore, their position in the vast kingdom of nature of which they are members, and determining the names by which they shall be called. The genetical classification is the ultimate historical fact which the historical method of linguistic study directly aims at establishing. With its establishment are bound up those more general historical results, for the ethnological history of mankind, which form so conspicuous a part of the interest of our science.

To subjects connected with this department of interest, the bearing of linguistic science on ethnology, we have next to turn our attention, occupying with them the remainder of the present lecture.

One of the first considerations which will be apt to strike the notice of any one who reviews our classification of human races according to the relationship of their languages, is its non-agreement with the current divisions based on physical characteristics. The physicists, indeed, are far from having yet arrived at accordance in their own schemes of classification, and the utter insufficiency of that old familiar distinction of Caucasian, Mongol, Malay, African, and American, established by Blumenbach, and probably learned by most of us at school, is now fully recognized. But it does not seem practicable to lay down any system of physical races which shall agree with any possible scheme of linguistic races. Indo-European, Semitic, Scythian, and Caucasian tongues are spoken by men whom the naturalist would not separate from one another as of widely diverse stock; and, on the other hand, Scythian dialects of close and indubitable relationship are in the mouths of peoples who differ as widely in form and feature as Hungarians and Lapps; while not less discordance of physical type is to be found among the speakers of various dialects belonging to more than one of the other great linguistic families.

Such facts as these call up the question, as one of high practical consequence, respecting the comparative value of linguistic and of physical evidence of race, and how their seeming discrepancy is to be reconciled. Some method of bringing about a reconciliation between them must evidently be sought and found. For neither linguistic nor physical ethnology is a science of classification merely; both claim to be historical also. Both are working toward the same end — namely, a tracing out of the actual connection and genealogical history of human races — and, though each must follow its own methods, without undue interference from without, they cannot labor independently, careless each of the other's results. To point out the mode of reconciliation, to remove the difficulties which lie in the way of harmonious agreement between the two departments of ethnological science, I shall not here make the least pretence; such a result can be attained only when the principles and conclusions of both are advanced and perfected far beyond their present point. All that we can attempt to do is to notice certain general considerations bearing upon the subject, and requiring not to be lost from sight by either party; and especially, to point out the limitations and imperfections of both physical and linguistic evidence, and how necessary it is that each should modestly solicit and frankly acknowledge the aid of the other.

How language proves anything concerning race, and what it does and does not prove, was brought clearly to light in the course of our earliest inquiries into its nature and history. What we then learned respecting the mode of acquisition and transmission of each man's, and each community's, "native tongue" was sufficient to show us the total error of two somewhat different, and yet fundamentally accordant, views of language, which have been put forth and defended by certain authorities — the one, that speech is to man what his song is to the bird, what their roar, growl, bellow are to lions, bears, oxen; and that resemblances of dialect therefore no more indicate actual genetic connection among different tribes of men than resemblances of uttered tone indicate the common descent of various species of thrushes, or of bears, inhabiting different parts of the world: the

other, that language is the immediate and necessary product of
physical organization, and varies as this varies: that an Englishman, a Frenchman, and a Chinaman talk unlike one another because
their brains and organs of articulation are unlike; and that all En-
glishmen talk alike, as do all Frenchmen, or all Chinamen, because,
in consequence of their living amid similar physical conditions, and
their inheritance of a common race-type, their nervous and muscular systems minutely correspond. And doctrines akin with these are
more or less distinctly and consciously implied in the views of those
who hold that language is beyond the reach of the free-agency of
men, and can be neither made nor changed by human effort. All who
think thus virtually deny the existence of such a thing as linguistic
science, or reduce it to the position of a subordinate branch of physiology: speech becomes a purely physical characteristic, one among
the many which by their common presence make up man, and by
their differences distinguish the different varieties of men; and it
would be for the physicist to determine, here, as in the case of other
physical characteristics, how far its joint possession indicated specific unity, or how far its diversities of kind indicated specific variety. All these false theories are brushed away at once by our
recognition of the fact that we do not produce our speech from
within, but acquire it from without ourselves; that we neither make
nor inherit the words we use, whether of our native tongue or of any
other, but learn them from our instructors.

But from this it also follows that no individual's speech directly
and necessarily marks his descent; it only shows in what community
he grew up. Language is no infallible sign of race, but only its
probable indication, and an indication of which the probability is ex-
posed to very serious drawbacks. For it is evident that those who
taught us to speak, of whose means of expression we learned to
avail ourselves, need not have been of our own kith and kin. Not
only may individuals, families, groups of families, of almost every
race on earth, be, as at present in America, turned into and absorbed by one great community, and made to adopt its speech, but a
strange tongue may be learned by whole tribes and nations of those
who like our negroes, are brought away from their native homes,
or, like the Irish, have lived long under a foreign yoke, or like the
Celts of ancient Gaul and Spain, have received laws, civilization,
and religion from another and a superior race. Languages unnum-
bered and innumerable have disappeared from off the face of the
earth since the beginning of human history; but only in part by reason of the utter annihilation of the individuals who had spoken them;
more often, doubtless, by their dispersion, and incorporation with
other communities, of other speech. Everywhere, too, where the
confines of different forms of speech meet, there goes on more or

less of mixture between them, or of effacement of the one by the other. Yet, on the other hand, mixture of language is not necessarily proof of mixture of race. We can trace the genesis of a very large part of our own vocabulary to the banks of the Tiber, but hardly the faintest appreciable portion of our ancestry is Roman. We obtained our Latin words in the most strangely roundabout way: they were brought us by certain Germanic adventurers, the Normans, who had learned them from a mixed people, the French, chiefly of Celtic blood; and these, again, had derived them from another heterogenous compound of Italian races, among whom the Latin tribe was numerically but a feeble element.

Of such nature are the difficulties in the way of our inferring the race-connections of an individual or of a community with certainty from the relations of the language which either speaks. They are of undeniable force and importance, and must be borne constantly in mind by every one who is pursuing investigations, and laying down conclusions, in linguistic ethnology. They drive him to seek after some other concurrent test of descent, which shall serve to check and control his own results; and they make him court and welcome the aid of the physicist, as well as of the archaeologist and the historian.

But, notwithstanding this, their consequence, and their power to invalidate linguistic evidence, must not be overrated. They concern, after all, what in the grand sum of human history are the exceptions to a general rule. It still remains true that, upon the whole, language is a tolerably sure indication of race. Since the dawn of time, those among whom individuals were born, of whom they learned how to express their mental acts, have been usually of their own blood. Nor do these difficulties place linguistic evidence at any marked disadvantage as compared with the physical. They are, to no small extent, merely the effect, on the side of language, of the grand fact which comes in constantly to interfere with ethnological investigations of every kind: namely, that human races do not maintain themselves in purity, that men of different descent are all the time mingling, mixing their blood, and crossing all their race-characteristics. Fusion and replacement of languages are impossible, except when men of different native speech are brought together as members of the same community, so that there takes place more or less of an accompanying fusion of races also; and then the resulting language stands at least a chance of being a more faithful and intelligible witness of the mixture than the resulting physical type. That the modern French people, for example, is made up of a congeries of Celtic, Germanic, and Italian elements is to a certain extent — although only the aid of recorded history enables us fully to interpret the evidences — testified by the considerable body

of the Celtic and Germanic words mixed with the Latin elements of
the French language; but no physicist could ever have derived the
same conclusion from a study of the French type of structure. The
physicist claims that there may be a considerable infusion of the
blood of one race into that of another, without perceptible modification of the latter's race-type; the intruded element, if not continu-
ously supplied afresh, is overwhelmed and assimilated by the other
and predominant one, and disappears: that is to say, as we may interpret the claim, its peculiarities are so diluted by constant re-
mixture that they become at last inappreciable. In any such case,
then, traces discoverable in the language may point out what there
is no other means of ascertaining. It is true that, on the other hand,
the spread and propagation of a language may greatly exceed that of
the race to which it originally belonged, and that the weaker numer-
ical element in a composite community may be the one whose dialect
becomes the common tongue of all. Thus the Latin swept away the
primitive tongues of a great part of southern and central Europe,
and has become mingled with the speech of all civilized nations, in
the Old world and the New. But we are not rashly to infer that such
things have happened over and over again in the history of the world.
We have rather to inquire what influences make possible a career
like that of the Latin, what lends the predominant and assimilating
force to a single element where many are combined. And, as was
pointed out in the fourth lecture, we shall find that only superior
culture and the possession of a literature can give to any tongue
such great extensibility. The Persians, the Mongols, have at one
period and another exercised sway over an empire not less extensive than the Roman, but their languages were never spread far beyond the limits of the peoples to which they properly belonged. The
German tribes, too, conquered in succession nearly every kingdom
of Europe; but it was only in order to lose themselves and their dialects together, almost undiscoverably, in the communities and languages into which they entered. Nay, even the wide-spread Greek
colonies, with the superiority of Greek culture to aid them, were
not able to make the Greek the tongue of many nations. There was
an organizing and assimilating force in Roman dominion which the
world has nowhere else seen equalled. And if the career of the
Arabic furnishes something like a parallel to that of the Latin, it is
due, not to the sword of Islam, but to the book, and to the doctrine
and policy which the book enjoined and the sword imposed. Since,
then, such movements must be connected with culture and literature,
they cannot but leave their record in written history, and find there
their explanation. Nor could there occur in every region or in every
period such an inpouring and assimilation of nationalities as is now
going on among us; it is only possible under the conditions of

civilized life in the nineteenth century, and the historical conditions which have been created here. The wild and uncultivated races of the earth generally are simply maintaining themselves by growth from generation to generation, taking in no immigrants, sending out no emigrants. Culture makes an astonishing difference in the circumstances and fates of those portions of mankind over which its influence is extended, and it would be the height of folly to transfer to barbarous races and uncivilized periods of human history analogies and conclusions drawn from the history of cultivated nations and tongues. The farther we go back into the night of the past, the greater is the probability that the limits of race and speech approximately coincide, and that mixture of either is accompanied by that of the other.

And if, in certain circumstances, a race may change its tongue, while yet retaining in its physical structure evidence of its descent, a race may also undergo a modification of physical type, and still offer in its speech plain indications of its real kindred. If the talk of our colored citizens does not show that they were brought from Africa, neither do the shape and bearing of the Magyars show that they came from beyond the Ural, nor those of the Osmanli Turks that their cousins are the nomads of the inhospitable plateau of central Asia. This is the grand drawback to the cogency of physical evidence of race, and it fully counterbalances those which affect the cogency of linguistic evidence, rendering the aid of the linguist as necessary to the physical ethnologist as is the latter's to the linguistic ethnologist. Physical science is as yet far from having determined the kind, the rate, and the amount of modification which external conditions, as climate and mode of life, can introduce into a race-type; but that, within certain undefined limits, their influence is very powerful, is fully acknowledged. There is, to be sure, a party among zoologists and ethnologists who insist much upon the dogma of "fixity of type," and assert that all human races are original; but the general tendency of scientific opinion is in the other direction, toward the fuller admission of variability of species. The first naturalists are still, and more than ever, willing to admit that all the differences now existing among human races may be the effects of variation from a single type, and that it is at least not necessary to resort to the hypothesis of different origins in order to explain them. In the fact that Egyptian monuments of more than three thousand years' antiquity show us human varieties and canine varieties, bearing the same characteristics as at the present day, there is nothing to disturb this conclusion; for, on the one hand, a period of three thousand years is coming to be regarded as not including a very large part of man's existence on the earth; and, on the other hand, such a fact only proves the persistency which a type

may possess when fully developed, and is of very doubtful avail to
show the originality of the type. Something analogous is to be seen
in language. The speech of our rude Germanic ancestors of the
same remote period, had we authentic record of it, would beyond
question be found to have possessed already a general character
clearly identifying it with Germanic tongues still existing, and
sharply sundering it from Greek, from Slavonic, from Celtic, and
all the other Indo-European branches; yet we do not doubt that the
Germanic type of speech is derived, a secondary one. In settling
all these controverted points, in distinguishing between original diversity and subsequent variation, in establishing a test and scale for
the possibilities and the rate of physical change, the physical ethnologist will need all the assistance which historical investigations
of every kind can furnish him; and the greater part must come to
him from the student of language.

As the Indo-European family of language is that one of which
the unity, accompanying a not inconsiderable variety of physical
type in the peoples who speak its dialects, is most firmly established, and as therefore it may naturally be regarded as furnishing
a prominent illustration of the bearing of linguistic conditions on
physical inquiries into the history of man, it is perhaps worth our
while to refer to a theory respecting Indo-European speech which
has found of late a few supporters of some note and authority, and
which, if accepted, would altogether deprive it of ethnological value.
The assertion, namely, is put forth, that the apparent unity of languages of this family is not due to a prevailing identity of descent in
the nations to which they belong, but to the influence of some single
tribe, whose superior character, capacity, and prowess enabled it
to impose its linguistic usages on distant and diverse races. By
some it is even assumed that the correspondence of words and
forms exhibited by the so-called Indo-European tongues are not
fundamental and pervading, but superficial, consisting in scattered
particulars only, in such designations of objects and conceptions as
one race might naturally make over into the keeping of another,
along with a knowledge of the things designated. This assumption,
however, the expositions, and reasonings of our fifth and seventh
lectures will have shown to be wholly erroneous: the correspondences in question are fundamental and pervading: they constitute
an identity which can only be explained by supposing those who
founded these tongues to have been members together of the same
community. Others, who know the European languages too well to
maintain respecting their relations any so shallow and untenable
theory, yet try to persuade themselves that the analogy of the Latin
will sufficiently account for their extension over so wide a region;
that, as Etruscans, Celts, Iberians, Germans, learned to speak a

tongue of Roman origin, so the populations of Europe and Asia, of diverse lineage, learned to speak a common Indo-European dialect; and that, accordingly, the differences of Greek, Sanskrit, Celtic, and Slavonic are parallel to those of Italian, French, and Spanish. But this theory, though more plausible and defensible than the other, is hardly less untenable. It exhibits a like neglect of another class of linguistic principles: of those, namely, which underlie and explain the abnormal extension of tongues like the Latin and the Arabic: we have more than once had occasion to set them forth above. In order to establish an analogy between the history of Latin and that of Indo-European speech, and to make the former account satisfactorily for the latter, it would be necessary to prove, or at least to render probable, the existence in a very remote antiquity of those conditions which in modern times have been able to give such a career to the language of Rome. But, so far as we can at present see, there must have been a total lack of the required conditions. Force of character, warlike prowess, superiority of inherent mental capacity, undeveloped or partially developed, the Indo-Europeans may probably have possessed, as compared with the more aboriginal races of Europe; but these are not the forces which enable the language of a small minority to stifle that of the masses of a people and to take its place; if it were so, southern Europe would now be talking Germanic instead of Romanic dialects. The rude beginnings of a higher civilization, as metals, instruments, seeds, domestic animals, arts, may possibly have been theirs; yet even these would merely engraft upon the languages of the peoples to whom they were made known certain words and phrases. Only the resources of an enlightened culture, supplemented by letters, literature, and instruction, could give to any tongue the expansive force demanded by the theory we are considering; and of these, it is needless to say, no traces are to be found in Indo-European antiquity. We have no good ground, then, for doubting that the great extension of the languages of our family was effected by the usual causes which act among uncultivated tongues: that is to say, mainly by the growth, spread and emigration of a single race; by its occupancy of ever new territory, accompanied with the partial destruction and partial expulsion, sometimes also with the partial incorporation and absorption, of the former inhabitants; the element of population which inherited the speech and institutions of the original Indo-European tribe being ever the predominant one in each new community that was formed. How many fragments of other races may have been worked in during the course of the family's migrations — how far the purity of blood of one or another of its branches or sub-branches may have been thus affected by successive partial dilutions, so that some of their present peculiarities of type are attributable to the mixture — is, of course, a legitimate

matter for inquiry, and one upon which we may even look for information from their languages, when these shall have been more nar-
rowly examined. But upon the whole, in the light of our present
knowledge, we are justified in regarding the boundaries of Indo-
European speech as approximately coinciding with those of a race;
the tie of language represents a tie of blood.

If the limitations and imperfections of the two kinds of evidence
are thus in certain respects somewhat evenly balanced, there are
others in which linguistic evidence has a decidedly superior practical value and availability. The differences of language are upon a
scale almost infinitely greater than those of physical structure.
They are equal in their range and variety to those found in the whole
animal kingdom, from the lowest organisms to the highest, instead
of being confined within the limits of the possible variation of a single species. Hence they can be much more easily and accurately
apprehended, judged, and described. Linguistic facts admit of being
readily collected, laid down with authentic fidelity, and compared
coolly, with little risk of error from subjective misapprehension.
They are accessible to a much greater number of observers and investigators. Exceptional capacity, special opportunity, and a very
long period of training, are needed to make a reliable and authoritative describer of race-characteristics. It is true, that to distinguish from one another very diverse types, like the European and
African, is a task which presents no difficulty. But, though we
should all, in nine cases out of ten, recognize a native of Ireland at
sight, who among us could trust himself to make a faithful and tell-
ing description of the ideal Irishman, such that, by its aid, a person
not already by long experience made familiar with the type would
recognize it when met with? The peculiarities of the native Irish
dialect, however, are capable of being made unmistakably plain to
even the dullest apprehension. A few pages or phrases, often even
a few words, brought back by a traveller or sojourner in distant
lands from some people with which he has made acquaintance, are
likely to be worth vastly more for fixing their place in the human
family than the most elaborate account he can give of their physical
characteristics. Photography, with its utter truth to nature, can
now be brought in as a most valuable aid to physical descriptions,
yet cannot wholly remove the difficulty, giving such abundant illustration as shall enable us to analyze and separate that which is national and typical from that which is individual and accidental. This
last, indeed, is one of the marked difficulties in physical investigations. Two persons may readily be culled from two diverse races
who shall be less unlike than two others that may be chosen from
the same race. While, on the contrary, words and phrases taken
down from the lips of an individual, or written or engraved by one

hand, can be no private possession; they must belong to a whole community.

The superior capacity of the remains of language to cast light upon the affinities of races needs only be illustrated by an instance or two. What could have impregnably established the ethnological position of the ancient Persians like the decipherment of the inscriptions of Darius and his successors, which show that they spoke a dialect so nearly akin with those of Bactria and India that it can be read by the latter's aid? What could exhibit the intimate mixture of races and cultures in the valley of the Euphrates and Tigris, and the presence there of an important element which was neither Indo-European, nor Semitic, except the trilingual inscriptions of the Mesopotamian monuments? What a pregnant fact in African ethnology will be, if fully and irrefragably proved, the relationship of the Hottentot dialects with the ancient Egyptian! What but the preserved fragments of their speech could have taught us that the Etruscans had no kindred with any other of the known races inhabiting Europe? And when would physical science ever have made the discovery that the same thing is true of the Basques, whom yet it has all the opportunity which it could desire to study? But the most important of the advantages belonging to linguistic science, in its relation to ethnology, is that to which allusion was made at the very outset of our discussions: namely, that language tells so much more respecting races than lies within the reach or scope of the physicist. In every part and particle, it is instinct with history. It is a picture of the internal life of the community to which it belongs; in it their capacities are exhibited, their characters expressed; it reflects their outward circumstances, records their experiences, indicates the grade of knowledge they have attained, exhibits their manners and institutions. Being itself an institution, shaped by their consenting though only half-conscious action, it is an important test of national endowment and disposition, like political constitution, like jural usage, like national art. Even where it fails to show strict ethnic descent, it shows race-history of another sort — the history of the influence which, by dint of superior character and culture, certain races have exercised over others. The spread of the Latin has swept away and obliterated some of the ancient landmarks of race, but it has done so by substituting another unity for that of descent; its present ubiquity illustrates the unparalleled importance of Rome in the history of humanity.

For these reasons, and such as these, the part which language has to perform in constructing the unwritten history of the human race must be the larger and more important. There are points which physical science alone can reach, or upon which her authority is superior: but in laying out and filling up the general scheme, and

especially in concerting what would else be a barren classification
into something like a true history, the work must chiefly be done by
linguistic science.

The considerations we have been reviewing will, it is hoped,
guide us to a correct apprehension of the relations of these two
branches of ethnological study. Discord between them, questions
as to respective rank, there is or should be none. Both are legitimate and necessary methods of approaching the solution of the same
intricate and difficult question, the origin and history of man on the
earth — a question of which we are only now beginning to understand
the intricacy and difficulty, and which we are likely always to fall
short of answering to our satisfaction. There was a time, not many
years since, when the structure and history of the earth-crust were
universally regarded as a simple matter, the direct result of a few
fiats, succeeding one another within the space of six days and nights:
now, even the school-boy knows that in the brief story of the Genesis
are epitomized the changes and developments of countless ages, and
that geology may spend centuries in tracing them out and describing
them in detail, without arriving at the end of her task. In like manner has it been supposed that the first introduction of man into the
midst of the prepared creation was distant but six or seven thousand
years from our day, and we have hoped to be able to read the record
of so brief a career, even back to its beginning; but science is accu-
mulating at present so rapidly, and from so many quarters, proofs
that the time must be greatly lengthened out, and even perhaps many
times multiplied, that this new modification of a prevailing view
seems likely soon to win as general an acceptance as the other has
already done. And the different historical sciences are seeing more
and more clearly their weakness in the presence of so obscure a
problem, and confessing their inability to give categorical answers
to many of the questions it involves.

Such a confession on the part of linguistic science, with reference to one point of the most fundamental interest and importance in
human history, it next devolves upon us to make.

A second question, namely, which cannot but press itself upon
our attention, in connection with the survey we have taken of the
grand divisions of human speech, is this: What is the scope and
bearing of the division into families? Does it separate the human
race into so many different branches, which must have been independent from the very beginning? Does linguistic science both fail
to find any bond of connection between the families and see that no
such bond exists? Or, in short, what has the study of language to
say respecting the unity of the human race?

This is an inquiry to which, as I believe, the truths we have
established respecting the character and history of language will

enable us readily to find a reply. But that reply will be only a negative one. Linguistic science is not now, and cannot hope ever to be,
in condition to give an authoritative opinion respecting the unity or
variety of our species. This is not an acknowledgement which any
student of language likes to make; it may seem to savor, too, of
precipitation on the part of him who makes it; of a lack of faith in
the future of his science — a science which, although it has already
accomplished so much, has yet confessedly only begun its career.
That those linguistic scholars — for such there are — are over-hasty
and over-credulous who suppose themselves to have proved already,
by the evidence of language, that all mankind are akin by blood as
well as by nature, will be conceded by many who are yet unwilling to
give up all hope of seeing the proof one day satisfactorily made out.
Let us, then, enter into a brief examination of the point, and a consideration of the grounds upon which is founded the view we have
taken.

     To show, in the first place, that linguistic science can never
claim to prove the ultimate variety of human races will be no long
or difficult task. That science, as we have seen, regards language
as something which has grown up, in the manner of an institution,
from weak and scanty beginnings; it is a development out of germs;
it started with simple roots, brief in form and of indeterminate
meaning, by the combination of which words came later into being.
And the existing differences of speech among men are, at least to a
very considerable extent, the result, not of original diversity, but of
discordant growth. Now we cannot presume to set any limits to the
extent to which languages once the same may have grown apart from
one another. It matters not what opinion we may hold respecting the
origin of the first germs of speech: if we suppose them to have been
miraculously created and placed in the mouths of the first ancestors
of men, their present differences would not justify us in believing
that different sets must have been imparted to different pairs, or
groups, of ancestors; for the same influences which have so obscured
the common descent of English, Welsh, and Hindustani, for example,
may, by an action more prolonged or more intense, have trans-
formed germs originally common beyond even the faintest possibility of recognition. And if, on the other hand, we regard them as
originated by the same agency which has brought about their later
combinations and mutations, by men, namely, using legitimately and
naturally the faculties with which they have been endowed, under the
guidance of the instincts and impulses implanted in them — and no
linguist, certainly, as such, has any right to deny at least the possibility of this origin of language — then the case is yet clearer. For
we cannot venture to say how long a time the formation of roots may
have demanded, or during what period universal language may have

remained nearly stationary in this its inceptive stage. It is entirely conceivable that the earliest human race, being one, should have parted into disjoined and thenceforth disconnected tribes before the formation of any language so far developed and of so fixed forms as to be able to leave traceable fragments in the later dialects of the sundered portions. These possibilities preclude all dogmatic assertion of the variety of human species on the part of the linguist. Among all the known forms of speech, present and past, there are no discordances which are not, to his apprehension, fully reconcilable with the hypothesis of unity of race, allowing the truth of that view of the nature and history of speech which is forced upon him by his researches into its structure. It is certain that no one, upon the ground of linguistic investigations alone, will ever be able to bear witness against the descent of all mankind from a single pair.

That no one, upon the same grounds, can ever bear witness in favor of such descent is, as it appears to me, equally demonstrable, although not by so simple and direct an argument, and although the opinions of eminent authorities are at variance upon the point, and may fairly continue to be so for some time to come, until more of the fundamental facts and principles in linguistic science shall have been firmly established and universally accepted than is the case at present. We have here no theoretical impossibility to rely upon; no direct argument from necessary conditions, cutting off all controversy. As the linguist is compelled to allow that a unique race may have parted into branches before the development of abiding germs of speech, so he must also admit the possibility that the race may have clung together so long, or the development of its speech have been so rapid, that, even prior to its separation, a common dialect had been elaborated, the traces of which no lapse of time, with all its accompanying changes, could entirely obliterate. Nay, he was bound to keep that possibility distinctly before his mind in all his researches, to cherish a hope of making language prove community of blood in all members of the human family, until conscientious study should show the hope to be groundless. The question was one of fact, of what existing and accessible testimony was competent to prove; it was to be settled only by investigation. But I claim that investigation, limited as its range and penetration have hitherto confessedly been, has already put us in condition to declare the evidence incompetent, and the thesis incapable of satisfactory proof.

In order to make clear the justice of this claim, it will be necessary to recapitulate some of the results we have won in our previous discussions.

The processes of change which are constantly at work in language, altering both the form and the meaning of its constituent words, were set forth and illustrated with sufficient fulness in our early lectures. The degree of alteration which they may effect, and the variety of their results, are practically unlimited. As they can bring utter apparent diversity out of original identity, so they can impress an apparent similarity upon original diversity. Hence the difficulties which beset etymological science, its abuse by the unlearned and incautious, the occasional seeming arbitrariness and violence of its procedures, even in skilled and scientific hands. Voltaire's witty saying, that in etymologizing the vowels are of no account at all, and the consonants of very little — to which he might have added, that the meaning is equally a matter of indifference — was true enough as regarded the science of his day; but we must also confess that in a certain way it possesses an applicability to that of our own times. Even modern etymology acknowledges that two words can hardly be so different, in form or in meaning, or in both form and meaning, that there is not a possibility of their being proved descendants of the same word: any sound, any shade of idea, may pass by successive changes into any other. The difference between the old hap-hazard style of etymologizing and the modern scientific methods lies in this: that the latter, while allowing everything to be theoretically possible, accepts nothing as actual which is not proved such by sufficient evidence; it brings to bear upon each individual case a wide circle of related facts; it imposes upon the student the necessity of extended comparison and cautious education; it makes him careful to inform himself as thoroughly as circumstances allow respecting the history of every word he deals with.

Two opposing possibilities, therefore, interfere with the directness of the etymologist's researches, and cast doubt on his conclusions. On the one hand, forms apparently unconnected may turn out to be transformations of the same original: since, for example, the French évêque and the English bishop, words which have no common phonetic constituent, are yet both descended, within no very long time, from the Greek episkopos; since our alms comes from the Greek eleēmosunē; since our sister and the Persian χāhar are the same word; since the Latin filius has become in Spanish hijo; and so on. On the other hand, what is of not less importance in its bearing upon the point we are considering, he must be equally mindful that an apparent coincidence between two words which he is comparing may be accidental and superficial only, covering radical diversity. How easy it is for words of different origin to arrive at a final identity of form, as the result of their phonetic changes, is evident enough from the numerous homonyms in our own language, to which we have more than once had occasion to refer. Thus, sound in "safe and sound" comes from one Germanic word, and sound in "Long Island Sound" from another; while sound, 'noise', is from the Latin <u>sonus</u>. So we have a <u>page</u> of a book from the Latin <u>pagina</u>, and a <u>page</u> in waiting from the Greek <u>paidion</u>, 'a little boy', we have <u>cleave</u>, 'to stick together,' from the Anglo-Saxon <u>clifian</u>, and <u>cleave</u>, 'to part asunder,' from the Anglo-Saxon <u>clufan</u>; and numberless other instances of the same kind. Fortuitous coincidences of sound like these, in words of wholly independent derivation, are not less liable to occur between the vocables of different languages than between those of the same language; and they do so occur. It is, further, by no means infrequently the case that, along with a coincidence, or a near correspondence, or a remoter analogy, of sound, there is also an analogy, or correspondence, or coincidence, of meaning — one so nearly resembling that which would be the effect of a genetic relationship between the two words compared as to give us an impression that they must be related, when in fact they are not. Resemblances of this sort, of every degree of closeness, do actually appear in abundance among languages related and unrelated, demonstrably as the result of accident alone, being mistaken for signs of genetic connection only by incompetent or heedless inquirers. Thus, an enterprising etymologist, turning over the pages of his Hebrew lexicon, discovers that the Hebrew root <u>kophar</u> means 'cover'; and he is at once struck with this plain proof of the original identity of Hebrew and English: whereas, if he only looks a little into the history of the English word, he finds that it comes, through the Old French <u>covrir</u>, from the Latin <u>coöperire</u>, made up of <u>con</u> and <u>operire</u>; which latter is gotten by two or three steps of derivation and composition, from a root <u>par</u>, 'pass': and this puts upon him the necessity, either of giving up his fancied identification, or of making out some degree of probability that the Hebrew word descended, through a like succession of steps, from a like original. Another word-genealogist finds that <u>lars</u> in ancient Etruscan meant 'a chief, a headman,' and he parades it as an evidence that the Etruscan was, after all, an Indo-European language: for is not <u>lars</u> clearly the same with the Scottish word <u>laird</u>, our <u>lord</u>? He is simply regardless of the fact that <u>laird</u> and <u>lord</u> are the altered modern representatives of the Anglo-Saxon <u>hlaford</u>, with which <u>lars</u> palpably has about as little to do as with <u>brigadier-general</u> or <u>deputy-sheriff</u>. A Polynesian scholar, intent on proving that South-Sea islanders and Europeans are tribes of the same lineage, points out the almost exact coincidence of the Polynesian <u>mata</u> and the modern Greek <u>mati</u>, both signifying 'eye': which is just as sensible as if he were to compare a (hypothetical) Polynesian <u>busa</u>, 'a four-wheeled vehicle,' with our '<u>bus</u> (from <u>omnibus</u>): for <u>mati</u> in Greek is abbreviated from <u>ommation</u>, diminutive of <u>omma</u>, 'eye,' and has lost its originally significant part, the syllable <u>om</u>, representing the root <u>op</u>, 'see.'

These are only a few samples of false etymologies, selected
from among the thousands and tens of thousands with which all linguistic literature, ancient and modern, teems; which have been
drawn out, with infinite expenditure of ill-directed ingenuity and
misapplied labor, from the vocabularies of tongues of every age and
every clime. There is not one among them which has not a much
higher primâ facie plausibility than the identity of évêque and bishop,
or of filius and hijo, or than numberless others of the true etymologies established upon sufficient evidence, by the scientific student of
languages: but their value is in seeming only; they are baseless and
worthless, mere exemplifications of the effects wrought by the process we are considering — the process which brings out accidental
analogies, phonetic and significant, between words historically unrelated. The greater portion of false etymologies are to be ascribed
directly to its influence; and their number is a sufficient and striking proof of the wide extent of its action, the frequency and variety
of the results it produces.

The fact is well established, that there are no two languages
upon the face of the earth, of however discordant origin, between
which may not be brought to light by diligent search a goodly number of these false analogies of both form and meaning, seeming indications of relationship, which a little historical knowledge, when
it is to be had, at once shows to be delusive, and which have no title
to be regarded as otherwise, even if we have not the means of proving their falsity. It is only necessary to cast out of sight the general probabilities against a genetic connection of the languages we
are comparing (such as their place and their period, their nearer
connections, and the pervading discordance of their structure and
material), and then to assume between them phonetic transitions not
more violent than are actually proved to be exhibited by other
tongues — and we may find a goodly portion of the vocabulary of
each hidden in that of the other. Dean Swift has ridiculed the folly
which amuses itself with such comparisons and etymologies, in a
well-known caricature, wherein he derives the names of ancient
Greek worthies from honest modern English elements, explaining
Achilles as 'a kill-ease,' Hector as 'hacked-tore,' Alexander the
Great as "all eggs under the grate!" and so on. This is very ab-
surd; and yet, save that the absurdity of it is made more palpable
to us by being put in terms of our own language and another with
which we are somewhat familiar, it is hardly worse than what has
been done, and is done, in all soberness, by men claiming the name
of linguistic scholars. It is even now possible for such a man to
take an African vocabulary, and sit deliberately down to see what
words of the various other languages known to him, he can explain
out of it, producing a batch of correspondences like these: abetele,

'a begging beforehand' (which he himself defines as composed of a, formative prefix, be, 'beg,' and tele, 'previously'), and German betteln, 'beg' (from the simpler root bit, bet, our bid); idaro, 'that which becomes collected into a mass,' and English dross; basile, 'landlord' (ba for oba, 'master,' si, 'of,' and ile, 'land'), and Greek basileus, 'king': and the comparer, who is especially versed in the mathematical doctrine of chances, gravely informs us that the chances against the merely accidental character of the last coincidence are "at least a hundred million to one." More than one unsound linguist has misled himself and others by calculating, in the strictest accordance with mathematical rules, how many thousand or million of chances to one there are against the same word meaning the same thing in two different and unconnected languages. The calculation is futile, and its result a fallacy. The relations of language are not to be so simply reduced to precise mathematical expression. If words were wholly independent entities, instead of belonging to families of connected derivatives; if they were of such precise constitution and application as so many chemical formulas; if the things they designated were as distinct and separate individualities as are fixed stars, or mineral species, or geographical localities — then the calculations of chances would be in place respecting them. But none of these things are true. The evidences on which linguistic science relies to prove genetical connection are not identities of form combined with identities of meaning: forms may differ as much as hijo and filius; meanings may differ as much as German bekommen, 'get,' and English become, 'come to be' and become, 'suit'; form and meaning may differ together to any extent, and yet the words may be one and the same, and good evidences of relationship between the languages to which they respectively belong. Not literal agreement, but such resemblances, nearer or more distant, clearer or more obscure, as are proved by supporting facts to have their ground in original identity, make satisfactory evidence of common descent in language.

Here, then, is the practical difficulty in the way of him who would prove all human speech a unit. On the one hand, those fortuitous coincidences and analogies which any given language may present with any other with which it is compared form a not inconsiderable body, an appreciable percentage of its general stock of words. On the other hand, the historical coincidences and analogies traceable between two languages of common descent are capable of sinking to as low, or even to a lower, percentage of its vocabulary. That is to say, there may be two related tongues, the genuine signs of whose relationship shall be less numerous and conspicuous than the apparent but delusive signs of relationship of two others which derive themselves from independent origins. The former have been

so long separated from one another, their changes in the meantime
have been so pervading, that their inherited points of resemblance
are reduced in number and obscured in character, until they are no
longer sufficient to create a reasonable presumption in favor of
their own historical reality; they are undistinguishable from the
possible results of chance. As we saw in the sixth lecture (p. 243),
evidences of genetic connection are cumulative in their character;
no single item of correspondence is worth anything until there are
found kindred facts to support it; and its force is strengthened with
every new accession. And, in the comparison of languages, the point
is actually reached where it becomes impossible to tell whether the
few coincidences which we discover are the genuine traces of a
community of linguistic tradition, or only accidental, and evidence
of nothing. When we come to holding together the forms of speech
belonging to the diverse families, linguistic testimony fails us; it
no longer has force to prove anything to our satisfaction.

To demonstrate that this is so, we do not need to enter into a
detailed examination of two tongues claimed to be unrelated, and
show that their correspondences fall incontestably short of the
amount required to prove relationship: we may take a briefer and
directer argument. We have seen that the established linguistic
families are made up of those dialects which exhibit traceable signs
of a common historic development; which have evidently grown together out of the radical stage (unless, as in the case of the monosyllabic tongues, they have together remained stationary in that
stage); which possess, at least in part, the same grammatical structure. There are some linguistic scholars who cherish the sanguine
hope that trustworthy indications of this kind of correspondence may
yet be pointed out between some two or three of the great families;
but no one whose opinion is of one straw's weight thinks of such a
thing with reference to them all. So discordant is the whole growth
of many of the types of speech that we can find no affinities among
them short of their ultimate beginnings: if all human speech is to
be proved of one origin, it can only be by means of an identification
of roots. To give the investigation this form, however, is virtually
to abandon it as hopeless. The difficulties in the way of a fruitful
comparison of roots are altogether overwhelming. To trace out the
roots of any given family, in their ultimate form and primitive signification, is a task whose gravity the profoundest investigators of
language are best able to appreciate. Notwithstanding the variety of
the present living dialects of the Indo-European family, and the
noteworthy preservation of original forms on the part of some among
them, their comparison would be far enough from furnishing us the
radical elements of Indo-European speech. Even the aid of the ancient tongues but partially removes the difficulty; and, but for the

remarkable and exceptional character of the Sanskrit, our knowledge
of that stage in the history of our language out of which its present
grammatical structure was a development would be but scanty and
doubtful; while we have been compelled to confess (in the seventh
lecture) that we know not how far even so primitive a stage may lie
from the absolute beginning. The corresponding condition of Semitic speech, its foundations of triliteral roots, is to no small extent restorable; but we have seen that these roots are themselves
the products of a strange and highly perplexing development, beneath which their actual origin is not yet discernible. Among the
different great branches of the Scythian family, the recognizable
radical coincidences are hardly sufficient, if they are sufficient, to
establish their unity as proceeding from the same stock: a reliable
basis for comparison with other families is certainly not furnished
us here. Nor was the Scythian the only family in establishing whose
unity we were obliged to add the evidence of morphological structure to that of material correspondences: there were at least two,
the monosyllabic in south-eastern Asia and the American, which
were founded almost solely on accordance of type. And the former
of them is a striking illustration of the power of phonetic corruption
to alter and disguise the bare roots of language, without help from
composition and fusion of elements. If we cannot find material correspondences enough between the pure radicals of Chinese, Siamese,
and Burmese to prove these three tongues akin, but must call in, to
aid the conclusion, their common characteristic of monosyllabism,
what hope can we possibly entertain of proving either of them akin
with Mongolian or Polynesian, for example, with which they have no
morphological affinity? Who will be so sanguine as to expect to
discover, amid the blind confusion of the American languages, where
there are scores of groups which seem to be totally diverse in constituent material, the radical elements which have lain at the basis
of their common development? Apparent resemblances among apparent roots of the different families are, indeed, to be found: but
they are wholly worthless as evidences of historical connection. To
the general presumption of their accidental nature is to be farther
added the virtual certainty that the elements in which they appear
are not ultimate roots at all, but the products of recent growth.
There is nothing, it may be remarked, in the character of ultimate
roots which should exempt them from the common liability to exhibit fortuitous coincidences, but rather the contrary. The system
of sounds employed in the rudimentary stage of linguistic growth
was comparatively scanty, the circle of ideas represented by the
roots was narrow and limited, the application of each root more
vague and indeterminate; hence accidental analogies of form and
meaning might even more reasonably be looked for between the

radical elements of unconnected families than between their later
developed words.

For these reasons it is that the comparison of roots is not
likely to lead to any satisfactory results even in the most favorable
cases, and cannot possibly be made fruitful of valuable and trustworthy conclusions through the whole body of human language.
There are, it is true, not a few philologists — and among them some
authorities deserving of the highest respect — who hold that correspondences enough have been found between Indo-European and Semitic roots to prove the ultimate connection of those two families
of language: but the number is yet greater of those who regard the
asserted proof as altogether nugatory. The attempt has been made
above (in the eighth lecture) to show that the governing presumption
in the case is not a purely linguistic one, but rather a historical;
and it is one which is quite as likely to be weakened as to be
strengthened by the results of future researches. But, as regards
the point now under discussion, the admission or rejection of a
genetic tie between these two particular families, or even between
these and the Scythian and Chinese, would make no manner of difference; there would still remain the impossibility of extending a
like tie, by linguistic means, to the other great families.

Our general conclusion, then, which may be looked upon as in-
controvertibly established, is this: if the tribes of men are of different parentage, their languages could not be expected to be more
unlike than they in fact are; while, on the other hand, if all mankind
are of one blood, their tongues need not be more alike than we actually find them to be. The evidence of language can never guide us
to any positive conclusion respecting the specific unity or diversity
of human races.

Notes

1. Lectures, first series, eighth lecture.

2. In his Letter on the Classification of the Turanian Languages, p. 21 seq.; see also his Lectures, first series.

3. See his paper, "Contribution to the Morphology of Language,"
in the Memoirs of the Academy of St. Petersburg, Vol. i, No. 7
(1859); also, the Introduction to his work, the German Language
(Stuttgart, 1860), p. 11 seq.

4. Of course the parallel is to be regarded as only an imperfect
one; though these three words are to our apprehension primitives,
they are far from being ultimate roots; they all either contain formative elements added to such a root, or have possessed and lost
them; each is, to be sure, employable as noun, adjective, or verb,

without change of form, yet not, like Chinese roots, in virtue of an
original indefiniteness of meaning, but as one distinct part of speech
is in our usage convertible directly into others; nor can it be said
that, even as they stand, they are altogether formless; for each is
defined in certain relations by the absence of formative elements
which it would otherwise exhibit: water is shown to be singular by
lacking an s, fish and like to be plural by the absence of s from like.

 5. Professor Schleicher, indeed, adopts this emblem as that of
the Indo-European root also, since he holds the view, briefly stated
and controverted above (in the eighth lecture, p. 293), that the radicals of our family were originally liable to a regular variation, of
symbolic significance, for purposes of grammatical expression. I
regard it, on the contrary, as the weak point in his system, as applied by himself, that it does not distinguish an internal flection like
the Semitic — which, so far as we can trace its history, is ultimate
and original, and which continues in full force, in old material and
in new formations, through the whole history of the languages —
from one like the Indo-European, which is rather secondary and
accidental, constantly arising in new cases under the influence of
phonetic circumstances, but never winning a pervading force, and
in many members of the family hardly taking on anywhere a regular
form and office, as significant of relations.

 6. See the latter's Charakteristik etc., pp. 70, 327.

CHAPTER EIGHTEEN

EDUARD SIEVERS

FOUNDATIONS OF PHONETICS

From Grundzüge der Phonetik zur Einführung in das Studiu
der Lautlehre der indogermanischen Sprachen
(Leipzig: Breitkopf & Härtel, 1901⁵), pp. 1-9, 267-69, 27ʑ

The most definitive achievement of nineteenth-century
linguistics may be in articulatory phonetics. By the end of
the century Jespersen, Sweet, Sievers and others had gained
a control of the subject which has been surpassed only in
details. Accordingly, sections from one of the standard
works on phonetics have been chosen as the last in this anthology.

These sections indicate that Sievers held some linguistic views which we generally consider characteristics
of more recent linguistics. Section 11 stresses the importance of system in language; entities are to be defined in it.
Section 14 speaks of "individual sounds" as abstractions
which are dependent on the point of view of the linguist;
this statement is not unlike definitions of the phoneme given
in the 1930's. Possibly most notable is Sievers' insistence
that the sentence is the minimum linguistic unit. Like other
views given in these few sections, this is remarkably in
keeping with those held today; one wonders why it had so
little influence in 1876 and during the subsequent decades
when Sievers' handbook was revised, reprinted and widely
used.

Sievers' views on historical linguistics seem equally
contemporary. Sound change is a modification of Bildungs-
faktoren — formative features. Sound law is temperately
defined. These excerpts may illustrate that students will
derive greater profit by reading the outstanding works of
the neogrammarians and their predecessors than by reading about them.

257

I. Present Position, Goals and Methods of Phonetics

1. By phonetics we mean the study of the forming of speech, that is, of the production, the characteristics and the use of sounds in the forming of syllables, words and sentences, and finally of the general conditions of their change and decay. Phonetics, then, is a border area between physics, insofar as it is concerned with the acoustic analysis of individual quantities of sound, physiology, insofar as it investigates the functions of the organs which are used in producing and perceiving speech, and finally linguistics, insofar as it gives information about the nature of one of its important aims.

2. Only for the two above-mentioned scientific disciplines can the investigation of the origin and the nature of the individual sounds from which a language is constructed be an end in itself. For the linguist, phonetics is only an ancillary science. Accordingly the interest of the individual disciplines in its different sub-areas will vary. The task and most important goal of scientific investigation is to ascertain the general, basic laws concerning the nature, formation and utilization of the speech sounds. The linguist's task on the other hand is to pursue these basic laws into all the ramifications which have taken place in the various languages and dialects and to make the results of this specialized research useful to his scholarly aims. The natural scientist will accordingly be concerned with the general, the theoretical, while the linguist is primarily interested in the specific data and their particular application to the material to the study of which he dedicates himself.

3. Within the wide area included in the study of language, the studies which are directed at the investigation of living languages undoubtedly have the most direct and practically significant part in the discoveries relating to the nature of linguistic phenomena, which phonetics is able to provide; for only on the basis of a knowledge of phonetics can the facts in the pronunciation of the various idioms be determined. The recognition of the accuracy of this statement has become increasingly widespread, and accordingly practical phonetic research has striven more and more to meet the needs of the modern study of language. It has directed itself particularly toward obtaining reliable material for study while limiting theoretical discussion as much as possible, and reducing this material to simple rules in keeping with practical demands. The success which these attempts have had, is adequate proof that the path begun was the correct one for the solution to this undertaking. It seems all the more doubtful whether the unduly great emphasis placed upon the so-called experimental phonetics with its purely mechanical measuring and representation, even by some who formerly represented the practical position, will in the long run work more to the advantage than to

the detriment of the physiological side of the discipline, notwithstanding a series of results with practical value, which experimental phonetics has thus far produced.

4. The relation of phonetics to historical-comparative linguistics is also different from its role for the investigator of living
languages. The practical aspect of phonetics is here important
only insofar as it may be necessary to ascertain the pronunciation
of the living members of a language or dialect group whose history
is to be investigated. The linguist needs such identification especially to augment the incomplete pictures of linguistic phenomena
which the incomplete writing systems of ancient and modern times
afford; for only too often do these systems conceal peculiarities of
pronunciation which are of importance in the development of the
language. But the center of the interest that linguistic research has
in phonetics surely lies in another area. Phonetics must enlighten
the historical linguist first of all concerning the nature, the development and the relationships of the various phonetic processes
whose beginning and end he has determined by means of a historical
study of language. It can do this because it shows him series of de-
velopmental stages in the comparison of living languages and dialects, which in turn, by suggesting analogies, lead him to reliable
conclusions concerning the course of development of the individual
language, and because it represents for him, in paradigm form, the
relationship between the force which conditions linguistic change
and the individual examples of the resulting change, again from the
example of living language. The historical linguist, then, needs detailed, individual descriptions of the pronunciation of a given idiom
less than does a scholar who is investigating a modern language;
and he has even less need to construct a general system in which
the individual sounds of the various languages are once and for all
ordered according to a definite arrangement. One can even say that
while for the theoretical phonetician the system and the precise
analysis of individual sound classes and sounds which result from
it stand in the center of interest, the historical linguist who pursues
the historically attested changes and shifts of precisely these formations will derive the most benefit from systematic consideration
precisely of the points of contact between the individual subclassifi-
cations which the systematizer sets up and tries to keep distinct as
best he can.

5. It would be impossible for any single presentation of phonetics to do justice to the demands of all the above-mentioned areas
of interest. For the phonetician with interests in science, the specialized linguistic material which is necessary for the philologist
and linguist will scarcely ever be available in any quantity. Moreover he lacks interest, since even a very large accumulation of

material can offer him no real help in the formulation of the general statements concerning language formation, for which he is striving. Still further afield for him are the historical linguist's problems of the development of language. And again only the smallest number of those who lean toward philology will want to or be able to follow the scientist in the details of his anatomical, physiological and physical research. Granted that some one individual might succeed in assembling all the knowledge necessary for presenting a comprehensive survey of phonetics, and in putting this down in a textbook of general phonetics, such a work would still not meet the needs of the student, who, after all, almost invariably approaches phonetics with a limited range of interest and accordingly brings to the subject an understanding for only one or the other portion of it, not for all.

6. Because of these considerations it seems necessary to abandon all thoughts of a general survey of phonetics in favor of individual presentations which direct greater attention to the particular requirements of the various areas of interest, while touching upon only the most essential aspects of the subject as a whole, and that but briefly. The present study, for example, is aimed at one such specialized field. In the first place it is intended to be an introduction to the study of the phonology of the older Indo-European languages, approximately in the extent to which they are represented in the "Library of Indo-European Grammars"; and it tries to do justice to this task by orienting the reader through selected examples about a number of phonetic problems which are pertinent to an understanding of the development of Indo-European phonology. Anything else which is included to make the presentation of the material more complete is intended only as an incidental supplement through which the author attempted, to the best of his ability, to make the book useful to historical linguists outside the field of Indo-European. It will be obvious that the book, because of this emphasis on the historical aspect, is not aimed at the scientist; nor does it meet the needs of the specialist in modern languages, and is useful in their teaching only insofar as that which is of use to the historical linguist may also be of use in language teaching.

7. It lies in the very nature of the problem that a certain amount of work with the spoken language is indispensible for any training in phonetics. A mere description will never be able to convey accurately all the fine points of pronunciation which determine the real character of a language or dialect, and along with it often the particular direction of its further development, while the ear trained through oral practice is readily able to grasp these. It may be most readily possible to present the basic scientific laws of language formation theoretically while keeping them generally understandable. But the greater phonetics is to be made useful for the

practical purposes of teaching languages or linguistic research, the
more instruction of the teacher must be replaced by direct observation on the part of the learner himself. A textbook of phonetics,
then, if it is to be useful to the student of linguistics, must be essentially nothing other than an introduction to the proper use of observation, which in turn affords the student the solid foundation for
the practical utilization of the phonetic principles which have been
acquired in this way.

8. It follows that the task of the language teacher, whose field
of observation is limited essentially to the normal pronunciation of
the language he is teaching, is relatively simple. The scholar en-
gaged in research, on the other hand, cannot consider such restric-
tion. The more complicated the phonological problems whose solution he is seeking may be, the more comprehensive and secure his
survey of the conditions of development of living idioms must be, if
he is to avoid continually exposing himself to the danger of reaching
for false means of explanation.

9. Above all, the serious student of language who hopes to re-
alize concrete profit for his science through the study of phonetics
must strive from the beginning to free himself from a number of
prejudices to which the scholar is driven, partially through the
schools, partially through the practical activity of living, and from
which learned circles are least of all free. The first of these prejudices is the opinion that normal or natural speech is found only in
the languages of writing or culture. The necessary presupposition
for this doctrine, the basic unity of languages, exists only on paper;
a tremendous number of opinions will, therefore, become entangled
in an insoluble conflict if, in accordance with bad habits of the past,
the individual arbitrarily attributes his own pronunciation to the
letters of a writing system, and makes this the only basis for his
conclusions concerning foreign languages. And even if there did
actually exist somewhere a relatively large entity within a language
(a phenomenon which could only be developed, as experience shows,
through artificial cultivation starting from a writing system transmitted from an earlier period of the language), how could the views
derived from it help to explain the development of language, which
so often moves from a condition of simplicity to one of complexity?
Furthermore, the individual modern languages are too distant from
one another to permit with requisite certainty from comparison of
them alone relatively general statements concerning the development of sounds and of speech. Dialects must be used to fill the gap,
since they alone are in a position to supply the links missing in the
standard languages. Furthermore, dialects are generally in a position to give the observer a much clearer picture of the consistency
of pronunciation and the development of sounds than do the written

and standard languages, which at any time not only exhibit a mixture of sound and speech forms, having widely divergent origins, but also are constantly subject to a large number of unpredictable influences from individual speakers than is the idiom of the lower classes which is transmitted only through the unconscious and therefore more steady tradition of oral communication.

10. Each linguist must accordingly use dialects which are familiar to him from his youth as the starting point for all studies in phonetics. If an actual folk dialect is not available to him, he must at least adhere to the natural and easy colloquial speech of the educated people of his home, and not to the generally artificially contrived and therefore often contradictory manner of speaking of the schools, the pulpit, the theater, or the drawing room. Only when he has achieved complete clarity with regard to all phonetic phenomena of his own dialect should he turn to the study first of related dialects and languages, and finally to those more distant. If it is feasible, one should attempt to attain perfect fluency in one or more dialects.

11. Some additional comments will be found below, in the concluding remarks to chapter 11, especially concerning the particulars of examining the sound systems of related dialects as one's study progresses. But even here it must be pointed out most emphatically that the tasks of historical phonetics cannot be solved with a mere statistical consideration of individual sounds and their changes. For in general it is not the individual sound which undergoes change according to certain universally valid laws, but rather there is usually a corresponding development of corresponding series of sounds in corresponding positions (cf. for example the uniform shift of the series of tenues, mediae and aspiratae in the Germanic consonant shift, or the transformation of entire vowel systems through increase or diminution of the specific articulation of the vowels, etc.); generally specific points of view can also be discovered which help explain the change of one such series of sounds from the overall constitution of the system as well as of the particular position of that series in it.

12. Above all, then, one should seek an exact insight into the structure of every phonological system which must be treated. One will do well always to remember that this is determined not so much by the number of sounds themselves which happen to be mixed together in the system as by the relationship of these individual members with one another; and furthermore that the acoustic impression of a sound is not the essential thing, but rather the manner in which it is formed. For what we call sound change is just a secondary result of modifications of one or more of this kind of formative factors through whose interaction a sound is produced.

13. It must be emphasized that the acquisition of such phonetic

training, as that emphasized here from the start, is no easy matter. It requires a tireless, lengthy training of the speech organs, and particularly in connection with the last statement of the hearing. For on the one hand the ear tends to be deaf to a certain extent to sounds which are foreign to it or to the differences of these from sounds which are familiar to it; or when a difference is actually perceived, we often hear intermediates somewhere between the unfamiliar and our own sounds, which arise only through the fact that the impression of one's own sounds blends with that of the corresponding unfamiliar sounds which are heard. On the other hand, because of the insensitivity of hearing to minor differences in the impression of sounds, we often run the risk of attributing such articulations to unfamiliar sounds which one can grasp only through hearing, by means of which one can approach the acoustic effect of them in attempts at imitation, but quite often one's own articulation does not correspond to the unfamiliar ones. One will therefore be able to say that a preliminary conclusion in phonetic training in this direction has only been acquired when the observer is able to perceive correctly any unfamiliar sound, preferably by ear alone, and to characterize it according to its position in its own system as well as its relationship to corresponding sounds of other systems. Cautious occupation with experimental phonetic studies may now and then be useful as a preliminary step in attaining this goal, because it can occasionally clear up deficiencies in the powers of observation especially for the indifferent beginner, which have thus far gone unnoticed. But only he who succeeds in sharpening his senses to such an extent that he need no longer remain subject to the often deceptive, dead apparatus attains complete mastery over his attainment.

14. Current grammatical practice usually takes letters or sounds as a starting point, and then builds up to consideration of syllables, words, and sentences. But it is self-evident that a phonetics which proceeds very systematically would have to begin with the investigation of the sentence, because only the sentence exists in the spoken language as an entity which is given by itself and which can be directly observed. The word, the syllable, the individual sound often take on different forms in the "sentence" (this word is understood in the broader sense in which it is generally used; for the problem itself cf. below, 611 ff); and the individual sound often does not even exist isolated in speech in the absolute form in which it is generally presented in grammars. Therefore the sentence ought to be investigated first, with all the variations which it can experience in oral expression (e.g. those, which the same "sentence" experiences when it is used as simple declarative, as exclamatory, as interrogative, etc., and the like). Only after one has

learned to take these variable characteristics of the sentence into
consideration should one go on to the analysis of the sentence itself, that is, to the investigation of the individual rhythmic groups
of speech (620 ff.) and of the syllables as components of these rhythmic groups. Only to this should the analysis of syllables as such
and of their individual sounds be attached. That which finally results as definition of the individual sound is in the end largely an
abstraction dependent on arbitrarily selected points of view which
is made from the frequently variable forms under which this so-
called individual sound can appear in continuous human speech. For
practical reasons it is customary also in the study of phonetics to
proceed from the simplest elements to the more complex formations, and this generally adopted method is also retained in the
present work. If, however, one adheres to this method, one must
always bear in mind the important fact, that we have by no means
exhausted all that there is to be said about the nature of the individual sound in living speech with the few things we can express
concerning the artificially isolated individual sound. In any case,
the construction of a mere sound system, however important it may
be in itself, always remains one of the most elementary tasks of the
phonetician, in whose realm all the various phenomena of spoken
language fall. One should not, then, be content with the study of
sounds per se, but must examine with equal exactitude the formation
of syllables, of rhythmic units and sentences, always with one's native language as the starting point. The knowledge thus obtained
must then be tested by comparing other living languages and dialects, and only when one finds that he is completely equipped for
these, should he proceed to the application of phonetic criteria for
the elucidation of older stages of speech and their gradual change
to their modern representatives.

IV. Sound Change and Sound Development

722. It is usual for the traditional pronunciation of the individual forms of speech, (sounds, groups of sounds, syllables, rhythmic
groups, etc.), to change in the course of time. Instead of the early
OHG gasti, for example, there is the later (common OHG) gesti and
in its stead late OHG and MHG geste; OHG piligrîm with m corresponds to the Latin peregrinus, with n; and the MLG bersten with
the sequence er corresponds to the OLG brestan, with re, etc. The
term "change in pronunciation" best describes the results of such
modifications; but instead the form "sound change" has come into
use. And this term is acceptable when one considers that even the
sum total of the changes in the pronunciation of complicated

formations (as of a sound group, a syllable, a word) are composed of the changes which the individual sounds of these complexes undergo.

723. Every sound change is based upon inadequate reproduction of the traditional pronunciation. The formation of new forms of pronunciation then originates with a single individual or with a group of individuals and only through imitation are such individual innovations spread adequately throughout larger parts of a speech community, or even its entirety. In the process it is rather unimportant for the further development of a language where the innovation begins, whether within one and the same generation of speakers or in the process of transmitting speech from one generation to the other. Apparently both forms of innovation have a characteristic role in language change.

725. Causes of the Sound Change. Even today the opinion is very widespread that all sound change proceeds from striving toward an easier manner of pronunciation, or in other words that it is always based on a decrease of effort ("sound weakening") and never on an increase ("sound strengthening"). We can admit that many phenomena in the development of languages may be brought under this heading, but in the generality with which the statement is produced it is definitely false. Its incorrectness can readily be seen, even from a very superficial examination of the various historically attested directions of sound development. When an original tenuis becomes a media, that is, when a fortis becomes a lenis, as in the change from Latin patrem to Italian padre, and when this lenis disappears completely as in the corresponding Provençal paire, French père, this clearly must be designated as an instance of weakening. But also the directly opposite series of development is found, as for example on Germanic soil, where we see a ddj arise from simple j (Gothic twaddje from *twaije, etc.) and all original mediae change to tenues or affricates (Gk déka, Lat. decem, Gothic taíhun, OHG zĕhan). The sphere of the vowels is similar. For example, the same languages frequently enough (if partly in different periods) show simplification of diphthongs to long vowels and diphthongization of originally simple vowels (OHG mêr, lôn as opposed to Goth. máis, láun; and OHG hiar, fuor as opposed to Goth. hêr, fôr; or Ital. oro beside Lat. aurum and Ital. buono, Pietro beside Lat. bonum, Petrum etc.) Particularly interesting phenomena along this line are found in languages like Danish, which forms its initial tenues very energetically and with strong aspiration, whereas in medial or final position following a vowel it has permitted them to sink to fricatives of very little energy or even to disappear completely.

726. These few examples are sufficient to show that if the concept of the simplification of pronunciation is to be retained at all, it

must be conceived in a very relative sense (often it will be a question of nothing more than simple fashion). In general it must be carefully noted that differences in difficulty of producing speech sounds are extremely minute, and that actual difficulties with regard to imitation generally exist only with regard to unfamiliar sounds. Just as every part of the human body is particularly trained through special practice for the one service which it performs every day, but becomes less suited or even completely useless for other tasks, so the human speech organs attain a complete mastery of all the articulatory movements, which are required for one's native language, through the practice in the production of sounds and groups of sounds in this language which one carries on continually since childhood. But only of these sounds! After the organs of speech have received special training for and through the service determined for them, everything which falls outside the limits of the familiar articulatory movements seems difficult. Naturally this applies with regard to the sounds of one language as well as another: the Englishman has the same difficulty in pronouncing the German ch or the uvular or tongue trilled r or the dorsal d, t as the German speaker has in imitating the English th or the cerebral r or the cerebral d, t, etc. Such difficulties, however, play a role of course only in the transfer of a language from one people to another (accordingly by speech borrowing in the broadest sense of the word).

732. The word sound law, as one sees, is not to be conceived in the sense in which one speaks of natural laws. It is not meant to imply that under certain given conditions a certain result must necessarily follow everywhere; but it should merely indicate that, if somewhere under certain conditions a shift in the manner of articulation has occurred, the new manner of articulation must be applied without exception in all instances which are subject to exactly the same conditions.